£25.00

KU-631-222

WITHDRAWN

Napier Polytechnic Library

3 8042 00056 4727

Demolition

**General Editor**: Colin Bassett, B.Sc., F.C.I.O.B., F.F.B.

*Other related titles*

Estimating Applied to Building (5th edition) *W. Atton*

Construction Projects: Their Financial Policy and Control *R. A. Burgess*

Building Production and Project Management *R. A. Burgess and G. White*

Demolition Waste *Environmental Resources Limited*

Building: The Process and the Product *D. R. Harper*

The Anatomy of Quantity Surveying *G. A. Hughes*

A New Approach to the (JCT) 1980 Standard Form of Building Contract *G. P. Jones*

A New Approach to the (JCT) 1980 Standard Form of Nominated Sub-Contract *G. P. Jones*

Building Law Reports *H. Lloyd and C. Reese*

Comprehensive Guide to Town Planning Law and Procedures *R. McKown*

Tendering and Estimating Procedures *J. A. Milne*

Building Contract Conditions (Revised edition) *R. Porter*

# Demolition

*Colin E. Topliss,* LIOB, M Inst DE, MICW, MSST, MFB,
*formerly Chief Inspector for the Demolition and Dismantling Industry Register*

*Construction Press*
*London and New York*

Construction Press
Longman House
Burnt Mill, Harlow, Essex, UK

A division of Longman Group Ltd, London

*Published in the United States of America
by Longman Inc., New York*

© Construction Press 1982

All rights reserved. No part of this publication may be
reproduced, stored in a retrieval system, or transmitted
in any form or by any means, electronic, mechanical,
photocopying, recording, or otherwise, without the
prior permission of the Copyright owner.

*First published 1982*

---

**British Library Cataloguing in Publication Data**

---

Topliss, Colin
  Demolition.
  1. Wrecking
  I. Title
  690'.26        TH153
  ISBN 0-582-41110-6

**Library of Congress Cataloging in Publication Data**

Topliss, Colin E.
  Demolition.
  Bibliography: p.
  Includes index.
  1. Wrecking. I. Title.   II. Series.
  TH153.T66           690'.26        81-8444
  ISBN 0-582-41110-6                 AACR2

---

Printed in Great Britain by
William Clowes (Beccles) Ltd
Beccles and London

NAPIER COLLEGE THE DUNNING LIBRARY

AC 84 /102866 /01    ON 184 001131

MERCHISTON    690.26 TOP    SUP JS

CON 05824/1106    PR 25-00

# Contents

# Preface

The writing of this book was prompted by the Publishing Company, Longman Group, Ltd., advertising in the trade journal 'Building Technology & Management' for authors specialising in various disciplines in the construction industry. One of these disciplines being demolition.

The contents of this book lies somewhere between the history of the industry through the eyes of the National Federation of Demolition Contractors since becoming an officially constituted body, my own interpretation of various legislation and an academic text.

The book is aimed at all sections, the professional, the contractor, the operator, students, and the general public who are always attracted to a demolition site.

Inevitably there are many quotations, tables, reports, etc., with several combined or independent sources which it would take much research to catalogue.

In the production of the book only metric units have been used. While it is understood that S.I. units are the present standard most material being demolished will be British units.

This book would not have been written without the initial and continued help and encouragement of a number of people in the industry and Public and Local Authorities whose help I gratefully acknowledge.

Colin E. Topliss

# Acknowledgements

The author is indebted to the following for permission to reproduce copyright material:

British Standards Institution for extracts from the Code of Practice – CP94: 1971: W. H. Lunning for our Appendix 9 from Atom (Nov 1978); National Federation of Demolition Contractors for our Appendices 2 and 3; Demolition Industry Conciliation Board for our Appendix 4; Mr J. B. Spaull for section on Lead in our Appendix 8; London and Southern Counties Demolition Industry Training Group for section on Hazards affecting eyes ears skin and lungs in our Appendix 8; The Controller of Her Majesty's Stationery Office for sections on Accidents to children on building sites and Inspections and tests in our Appendix 8. and for extracts from various Acts, Bills and Statutory Instruments; P. A. Griffiths for our Figs. 1.1, 1.4, 2.3, 3.4, 3.5, 3.7, 3.8, 3.9, 5.11, 5.19, 5.29, 8.1 and 8.8; R. E. Willment for our Figs. 1.2 and 2.4; Manchester Evening News for our Figs. 2.1 and 8.21; D. Watson for our Fig. 2.2; Embassy Demolition Ltd. for our Fig. 3.2; Palmers Scaffolding Ltd. for our Figs. 3.6, 5.6 and 5.12; Burnthills Demolition Ltd. for our Figs. 4.2, 8.13 and 8.14; London Demolition U.K. Ltd. for our Fig. 4.3; A. Ogden & Sons (Demolition) Ltd. for our Fig. 4.4; M. Bishop for our Figs. 4.5 and 8.4; British Steel Corporation for our Fig. 8.5; Cement & Concrete Association for our Figs. 4.7, 4.8, 4.9, 4.10, 4.11, 4.12, 4.13, 4.14, 4.15, 4.16, 4.17, 4.18, 4.19, 4.20, 4.21, 4.22 and 4.23; Geo. Robinson Demoliton Ltd. for our Fig. 4.28; Portasilo Ltd. for our Fig. 4.29; L. C. Kemp for our Fig. 7.2; T. B. Greenham for our Fig. 8.2; Leyland Trucks Ltd. for our Fig. 8.3; Leibherr (Great Britain) Ltd. for our Figs. 8.9 and 8.10; La Bounty Co. Ltd. for our Fig. 8.12; Leverton Caterpillar Co. Ltd. for our Figs. 8.11, 8.16 and 8.18; Marubeni-Komatsu Ltd. for our Fig. 8.15; Clifford Devlin Transport Ltd. for our Fig. 8.17; Hyscot Hydraulics Ltd. for our Figs. 8.19 and 8.20; Simon Engineering Dudley Ltd. for our Figs. 8.22, 8.23 and 8.24; Ruston-Bucyrus Ltd. for our Figs. 8.25 and 8.26.

The author would also like to thank the following individuals and companies for their valuable assistance during the research and preparation of this book:

L. C. Kemp, Chairman CITB; P. A. Griffiths, Charles Griffiths Ltd; G. P.

Henderson, T&GWU; R. E. Willment, Willment Bros. Ltd; W. H. Lunning, UKAEA; National Federation of Demolition Contractors; Construction Industry Training Board; Demolition Industry Conciliation Board; Transport and General Workers Union; United Kingdom Atomic Energy Authority; R. I. Almond, University of Manchester and the late Douglas Short.

# Introduction

The importance of the demolition and dismantling industry within the building and civil industry cannot be overemphasized, but sadly is all too often overlooked.

It is important to refer to the demolition and dismantling industry and not demolition in isolation as there are clear and distinct differences. The word 'demolish' means to destroy or knock to pieces. This means that the components cannot be used again in their present form. The word 'dismantle' means to take to pieces carefully. This means that the components can be used again.

Demolition, being the first stage of any redevelopment, becomes a very important part of the construction industry; therefore the safe and efficient manner with which buildings are demolished is or should be important to the building and civil engineering industry and the client. The more efficient is the demolition or dismantling contractor, the faster the sites are cleared of the existing structures and redevelopment can take place. This redevelopment can take the form of whole renewal areas within city centres for commercial use, urban redevelopment after clearing slum dwellings, the rebuilding of industrial sites and new road building.

Demolition, as we know from statistics, is one of the more dangerous sections of the building and civil engineering industry, and yet that fact is the one to which the least thought is given when planning a project.

The clearance of the site is the first element of planning for any redevelopment, and yet in practice demolition and dismantling and the appointment of the contractor is more often than not the last thought and the last appointment made. Often the appointment of the demolition contractor is left in the hands of a main building or civil engineering contractor and is relegated to the bottom of the scale of importance.

One of the main complaints of demolition contractors is that they are very rarely consulted on methods of demolition or time required to complete the contract in accordance with statutory requirements. They are usually asked to give a budget price by the main contractor to comply with the specification, and the next the demolition contractor knows is when a competitor (very often unqualified) is seen on site doing the work without the scaffold and other safety precautions which the specification calls for and which the genuine contractor has included in his quotation.

As much as 85 per cent of demolition and dismantling is carried out in Great Britain by government departments, local authorities or other statutory authorities and nationalized industries; therefore, the industry should not be classed as a necessary evil which must be tolerated. In fact the demolition and dismantling industry is a highly skilled specialist operation and should be give the importance and time which the skill demands.

Despite the skill required to demolish or dismantle in a safe and economic manner little research has been carried out until quite recently. What was carried out previously was often done on an individual basis by some of the large contractors for their own individual use.

More recently the National Federation of Demolition Contractors (NFDC) have carried out an investigation into new methods and techniques, and research into problems associated with demolition of modern structures and components. It is largely due to the individual members of the NFDC that salvage of material from conventional demolition sites has become a thriving industry in itself, allowing restoration work to be carried out in material in keeping with the original.

It is with regret that some blame for the inherent bad practices must be laid at the doors of certain individual contractors in the industry. As has been previously stated, demolition and dismantling is a very arduous and dangerous industry. Once the contractor has removed the 'cream' of any salvage, he could be tempted to take risks to attempt to complete a contract as quickly and cheaply as possible. When this attitude of mind prevails the safety of the operatives and the general public are at great risk, as this is when most accidents occur.

The contractor is not always the villain. In a number of instances it has been found that the site supervisor – or in some cases the operatives themselves – are at fault if they can see a method of removing a valuable piece of material before the proprietor of the company becomes aware of its existence. Whoever is to blame for this approach, the ultimate responsibility must be with the contractor.

A more constructive modern approach is essential for the industry to progress to the importance it should have. Most of the problems suffered by the industry today can, and should, be attributed to the attitude of previous generations who, by their approach to the work and lack of safety precautions gained little or no respect from the rest of the building and civil engineering industry and from the general public. This attitude and approach is being gradually overcome by training and education, but all too often is resorted to when problems are encountered.

During the last 40 years we have witnessed a dramatic change in methods of construction, including materials used and the way buildings are designed. Forty years ago there were few multi-storey buildings let alone pre-stressed or post-tensioned multi-storey structures. With the advent of this type of structure comes the eventual problem of the demolition of such structures. It is only in latter years that any consideration has been given at the design stage (and then on a very limited scale) to the problems which may occur during the eventual demolition of such structures. On the initiative of the NFDC an attempt is being made to remedy this with strong lobbies to government bodies, professional associations and other interested parties.

Each building, although identical in design and construction, can pose its own problems when it comes to demolition or dismantling. Therefore each unit is unique as far as planning is concerned, even on a contract which has a number of identical structures. New methods have been developed as and when new problems have arisen. More sophisticated equipment is being developed and used, sometimes to adapt to new methods and sometimes to overcome the problem associated with the shortage of skilled labour.

The demolition and dismantling industry consists in the main, of family concerns who have for generations carried out this type of contract. Although these family contractors still exist and play a very important role in the industry, modern methods and current legislation has demanded a more professional and organized approach. The NFDC as a body operating at national and regional level, along with the other authoritative bodies discussed and detailed in Chapter 1 have and are continually playing an important role in the promotion and expertise required to project the industry forward as a highly specialized industry, using skilled operatives who require a general knowledge of all elements of the building and civil engineering industry, in addition to each one's own individual skill as an experienced demolition operative. Few other trades within the construction industry can boast this knowledge.

## Chapter 1

# Authoritative bodies

*The National Federation of Demolition Contractors*

Before 1939 there was little or no large-scale redevelopment in Great Britain, therefore there was no urgent need to clear sites in our inner cities for new buildings.

With the advent of the Second World War and the major destruction of large areas of urban development in the large cities throughout Great Britain, people in authority in national and local government had to look to some organization other than the armed forces to clear the mass of rubble left by the frequent bombing raids, and the disruption this caused to the rescue services attempting to extinguish fires and save lives.

Prior to 1939 the industry we know today did not exist. No trade organization had been established and demolition was carried out by individuals, mainly family businesses and what could be described as general contractors who, by wheeling and dealing, allowed the image of the industry to start at an all-time low because many contractors preferred to make a quick profit without thought for the safety of their employees or the general public. Profit was the only motive without any thought for their future as an individual company or for the industry as a whole.

However, there were a few exceptions to the norm, and some prominent specialist demolition contractors fought to promote the good name of the industry at that time. They fought a losing battle because the client and people in authority, or their agents continued to place contracts with unscrupulous tenderers, who, as I have previously stated, were interested only in removing the valuable items from the site for a quick profit and then more often than not disappeared, leaving what can only be described as resembling a battle-field with the resultant problems for some other contractor to clear.

I regret that all too often the same conditions prevail today. The experiences of the client and his agents do not seem to have been heeded, but today, with legislation and control as they are, speedy action can, and in most cases is, being taken.

The National Federation of Demolition Contractors (NFDC) was formed in the early part of the Second World War after discussions starting in 1940, when the then Ministry of Works and Building called together a nucleus of demolition and dismantling contractors with the prime task of organizing themselves into a proper body to help clear the devastation (Fig. 1.1).

The birth of the NFDC had taken place.[1]★ The first appointment being Mr G. A. Warley, FCA, as secretary with offices in Bloomsbury Square, London.

The constitution of the NFDC was finally agreed on 28 October 1941[2] and the first President elected was the late Mr Charles S. Willment (Fig. 1.2). The Federation was organized on a regional basis[3] shown in Fig. 1.3, and elected a Council consisting of a President, a Vice-President and the chairmen from each of the five regions to form the Council. The National Federation of Building Trade Operatives, who were the union which represented the operatives in the industry, was approached and both sides got down to the task on hand.

This task on a national basis was to organize teams of workers to clear the destruction and devastation as quickly and economically as possible. The government and local authorities needed the co-operation of the NFDC to be able to mobilize labour throughout the British Isles. As local authorities had little or no emergency powers in those days, the Federation was needed to be able to control and direct labour as and where it was most needed without delay.

*Fig. 1.1*   The scene at the House of Commons after a bombing raid in the early days of the Second World War

*Fig. 1.2*   Charles Willment – Founder President of the NFDC

The Ministries of Works and Building and Housing formed 'reconstruction panels' with the prime objective of controlling all directed labour following the bombings. These panels were honorary appointments during the crisis, and appointments were made from prominent experienced members of the newly formed NFDC.[2]

The Directorate of Emergency works issued letters of authority to these reconstruction panels allowing them considerable latitude in their own movement and that of labour in the area of their control. The Directorate advised the fullest co-operation of all local authorities, police and other official bodies.

The control and co-operation during the war years served the NFDC well when the war finally came to an end, and the problems of demolition and dismantling changed. The NFDC Council and members now realized that the strength and co-operation gained throughout the war must not be lost or forgotten.

At the end of the war the whole of the construction industry was in disarray and the demolition and dismantling industry was no exception. Numerous restrictions had been imposed on all rebuilding and various types of licences had to be obtained before any work could take place.

The NFDC had now to look to the future. To progress, the Council decided to alter the constitution and form a constitution limited by guarantee. This was approved on 26 February 1946. The original five regions were retained with an elected National Council still being the controlling authority.[4] The Federation's Memorandum and Articles of Association have from time to time been

---

* References for all chapters are in Appendix 10, pp. 355–8.

Fig. 1.3  Regional organization of the NFDC

amended, but the basis of the 1946 constitution remains.

When the NFDC was first constituted the subscription was based on numbers employed and the voting rights based on that criterion. Since 1973, when the Articles were revised a flat rate of subscription was introduced and is still in being.

The constitution of the NFDC today allows for the elections of a President and Vice-President who are elected annually at the annual general meeting, and the remainder of the Council is made up of honorary life vice-presidents, who are the past presidents of the Federation. Each of the five regions elect a chairman and one or more council members as that region's representatives at the National Council.

During the forty years since it was formed, the NFDC has been accepted as the official negotiating body for the industry by government departments, local authorities, professional associations and trade unions. Its members offer a fully comprehensive range of services, including the demolition and dismantling of all types of structures, site clearance and excavation, making safe dangerous structures, plant dismantling and foundations and general site works. The views of the Federation as an official body, or its members as individuals, are often sought by various statutory bodies or government departments, and a close liaison has always been evident between the Federation and the Health and Safety Executive (HSE).

The Federation is represented on many government and other committees and outside bodies, including the Joint Advisory Committee for Health and Safety in the Construction Industry,[5] and a number of BSI code-drafting committees.[6]

In 1967–68 the NFDC and the Ministry of Defence negotiated an agreement whereby the armed forces would not carry out works of demolition normally carried out by civilian demolition contractors without the prior knowledge and approval of the NFDC and the appropriate trade unions. This arrangement was set in print in the *Blue Book*, a document held by the NFDC and others as a guide to these agreements, and also ensuring that the possibility of the use of the armed forces as cheap labour would be eliminated.[7]

A number of notable achievements have been made by the NFDC which has led to an improved service given by NFDC members to their clients.

1. The Form of Direct Contract which has been designed especially for works of demolition and dismantling. A revised edition was published in 1974.[8] (Appendix 3)

2. The NFDC participation along with the respective trade unions in the Demolition Industry Conciliation Board and the establishment of a nationally approved Working Rule Agreement.[9] (Appendix 4)

3. A Standard Specification for Demolition and Associated Works in the Clearance of Existing Buildings and Structures – 1976. (Appendix 2)

4. A Schedule of Daywork Charges. The law does not allow the Federation

to recommend this document as all contractors are free to quote and agree whatever price they wish for daywork. This document, however, is a fair guide to the client and the contractor with due and reasonable allowance for profit, overheads, etc.

5. The Federation instigated the formation of a British Standards Committee for the preparation of a Code of Practice for the demolition industry which resulted in the publication of CP94: 1971 – *Demolition* (Ch. 3) which is a guide to safe basic practice and which should be adopted and followed by all employers engaged in works of demolition.

6. The Institute of Demolition Engineers was formed by the Federation to provide a professional platform and a recognized technical qualification for senior personnel to promote the highly skilled nature of demolition techniques and management.

7. The Federation also sponsors 'The Charles Willment Memorial Prize' which is an annual award at a civil engineering college, to a student who in the opinion of the adjudicators has contributed most to college life. The trophy takes the form of a silver cup, with an additional money prize. The trophy is to commemorate the late Charles S. Willment, Founder President of the Federation.

8. In 1974, the Federation in association with the appropriate trade unions established the Demolition and Dismantling Industry Register (DDIR), which was a system of voluntary registration for contractors who meet certain criteria.

9. The European Demolition Association (EDA) was founded in 1976, the founder-members being the NFDC, along with the demolition associations of West Germany and Holland. The offices of the EDA are in The Hague and the first Secretary-General was Dr Robert Basart. Mr Peter A. Griffiths, Managing Director of Charles Griffiths Ltd, Past-President of the NFDC and Founder-Chairman of the Demolition and Dismantling Industry Register (Fig. 1.4) became Founder-President of the Association with the other two associations supplying the two vice-presidents. An executive committee of the EDA meets on a regular basis for the interchange of ideas on all aspects of the industry and new techniques.

10. Looking to future problems as early as 1972, the Federation considered that the removal of tensioned components in structure would pose one of their greatest problems as very little research had been carried out in Great Britain.

   In 1973, after considerable discussion, the Federation set up a Joint Liaison Committee to look into the problem and invited the following interested organizations to participate and report on their findings with recommendations: the Institute of Structural Engineers; the Institute of

*Fig. 1.4*   Mr P. A. Griffiths – Founder – President of the European Demolition Association, Founder-Chairman of the DDIR and Past-President of the NFDC

Civil Engineers; the Concrete Society; the Cement and Concrete Association; and the Royal Institute of Chartered Surveyors (Ch. 4, Tensioned Structures). The complete report can be obtained from the NFDC.

As a result of all these achievements the Federation can boast that it enjoys a close and friendly relationship with both client and employee alike. The client can be safe in the knowledge that the work will be carried out in a safe, efficient and economical manner by fully trained employees who are supervised by experts, using the most up-to-date methods and techniques in demolition today.

The Federation are proud to state that the employment of an NFDC member ensures that the work will be carried out in a proper and safe manner. Membership is restricted to contractors who can prove they have carried on the business of a demolition contractor for a minimum of five years, and who can supply proper and suitable references to substantiate the fact. They must employ sufficient trained operatives to carry out work they undertake, and to carry out such work in accordance with the Code of Practice CP94: 1971, the Working Rule Agreement and other statutory obligations and legislation.

Throughout the forty years of its existence the NFDC has placed great emphasis on its family ties with companies passing from father to son; you will see numerous examples of this in these pages, but none greater than that of the present President of the NFDC, Roger Willment. The clock has travelled full

7

circle, not only within the company, Willment Bros. where Mr Willment is Chairman and Managing Director but as President of the NFDC in 1980. Mr Willment carries on in the tradition of his father and Founder-President in 1940, and although we are not fighting a tactical war today as in 1940, the problem the industry is facing is an economic war where the enemy is not always known and the remedy is often even more remote.

## The Demolition Industry Conciliation Board

Almost forty years ago the newly-formed NFDC signed an agreement with the National Federation of Building Trade Operatives, thus setting into being the Demolition Industry Wages Board. This agreement and signing automatically led to the establishment of the Demolition Industry Conciliation Board (DICB) and the establishment of the Working Rule Agreement.[9]

The DICB is the official negotiating body for the industry and provides the platform from which national and local problems can be considered by both sides of industry – employers and operatives – and a solution found. The constitution of the Board is representative of both sides of industry and is made up of representatives of the following: the National Federation of Demolition Contractors; the Transport and General Workers Union (TGWU); the General and Municipal Workers Union; and the Union of Construction, Allied Trades and Technicians. Each body can appoint three representatives to the Board and are individually responsible for the election of these honorary positions, and together they form the employers' side and the operatives' side on the Board. The Chairman and Vice-Chairman are appointments made directly by the Board and again are honorary positions.

Two secretarial appointments are made, one from the employers' side and one from the employees' side. At present the NFDC, who appoint the employers' secretary, nominate their national secretary to that position, and the employees' representative is taken from the major union (TGWU). Currently Mr George Henderson who is National Secretary of the Building, Construction and Civil Engineering Group and the Building Craft Section of the TGWU is the employees' secretary.

The main function of the Board is the annual negotiations on new wage rates and terms and conditions for the employment of labour in the industry. Once these new rates and terms and conditions are agreed they are incorporated into the DICB – Working Rule Agreement and through the joint secretaries a promulgation notice is published which is then circulated to all parties affected by such changes.

The Working Rule Agreement (WRA) (Appendix 4) is similar to those, issued by the other main construction negotiating bodies, but is designed to meet the specialist nature of the work and the operatives employed within the industry. It will be noted in Appendix 4 that certain categories of employees occur which are not evident in other construction groups. The WRA also details minimum rates for such operatives, and also calls for the operation of the Building and Civil Engineering Holiday Management Scheme Ltd, holidays with pay and the death benefit scheme, as detailed in sections 8 and 17 of the WRA.

All working rule agreements are those which formed the basis of the Fair Wages Resolution of Parliament October 1946,[10] which states that:

'The Contractor shall in the execution of the Contract, observe and fulfil the obligation upon contractors specified in the Fair Wages Resolution passed by the House of Commons on the 14 October, 1946 and as described below:–

'1A.   The Contractor shall pay rates of wages and observe hours and conditions of labour not less favourable than those established for the trade of industry in the area where the work is carried out by machinery of negotiation or arbitration to which the parties are organisations of employers and trade unions representatives respectively of substantial proportions of the employers and workers engaged in the trade or industry in the district.

'1B.   In the absence of any rates of wages, hours or conditions of labour so established the Contractor shall pay rates of wages and observe hours and conditions of labour which are not less favourable than the general level of wages, hours and conditions observed by other employers whose general circumstances in the trade or industry in which the Contractor is engaged are similar.

'2.   The Contractor shall in respect of all persons employed by him (whether in execution of the contract or otherwise) in every factory, workshop or place occupied or used by him for the execution of the contract comply with the general conditions required by this Resolution. (Before a Contractor is placed on an approved list for invitation to tender, the Department or Authority must obtain from the Contractor an assurance that to the best of the Contractor's knowledge and belief he complies with the general conditions required by this Resolution.)

'3.   In the event of any question arising as to whether the requirements of the Resolution are being observed, the question shall, if not otherwise resolved, be referred to the Department of Employment for a decision by an independent Tribunal.

'4.   The Contractor shall recognise the freedom of his employees to be members of trade unions.

'5.   The Contractor shall at all times during the continuance of a contract display for the information of his employees in every factory, workshop or place occupied or used by him for the execution of the contract a copy of the Resolution.

'6.   The Contractor shall be responsible for the observance of the Resolution by sub-contractors employed in the execution of the contract, and shall if required notify the Department or Authority of the names and addresses of all such sub-contractors.

Note: UNLESS A COPY OF THE APPROPRIATE WORKING RULE AGREEMENT IS READ IN CONJUNCTION WITH THE FAIR WAGES RESOLUTION an accurate interpretation cannot be considered.'

## The Demolition and Dismantling Industry Register

On 29 May 1970 the Robens Committee were appointed with the following terms of reference:

> To review the provision made for the safety and health of persons in the course of their employment (other than transport workers while directly employed on transport operations and who are covered by other provisions) and to consider whether any changes were needed:
>
> (1)  the scope and nature of the major relevant enactments, or
> (2)  the nature and extent of *voluntary* action concerned with these matters and
>
> to consider whether any further steps were required to safeguard members of the public from hazards, other than general environmental pollution, arising in connection with activities in industrial and commercial premises and construction sites and to make recommendations.

The whole theme of the report stressed self-regulation throughout industry on a voluntary basis and operated by industry-based organizations. It went on to say that each industry has its own particular interests and problems.

The problems facing the demolition industry are the 'Lump' and the whole casual approach to the industry.[11] The term 'Lump' as was referred to in the criteria of the DDIR is derived from the payment of a lump sum for a specific piece of work in the construction industry. As such it is used to describe labour-only sub-contracting, self-employment or agency labour. The term is often used to distinguish between bona-fide labour-only and self-employed and those who choose to abuse the system. A bona-fide labour-only sub-contractor is a term used to describe a contractor who directly employs his labour and observes the national working rule agreement, i.e. DICB–WRA. The genuine self-employed man is less easy to define, but is generally thought of as the jobbing specialist. A construction industry census in 1966 quoted almost 250 000 self-employed, broken down into 66 000 as employers and the remainder not employers.[12]

In 1971, the Finance Act initiated the system of tax exemption certificates as a means of control in the construction industry.[13] The number of certificates could only provide a rough guide to the numbers involved, but by the end of 1972 just over 350 000 certificates had been issued. It was also estimated that a further 50 000 labour-only firms had formed registered companies. Companies House registered some 52 000 companies in 1972, compared to just over 29 000 in 1970. In 1970, the official Inland Revenue estimate was that bogus self-employment was costing the exchequer £10 m. per year in tax evasion.

One other main cause for concern and objection to the self-employed concerned safety, or the lack of safety, but no official figures have been produced on this subject. One prominent report as far back as 1968 stated:

> At its worst, labour-only sub-contracting produces faulty work by irresponsible men concerned only in wresting the greatest possible gains from the industry in the short run, and unrestrained by their own standards or by the control of management.

It was against this background that the industry and trade unions approached government to form the DDIR, and in August 1975 a Ministerial Circular 75/75 was issued to all local authorities in England and Wales[14] and Finance Circular 46/1975 in Scotland.[15] These circulars set out the requirements of registration and advised all local authorities and official bodies to follow the advice in the document. The DOE/PSA Contracts Department incorporated the details in their own contract notes for all contracts officers to follow.[16]

From these initial moves DDIR[17] was founded. It was in the form of a voluntary register set up to deal with the problems caused by 'Lump labour', to promote safety within the industry and to control and monitor companies who wish to be registered. The Register was governed by an independent Registration Council which was representative of all interested sections of industry and was made up as follows:

1. Representatives from each side of the DICB, i.e. employers and trade unions which are represented by the NFDC, the TGWU, the General and Municipal Workers Union and the Union of Construction, Allied Trades and Technicians.

2. Representatives from the British Scrap Federation and the National Federation of Master Steeplejacks and Lightning Conductor Engineers.

3. Two registrars from each side i.e. employers and trade unions.

4. Observers appointed by the DOE and by Local Authority Associations including Scotland.

The Register was self-financing through the initial registration fee and an annual subscription. Registration was opened on 1 April 1974 when companies from (1) and (2) above were invited to register. Government approval was sought and received and is referred to in the DOE Ministerial Circular 75/75 issued in August 1975 previously quoted.

Membership of the Register was open to contractors engaged in demolition or dismantling who undertake as follows:

1. To observe the recommendations of CP94: 1971 – *Demolition*, as amended.
2. To abide by the terms and conditions of one of the following national negotiated WRAs.
   (a) The DICB # WRA.
   (b) The Joint Conciliation Committee for the Iron, Steel and Non-Ferrous Scrap Industry WRA ('the British Scrap Federation WRA').
   (c) The National Joint Council for the Steeplejack Industry WRA.
3. To operate such safety training schemes for employees as the Registration Council shall prescribe and/or approve from time to time.

At present a pilot Safety Training Scheme is being operated by the NFDC in conjunction with the CITB and other interested bodies in the southern region of the country. When this pilot scheme is firmly established, other groups will be formed and developed. In the meantime all contractors are bound to adopt the best safe working practices, and to undertake training, and are reminded of their legal requirements with regard to the Health and Safety at Work etc. Act 1974, and all other statutory obligations.

There was an initial registration fee, payable on application and was non-returnable in any event. In addition there was an annual subscription, payable on admission, then subsequently on 1 April in each year. This fee was an amount fixed by the Registration Council from time to time. The Council had powers to prescribe detailed rules and regulations for the operation of the Register, and registered contractors were bound by the Council's rulings.

The Registration Council met six times per annum, the two working committees, the Membership and Disciplinary Committee and the Finance Committee, met monthly, to approve new memberships, disciplinary matters and financial and administrative control of the Register.

The Registration Council had the power to expel or otherwise discipline registered contractors for non-compliance with its requirements, and any disciplinary decisions could be made public. The inspectorate, through the Chief Inspector, were responsible for checking that all the undertakings were being observed. These inspections required the following information listed 1–13 below to be available for checking, after which the Inspector would require to visit sites in the course of operations and inspect plant and equipment and facilities for the maintenance of this equipment.

1. Wage records.
2. Tax records (PAYE) and receipts from tax office.
3. Holiday with pay cards – where applicable and registered number.
4. CITB registration number – or other approved State Training Board registered number.
5. Insurance coverage, to include for demolition and/or dismantling. A letter from your broker would be accepted.
6. Accident Book – BL-510.
7. General Register – F36.
8. Written Company Safety Policy.
9. Trade association membership and registered number.
10. Tax exemption certificate – 714 – (Finance Act). If not already supplied a photo-copy of the 714 certificate to be supplied and retained on file.
11. Details of plant owned.
12. Category of labour employed.
13. List of current contracts with details of a site to be visited by the Inspector.

All new applicants underwent such examination before any recommendations were made to the Registration Council and all existing registered contractors underwent spot inspections to ensure they maintained the required standard. The new applicants and registered contractors were required to co-operate with the inspectorate.

The Register was open to all contractors willing to comply with the registration criteria and who signed the declaration on the application form. Once the contractor had proved qualification and the Registration Council accepted the registration, the applicant's name was entered in the Register and given a registration number. This number was proof to any client that registration exists.[18]

In the event of an unfavourable decision and the applicant failed to become registered he had the right of appeal to an independent Appeals Tribunal, which also heard appeals against disciplinary decisions of the Registration Council.

Registered contractors were issued with a registration certificate and were entitled to use the Register's insignia on their stationery.

Unfortunately in early 1981 the government issued a statement withdrawing support for the DDIR, saying it was strong enough to be self-supporting in technical terms (the Register being financially self-supporting). The trade federations who were party to the Register (the NFDC, the British Scrap Federation and the Federation of Master Steeplejacks and Lightning Conductor Engineers) decided they would withdraw support, saying that without official support the strength of the Register had been undermined. The demise of the DDIR therefore took place at the end of the financial year on 31 March 1981.

In the opinion of the author the decision of the Federations to withdraw and subsequently allow the closure of the DDIR was the most retrograde step the industry has taken. As *the only truly independent voice* representing the whole of the demolition and dismantling industry, free from influence from official bodies as well as the federations, the DDIR could have helped to promote a more favourable image than the tarnished one the industry in general appears to create. No industry or individual company should be above change for the betterment of that industry, especially when the safety record cries out for change. Only time will tell if the above observations of the author are correct.

## The Institute of Demolition Engineers

Demolition, as we know, is a very specialized craft, therefore the people who supervize and specify works of demolition have the right to be represented by a professional association in the same manner as other sections of the construction industry, not only to look after their professional well-being but to give them a platform to discuss with their contemporaries problems common to all sections of the construction industry when dealing with demolition engineering and associated works.

The Institute, along with all professional associations, has a reputation to maintain for professional ethics, therefore a code of conduct has to be maintained among its members. Should any member be in breach of conduct and found guilty, disciplinary action would have to be taken.

The Institute of Demolition Engineers[19] was first discussed in the mid-1970s and came into being in 1978, as a charitable trust with the prime objective of advancing demolition as a profession and to establish beyond doubt that from 1980 onward the promotion of demolition as a science must be recognized in order to create safe and modern working practices in the interest of the public at large, not only in Great Britain but throughout the world.

Membership of the Institute takes three different forms:

1. Fellows.
2. Members.
3. Associate Members.

*Fellows.* As the name implies this is the most senior grade of membership and is open to those who have:

either    (a) Had at least ten years of practical experience in a senior management capacity in the demolition industry; and

(b) Made outstanding contributions to the industry; or

(c) Made an original contribution to the science or practice of demolition engineering submitted in the form of a thesis.

*Members.* This grade of membership is open to those who have:

(a) Had at least five years' practice and responsible experience in the industry at management level; or

(b) Submitted a paper to an approved standard on some topic of demolition engineering or passed examinations set by or with the approval of the Institute.

*Associate Members.* Open to those who are qualified in some other profession, but who in their work are closely associated with the industry.

Other classes of membership such as 'student' and 'corporate' will be considered by the Institute in due course.

All applications for membership of the Institute has to have two members to propose the applicant. The Institute, in its absolute discretion, retains the right to elect an applicant to membership. A permanent sub-committee of the Council Management of the Institute has been formed to deal with applications for membership, and where appropriate, to hold examinations to assist in assessing the character and qualifications of those who apply. The Institute will provide a syllabus from time to time for examination purposes so that applicants may know the standards required of them and prepare themselves accordingly. These standards are essential for the Institute to judge and be judged by the quality of its membership.

The Institute as a body recognizes that the task of promotion is very demanding and considers the need for much wider public appreciation of the role to be played by the demolition engineer in the redevelopment of our country as a whole. Through past experience and events such appreciation will not be easy to bring about.

To this aim the Institute has embarked on a policy of participation in any form of discussion on the safest and most efficient techniques of demolition engineering, whether it be within the industry or allied professions, government or with other statutory bodies, the British Standards Institute or anyone else.

The Institute has agreed to set up working parties on any aspect of demolition engineering where further research of existing methods or scrutiny or innovations are required and will, from time to time, publish papers setting out their findings.

It will, when finance permits, sponsor the research of independent groups where this can be seen to be for the advancement and betterment of demolition engineering. It is also intended that the Institute should offer the industry a panel of arbitrators on any question related to demolition engineering, also to supply a panel from time to time for seminars and give lectures on demolition engineering.

It has been emphasized that the role of the Institute will not be to give free advice on commercial matters although every assistance possible will be given.

The Institute is managed by a Council of Management, the membership of which collectively and individually seeks to combine the greatest talent and experience for the furtherance of the professsion of demolition engineering. Members of the Council are elected annually in accordance with the rules.

## Chapter 2

# Planning and statutory requirements

## The client and the professional

Before any works of demolition or dismantling can be undertaken there must first be a client. The client can be any one of a number of individuals, commercial undertakings or official bodies. As approximately 85 per cent of all demolition contracts in Great Britain are carried out for, or on behalf of, official bodies, government and local government plays an important part in the industry.

Complications occur for the demolition contractor and the client because most professions within these official bodies undertake demolition. The contract can be in the control of the architect, surveyor, engineer, estates, housing and, in some cases, the more remote professions not normally associated with the industry such as planning and welfare departments.[1] The situation often becomes more complicated when one of the former professions carries out the client roll as agent to one of the other professions listed.

We ask ourselves, why does the client require the demolition carried out in any case? The answer is very simple. The client requires the site cleared of the existing structure for various reasons such as have been stated in the Introduction.

The client usually sets out his requirements in a brief to the professional planning the work. In most cases a predetermined budget has already been established by the client for the overall project. At this stage little or no thought has been given to the works of demolition other than the fact that the existing structure must be removed. At this stage, the professional supervising authority have made their first mistake in not considering the first and most important element in any redevelopment project.

## The contractor

During his tendering the main contractor has in many cases, himself, gone out to tender on various specialist elements within the contract, namely demolition heating and ventilation, electrical and many others.[2] Even at this stage insufficient importance is placed on the demolition contract and more often than not the main contractor, who has asked for possibly up to three individual prices from demolition contractors for his budget to be able to submit his firm tender to the architect, now goes out to tender again to allow him to obtain the lowest price in the market, thereby allowing his profit margin to be extended. Needless to say the bona-fide demolition contractor who has submitted a fair price to include all statutory requirements,[3] scaffolding and hoarding to safeguard the public becomes aggrieved, especially when he has been instructed in writing to include for all these.

Not all main contractors, may I say, adopt this method, but regretfully all too many do and even one is too many to allow for fair and equal tendering. Once a contract has been agreed between the main contractor and the demolition sub-contractor, the main contractor will tend to squeeze the contract time allowed for demolition, thereby giving other trades more room to manoeuvre should things go wrong later in the contract. The demolition contractor can agree to work under what conditions he considers most advantageous to him as an individual, although the NFDC has published suitable documents in the form of Standard Form of Contract[4] and a Standard Specification[5] as detailed in Appendices 2 and 3.

These documents allow for the work to be carried out with due thought for statutory requirements and the correct employment of labour under conditions to meet all the health and safety legislation applicable.

Before a demolition contractor can submit a realistic tender he must first be acquainted with all the conditions to be imposed and under what terms he is to operate.

Nevertheless, the professional, usually an architectural practice, has the site surveyed and prepares sketch drawings for discussion with the client. Once these have been approved, final plans and specifications are prepared and submitted to the local authority for planning and building regulation approval. Even at this stage it is usually only noted on the plans that existing buildings are to be demolished. In most cases, unless a preservation order is in being on the buildings, approval is given for the development to proceed.

## Tender procedure

From now on the architect is working against the clock because the client requires the completed project as soon as possible to achieve a return on their investment. The working drawings, bills of quantities and the specifications[6] are prepared, and even though the demolition is itemized in the bill of quantities scant attention is given to the actual work of demolition, and more often than not no detailed specification is prepared for the actual demolition work even though it is the first contract to be undertaken and any work programme must be affected by the time taken to carry out that part of the contract.

It is a sad reflection on the other professions and trades in the construction

17

industry, that when it comes to preparing a bar chart for a project, planning usually starts after demolition, allowing ample time for other elements of the contract and relegating the time allowed for demolition to that of least importance.

By this time the preparation of contract documents is well advanced for the project as a whole and invitations to tender for the overall project are advertised in the trade journals or negotiated with a demolition contractor if circumstances allow. When out to tender on a competitive basis certain rules are followed cumulating in a date being set for the return of tenders. On negotiated tenders the procedure differs slightly, but in the end a tender figure is agreed with a main contractor and given approval by the client for the project to proceed. A considerable amount of preliminary information is required either from the client or the main contractor before tendering to allow these conditions to be reflected in the tender figure. In addition, a clear and precise definition of the scope of the contract[7] is required.

The demolition contractor will require the following information:

1. Commencement dates and duration of the demolition contract.
2. Messing and toilet facilities, can they use the facilities supplied by the main contractor?
3. If first aid is supplied by the main contractor are these facilities available for his use also?
4. Has the demolition contractor free and clear access to the site or is this shared with the main contractor or others?
5. Details of any services to be retained and plans showing position of all existing services.
6. If any material is to be retained (a) who becomes responsible for security of material? (b) where is material to be stored?
7. Has the demolition contractor to supply site security or is this already allowed for in the main contract?
8. Is the demolition contractor to allow for any hoardings, scaffold, fencing, lighting, etc?
9. The precise area of the site and any areas not accessible to the demolition contractor.
10. Location and depth of any basement and if they are to be retained. If they are to be retained, under what conditions and any involvement required by the demolition contractor. If they are to be filled, what specification of fill material is required and should it be layered and compacted by mechanical means?
11. To what levels is the site to be reduced to and does that include all foundations and solid matter?
12. Is it the responsibility of the demolition contractor or the main contractor to obtain statutory approvals, licences, etc?
13. Are any materials or fittings not removed prior to the demolition commencing to become the property of the demolition contractor?

14. Have any buildings, containers, areas, etc. been contaminated or used for toxic, explosive or radioactive material?
15. Has the client or the public any right of way through the site during the contract and if so what precautions are necessary?
16. What insurance and indemnities are required to be carried by the demolition contractor?

The detailing and description of demolition work so that a true estimate can be arrived at, is very difficult. The architect cannot prepare a set of drawings similar to that for the main contractor, therefore he has to rely on his past experience of previous contractors or seek the guidance of such organizations as the National Federation of Demolition Contractors.

Demolition and dismantling contracts can be undertaken in one or two ways, either as a main contractor direct with the client or as a sub-contractor to a main contractor.

The category of the demolition contractor is also an important factor in selection for an approved list, as not all contractors are experienced or in fact competent to undertake all types of demolition and dismantling.[8] The client or his advisers must ensure the contractual competence and financial viability of any demolition contractor and must not rely on verbal assurances as the risks involved are extremely high in relation to the value of the demolition contract. Before any work of demolition is started the site and adjoining buildings should be surveyed in minute detail both internally and externally to ascertain the structural stability and condition of these buildings (Fig. 2.1).

The survey should take the form of a joint survey between the representative of the demolition contractor and a representative of the owner of these adjacent buildings, noting any structural cracks and damage, any subsidence, any roof damage and in fact anything which may lead to a claim for compensation at a later date. Photographs of areas of damage are always useful in case of disputes. Once the survey is complete and agreed both parties should sign and agree the survey report and each party take a copy for reference. It is always advisable to notify the main contractor who may require to be in attendance and receive a copy of the report.

## Before work starts

Certain checks should be carried out before any structure is removed. These can be carried out by the client, the main contractor or the demolition contractor, but at all times the demolition contractor should ensure that he has all the relevant information.

This, in fact, is a comprehensive check list on: the age of the structure; its state of preservation. The state of preservation should be obvious to a trained building surveyor, but the method of construction is not always evident; therefore it is always advisable to consult your local authority who holds the original

19

*Fig. 2.1*  Scaffold collapse caused by overloading and lack of adequate site survey prior to demolition

plans.

The age and condition of adjacent property is of prime importance, as they may be relying for support on the property to be demolished. Support rights, party rights, party wall agreements with adjoining owners, boundary walls, etc. all need to be checked. Careful examination of the property to be demolished and adjacent property is necessary to establish the siting of cellars, basements, underground tanks and wells, etc. The local authority requirements must be checked regarding licences, scaffolds, hoardings, etc. for the protection of the public and passing traffic.

### Building or structure check

1   *On what type of ground is the structure erected?* (Some soils, notably clay, can transmit shock waves a considerable distance and therefore do damage elsewhere.)

2.   *Check the condition of roof trusses.* In framed structures, what is the type of framing – steel, cast iron, wrought iron, concrete (cast *in situ*, precast, prestressed)? Are any unbalanced forces likely to occur?

3.   *Walls* – which are load bearing?
   - which have been reduced in thickness by cupboards, fireplaces, etc. and will, therefore, need protective support?
   - what is the condition and thickness of any walls or gables that are to remain?
   - what effect might the removal of buttress walls have on any surrounding structure?

4.   *Staircases, balconies, cornices* – where the construction is cantilevered, what type of support or counter-weighting has been used?

5.   *Pre-stressed concrete and multi-storey structures* – what system of stressing and construction was used? This information is vital to ensure safe working. (These structures, which have become increasingly popular in recent years, present serious dangers in future demolition work.) It is therefore necessary to:
   (a) check with the original contractor;
   (b) enquire from the local authority;
   (c) have the structure inspected by a specialist engineer.

6.   *Basements, cellars, etc.* – do these extend beneath pavements (either in the property to be demolished or in that adjacent)? Do they require filling?

7.   *Wells and springs* – check depth and position.

8.   *Storage tanks* (above or below ground) – check depth and/or position. Check what they were used for (e.g. petrol) in case other risks arise; as necessary, make them clean and safe to work on, e.g. for petrol tanks:
   (a) flood tank with water and seal ventilation holes;
   (b) flush out petrol vapour–air mixture by pumping in nitrogen; or
   (c) introduce solidified carbon dioxide (dry ice).

9.   *Structures known to be dangerous* – check with local authority on:
   (a) type of construction;
   (b) cause of damage.

10. *Lightning conductors* – check for radioactivity. On older types, a millicurie source of radium was sometimes fitted to the top. Since radium has a half-life of 1620 years, old conductors might well be radioactive.

11. *Original plans* – wherever possible locate and examine, though it must be admitted this is often impossible. If the nature of construction remains uncertain, a site investigation should be made by a specialist engineer.

12. *Examine the structure for any signs of a bench-mark.* These are Ordnance Survey markings, usually in two forms:
    (a) a brass plate, 180 mm × 100 mm inscribed:

    O     S
    ___

    B     M

    Above the broad arrow is a small cavity into which a spirit level can be set.
    If these plates are salvageable, they should be returned to the nearest Ordnance Survey Office.
    (b) a broad arrow, with bar above it, chisel-cut into brickwork or masonry. If either form exists on the structure to be demolished, at least make sure that the local Ordnance Survey Office is informed.

13. *Check that whatever has to be left will remain stable*, i.e. walls may need shoring, steam, acid or other pipe-work may need additional support.

14. If *street closures* or *traffic diversions* are likely to become necessary, make arrangements with the local authority.

## Public services

Check with the appropriate statutory undertaking to locate drains, electricity, gas, water, telephone lines, etc. Arrangements should be made for diversion, removal or, where they have to remain, for protection, and for any pipes connected to foul sewers to be sealed off (sewer gas is both toxic and explosive). A temporary water supply will often be needed so that spraying, to keep down dust, can take place.

## Statutory requirements[3]

Before any demolition work takes place, the owner of the building must notify, as appropriate:

1. the local authority under the Public Health Act 1961 (section 29);
2. the District Surveyor in the Inner London Area under the London Building Act (Amendment) 1939;
3. the Building Authority of Scottish Burghs or Counties under the Building (Scotland) Act 1959 (sections 6 (1) and 6 (6)).

(a)

(b)

*Fig. 2.2*   Types of hoarding: (a) plywood; (b) corrugated metal

Where demolition work could affect other property, the owner of the building must notify the other owners so that full agreement can be reached on matters of support, protection, disturbance, etc. For example, shoring or weather-proofing of adjoining party walls may have to be carried out prior to demolition. Her Majesty's Factory Inspectorate must be notified whenever construction work (including demolition) is expected to last for more than six weeks (Factories Act 1961, section 127 (7). All demolition contractors must satisfy themselves that these notifications have been made before work commences.

## On site

### General precautions

Irrespective of the actual method of demolition to be employed, the following items are of special significance:

1. Hoardings, minimum height 2.5 m, should be erected round the site (Fig. 2.2). On isolated sites, where there is no public access, a clearly defined danger area should be marked by pole or rope barriers with warning notices attached.
2. Wherever other operatives, the public, passing traffic or adjacent buildings of lower height need to be protected, fans should be erected at first floor level – minimum ten scaffold boards wide, with a splayed upstand minimum four boards high. If the building comprises four or more floors, then additional fans should be erected at alternate floors (Fig. 2.3).
3. Wherever possible, windows should be taken out before work starts to avoid damage by broken glass, etc. Window-frames should be left in to help maintain wall strength.
4. Window, door and other openings should be boarded.
5. Internal lift entrances should be boarded.
6. Access to all areas where flooring has been removed should be barred with at least one board to indicate danger.
7. Stone balconies and stone cantilever projections should be cut off before the main demolition starts.
8. Where scaffolds are to be used for work on stone-faced buildings and those with heavy overhanging cornices or string courses, a mason's scaffold is recommended.
9. All external metal staircases or ladders should be carefully inspected before use.
10. Once disturbed, stone staircases should not be used at all since they can no longer be regarded as safe access.
11. Staircases should be kept free from debris.
12. Timber, taken out during demolition work, should have any projecting nails and screws flattened or removed.

13. Personnel protection:
    Wearing of safety boots is vitally important.
    Safety helmets (type BS 2826 preferred) are always advisable.
    Light goggles in high winds or dusty conditions.
    Special goggles where burning equipment is being used.
    Safety belts/harness for all men liable to fall when working in isolated or awkward positions, especially if pneumatic, electric or burning equipment is in use.
    (All protective equipment should be to BS specification)
14. Strict control should be exercised over the burning of rubbish – especially where large amounts of old timber are being burnt, flames fanned by a breeze can easily get out of hand.

*Fig. 2.3* The erection of protective scaffold, fans and hoardings around a demolition site

15. Particular attention is required to fire precautions whenever thermic lances or oxyacetylene cutting equipment are being used and to the dispersal of fumes from burning old paint when flame-cutting old painted steelwork.
16. Explosives must be properly stored.

The contractor can now proceed to start the work of demolition. The type of structure to be demolished will determine the method which is adopted. Usually any material of value is removed as soon as practicable, followed by the stripping and removal of internal fixtures and fittings, followed in a progressive manner by the roof covering, roof timbers and finally the superstructure.

When the demolition contractor has been successful in open competition there is usually a penalty clause built into his contract, therefore he is always mindful of the need to complete in the stipulated time without the penalty – which is almost always monetary – being invoked. This has to be considered when first tendering, but at this stage in the contract he must rely on his own resources, including proper use of his plant and equipment, but more important the availability of sufficient experienced demolition operatives supervised by a competent foreman and controlled by an experienced manager.

When the NFDC was first incorporated the supply and quality of labour was in abundance; albeit not experienced in modern techniques which have de-

*Fig. 2.4* Typically labour-intensive demolition site in the early days of the NFDC

veloped in recent years, they were eager to work (Fig. 2.4). The present-day labour force, although more mechanically orientated, demand better conditions, and quite rightly so, but also fail to produce the conscientious pattern of work and timekeeping once evident.

With all the problems, legislation and the restrictions imposed on the contractor from all levels of society there comes a fine balance between profit and loss on a contract. This balance is not always conducive to good relations between employer and employee, but is a very important factor in the life of the contractor. Without the contractor there can be no employee.

## Chapter 3

# The Code of Practice – CP94:1971 – Demolition
# UDC 69.059.6

The Code of Practice, like all other codes, is a document published by the British Standards Institution and can be obtained from suppliers of British Standard publications.

The British Standards Institution was founded in 1901 and incorporated by Royal Charter in 1929.[1] The principal aims of the Institution are to co-ordinate the efforts of producers and users for the improvement, standardization and simplification of engineering and industrial materials; to simplify production and distribution, to eliminate the waste of time and material involved in the production of an unnecessary variety of patterns and sizes of articles for one and the same purpose, to set up standards of quality and dimensions and to promote the general adoption of British Standards. The Institute endeavours to ensure adequate representation of all points of view. There has to be a recognized need to be met, with a strong body of opinion in favour of that need, before the approval of a British Standard.

This Code of Practice was prepared by a committee convened by the Code of Practice Committee, who specialize in building and was first published under the authority of the Executive Board on the 21 May 1971.[1] The Code also refers to scaffolds and the safe use of cranes.

As stated elsewhere, the Code of Practice is not mandatory but is a recommendation.[2] Nevertheless, the contents of the Code have been devised by a committee of people with expert knowledge and experience in the industry and, although not legally enforceable, could and would be used by the courts as a way of indicating recommendations and working practices in the industry. Compliance with the Code of Practice does not exclude a contractor from other relevant statutory and legal requirements.

The Code[3] itself covers all aspects of procedures involved in demolition including: 1. General; 2. Procedures; 3. Protective precautions; 4. Method of demolition; 5. Recommendations for various types of demolition of structures.

There are a number of sketches and tables in the Code of Practice setting out safety requirements, and although it is not proposed to go into details on the content of the Code it is necessary to say that any person contemplating carrying out demolition as client, contractor or anyone involved in the project should, as a first priority, obtain and study a copy of the Code. For any part not under-

28

stood, they should immediately seek expert advice.

As certain items such as method, recommendations and illustrations listed in the Code are covered in separate chapters of this book it is unnecessary to duplicate such details in this chapter. It is, however, necessary to highlight certain important sections in the Code of Practice and these are set out below.

*Section 2.2.1. Insurance*

We all know that full and adequate insurance is required to carry out any work in construction in Great Britain. It is not always obvious at first sight of the policy that adequate insurance cover is in being, and regrettably not all insurance brokers know or care what is adequate. An annual insurance is not always sufficient – therefore the main contractor and/or the client should look closely at the small print and schedule to ascertain what is covered and the amount of cover in force. Being aware after an accident or occurrence is not enough.

It has not been unknown for a unscrupulous demolition contractor to take out limited cover to obtain the contract and then have the policy terminated. Most reputable demolition contractors take out full and adequate annual policies for works of demolition and dismantling, and should additional cover be required they obtain endorsements to the policy to cover such work.

Because of the high risk in the demolition and dismantling industry a number of insurance companies are reluctant to carry policies for demolition and dismantling contractors. There are sufficient insurance companies willing to provide competitive quotations providing always that the company requiring the cover is not classed as a 'high risk' policy.

*Section 2.2.2. Statutory notices*

It is a requirement that any demolition work which is expected to last more than *six weeks* should be reported to HM District Construction Inspector of Factories before the work commences. In a large number of cases this is not done for a variety of reasons, some out of ignorance of the requirements, others simply so that the Inspector is not aware of the contract. This can be for one reason only: that is, to allow the contractor free and unhindered access to break the law to some degree or other. The contractor and/or the client must know at the time of tendering approximately how long the contract should take, and it is at this stage that the Inspector should be notified.

*Section 2.2.4. Assigning or under-letting*

Most contracts, in fact all national and local government contracts, contain a clause which precludes the under-letting or sub-letting of any or part of a contract without written permission, and yet numerous occasions occur when this happens and only come to light when an accident or site inspection occurs. No genuine client or main contractor would withhold permission, but is required to know to be able to safeguard himself as well as the demolition contractor.

(a)

(b)

*Fig. 3.1(a)*   Dangerous, partly demolished, building without any control or supervision.
   *(b)*   Unfenced or unhoarded site with total lack of concern for public safety

*Section 2.2.5. Supervision*

The Code is clear with regard to this section, with the emphasis being on the word 'competent'. It is not sufficient to say to an operative, 'you can be in charge to look after things'. A competent foreman must be aware of, and understand, legislation and safety requirements and be able to interpret the client's specification. The larger contractors employ not only very experienced foremen but site engineers and consultants to advise on dangerous areas not normally found in conventional demolition.

*Section 3.3.1. Safety and convenience of third parties*

This, in my opinion is the one section which is ignored and abused by more contractors' clients and everyone connected with the industry. The paragraph within this section I refer to is 'properly secured or closed against entry at all times when demolition operations are not in progress and that the buildings or structures are left in a safe condition at the close of each day's work'. How often do you see an open demolition site when, for instance, the operatives have gone for their break, or during non-working hours? I regret that this occurs all too often, and children and the public at large are put at risk because no one considered it necessary or, more to the point, thought it too expensive to fence the site against access (Figs. 3.1(a) and (b)).

The best example of compliance with this section of the Code of Practice can be seen in most London boroughs where the specified requirements are for a 2.438 m high corrugated fence to surround the sites as in Fig. 3.2(a) and (b). A

(a)                                                    (b)

*Fig. 3.2*   (a) and (b) Typical corrugated metal hoardings specified by most London boroughs

*Fig. 3.3* Potentially dangerous situation – the public right of way has not been diverted, leaving open access to dangerous structures

very bad example[4] of non-compliance can be seen in Fig. 3.3, where not only is there no protection but there is clear evidence that a public footpath across the site is used by the public alongside a partly demolished dangerous building. This standard is not acceptable and should be eliminated by closer supervision by supervising officers and clerks of works.

*Section 3.4.1.    General*

In respect of adjacent property, the contractor must, in his original survey, have agreed with the adjacent owners or occupiers whether permanent or temporary weather-proofing is to be applied to all or any exposed perimeter walls on their property, and if any permanent or temporary supports are required. The exposed walls may require rendering as a permanent weather-proofing or a liquid or polythene membrane fixed to the walls as a temporary measure. Should the use of shoring be required, whether temporary or permanent, the advice of an expert structural engineer should always be sought. The three types of shoring used by or on behalf of the demolition contractor are raking shores (Fig. 3.4), flying shores (Fig. 3.5) and dead shores. One of the best examples of the dead shore is the adjustable metal prop with a flat top and bottom plate and a slot and screw adjustment within the length of the prop (Fig. 3.6). Its versatility means that it can be used with both modern and traditional formwork systems; it is economical inasmuch as it is re-usable, can be erected quickly by unskilled labour without any additional or special tools, has a large range of adjustment and is easy to handle. All adjustable props should conform to BS 4074:1966. It should always be noted that any shoring is designed to be used as a support and should not be erected in such a way that it may in fact push the building it is

*Fig. 3.4*   The use of timber raking shores constructed through an existing concrete floor

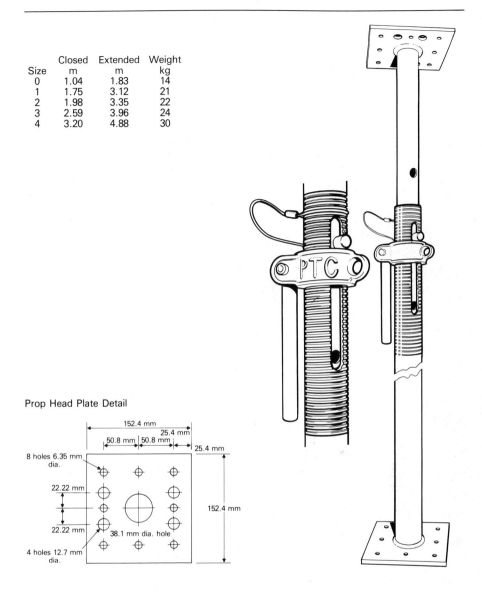

| Size | Closed m | Extended m | Weight kg |
|------|----------|------------|-----------|
| 0 | 1.04 | 1.83 | 14 |
| 1 | 1.75 | 3.12 | 21 |
| 2 | 1.98 | 3.35 | 22 |
| 3 | 2.59 | 3.96 | 24 |
| 4 | 3.20 | 4.88 | 30 |

Prop Head Plate Detail

*Fig. 3.5* (facing page) The use of timber to construct flying and dead shoring

*Fig. 3.6* Adjustable prop for use as a dead shore

*Fig. 3.7*  The use of scaffolding to construct raking shores

*Fig. 3.8*  The use of scaffolding to construct flying shores between two adjacent buildings

designed to retain.

It is common practice today for tubular scaffolding to be used for all types of shoring, and Figs. 3.7 and 3.8 are clear examples of the use of tubular scaffolding for raking and flying shores. Numerous examples of shoring are illustrated in Chapter 5.

*Section 3.3.5.    Excavation and removal of redundant petroleum tanks*
Always and without exception seek the advice of the Local Authority Petroleum officer, the Local Fire Officer and the Health and Safety Executive before the removal of any tank or fittings which has had, or you *suspect* may have had, petroleum spirits or other flammable or explosive liquid stored in them, no matter how much time has elapsed since they were last used.

Inexperienced handling can be dangerous and can cause an explosion, often with the loss of life or serious accidents. Always display adequate notices around any tank being removed and on any vehicle being used to transport a redundant tank away from a site for re-use or disposal elsewhere.

*Section 5 – and all sections*
Ensure that you know the composition and make-up of any component you are

*Fig. 3.9*   The use of a hydraulic lift as a safe working platform

proposing to remove. Make sure a detailed survey has been carried out by an expert. We all consider we know best until an accident happens, yet when it happens we can and should learn by our mistakes – mistakes which are all too often fatal.

Finally, although not detailed in any one section as it is relevant to all demolition and dismantling, ensure you always work from a safe working platform. This platform can be from a permanent floor not being removed, scaffolding or a portable mechanical type of platform as illustrated by the Simon Chair type in Fig. 3.9 and described in Chapter 7.

The Code gives various recommendations and explanations which have been tried and tested over many years by experts in the field of demolition and dismantling and is there for the guidance of others.

Always plan ahead and prepare a programme of work before you start. Seek the advice of your local Health and Safety Executive or other experts in their specialized fields.

## Chapter 4

# Demolition techniques

## *Conventional structures*[1]

When buildings and other structures have been designed in the past, little or no attention has been given to the question as to how these buildings and structures are to be demolished when their economic, commercial or structural life has expired.[2]

It can be assumed that the architect and structural engineer have never given any thought to the destruction of their creation, and until recently would have given little co-operation to such research. Morever, until recently the buildings and structures being demolished were constructed of material such as brick and stone with timber components and conventional roofs. These materials were easy to dispose of or to re-use.

Modern building techniques have seen the increased use of concrete not only in the frame of new constructions but in complete units. The method of construction varies and is detailed later in the chapter. With this increased use of concrete in construction since the end of the Second World War comes the problem for demolition contractors of how to dispose of this material when demolition arises.

Research is already taking place throughout the world as to the best methods of demolition and disposal of pre-stressed and tensioned buildings[3] and in fact the labour required in such work.

A number of physical as well as environmental problems will need to be considered not only for future work of demolition but in the design of buildings and structures which one day will be demolished or dismantled, namely:

1. Can a building be designed so that it can be dismantled to some degree and the components re-used or removed to other areas for disposal?

2. Research and design of new plant and equipment to reduce and eliminate dust and noise which will become increasingly unacceptable in densely populated areas as the population become aware of environmental pollution.

3. The increased volume of material to be disposed of and the diminishing number of areas acceptable and classified as disposal points.

4. With disposal points becoming limited can this material be recycled and re-used as aggregate thereby eliminating two problems? One of disposal of the demolished material and one of excavation for supplies of aggregate for use in the construction industry.

5. The less acceptable methods by the labour force of the strenuous physical effort demanded by the present plant and equipment. (An example of this being the pneumatic hammer used by demolition operatives and the physical damage they can cause.)

The economic life of a building or structure depends on many aspects, none being more important than care and maintenance. Nevertheless, the life of a building can vary between eight and eighty years, therefore it can be assumed that in the near future a considerable number of concrete as well as brick and stone structures will have to be demolished. With the concrete stressed and tensioned structures comes the problem (see *Tensioned structures* on pp 51–61)

It was estimated that in the whole of the EEC[4] in 1975 something like 800 million tons of concrete were produced. We accept that not all of this will be demolished in the near future. Nevertheless, if that rate of growth continued this would account for something in the region of £7000 m. worth of concrete, most of which would be required to be demolished each year. Although these are only estimated figures it shows clearly the problems ahead facing the demolition contractor as well as the designer.

At present about £500 m. is spent throughout the EEC on the demolition of concrete structures. This figure will increase as society demands more and more sophisticated conditions, and although problems are already emerging all too little attention is being placed on conventional techniques which are listed below.

### Hand demolition

Normally carried out by operatives using manually operated or portable tools such as mattocks in the southern areas of the country or long bars in the North or Scotland, shovels, pneumatic hammers, drills, etc. Cranes and lifting appliances are often used to supplement the labour and provide a means to support and lower structural members while they are being cut and lowered to the ground.[5]

Structures that are to be demolished in this way normally[6] have any salvageable material removed prior to demolition. The floors or parts of the floors are usually removed before any structural demolition takes place to allow the free fall of debris from roof and upper floors, otherwise there would be a build-up of debris on the upper floors which would cause an overload and could bring about premature collapse. Floors to be opened up must retain structural stability and must be secured by barriers when not in use. Debris must never be allowed to accumulate on retained floor areas to the extent where an overload situation becomes evident. The removal of debris through the open floors should never be allowed to build up against outer walls or structural components below the level at which work is being carried out, or at ground floor level to the extent where lateral pressure against these walls could cause premature collapse. Under normal circumstances the roof covering and roof timbers are removed in reverse order to that of erection.

In the case of hand demolition, wherever practicable, all demolition material should be lowered to the ground by means of a properly constructed chute or the use of a skip and lowered by crane. If it is intended to drop or throw material a lookout man should be so positioned on the perimeter of the fall area to confirm when it is safe to drop any material. The fall area must always be sufficiently clear of any other work area, public highway, footpath or adjacent property so as not to be classed as dangerous because of flying debris.

On the completion of work at the end of the day the supervisor should ensure that all walls, floors and supports are left in a structurally stable condition. Access to these properties should be prevented at all times when work is not taking place. Where only partial demolition is taking place the demolition contractor must ensure through his structural engineer that the structure to be retained remains stable at all times and a constant check and report commissioned for these parts.

Hand demolition is used on restricted sites, is labour-intensive and tends to be slow and laborious.

### Demolition ball

The crane capacity must be adequate to cope with the weight of the ball the contractor proposes to use when the crane is at the full radius of its swing. All safety equipment on the crane must be in good working order, the crane operator should be trained and experienced in the use of the crane and must be conversant with the limits to which the machine has been designed.[6] The supervisor must also be competent and conversant with the capabilities of the machine. The ball (Fig. 4.1) should also be used with a drag line so that it can be kept under the control of the operator at all times. Slewing with the ball imposes additional stress on the jib and should not be allowed. The roof of the machine to which the ball is fixed should be reinforced to withstand falling debris, all windows should be protected by a mesh cage or similar protection and glass should be reinforced.

Before any balling takes place the contractor must ensure that the area to be demolished has been checked to ensure that no operative is within and lookouts posted to stop any operatives gaining access during the operation. Checks should be made before recommencing work after lunch break or similar stoppage. As with hand demolition, floors should be removed to allow free fall of debris so that a build-up of material cannot exert lateral pressure against structural walls. Tall structures in excess of 30 m should be reduced by hand before using the demolition ball.

Buildings to be demolished that are attached to one which has to remain

41

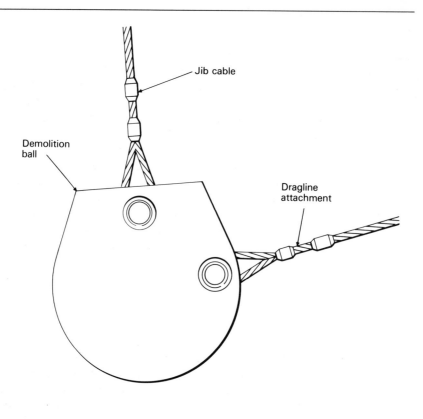

| Weight kg | Overall length mm | Overall width mm |
|---|---|---|
| 508 | 520 | 518 |
| 762 | 609 | 584 |
| 1016 | 654 | 648 |
| 1270 | 724 | 699 |
| 1524 | 756 | 724 |
| 2032 | 845 | 825 |

*Fig. 4.1*  Specification of demolition balls

should first be detached by hand demolition, leaving a clear span of at least 6 m between before the use of a ball is considered. All parts of all structures should be left in a stable condition at the end of each day. This method is highly dangerous unless a very experienced crane operator is used. Not recommended when the retention of components is essential. Slow and laborious when used on reinforced concrete.

Pusher arm

The machine should only be used in accordance with manufacturer's instructions[6] and should be fitted with a deflector plate (Fig. 4.2) to eliminate the possibility of back fall of debris on to the cab of the machine. The operator should be trained and fully conversant with the machine. The machine should have sufficient working space to allow it to manoeuvre and for the free fall of debris. Local authority permission must be obtained before this type of operation can take place from a public highway.

Buildings demolished by this method should first be reduced to such a height as to allow safe working of the machine, and if attached to adjoining buildings should be broken away as specified for balling. The structure should be reduced in height by pushing small sections at a time. The pusher arm should engage the building no more than 1 m from the top of the remaining structure. This method not only allows for more speedy demolition but ensures the pusher arm does not impose undue stress on the jib of the machine.

Deliberate collapse

Before any demolition contractor undertakes this method the advice and retention of a structural engineer is necessary. This method can only be undertaken when the whole structure is to be demolished, as this method relies on the removal of components to effect total collapse. The most advantageous site for this method is a level site with adequate area surrounding to allow free fall away from operatives and equipment. It is not advisable for section by section demolition of a structure, but if this is done the engineer must ascertain that the structure left standing remains stable at all times.[6]

Pulling by wire rope

This is another form of demolition by deliberate collapse. This type of demolition requires large areas of open space around the building to be demolished. All sections of the building to be removed in this way must be wired up prior to any demolition taking place, and the free ends of the pulling cables left in a convenient area not to be covered by previous pulling. This method requires a tracked machine of suitable size or a winch anchored to the ground. The cable used must not be less than 25 mm in diameter and the pulling device should be located at a distance not less than one and a half times that of the structure being demolished.

It is advisable to have a second cable already installed as a replacement on a difficult structure so that if the first cable breaks you are not required to enter an unstable structure to refix the replacement cable. The cable should be inspected after each pull to ascertain its condition.[6]

Before consideration of this method any structure being demolished must be completely detached from adjoining property. Demolition by this method can

*Fig. 4.2*  Hydraulic excavator with deflector plate fitted to the demolition arm and metal protector fitted to cab

cause nuisance from dust and the uncontrolled collapse can often be time-consuming during clearing operations.

## Explosives

Demolition should only be carried out by a competent explosive specialist[6] who holds licences to store and work the explosives. There are numerous types of explosives available with a wide range of detonators for use on various types of demolition. It should not be assumed that explosives operators in industries such as quarrying and agriculture or in the armed forces are sufficiently experienced to take control of this type of work in demolition. The storage and conveyance of explosives must always comply with the 1875 and 1923 Explosives Act and any subsequent orders.

The explosives operative should have a certificate of competence in the use of explosives for demolition and civil engineering works, should be not less than twenty-one years of age and should have a minimum of one year's experience before being placed in charge of an explosives operation.

The operative should know and understand the following:

1. The law relating to storage of explosives.
2. The law relating to conveyance of explosives.
3. The characteristics of the explosives which he uses daily. (In simple terms their velocity of detonation and work output related to the cartridge weight.)
4. Simple electrical terms, and be capable of calculating resistance in ohms, to ensure that an electrical exploder unit always has greater output than the resistance it has to overcome.
5. Simple electrical circuits and their functions: series, parallel, how to avoid short-circuits, latent electricity in structures.
6. Not to use electric initiation during thunderstorms or conditions of high static electricity.
7. Safe methods of handling explosives (piercing cartridges, cutting cartridges, conveyance about the site, loading into holes, fixing detonators, etc.)
8. Calculating burden, spacing, depth of holes relative to the charge weight and the degree of fragmentation required in the various masses and materials with which he can be called upon to work.
9. Safety of other persons on site and the public at large when carrying out blasting operations.
10. The amount of protection afforded by blasting mats and blankets, also advising what other protection of vital plant and equipment may be necessary.
11. The degree of security necessary to fire a particular blast and the protection of the danger area (signals, guards, fences, etc.) Safety checks and the dismantling of the operation.

(a)           (b)

(c)           (d)

*Fig. 4.3* Series time sequence in blowing a cooling tower using explosive charges at Swindon power station by London Demolition (UK) Ltd .

12. How to deal with misfires.
13. Some knowledge of the effects of explosives in terms of air blast.
14. The effects of explosive forces through the ground and how they affect structures.
15. How to drill holes, and how to obtain the best results from a charge by spacings and angling of the holes.
16. Procedure to be adopted in an emergency.

Before a company can obtain a licence they should have a properly constructed and licensed explosives store. The directors or management should have a working knowledge of the Explosives Act relating to the storage and conveyance of explosives and all other relevant Acts. The company should employ at least one operative who has a certificate of competence in the use of explosives.

Demolition by explosives differs from most other types of blasting in as much as one rarely has a second chance to experiment, as in most cases it is a once-only situation. The hazards caused by an incorrectly positioned charge can have disastrous effects and leave a structure in an unsafe condition.

There are two obvious advantages of this type of demolition. Speed of removal of the structure and safety for other operatives in as much as no one need be in the immediate area of demolition and the work can then be carried out by remote control from a safe distance. Figures 4.3, 4.4 and 4.5 illustrate the safe and speedy use of explosives in demolition.

The disadvantages are threefold: first, the storage of explosives on site when these could be stolen or otherwise tampered with; secondly, when used the damage caused by flying debris; third, the danger to other buildings caused by blast where the effects of airborne of ground-transmitted shock waves can be underestimated.

More recently, delayed fuses have been used with success. These fuses cause a slight delay between the firing of small charges which in fact represents the same effect as a much larger charge without the problems of excessive noise and less risk from flying debris.

A checklist should be operated when using explosives and should determine:

1. A safe and prearranged escape route should anything go wrong.
2. Ensure the public are kept at a safe distance at all times.
3. Ensure the operation has been pre-planned and the whole team is aware of the procedures to be used.
4. Plan and operate an adequate warning system and ensure all personnel are aware and understand.
5. Have a predetermined procedure to operate should a misfire occur.
6. Seek the approval of the police and co-operate with them to control the public.

The Home Office demand strict control on the sale and storage of explosives,

*Fig. 4.4(a)*   Use of explosives in demolition – before

*Fig. 4.4(b)*   Use of explosives in demolition – during

therefore anyone considering their use must first obtain advice from the nearest main police station.

### Demolition by expansion

This method is used more to break up material such as concrete rather than actual demolition. After drilling a hole in the concrete or masonry a metal cylinder is inserted, expansion is then obtained by small pistons or cylinders which produce outward displacement, thereby cracking the structure. Another method is to insert a liquid $CO_2$ cartridge into the holes after drilling, which, when the gas expands, will create considerable outward pressure. This is known as the **cardox** method. This method, although slow, allows for working in close proximity to other buildings.

### Thermic lance

This method has been widely used in the steel industry for a number of years. The main danger with this method is that an inexperienced operator could suffer severe burns. The components used are a lance holder, a thermic lance which is constructed of 19 mm metal pipe approximately 3 m in length and packed with mild steel rods, adequate supplies of oxygen and a means of ignition.[6] The tip of the lance is pre-heated to 1000 °C, oxygen is then fed into

*Fig. 4.4(c)* Use of explosives in demolition – after

*Fig. 4.5*   The end results in the use of explosives in demolition

the lance and the mild steel rods ignite producing a flame in excess of 2500 °C, enough to melt the reinforcing and the concrete. Operatives should always wear protective clothing and be aware that the cutting of certain materials can produce toxic fumes.

### Hydro laser (water jet)

This is a method used to cut cement grout to realize components. At present the pressure required to cut concrete is 379 225 kN/m$^2$, and at the time of writing a suitable pump has not been developed to produce such force. The cutting of grout needs something in the region of 68 950 kN/m$^2$.

### Radar (microwaves or the eddy current)

The principle of these methods is to pass the microwave energy into the mass, the transfer of energy causes heat and the mass becomes hot and any liquid absorbed may vaporize. On concrete this method causes steam within the concrete, thereby causing cracking to occur by steam pressure.

### Diamond saws and drills

These are useful when only partial demolition is taking place and areas of floor or wall are required to be cut away. The main advantage is that a clean cut can be obtained. The cutters are bulky and require a firm base to work. The depth of cut is limited, thereby restricting the use of this method to specialized areas.

### The slageater

A semi-automatic machine used mainly in the removal of slag and linings from inside blast furnaces. This method has the advantage of the operator being well away from the area of operation.

### Cryogenic method

This method is, in simple terms, the quick freezing of material (usually steel) in a restricted area at which time it is brittle and can be easily removed. This method which has limited although important use, is expensive to use and time consuming. Details of the cryogenic method and the supply of material should be obtained from the British Oxygen Co. Ltd, Technical Services Department.

## Tensioned structures

The possibility of unfortunately witnessing an uncontrolled projectile when passing a large demolition site is ever increasing. This projectile could be a large tensioned concrete component that some unsuspecting demolition operative has, through his lack of knowledge, launched into space.

The seriousness of this situation has to be emphasized in any way possible to bring to the attention of designers and the public at large what could be in store for them when a tensioned structure is demolished.

The danger which exists is the vast amount of energy created in these modern structures by the tensioned method of construction, and when the time occurs for demolition to take place and that stored energy is accidentally released prematurely by the cutting through of the steel tensioned bars, the building would react like a bomb and explode with missiles flying in all directions. This would not only inevitably kill the demolition operative concerned and several of his colleagues but must surely put the public at great risk.

Most of these tensioned buildings are in densely populated areas or units which employ a vast number of personnel, therefore the effect would be a major disaster.

Some while ago the NFDC published a pamphlet *The Bomb in Every High*

*Fig. 4.6* The 'special building' plaque as recommended by the NFDC for buildings containing stressed concrete

*Street* to try to outline the potential dangers of pre-stressed concrete structures being demolished without knowledge of their destructive powers. It is often said and written that this type of statement is scaremongering and only goes to promote the 'cause'. *This is not so* and it must be stressed that to be aware of any problems and their cause prior to any happening should be the concern of all in authority, and the public at large should also assist in the promotion of such measures.

In post-war years the need to design bigger, higher and more complex buildings using modern technology such as pre-stressed concrete without any thought as to what would be required when the inevitable day for demolition arrived, is still to a large extent still occurring without any recorded facts regarding methods of demolition.

The NFDC were so concerned with the risk attached to the ever-increasing number of tensioned structures being built that some years ago they made a valiant attempt to promote the idea of placing a plaque on all new building having in their construction the potential hazards of any tensioned components. The plaque was to take the form of the outer circle of the NFDC logo with a special building (SB)[7] and number internally. It was suggested the plaque be placed in a prominent position in the entrance to the building and a register kept of all such plaques issued (Fig. 4.6). Regretfully, only one local authority, the City of London, took up the challenge and adopted the SB plaque, and yet throughout Great Britain this type of structure is still being constructed and approved for construction by our planning authorities both at local and national level.

There is little documented evidence available on the demolition of tensioned structures and little research has been carried out. In 1975 the NFDC instigated the formation of the Joint Liaison Committee (JLC) on the *Demolition of Pre-Stressed Concrete Structures*[7] which outlined the problems associated with tensioned structures and presented possible solutions.

The concern shown by planners, designers and constructors as a whole leads one to believe that once again, without the NFDC who promoted this study along with such associations, institutions and societies who made up the Committee, there would have been no progress achieved in identifying such buildings for future generations.

The main problems which appear to be facing the demolition industry is first the keeping of all related information on this type of structure. Here it would seem logical for an organization such as the DDIR to keep in such a form as microfilm all such records, and as suggested by the JLC report this could be funded by local authorities and the owners of such buildings. There would be numerous problems to overcome to identify existing buildings, but unless a start is made the problem only multiplies. The other problem that exists is technology. Not so much in design of such structures, as this has been tried and tested for a number of years, but little or no experience is available on how to release the tension on units incorporated into buildings.

There are a number of methods of pre-stressing concrete as catalogued in the JLC report on the *Demolition of Pre-Stressed Concrete Structures*, some of these are illustrated in the photographs which can be seen in Figs. 4.7–4.23. The use of pre-stressed concrete in buildings has only occurred since around 1946 therefore, the need for large-scale demolition of such structures has never arisen.

*Fig. 4.7*　Typical pre-stressed 'T' beam

*Fig. 4.8*　Typical standard box beam (hollow core). *Note*: wire burnt off close to concrete surface

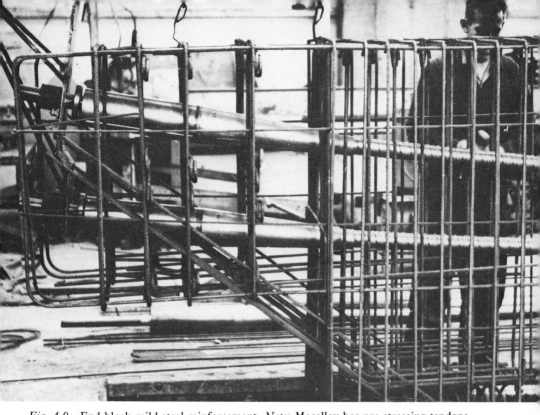

*Fig. 4.9*   End block mild steel reinforcement. *Note*: Macalloy bar pre-stressing tendons

*Fig. 4.10*   Continuous beam pre-stressing construction

Fig. 4.11  Macalloy system of pre-stressing.
Note: thread projecting beyond nut may or may
not be cut off before protective concrete is cast

Fig. 4.12  Freysinnet system of anchorage

Fig. 4.13  Freysinnet system of anchorage (end view)

Fig. 4.14    Multiple-wire opposed anchors    Fig. 4.15    Single opposed strand anchors

Fig. 4.16    Circumferential pre-stressing with strand anchors cast into buttresses. *Note*: vertical pre-stressing using Macalloy bars

Fig. 4.17   Circumferential pre-stressing systems to tanks

Fig. 4.18   Typical example of the Magnel-Blaton wedge anchor

Fig. 4.19   Another example of the Magnel-Blaton wedge anchor

Fig. 4.20   Wires button headed into threaded anchor which is secured by locking pin

*Fig. 4.21*   Single wire anchorages

*Fig. 4.22*   Typical eight-wire anchorage using spiral reinforcement behind bearing plate

*Fig. 4.23* Stressing on tanks in an opposed type anchorage

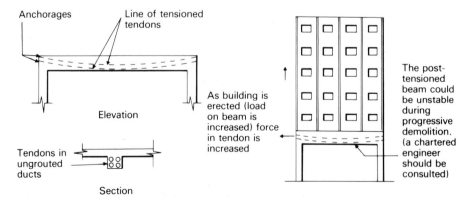

*Fig. 4.24* Post-tensioned beams

There are two basic methods of pre-stressing in use today, these being: (1) pre-tensioning; (2) post-tensioning (Fig. 4.24). The energy is contained in the high-tension steel cable used to give increased strength to concrete. The tendons are positioned in various locations to give high compression stresses where required in the section and a force equivalent to an average stress of about 6895 kN/m$^2$ over the whole cross-sectional area of the section is applied.

The problem facing demolition contractors is how to 'unstress' the building prior to demolition. One such method could be core testing, although extreme care would need to be adopted with this method because of the danger of cutting the actual tendons while drilling the core.

There are numerous very impressive buildings throughout the country which when the time comes no one will be certain how to remove. One such building which has previously attracted criticism – for other reasons – is Centre Point, a well-known London landmark which, although no one is considering demolishing it, will one day present a future generation of demolition contractors with an enormous problem.

In the USA the methods of explosion and implosion are widely used, and although not acceptable in Great Britain at this time to any great extent, may one day be the only solution to a problem which at present appears to have no solution.

## Industrial structures

Demolition of industrial structures in general follows the same procedure and legislation, although a number of other precautions have also to be taken into consideration, two of the main ones being as follows:

1. Is it total demolition; or
2. Is it partial with the remaining structure still 'live' and producing.

The type of structure in the industrial category which comes to mind where hidden hazards could cause serious injury or death as a result of toxic material and liquid being present, or the residue of such still remaining in tanks or vessels[8] or where crocidolite (blue asbestos)[9] or other fibrous material are present, are chemical works, power stations or heavy engineering or steelworks. When the demolition contractor moves in, the operatives often have to work in confined spaces where dangerous processes have taken place and where poisonous gases could still be present.

The chief risk to operatives in these situations where toxic or poisonous gases, fumes or vapour are present is that the operative could be totally ignorant of the fact, neglect to inform a supervisor and the result could be fatal.[10]

A typical such situation would be working in a confined space such as a duct, tank or vessel, and those less obvious but equally dangerous such as open tanks, vats, steel ladles, unventilated rooms, furnaces and ovens in which a concentrated build-up of gases can occur. These fumes can arise from within the area

## PERMIT-TO-WORK CERTIFICATE

|  |  |  |  |
|---|---|---|---|
| PLANT DETAILS (Location, identifying number, etc.) | | ACCEPTANCE OF CERTIFICATE | I have read and understood this certificate and will undertake to work in accordance with the conditions in it<br><br>Signed    Time<br>Date |
| WORK TO BE DONE | | | |
| WITHDRAWAL FROM SERVICE | The above plant has been removed from service and persons under my supervision have been informed<br><br>Signed    Date    Time | COMPLETION OF WORK | The work has been completed and all persons under my supervision, materials and equipment withdrawn<br><br>Signed    Time<br>Date |
| ISOLATION | The above plant has been isolated from all sources of ingress of dangerous fumes, etc.<br>Signed<br>The above has been isolated from all sources of electrical and mechanical power<br>Signed<br>The above plant has been isolated from all sources of heat<br><br>Signed    Time<br>Date | REQUEST FOR EXTENSION | The work has not been completed and permission to continue is requested<br><br>Signed    Time<br>Date |
| CLEANING AND PURGING | The above plant has been freed of dangerous materials<br>Material(s):    Method(s):<br><br>Signed    Time<br>Date | EXTENSION | I have re-examined the plant detailed above and confirm that the certificate may be extended to expire at:<br><br>Further precautions:<br><br>Signed    Time<br>Date |
| TESTING | Contaminants tested    Results<br><br>Signed    Time<br>Date | THIS PERMIT TO WORK IS NOW CANCELLED. A NEW PERMIT WILL BE REQUIRED IF WORK IS TO CONTINUE | |
| I CERTIFY THAT I HAVE PERSONALLY EXAMINED THE PLANT DETAILED ABOVE AND SATISFIED MYSELF THAT THE ABOVE PARTICULARS ARE CORRECT<br>*(1) THE PLANT IS SAFE FOR ENTRY WITHOUT BREATHING APPARATUS<br>(2) BREATHING APPARATUS MUST BE WORN<br>Other precautions necessary:<br>Time of expiry of certificate:<br>*Delete (1) or (2)<br><br>Signed    Time<br>Date | | RETURN TO SERVICE | I accept the above plant back into service<br><br>Signed    Time<br>Date |

*Fig. 4.25* Permit-to-work certificate

by reason of material being disturbed by the demolition or dismantling or from outside, when fumes from a 'live' plant can filter through from adjoining areas not completely isolated. Sludge or sediment in the base of tanks and vessels will always be contaminated to a greater or less degree; therefore, before it is disturbed the advice of a chemist or supervisor who has been involved in the process must be obtained. The demolition operation itself can often cause toxic fumes, such as burning lead-painted surfaces[11] and the removal of plastics with a solvent adhesive base.

The use of oxy-propane cutting equipment in confined space will enrich the atmosphere and would increase the risk of spontaneous combustion. The reverse could arise in a tank which has been 'de-gassed' to remove toxic or flammable vapour. This process has made the atmosphere deficient in oxygen and the operative could be asphyxiated.

All such work in these confined spaces must be well supervised by highly trained supervisors and all necessary precautions taken at all times. No work should be carried out without a proper system of control, starting with a permit to work. This document could take the form of Fig. 4.25 as the *permit-to-work certificate*; the request for such a permit should be accompanied by a *request form* (Fig. 4.26) with the appropriate sections ticked and signed by a competent person.[12] The client who engages the demolition contractor to undertake such work should be responsible for the issue and control of such permits and should advise the contractor of any special risk involved. Client and contractor should themselves invoke their own procedure for rescue should an accident occur in accordance with the requirements of the Health and Safety at Work Act.

Before any demolition work is undertaken in such circumstances, all requests should be assessed by a competent person and the method study discussed. Most large demolition contractors employ competent consultant engineers or have available a chemist to discuss with the client the best possible approach. Entry into these dangerous areas should only be considered when no realistic alternative is available.

Before any plant is demolished, either partially or totally, the client should ensure that all precautions have been fulfilled to withdraw that area from service and ensure total isolation of that part of the work. In chemical works, for example, the closing of valves and similar steps are insufficient. These must be totally severed or removed, and blank ends fitted. The demolition operative may not be aware of any problem until he removes a wall or similar, and disturbs lining, insulation or other material at the same time.

The simple use of clear water or neutralizing solvent is often sufficient to render a toxic liquid harmless, although if washed into a drainage system could cause disastrous effects outside the area being worked, therefore extreme caution should always be exercised.[10]

If work has to be carried out in a contaminated area an approved breathing apparatus must be worn, and a lifeline held by a person outside the contaminated area, with the correct resuscitation apparatus on hand during the work.

The chemical industry can almost claim to 'specialize' in the production or

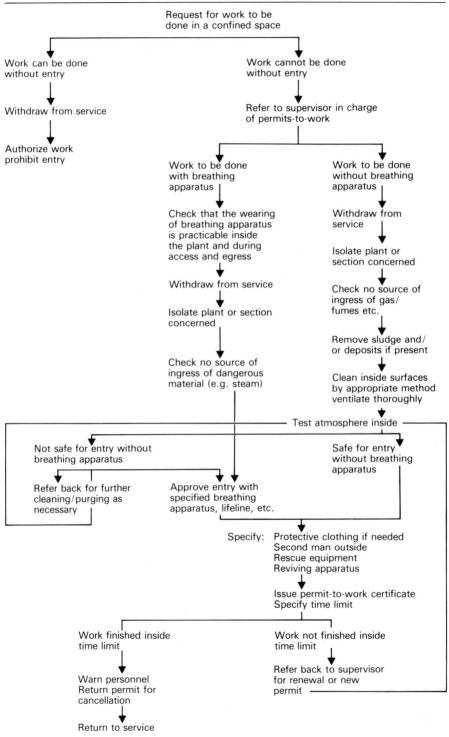

*Fig. 4.26* Request form

use of flammable liquids and gases. There is hardly a chemical plant which does not include a potential hazard from this source in its production or maintenance areas. Even if flammable liquids or gases are not a particularly hazardous feature of production, most laboratories are fertile sources of this particular hazard.

The more volatile nature of certain liquids and their low 'flash points' often create particularly acute problems. Many have vapour densities which are heavier than air and therefore tend to sink to ground level, spread over a considerable area, form explosive concentrations and become exposed to sources of ignition at low levels and at distances remote from the point of origin of the escape vapour or gas.

When a flammable gas or vapour is mixed with oxygen in certain proportions it can be ignited if there is a source of heat which can raise it locally to its ignition temperature. The spread of combustion is extremely rapid causing corresponding expansion and the resulting pressure which can build up within a fraction of a second to explosive force in an enclosed vessel or in the open often to fires of high intensity.

The chemistry of particular flammable vapours and gases varies considerably and each conforms to a different set of characteristics relative to the risk of fire and explosion. The determinants are the concentration of the vapour/gas-in-air which regulates its ability to catch fire and controls the rate of burning. Below certain concentrations and above others, some vapours will not burn at all, but within the 'explosive limits' these same vapours can be extremely unstable. Some chemicals have extremely low flash points (basically, the temperature at which it gives off vapour in sufficient concentration to support ignition). Indeed, a range of chemicals have flash points below atmospheric temperature so that under normal environmental conditions they commence to give off potentially dangerous vapour when open to the atmosphere. Other chemicals will release flammable vapour only after considerable heating. As mentioned above, each has a particular vapour density. If it is a vapour or gas lighter than air it will quickly dissipate into the atmosphere, but the denser the vapour the lower it will lie, tend to 'layer' – move laterally under the influence of draughts and other local atmospheric disturbances – and gradually spread into areas where it may become subject to ignition by a range of 'new' sources not under consideration at the point of usage. Ignition temperatures are variable and for many vapours, even low-pressure steam pipes at, say, 120 °C, can constitute a hazard. Figure 4.27 shows the 'auto-ignition temperature' of various vapour/air mixtures common in chemical manufacture relative to common sources of heat.[10] Note how low the risk threshold is even in the presence of sources of 'black heat'. Radiators, electric light bulbs, overheated cables, 'fag ends' abandoned carelessly, process steam pipes, etc. are all sources of heat sufficient to cause sensitive vapours to ignite.

At all times demolition or dismantling of this type of work should be supervised by the person who issued the permit to work and the time limits for working strictly adhered to. Once the work scheduled in the permit to work is com-

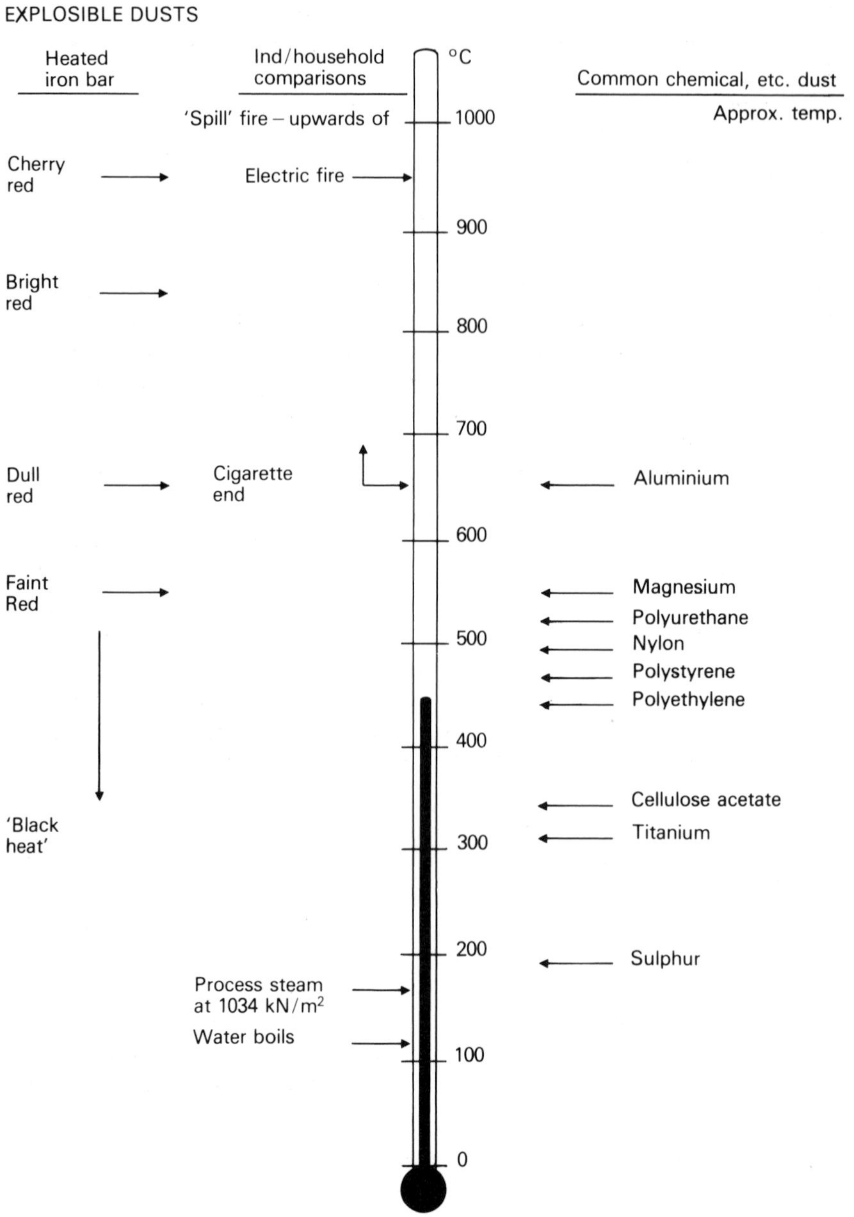

EXPLOSIBLE DUSTS

*Fig. 4.27* Automatic ignition temperatures

pleted, the permit should be cancelled and returned to the person who issued it.

The breathing apparatus to be used in such works must be approved by the Health and Safety Executive and of the kind which has the Certificate of Approval under the Chemical Works Regulations 1922. Lifelines must conform to BS 3776:1964 and should the use of harnesses be necessary, they should comply with BS 1397:1967.

## Explosible dusts

Many chemical processes, for example, powder-mixing, grinding, bagging, conveying, screening and sieving produce large quantities of dust.[13] Where they are a feature of production, the design engineers will no doubt have taken into account the potentially hazardous nature of the operation and design features will have been included to minimize risk and contain the effect of any explosion that may occur. Occasionally major plant breaks down and *ad hoc* methods are resorted to, or a new job or process comes along where the potential hazard is unrecognized, or an operator, through ignorance, creates a potentially hazardous condition through an 'unsafe act'. An example could be the operation of a pneumatic hammer chipping out a gelled synthetic resin within the confines of a reaction vessel which could, conceivably, produce a hazardous concentration of explosive dust created quite unwittingly by an operator with his mind on other priorities. In these situations a dust explosion could be initiated by a source of ignition and may result in injury and damage. Each year 'accidents happen' because workpeople are unaware of the explosive hazards inherent in operations which create concentrations of dust. Dust represents a fuel in the 'triangle of fire'.

Some dusts are so easily ignited that special precautions are advisable in handling them. In such cases they are usually produced in specially designed, totally enclosed plant or in an atmosphere rendered inert (i.e. the source of oxygen in the 'triangle of fire' is deprived). In the case of, for example, magnesium, the hazardous nature is covered by special regulations; other materials which produce highly hazardous dusts which may be met within a chemical works are aluminium, sulphur, aluminium stearate and metallic hydrides.

The remaining side in the 'triangle of fire', i.e. 'heat' can be completed in any number of ways which will be sufficient to initiate a dust explosion. The principal causes would be:

1. Hot surfaces and naked flames.
2. Cutting, burning and welding operations.
3. Friction sparks (as from grinding) and mechanical heat (e.g. hot bearings)
4. Electrical fires and sparks.
5. Static electricity.
6. Spontaneous combustion.

Obviously, this depends upon the chemical properties of the material. Many dust concentrations will ignite at very low temperatures relative to the heat sources common in factories and certainly many will ignite in the 'black heat' range. There is also a peculiar feature about ignition temperatures in that *layers* of dust have very considerably lower ignition temperatures than dust in *clouds*. In some cases, the difference can be over 200 °C. The effect of this is that when dusts are allowed to accumulate and settle, they can begin to smoulder, catch fire and initiate an explosion well below an apparently 'safe' temperature if this is related to dust cloud ignition temperatures. Furthermore, the ignition temperatures for dust in *layers* decreases as the depth of dust increases. For example a layer 150 mm deep may ignite 100 °C lower than a 12 mm layer. The variable nature of the ignition temperature of dust in consequence of its physical state makes it a particularly capricious problem requiring understanding and awareness to combat successfully.

A related problem is concerned with the 'ignition energy' of any spark which may initiate an explosion. This will be many times greater for dusts than for flammable gases and vapours. It is not unusual, however, for powdered products to contain flammable solvents, etc. and the 'ignition energy' required for an apparent dust would be more akin to that needed to initiate a fire or explosion in a flammable vapour. Both the ignition energy and the ignition temperature for the dust could be qualified by other components in a mix, and this condition could vary as the mix is formulated.

*Spontaneous ignition*

Dusts may be liable to spontaneous heating and consequent ignition. 'Dead spots' in conveyors or storage facilities can create a dangerous build-up of dust which may self-heat. While such spots should be 'designed out', regular, frequent and careful cleaning will guard against this tendency in dusts.

The problems of explosion control are often concerned with chemical or mechanical engineering features in plant design and modification. It would be inappropriate to become involved in these areas because, once a hazard is identified the legal obligation is on the company, under the Factories Acts 1961, section 31 to take all practical precautionary steps to prevent and restrict dust explosions, and this responsibility passes beyond the scope of safety representatives and supervisors except in general terms. Basically, however, control is dependent on a number of well-known principles which can be applied.

The key question to be asked is:

1. Is any process producing an explosible dust? If the answer is 'no' then ordinarily there is no hazard. If the answer is 'yes' the key questions which follow are:
   (a) What is the minimum concentration which will support an explosion?
   (b) What is the temperature at which an explosion could occur?
   (c) What energy in the source of ignition will be required to initiate an explosion?
   (d) What magnitude of problem will an explosion create? (The scale of operations, positioning, pressure of explosion, etc. will have to be taken into account.)

Dusts consist of particles of a solid material. As such, dusts have a much larger surface area than the solids from which they are formed. In the form of a cloud, each particle is surrounded by air, and certain conditions can exist where the rate of burning is many times greater than the solid state. Provided that the particle size and density is favourable, ignition will be followed by a rapid spread of flame through the dust cloud as successive zones reach ignition temperature. If the spread of flame is extremely fast, the expanding gases from combustion can create a pressure rise of explosive proportions. As the pressure waves advance, any compacted dust lying on surfaces, etc. will be dispersed into the air and may cause a secondary explosion even more violent than the original.

An explosion will only propagate through a dust cloud if the concentration lies between certain limits. Most dusts require a minimum concentration from 0.6 to 1.1 $g/cm^3$. This is broadly equivalent to the minimum explosive concentrations for, say, petroleum vapour. Because of the small size of particles in suspension even this apparently small concentration would appear as a dense cloud.

### Asbestos

When the Asbestos Regulations 1969 came into force in May 1970 the protection of workers from industrial disease which might arise from the inhalation of asbestos dust became a statutory obligation wherever asbestos materials are used in such a way as to give rise to the emission of dust dangerous to the health of employees.

The Asbestos Research Council[14] and the major companies of the UK asbestos manufacturing industry have had considerable experience in devising safer methods of production and processing of asbestos materials, as the record of improvement in their own factories testifies.

For the assistance of those who are now similarly concerned with the control of working conditions in accordance with the Asbestos Regulations 1969, the Environmental Control Committee has prepared a series of guides based on the experience of its members in many different sections of the asbestos industry.

### *The Asbestos Regulations – General*

The 1969 Asbestos Regulations[15] apply to all factories, construction and demolition sites where operations giving rise to the liberation of asbestos containing dust occur.

Regulations apply to:
1. Employers;
2. Employees;
3. Occupiers of buildings;
4. Self-employed persons;
5. Contractors' employees and others occupying the same building.

No young person under eighteen years of age may be employed where the regulations call for use of protective equipment.

Where thermal insulation materials containing blue asbestos fibre (crocidolite) are to be stripped and handled, Regulation VI requires that twenty-eight days' written notice prior to work commencing must be given to the local Factory Inspector. By consultation the Inspector may accept a shorter period of notice.

*Asbestos dust*

The application of the 1969 Regulations was based upon the amount of asbestos dust in the workplace. For this purpose threshold limits were set (see Health and Safety Executive notes for guidance entitled *Hygiene Standards for Asbestos and Measurement of Airborne Dust Concentration*).

The action required relating to the standards is summarized as follows:

(a)  Exposure to all forms of asbestos dust should be reduced to a minimum; and

(b)  In any case, occupational exposure to asbestos dust should never exceed:
*For crocidolite* 0.2 fibres/ml when measured over a 10-minute period
*For other types of asbestos* 2 fibres/ml when measurements are averaged over a 4-hour period; short-term exposure should not exceed 12 fibres/ml when measured over any 10-minute period.

*Note*:  'Fibres' means particles of length greater than 5 $\mu$m (micrometres), a diameter of less than 3 $\mu$m and having a length to breadth ratio of at least 3 : 1, observed by transmitted light under phase contrast conditions at a magnification of approximtely 500×.

These criteria were used in assessing whether or not these measurements were in compliance with the Asbestos Regulations and the Health and Safety at Work etc. Act,[16] at least until the Advisory Committee on Asbestos (ACA) had published its findings and recommendations. The final report of the ACA[17] as set up by the Health and Safety Commission (HSC) has now been published. Its recommendations of relevance to thermal insulation contractors are:

• the replacement of 'hygiene standards' with a new concept of 'control limit';
• a statutory ban on new applications of blue asbestos (crocidolite);
• with effect from 1 December 1980, tighter and statutory control limits for exposure to dust from white (chrysotile) and brown (amosite) asbestos;
• on completion of the government's monitoring programme on asbestos in the general environment, the assessment of the data in the light of medical evidence to determine whether any further action is needed;
• raw asbestos fibre and other loads liable to give rise to asbestos dust should be transported only in such a way as to prevent its escape.

The Committee concluded that there is no quantitative evidence of a risk to the general public from exposure to asbestos dust. In respect of worker exposure, the Committee has been unable to identify a threshold limit below which there is no evidence of adverse effect, and it suggests that any new control limits at the workplace should be linked with a continuing statutory requirement that exposure to all forms of asbestos dust should be reduced to the minimum that is reasonably practicable.

The report represents the culmination of the ACA's work, based on information provided and received by members since their appointment by the HSC, with the agreement of Ministers, in 1976. Against a background of medical evidence and increasing public concern, the Committee was set up to review the risks to human health arising from exposure to asbestos or products containing asbestos and to recommend whether further protection was required.

The first volume contains the main text of the report. It begins with an introduction to asbestos followed by descriptions of the uses of asbestos in the workplace and the ways in which the general public may come into contact with it. The medical effects of exposure are then considered and, in the light of the available information and existing control provisions, recommendations are made for new legal and administrative controls on exposure for those at work and the general public. For convenience, the first volume also includes summaries of the recommendations made in the Advisory Committee's two previous reports.

The second volume contains papers prepared for the Committee and used as a basis for this conclusions, together with a list of all those who submitted written evidence.

The Committee rejected an across-the-board ban on asbestos. As a general principle they take the view that control of any useful but hazardous material is preferable to the ultimate sanction of prohibition. It is very easy to say that a dangerous substance or process should be banned and to hope that that will solve the problem. In their view this is a gross over-simplification of a complex equation of interlinked factors.

For example, says the Committee, it ignores the possibility that such action may directly result in an increase in health or safety risks, such as fire, which asbestos either prevents or reduces. It also ignores the implications of statutorily enforcing substitution by materials or substances which appear suitable now, but may at a later date be found to constitute a health risk. The socio-economic consequences also need to be considered, the Committee adds.

Prohibiting certain types of asbestos or process may sometimes be justified, particularly where there is evidence of serious risk or where present or future controls are thought unlikely to be sufficiently effective. Such is the case with the application of asbestos in thermal insulation and by means of spraying, for which special recommendations were made in the Committee's first report; the Committee considered that new and more general applications of crocidolite should also be included in this category. It recommended that the import of raw crocidolite fibre (voluntarily stopped since 1971) should be statutorily banned and that the ban should be extended to the import of products containing crocidolite provided that the practical difficulties can be overcome.

The report discussed the various asbestos-related diseases such as asbetosis (fibrosis of the lung), lung cancer and mesothelioma (tumour of the chest lining

71

or abdominal cavity), the relative order of their frequency and the relationship of medical effects to fibre type.

From the evidence available, the Committee concluded that there is no apparent threshold below which exposure to asbestos dust entails no risk to human health. The Committee said that it was, therefore, inappropriate to continue to control exposure levels in terms of 'hygiene standards', as at present, since they imply levels of exposure below which exposure is safe.

Instead the Committee favoured the concept of 'control limits' which, it said, more accurately reflected the current state of information, taking account of the medical evidence and the ability of employers and others to control and reduce exposure to asbestos dust. It added: 'This new concept is intended to represent a realistic level of airborne concentration of dust, closely associated with the relevant legislation, above which no person should be occupationally exposed.'

The report discussed in detail how the Committee considered and rejected a number of approaches to setting control limits. Finally, in what the Committee described as 'the best available solution in a difficult situation', it concluded that the concept of 'control limits' should be based upon a principle of identifying the concentration of asbestos dust in the workplace at which further expenditure of effort to lower that level is out of all proportion to the reduction achieved in the risk of contracting asbestos-related diseases.

Within an overriding requirement to reduce exposure to asbestos dust to the minimum that is reasonably practicable, the Committee recommended a single control limit for each type of asbestos to serve as an upper limit on exposure from personal sample results, in most cases averaged over a four-hour period.

In 1969, HM Factory Inspectorate (now part of the HSE) adopted a limit of 0.2 fibres/ml in air for crocidolite averaged over ten minutes. The Committee said that no information had been presented on either the levels of exposure of the effects on the health of people outside the controlled working area to warrant a change in the numerical control limit for crocidolite at present.

However, since the Committee advocates four-hour sampling periods as the basis for determining compliance with all control limits, it proposed that exposure to crocidolite asbestos dust should also be subject to a control limit of 0.2 fibres/ml for a four-hour sampling period. The report says that, in view of the special precautions taken for working with crocidolite, this 'relaxation' of the limit is more apparent than real.

Applying the principles and criteria discussed above, the Committee recommended that the current standard of 2 fibres/ml for chrysotile and amosite should be reduced to *1 fibre/ml and 0.5 fibre/ml respectively (when averaged over a four-hour sampling period) with legal backing from 1 December 1980.*

The Committee reported there is no quantitative evidence of a risk to the general public from exposure to asbestos dust. The evidence of non-occupational risk submitted to them was not such as to, for example, recommend the removal of asbestos from existing buildings. The Committee concluded that no appreciable mortality from lung cancer can be associated with any degree of contamination by chrysotile to be encountered in the UK, either in the atmosphere or in buildings not under active construction or repair.

Escape of dust during transport of raw asbestos has been virtually eliminated by the use of freight containers, the Committee says. The report, therefore, recommended that the use of suitable freight containers for the import of raw asbestos should be made compulsory from 1 December 1980 and that, once the containers had been opened, loads liable to give rise to asbestos dust should be transported only in such a way as to prevent its escape.

The Committee found that, as the concentrations of asbestos in the general environment are much lower than those associated with work operations, the methods of measurement used in the workplace cannot readily be used outside.

The Committee noted that a programme to evaluate exposure to asbestos in the non-occupational environment, as recommended in its second report, had been started by the Department of the Environment and the HSE, and proposed that any further recommendations should await the results of this programme.

Other sections of the first volume of the report include methods of reducing atmospheric concentrations of, and exposure to, asbestos dust; removal, dismantling, stripping and demolition of asbestos; measuring dust outside the workplace and in buildings; disposal of asbestos waste; labelling of consumer products containing asbestos; the present legal and administrative controls for both workplaces and the general public; and the industry's estimates of the likely impact of reducing the control limits for chrysotile and amosite.

Experience and expertise are required if reliable information on dust concentrations is to be obtained. If in doubt, assistance can be sought from the following sources:

The Industrial Hygiene Division of HM Factory Inspectorate.
The Asbestos Research Council (ARC).
Your supplier in the asbestos industry.
Alternatively, there are recognized Consultancy Laboratories which are sometimes associated with universities.

Respiratory protection and protective clothing will usually be required wherever stripping thermal insulation is taking place. Unless dust can be reduced by wetting or controlled by dust-extraction equipment, all stripping operations will require respiratory protective equipment, often of the more sophisticated type such as positive pressure respirators or airline breathing apparatus. All stripping operations where crocidolite (blue) asbestos is involved will require this type of protective equipment (Fig. 4.28).

Respirators of a type approved by the Factory Inspectorate for use in asbestos-containing atmospheres must be used on a personal basis. These respirators should be kept in a dust-proof container when not in use, e.g. a plastic bag sealed with tape. Respirators should be cleaned, checked and maintained at regular intervals by a designated person. Before reissue to another person, respirators are to be disinfected (for further detailed information see the ARC Guide No. 1). The regulations require that all persons required to wear respirators shall be fully instructed in the proper use of the equipment.

The workers shall be provided with approved hooded overalls and appropriate headgear (for further detailed information see ARC Guide No. 1) which must be worn during the working period. At the end of each work period, or before taking a meal, loose fibres should be cleaned off the hooded overalls and appropriate headgear and footwear while still being worn, using vacuum cleaner equipment fitted with a special cleaning head designed for this purpose. The protective clothing should not be worn while walking to and from the place of work, as during this time the asbestos worker will be in contact with other people or will pass through clean areas.

Protective overalls should be vacuum cleaned, dampened if possible and sealed in polythene bags marked 'asbestos contaminated clothing' prior to launder-

*Fig. 4.28* Protective clothing for use by workers removing asbestos. *Note*: the mask and rubber boots and gloves that can be washed down

ing by a selected contractor. Workers must not be allowed to take their protective clothing away from the contaminated area.

Segregated changing and toilet facilities should be provided for workers to change into and out of the approved protective equipment, provision should be made for de-dusting and handling soiled protective equipment and personal washing facilities should be provided between the dirty and clean changing areas.

The dirty and clean lockers should be provided in the respective changing areas and segregated from non-asbestos workers' facilities (see Fig. 4.29 which includes specification).

Before asbestos removal takes place the area should be roped off and warning notices fixed in prominent positions. Screening may be required to reduce the asbestos dust levels in adjacent areas to safe levels. If a totally enclosed screened gangway between changing room and job has not been provided then a roped-off access way should be provided between the work and the decontamination unit.

*Stripping insulation*
This operation can give rise to very high dust levels, but these are capable of considerable reduction by pre-wetting and soaking.

It is likely that each job will require its own technique, e.g. non-absorbent surfaces will have to be punctured to permit water to be introduced into the insulation; this operation may be by a hollow probe drilled along its length to

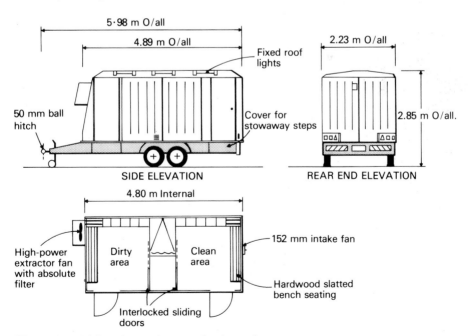

*Fig. 4.29*  Mobile asbestos decontamination unit

75

allow water to escape into the insulation, such probes in parallel being coupled to a suitable water supply. Care should be taken to prevent slurry forming as this will create hazards such as slippery floor and cleaning difficulties in open-mesh gratings. Alternatively, the wetting can be achieved by a fine, copious, low-pressure spray such that dust is not raised by impingement of the water on the insulation surface.

Insulation should be removed by sawing or cutting away. The insulation should not be allowed to fall, but should be placed in suitable plastic bags for removal from site and disposal by burying. Dry removal is generally used when stripping is required on operational plant. In all cases overalls and the appropriate approved respiratory protection must be worn.

The slurry should not be permitted to dry out, but be removed from all resting places while still wet.

In some cases it may be possible to employ a high-capacity extraction system to reduce the emission of dust to the atmosphere. If mobile or portable extraction equipment is used it should be of a type which has been tested and recommended as suitable for use on asbestos materials.

In order to notify the Factory Inspector of the intention to carry out work involving crocidolite (blue) asbestos as required in section VI of the Asbestos Regulations 1969, it is necessary before starting stripping operations to determine the type of asbestos involved. In most cases the presence of crocidolite is discernible by its rich lavender-blue colour, but sometimes material which has been installed for a long time may have become discoloured. If in doubt guidance can be obtained from universities which have suitably equipped laboratories, from each HM Factory Inspectorate or from the ARC. If crocidolite (blue) asbestos is identified, immediate written notice must be given to the Factory Inspector but, if, for any reason, the stipulated twenty-eight days is impracticable, notification should be given immediately by telephone. Special requirements for protection and identification of waste materials must be observed.

Where demolition of plant insulated with asbestos is taking place, it is recommended that the insulation should be stripped prior to the dismantling of plant or buildings. The regulations require all asbestos waste to be carried in closed receptacles which prevent escape of dust.

Asbestos materials should be placed in heavy-duty polythene bags. It is obligatory to label bags containing blue asbestos 'blue asbestos – do not inhale dust'. It is fairly common practice for demolition to use red bags and to label them 'asbestos waste' for white asbestos. These are to be sealed in an effective manner. Care should be taken when wire netting or expanded metal is included to prevent this piercing the bags. Polythene bags of 500 gauge, double-sealed bottom have been found satisfactory. When filled the neck should be twisted, tightly folded over and secured in position.

Bags containing asbestos should be placed in specialist skips and removed from the workplace at frequent intervals. Such bags should not be stored in any other way prior to disposal. Forms for disposal must be completed and submitted to local authorities prior to commencement of the work. (For further detailed information see the ARC Recommended Code of Practice for the *Hand-ling and Disposal of Asbestos Waste Materials.*)

Site hygiene is most important. General site clearing of removed asbestos should take place each day after work has ceased, with additional clean-ups as necessary. It is important to protect scaffold boards and equipment using non-slip polythene sheets or equivalent to prevent fibres landing on them. On completion of the asbestos removal the whole area should be washed or vacuumed down. On completion of final clean-up any screening used and cleanings should be put into the bags and sealed for disposal.

The firm should arrange a consultation with the appropriate local authority whenever it is proposed to change any arrangement for the disposal of waste. When new arrangements have been settled the firm should send a written notification to the appropriate local authority.

In England (other than Greater London), in Wales and in Northern Ireland the appropriate local authority in this matter will be the county borough council, borough council, urban district council or rural district council in whose area the waste is disposed of. In Greater London the appropriate authority will be a London borough council or the Common Council of the City of London. In Scotland the appropriate authority will be a town council or a county council. (*Note*: A copy of any notification sent to a London borough council should be sent to the Greater London Council since that Council is responsible for refuse disposal in London.)

Notification of removal or deposit of asbestos waste (in accordance with section 3 of the Deposit of Poisonous Waste Act 1972)

*Details to be provided*
Premises from which waste is to be removed.
Nature and composition of the waste.
Quantity which is proposed to be removed or deposited.
If waste is removed in containers, their number, size and description.
In the case of waste to be removed, the name of the person who is to undertake the removal.

*'Season ticket'*
Where similar consignments of a certain type of waste are being disposed of regularly or frequently, it is understood that the statute would be complied with if the required notice was given, saying, for example, that a specified quantity of waste was being removed and deposited on the same tip every week for the next twelve weeks. The appropriate local authority should be consulted where such an arrangement is desired.

*Notification*
Notification must be given to the responsible authorities not less than three days

(not counting Saturday, Sunday, Good Friday, Christmas Day or bank holidays) before the removal of waste takes place. The responsible authorities are, in the case of removal, the local authority and river authority or river purification board for the area in which the premises from which the waste is to be removed are situated.

In any case the local authority and river authority or river purification board for the area in which the waste is to be deposited must be notified. It is also recommended that a copy of the notice should be sent to the tip operator concerned. A copy of the notification must be given to the person or contractor who is undertaking the removal. It is recommended that a copy should also be provided for the driver of the vehicle used for transporting the waste from the manufacturer's premises to the tip.

There is no prescribed form for the giving of notice required by the Act, but a form drawn up by the Trade Effluent Joint Advisory Panel is regarded as suitable (Fig. 4.30).

*Notes on Fig. 4.30*

(a)  Completed copies of this Notice are to be given to the following:
     Part I   Each of the Authorities named in B (ii) and (iii)
              The operator of the tip named in C (i)
              Each of the Authorities named in C (ii) and (iii) (see note (e))
              The party named in E
     Part 2   Each of the Authorities named in B (ii) and (iii) and in C (ii) and
              (iii)
     The Local Authorities for the purpose of the Act are, in England and Wales, county borough councils, county district councils and the Greater London Council and in Scotland, county councils and town councils.

(b)  Enter the telephone number of the person signing this Notice (or that person's nominee) where he can be contacted during normal working hours.

(c)  A Part 1 Notice must be received by the relevant Authorities not less than 3 days before the date on which it is intended to deposit the waste (excluding Saturday, Sunday, Good Friday, Christmas Day and bank holidays).

(d)  Identify the land in sufficient detail to enable its location to be established beyond doubt.

(e)  Enter only if the Authorities are different from those named in B (ii) and (iii).

(f)  When the waste is to be carried to the place of deposit other than in distinctive loads (e.g. by conveyor or pipeline), state the mode of carriage.

(g)  When this Notice relates to deposit over a period, give an indication of the approximate frequency and amount of each deposit (e.g. tonne per day) and where applicable the end date of the period to which this Notice applies.

DEPOSIT OF POISONOUS WASTE ACT 1972

This copy for:

Serial number

Originators reference

Date of notice

Part 1 Notice of intention to remove and deposit waste given under s.3 (see note (a))

A (i) I certify that copies of this Part 1 Notice as hereunder completed have been served on the Authorities mentioned in B and C below

Signed ................

on behalf of ................

(person, firm or authority originating and/or disposal of waste)

(ii) Position held by signatory

(iii) His address and telephone number (see note (b))

B Removal

(i) Premises from which the waste is to be removed:

(ii) Name and address of the Local Authority for this area (see note (e)):

(iii) Name and address of the River Authority or River Purification Board for this area:

(iv) Earliest permitted date of removal (see note (c))

C Deposit

(i) Land where the waste is to be deposited (see note (d))

(ii) Name and address of the Local Authority for this area (see note (e))

(iii) Name and address of the River Authority or River Purification Board for this area (see note (e))

D Description of the waste

(i) Nature (general description)

(ii) Principal components (chemical, biological, etc.)

(iii) If in containers, state number, size and description: (see note (f))

(iv) Quantity (see note (g))

E Person, firm or authority who is to undertake removal

Part 2 Notice of deposit of waste given under s. 4 (see notes (a) and (h))

I certify that the waste described in D above was deposited on the land described in C above on

(date) ................ and that

the person who brought the waste to the tip was

(name) ................ an employer of

................

Date of notice ................

Signed ................

on behalf of (person, firm, or authority operating the tip where the waste was deposited)

*Fig. 4.30* Form for notification of removal or deposit of asbestos waste (Notes for completion of this form are set out on facing page)

(h)　A Part 2 Notice must be given to the relevant Authorities not more than 3 days following the date of deposit of the waste (excluding Saturday, Sunday, Good Friday, Christmas Day and bank holidays).

Where the Part 1 Notice relates to deposit over a period the relevant Authorities should be notified in the terms of a Part 2 Notice within 3 days in respect of each interim or daily deposit but the presentation of this information may be simplified if the Authorities so agree.

## Radioactive structures

We are all aware of the worldwide publicity the nuclear power industry attracts with such near-disasters as at Three Mile Island in the United States and the leak of radioactive material found at Windscale.

Although there is a strong environmental lobby against the building of new nuclear reactors and in fact the use of those already producing energy, there is a worldwide shortage of other forms of material such as oil for present and future energy needs of the world's population, therefore an alternative source of energy is required. It may not be ideal environmentally to use nuclear power, and yet controlled in a realistic manner it can be a worthwhile form of energy.

With the building of new reactors comes the problem of decommissioning redundant facilities. Increased attention is now being focused on the decommissioning of nuclear facilities when the time comes to withdraw them permanently from operational service. The United Kingdom Atomic Energy Authority (UKAEA) and the Central Electricity Generating Board (CEGB) are at the present time looking into methods for the demolition and dismantling of part or all of these redundant nuclear facilities, thereby making way for new and modern facilities to be built.

There will be numerous problems associated with the decommissioning which to date have been unknown in the field of demolition or, in fact, construction and civil engineering. The main problem will be to ensure that sufficient trained operatives are available when the time comes to commence the work.

There will obviously be unique problems associated with these projects, none being greater than the radioactive concrete and superstructure remaining, even when the nuclear fuel rods and radioactive material needed to charge the reactor have been removed. The need for special containers to remove the contaminated waste material from site and the remote-controlled equipment necessary to demolish such structures are only two of the many problems which have to be studied and a solution found. One method for the disposal of contaminated metals could be to use a redundant steelworks to melt them down, thereby removing some or all of the radioactivity, but again research must be carried out before any method could be considered safe.

The skills and experience within the demolition and dismantling industry are more than adequate to establish, along with the CEGB and the UKAEA, a vi-able agency with the resources which are capable of undertaking such a prog-ramme. Numerous independent laboratories, some within universities, are also available to give independent monitoring services for such projects, although it would be assumed that the CEGB and/or the UKAEA would supply a team of nuclear experts to control and continually monitor work during the whole of the decommissioning work.

A large part of the complex including the perimeter buildings which are not contaminated would be demolished by conventional methods and it would only be when the work of removing the reactor and associated building became necessary that the special precautions would be enforced.

An independent report is included as Appendix 9 to illustrate the work being undertaken throughout the world on the problems unique to this work and the research into the safest methods necessary for decommissioning of the Advanced Gas-cooled Reactor (AGR) at the Windscale complex.[18]

## Chapter 5

# Scaffolds in demolition

## *Scaffolds*

Scaffolds must be erected correctly and in compliance with current Factories Acts and Construction Regulations.[1] The ground must be firm enough to carry the weight of the scaffold and the load the scaffold will be carrying. The foundations must not be weakened by any excavations. Soleplates must be large and strong enough, with no fouling of any service covers and at right angles to any joists or rafters underneath. Standards must all be set on baseplates, and suitably spaced for the expected scaffold loading. Public footpaths and roadways must not be obstructed without a licence from the local authority. If a scaffold is to be placed within about 0.5 m of the kerbline, then a fender must be placed in the road to allow an equivalent amount of clearance. Lights must be set up to warn people after dark of the presence of the obstruction. All hoardings must be sufficiently tied. If corrugated sheeting is used, the hook bolts must be flush on the public side or covered with some sort of protection. Corrugated sheetings used for fan protections *must be* fixed with proper sheeting clips, and scaffolds which are to be sheeted *must* have extra 'through' ties. All boards exposed to high winds *must* be fixed. All couplers bearing loads *must* be the proper type. Trussed scaffolds *must* have sufficient 'through' ties at outrigger level, and cantilevers *must* have adequate counterweights. The stipulated headroom *must* be maintained over paths, roads, railways and waterways, and under power lines. Scaffolds and ladders must be used *only* for the purposes for which they have been designed. Handrails and toeboards *must* be fitted to any platform or landing from which a person could fall 2 m or more. Guys and buttresses must be fixed to *suitable* anchors. Keep a watch to make sure that no part of any scaffold (especially the ties) is removed before it is safe to do so. This last point applies particularly where other trades such as carpenters, plasterers and glaziers are working on a job nearing completion.

### Competent persons

All inspections, examinations and tests, and all annealing of scaffold structures must be done by (or under the immediate supervision of) competent persons.

But 'competent person' has no legally definable meaning. Whether any person is competent for carrying out any given examination, etc. must be decided by the employer. In the event of legal proceedings, the employer may be called upon to satisfy a court as to the competency of the person chosen. However, so far as examinations and inspections are concerned, the following extract from *A Comprehensive Guide to Factory Law* by Robert McKown (4th edn) may be helpful:

> The person chosen should have such practical and theoretical knowledge and actual experience of the type of machinery or plant which he has to examine, as will enable him to detect defects or weaknesses which it is the purpose of the examination to discover, and to assess their importance in relation to the strength and function of the machinery or plant.

In other words, the competent person must not only be able to discover defects, but must also be able to tell what effects they are likely to have. He must not only be able to detect faults – he must also, from his knowledge and experience, be able to assess their seriousness. The above definition is an unofficial one and it does not have the authority of law. It does, however, provide a useful working rule. It should never be assumed that a person is competent just because he has worked for a long time in particular trade. This competency should not be taken for granted, and the 'occupier' should satisfy himself that the man really is competent to the extent required. For some kinds of examinations, many factory or site occupiers call in outside experts employed by the manufacturers, insurers, or consultants. This is generally the best thing to do. However, there is nothing in the Factories Act to prevent an occupier from having such examinations made by one of his own employees – if he is satisfied that the employee is competent for the purpose.

Daily checks

As a matter of routine, the following features should be kept under permanent scrutiny.

*Before erection of the scaffold*
Check that the ground is capable of supporting the weight, and if in doubt seek professional advice; check that the materials (tubes, boards, fittings) are up to the standard required.

*During and after erection*
Ensure that baseplates are fixed under all standards; and the standards are plumb; with soleplates where necessary. Ensure that the standard and lift spacings are as specified and that the ledgers are horizontal. Ensure that there are sufficient ties and that they are of the type specified. Ensure that joints in standards and ledgers are staggered. Ensure that adequate dog-leg, transverse, longitudinal and (if necessary) plan bracings have been incorporated. Ensure that

83

fittings near joints are grouped as closely as possible, and that only specified fittings have been used. Ensure that the regulations have been complied with, particularly regarding platforms, guardrails, toeboards, ladders. Ensure that any gin wheels in use are secure, with properly safeguarded hooks (moused if necessary). Keep a check on all ropes for soundness. Display warning notices on any incomplete scaffolds.

*Support scaffolds* (and any for which drawings are issued)
In addition to the previous recommendations: check the structure against the drawing(s). Ensure that adequate and secure foot ties are installed. Comply with special requirements for distributing loads. Ensure strict accordance with the specifications.

*General*
If there are any doubts about the safety or stability of a scaffold – get professional advice.

## Scaffolding hazards

Many accidents are caused by very simple faults – such as misuse of tools, ladders not fixed, toeboards missing. Regrettably, some accidents are also caused by neglect of the Construction (Working Places) Regulations, 1966, and the Health and Safety At Work etc. Act 1974 – such as using a board which is seen to be defective, or using a board over an excessive span.

*Ties.* These must be adequate in number and quality, with one every other lift up and down and every 6 m across. At least 50 per cent of the ties must be 'through' (positive) ties – the rest can be reveal. Extra ties must be used if anything which may catch the wind is to be fixed to the scaffold (fans, sheetings).

*Ledgers.* These must be truly level. Any joints must be staggered, and the inclusion of sleeve couplers is desirable. Ledger bracings must be fixed to alternate standards on every platform, not to the handrails, etc.

*Boards.* To comply with BS 2482, all working platforms must be fully boarded out with 38 mm thick boards, supported by transoms or putlogs at *not more than* 1.500 m centres. The ends of the boards must overhang their last support by not more than four times the board thickness nor by less than 50 mm. They must be free from cracks, splits, large knots or any damage which could cause weakness in any way.

*Working platforms.* No rubbish or spare materials must be allowed to accumulate on any working platform, and nothing should be thrown down or allowed to fall.

*Baseplates.* Must be used under *every* standard.

*Soleplates.* Must be sound and sufficient, and must extend under at least two standards at a time. They must also extend at least one-third bay distance beyond the last standard in any row, and any joints must be placed within the middle third of the distance between two standards. They must be set at right angles to any joists or rafters underneath them. Highly finished floors must first be covered with something which will protect the floor and lessen the danger of slipping.

*Standards.* Must be *truly plumb*. A crooked or leaning standard will bow, and push the rest of the scaffold. All joints in standards must be staggered, so that no two are placed in the same bay.

*Sway bracing.* Also known as 'longitudinal' or 'façade'. Must be fitted through the full length of the scaffold at an angle as near 45 degrees as possible, and not more than 30 m apart.

*Dismantling.* Do not overload the lower lifts when passing down materials.

*Ladders.* No split stiles or missing or damaged rungs. All ladders in use *must* be fixed top and bottom, and must extend at least 1.200 m above the level of the landing point. Ladder landing points must be placed at not more than 9 m apart, and must be completely boarded out and finished with handrails and toeboards.

*Hoist towers.* Load-bearing couplers must be used at all connections. The ledgers and transoms must be fixed to the standards.

*Handrails and toeboards.* Required on any platform over 2 m high wherever there is a space through which a person could fall.

*Loadings.* See section on 'Scaffold loadings'.

*Other points.* Improper removal of parts, especially braces and ties. Any movements in the scaffold boards. Damage to or removal of guardrails and toeboards. Excavations near by, especially if affected by rain or traffic. Any damage from impacts by vehicles or plant. Use for propping formwork when not so designed. Vibrations from hoists and other plant. Any uses beyond design capability.

Checking scaffolds for faults

Scaffolds must be erected to comply with current Factories Acts and the Construction Regulations, and the scaffolder must ensure that: The ground is firm enough to carry the superimposed load of the scaffold and the loads on the scaffold, with baseplates of adequate strength and size to spread the loads. Baseplates are used under every standard, on good foundations and clear of any service covers, etc. Public roads and footpaths are kept clear of obstructions unless a licence has been obtained in advance from the local authority giving this permission. Where any part of a scaffold is within 460 mm of the kerbline, a stout fender is necessary in the road to ensure that pedestrians have at least that amount of space to walk in. Where the scaffold causes any obstruction, warning lights must be installed to operate during the hours of darkness. Where hoardings are erected, they must be firmly and adequately fixed with any dangerous projections on the inside (away from the public). Any projections towards the public side must be adequately wrapped or covered to prevent injuries to passers-by. Where any scaffold, gantry, etc. passes across a footpath or roadway, the minimum stipulated headrooms must be kept. Where any excavations are near scaffolds, active steps must be taken to ensure that the scaffold foundations will not be weakened. Wherever scaffolds will be near overhead power cables, the minimum safe working distances must be ascertained from the local electricity authority. The spacings between standards are suitable for the expected scaffold loadings. The correct types of fittings have been specified (e.g. load-bearing couplers for fixing ledgers to standards). The numbers and types of ties have been specified correctly, i.e. at least 50 per cent two-way positive ('through ties'). All working platforms higher than 2 m are fitted with proper handrails and toeboards. Where scaffolds are to be guyed or buttressed, suitable anchorages are provided. Where scaffolds are to be sheeted out with tarpaulins or other approved sheetings, extra ties have been provided. Where corrugated iron, etc. is used on temporary roofs, it is secured with hook bolts **and** sheeting clips. On scaffolds exposed to high winds, the boards are all lashed to the scaffolds. Soleboards on floors and roofs are always placed at right angles to joists or rafters, and the scaffold loadings checked very carefully. Trussed scaffolds are provided with sufficient two-way positive ties at outrigger level. Cantilevered scaffolds have adequate counterweights. Ladders are fixed in compliance with the regulations. On sites nearing completion, ties are not removed by unauthorized persons. Scaffolds are always erected in accordance with the specifications. Scaffolds are used only for the purposes for which they are designed. Scaffolds are never overloaded in any way.

Points to check before erecting a scaffold

The *foundation* on which the scaffold will be erected. Any *services* near the proposed scaffold, underground or overhead, such as power lines, telephone wires, any alarm systems and neon signs. *Adjoining properties*, where permission may be needed for any encroachment. *Public facilities* – such as bus stops, fire hydrants, fire escapes and fuel supply inlet points. *Excavations* near enough to affect scaffold foundations. *Access* – for placing materials before and after the scaffold is erected. *Local authority* rules and regulations. Possible *use* to which the scaffold may be subjected over and above the original design purpose. *Obstructions* which will require licences or permission. *Existing damage* to properties which may later be blamed on the scaffolders or other workmen. Positions for ties where they will be most effective. *Specifications* – work in strict compliance.

### Independent scaffold

This is the scaffold which (apart from necessary ties) stands completely free of the building. It consists of the two upright rows of standards, with horizontal ledgers running the full length and horizontal transoms placed at right angles to the ledgers. Tubular braces provide stability. The main applications for independent scaffolds are access for stonework on masonry buildings, access to solid or reinforced concrete structures and any other access which avoids direct attachment. For normal working convenience, the vertical distance between ledgers will usually be less than 2 m. The two rows of standards are spaced according to the load to be taken – very close for masonry work, to fairly wide for painting – within the limits of 1.5 to 2.5 m. The standards must always be plumb and set on baseplates, with good foundations such as soleboards on concrete, etc. Ledger spacing will vary from job to job. The most common height of lift will be 1.75 to 2 m. With 38 mm scaffold boards, transoms must be fixed to the ledgers or the standards at not more than 1.220 m centres. Transoms should always be fixed within about 300 mm of standards, to keep heavy loading away from the middle of the ledger. Bracing is necessary at every lift, to strengthen the scaffold and ensure rigidity, especially if it is being erected ahead of the building, as with new work. Ledger bracing must be fitted at alternate standards, for plumbing the scaffold. Wind bracing should be fitted from bottom to top, at about 45 degrees and at intervals of about 30 m. This holds the standards upright, prevents sideways movement and provides a safeguard against the possibility of any unforeseen collapse.

### Temporary scaffold/roof access

Figures 5.1, 5.2 and 5.3 are good examples in the use of tubular scaffolding as temporary access platforms erected at eaves level on any level on any building to ensure the demolition topman has protection against falls during the stripping of roofing material. Figure 5.1 allows for stacking material to be removed from the roof on to scaffold platform prior to lowering to ground. Figures 5.2 and 5.3 are for use purely as safety precautions against falls and are not designed for stacking roofing material against. The erection of scaffolding shown in Figs. 5.2 and 5.3 can only be carried out providing the upper walls of the building to be demolished are structurally sound and the design has been approved by the design engineer.

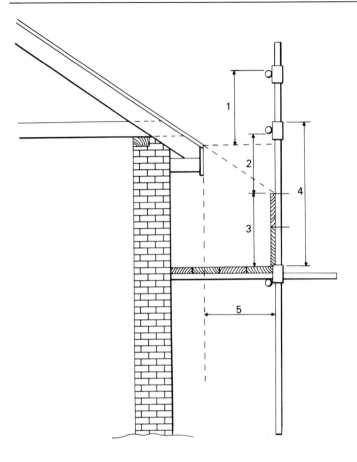

1. Top hand/guard rail not less than 0.432 m above eaves tiles.
2. Not more than 0.685 m between toeboard/catch barrier and handrail.
3. Toeboard/catch barrier at least 0.203 m high.
4. From platform to lower guard rail not less than 0.914 m.
5. Width of accessible working platform not less than 0.635 m.

*Fig. 5.1* Scaffold for roof with pitch exceeding 10°

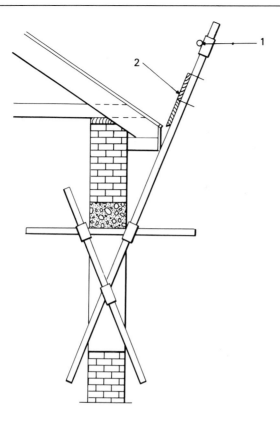

1. Guard/handrail not less than 0.914 m above roof and 0.685 m above scaffold/toeboard.
2. Toeboard/catch barrier at least 0.432 m above roof.

*Fig. 5.2*   Scaffold for roof with pitch exceeding 10°

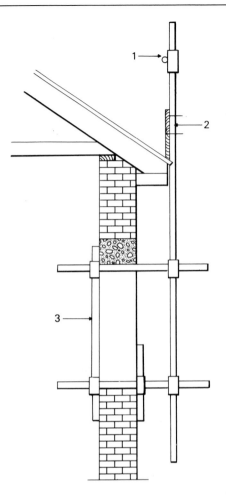

1. Guard/handrail not less than 0.914 m above roof and 0.685 m above scaffold to toeboard.
2. Toeboard/catch barrier at least 0.432 m above roof.
3. Scaffold tie tubes.

*Fig. 5.3*  Scaffold for roof with pitch exceeding 10°

S P E C I M E N

Top copy (lilac colour)
issued to Company

Undercopy (white)
retained.

### HANDING-OVER CERTIFICATE – SCAFFOLDING

Contractor . . . . . . . . . . . . . . . . . . . . . . . . . . . . . .   Date . . . . . . . . . . . . . . . . . . . . . . . . . . . . . . . .

Site . . . . . . . . . . . . . . . . . . . . . . . . . . . . . . . . .   Time . . . . . . . . . . . . . . . . . . . . . . . . . . . . . . . .

Description of section
handed over . . . . . . . . . . . . . . . . . . . . . . . . . . . . . . . . . . . . . . . . . . . . . . . . . . . . . . . . . . . . . . . . . .

. . . . . . . . . . . . . . . . . . . . . . . . . . . . . . . . . . . . . . . . . . . . . . . . . . . . . . . . . . . . . . . . . . . . . . . . . . .

. . . . . . . . . . . . . . . . . . . . . . . . . . . . . . . . . . . . . . . . . . . . . . . . . . . . . . . . . . . . . . . . . . . . . . . . . . .

Drawing No. . . . . . . . . . . . . . . . . . . . . . . . . . . . . . . . . . . . . . . . . . . . . . . . . . . . . . . . . . . . . . . . . . . . .
(where applicable)

Scaffolding as described above has now been completed and complies with the Construction
(Working Places) Regulations 1966. It is structurally sound and should be used and loaded in
accordance with our Quotation No. . . . . . . . . . . . . . . . . . . . . . . . . . . . . . . . . . . . . . . . . . . . . . . . . . . . .
(If no quotation (a) use only for . . . . . . . . . . . . . . . . . . . . . . . . . . . . . . . . . . . . . . . . . . . . . . . . . . . . . . .
         (b) loading to be . . . . . . . . . . . . . . . . . . . . . . . . . . . . . . working lifts with distributed
        load of. . . . . . . . . . . . . . . . . . . . . . . kN/m$^2$ . . . . . . . . . . . . . . . . . . . . . . per lift.)

The detail requirements of the Regulations with regard to guardrails – working platforms –
toeboards – bracing and ties have been complied with.

This scaffold must be inspected once a week (or following exposure to weather conditions likely to
have affected its strength or stability) by the *user* and the inspection recorded in the scaffold
register (Form 91 (Part 1) Section A). This inspection carried out under Regulation 22 is to ensure
that the scaffold continues to comply with the Regulations.

It is also the responsibility of every employer under Regulation 3 to see that the requirements
of the Regulations which apply to his own men are complied with.

N.B. Tarpaulin sheets (or other windsails) must not be fixed to a scaffold unless it has been
specifically designed to take them.

        Scaffold Contractor . . . . . . . . . . . . . . . . . . . . . . . . . . . . . . . . . . . . . . . .
        Depot . . . . . . . . . . . . . . . . . . . . . . . . . . . . . . . . . . . . . . . . . . . . . . . . . .
        . . . . . . . . . . . . . . . . . . . . . . . . . . . . . . . . . . . . . . . . . . . . . . . . . . . . .

**DO NOT REMOVE TIES**

*Fig. 5.4*   Handing-over certificate

SCAFFOLD CONTRAVENTIONS REPORT

Inspector: . . . . . . . . . . . . . . . . . . . . . . . . . . . . . .

Report No.: . . . . . . . . . . . . . . . . . . . . . . . . . .

Site: _____

FOR ACTION BY:

GF/Agent/Contracts Supervisor/
Scaffolder Chargehand

FOR INFORMATION TO:

Managing Director/Contracts
Director/File

| | Type of scaffold | Defect | Position of defect |
|------|------|------|------|
| 1. | | | |
| 2. | | | |
| 3. | | | |
| 4. | | | |
| 5. | | | |
| 6. | | | |
| 7. | | | |
| 8. | | | |
| 9. | | | |
| 10. | | | |
| 11. | | | |
| 12. | | | |

ANY OTHER DEFECTS:
Maintenance of registers is
Satisfactory/Not satisfactory

Signed: . . . . . . . . . . . . . . . . . . . . . . . . . . . . .

Date: . . . . . . . . . . . . . . . . . . . . . . . . . . . .

THIS SECTION TO BE DETACHED AND
RETURNED TO SCAFFOLDING INSPECTOR

Report No: _____ Date: _____

The following action has been taken
to rectify the contravention listed

ACTION TAKEN BY:

— — — — — — — — — — — — — —

Signed: . . . . . . . . . . . . . . . . . . . . . . . . . . . . . . . . . .

Date: . . . . . . . . . . . . . . . . . . . . . . . . . . . . . . . . . . .

*Fig. 5.5*   Scaffold defect report

Scaffold documentation

Before a scaffold can be operational, a handing-over certificate (Fig. 5.4) must be completed. The scaffold construction must undergo periodic inspections by a competent scaffolding supervisor and any defect must be noted on a report. similar to Fig. 5.5 which is issued to the appropriate authorities listed on the form.

Special scaffolds

In the main, these are designed by engineers. Technical advice and guidance should be sought before commencing the erection of any of the following kinds of scaffolds or scaffolding structures: Dead shore; Raking shore; Flying shore; Centring or support scaffold; Cantilevering with rolled steel joists; Temporary roofs or structures forming 'windsails'; Lighting towers; Masts of all kinds; Access scaffolds incorporating lifts; Staircases; Slung or hanging scaffolds with grids more than 2.5 m$^2$; Heavy suspended structures for holding reinforced concrete; Mobile scaffolds of any kind; Bridges for pedestrian or vehicle traffic; Stands, spectator platform and the like; Gantries taking static loads; Line crossings; Sealing end structures; Racking; System scaffolds over 18 m high; Free-standing structures over 12 m high; Trusses over 12 m above out-rigger level; Built-up beams; Boring rigs.

Fig. 5.6 is a good example of a special scaffold. It shows a cooling tower completely encased in tubular scaffolding with a hoist and platform incorporated in the structure.

Scaffold boards

This section includes part of B.S. 2482:1970 (Metric Units) for *Timber Scaffold Boards*, 38 mm × 225 mm. The term 'scaffold board' is generally used in the industry, but 'scaffold plank' is also used in some areas.

*Specifications*

Scaffold boards must be made from softwood, sawn-finished all surfaces, and must be suitable for use with metal scaffolding complying with BS 1139 and with timber scaffolding. They must be capable of holding a load of 6.7 kN/m$^2$ when supported at 1.200 m centres. The corners may be chamfered, round or square. The ends must be bound with hoop iron 25 mm wide and at least 0.9 mm thick, extending at least 150 mm along each edge. The hoop irons must either be sherardized to comply with British Standards, or must be galvanized. All hoop irons must be secured at each end of the board and on all edges with two large-headed clout nails at least 30 mm long, and must either be finished off to avoid any injuries or some other satisfactory protection provided. To comply with BS 2482, the dimensions of the scaffold boards must be:

Width: 225 mm, plus or minus 6 mm;
Thickness: 38 mm, plus or minus 3 mm.

Timbers in general use for making scaffold boards are as follows: *Spruce* (European or eastern Canadian); *Douglas Fir; Whitewood; Redwood.*

Other suitable but less generally used timbers are: *Pitch Pine; Western Hemlock.*

Scaffold boards *can* be made from any timber, *if the user is satisfied that it is suitable.*

*Scaffold board defects*

The following are among the defects commonly found: *Large knots; Crossgrain; Splits* and *shakes; Excessive warping; Bands missing from the end; Damage* (impacts, strains, nails, sawcuts); *Weakening* (oil, acids, alkalis (cement), etc.).

*Painting* a scaffold board is *Strictly forbidden*, as this could hide defects and also makes a slippery surface. Assessment of the defects in scaffold boards should take into account all the above features in total.

*Face knots* must not be more than 55 mm in diameter, and there must be at least 150 mm clear between any two face knots if they are to be regarded separately.

*Margin knots* must not be more than 40 mm in diameter, and if they are closer to each other than 150 mm, then their diameters must not add up to more than 55 mm total.

*Knot clusters* must not be more than 40 mm across in any direction, and if any clusters are closer together than 150 mm their total measurements must not add up to more than 55 mm.

*Arris knots* must not be more than 40 mm across on the face of the board, not more than 13 mm on the edge. They must not be any closer to each other than 150 mm nor add up in size to more than 55 mm.

*Splay knots* must not be more than 25 mm on the edge of the board. If they extend more than 40 mm on the face then there must be at least 150 mm clear between any two. No splay knot can be allowed which extends more than 55 mm on either face of the board.

*Edge knots* must not be more than 20 mm across in any direction.

*Wane or bark* must not extend more than 20 mm on any face or edge.

*Natural upsets* – deformations of the grain possibly caused by lighting or earthquake during growth. They are often microscopic, and can be the most dangerous fault of all. Keep a constant lookout for this fault, and reject any such board.

*Fig. 5.6* The use of special scaffold as an aid to the demolition contractor

## Baseplate

There are three main functions for a baseplate (Fig. 5.7): distributing the load from the standard; preventing any sideways movement; preventing damage to the tube. It is an essential part of any scaffold and must never be left out. No baseplate must ever bear directly on any fragile surface, and where the surface slopes, suitably shaped packings must be used to keep a level bearing. Baseplates are sometimes welded permanently to the tubes. Baseplates must be at least 23 226 mm² in area (just over 150 × 150 mm). If the plate is mild steel it must be at least 5 mm thick. If it is made of any other metal, then it must be thick enough to be capable of distributing the required load. If fixing holes are incorporated in the design, they must be diametrically opposed (opposite each other), 6 mm in diameter, not less than 50 mm from the centre of the plate and not less than 19 mm from the edge. The shank must be at least 50 mm in height.

## Standards

These are the tubes used as the vertical members of a scaffold. They transmit the vertical loads from the working platforms through the baseplates and the soleplates to the ground. Spacing may vary from a few hundred millimetres (300 mm or so) in a heavy-duty support scaffold, to 2.500 m in a light scaffold. Standard spacings are usually specified beforehand, but in any case they should be within the limits recommended in BS Code of Practice CP:97. All standards should be truly vertical without measurable lean in any direction. They should be checked for plumb all the way up, first on one side and then the other, to cancel out any errors. Joints in any two standards next to each other must be

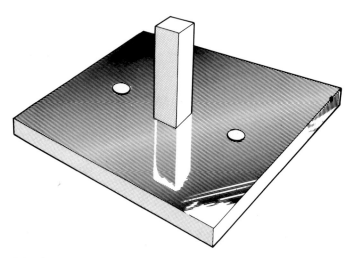

*Fig. 5.7* Metal baseplate

staggered in different lifts to spread them out. Any joints should be arranged to come as near to a ladder as possible and not more than 600 mm above the level of the platform. Spigot or sleeve couplers can be used. All standards must be set on baseplates, and special attention must be given to the solid support of any standard near excavations. For heavy-duty support scaffolds, standards are arranged in clusters. Any structural queries should be referred back to the design office.

Ledgers

These are the tubes running dead level along the full length of the scaffold, tying it together end to end. They also give support to other parts of the scaffold, such as the transoms, putlogs, puncheons or drop tubes and pick-ups, etc. They **must** be level, and fixed to the standards with load-bearing couplers. Joints in ledgers next to each other must be spread out to not more than one in any bay. Joints in ledgers may be secured with sleeve couplers, which must come within one-quarter to one-third of the distance between two standards – never near the middle. Different types of tubes (alloy and steel, or different gauges) must not be joined together. Height of lift between ledgers will be from 1.370 m on a bricklayers' scaffold to perhaps as much as 3.000 m on a multi-storey building. The recommended height of the first lift on all general-purpose scaffolds is about 2.600 m, to allow movement of men and materials underneath. If any of the above heights of lift have to be exceeded, then extra standards and bracings must be built into the structure. Scaffolds with lifts spaced at the maximum of 3.00 m can be used only for light work, and not more than one lift may be erected above the highest level of through ties (positive ties). Further guidance on ledgers is given in BS Code of Practice CP 97.

Transoms

These are the tubes which are fixed horizontally through the scaffold between the outside and inside ledgers. They tie the scaffold together and support the scaffold boards of the working platforms. Their weight-carrying capability is an important part of their purpose – tie tubes should **not** be used for supporting scaffold boards. Transom spacing depends on the loads to be carried and the thickness of the boards. Main transoms must be placed as near as possible to a standard, and never more than 300 mm away. Main transoms must never be removed without authority, intermediate transoms may be removed temporarily if it becomes necessary on non-working lifts. No transom must be allowed to project beyond the ledger in any place where it could constitute a hazard. Any transom extending more than two boards' width must be properly supported. Longitudinal or façade bracings which are sometimes attached to transoms must be fixed with load-bearing couplers. Transoms within striking distance of any gin wheel must be flush with the ledgers, to let the ropes run freely. Statutory

Regulations for transom spacing are:

| Board thickness | Transom spacing not more than |
| --- | --- |
| 32 mm | 1 m |
| 38 mm | 1.5 m |
| 50 mm | 2.5 m |

British Standards recommendation for transom spacing for the 38 mm boards is only 1.220 m to allow for the scarcity of high-quality timber. All boards in this category bear the BS kitemark on the end hoop irons.

### Putlogs

These are tubes either with one end ready flattened or with an adaptor fitted, which are inserted in a joint in the brickwork. They serve the same purpose as a transom, but they need no ledger on the inside of the scaffold. The span of the putlogs dictates the load the scaffold will support. Figures quoted in the Construction Regulations are the maximum permissible loads. If extra safety margins are required, the loads should be reduced or the spans shortened. As with transoms, spacing between putlogs depends on the loads, scaffold board thickness and timber quality. Main putlogs must be fixed to the standard or ledger with load-bearing couplers, and in any case not further than 300 mm from a standard. They must **not** be removed until the scaffold is being dismantled. Intermediate putlogs which are no longer supporting scaffold boards may be removed if a need arises. Putlogs which project from the scaffold are subject to the same considerations as transoms. Tie tubes must be placed so that they will not have to bear any weight which should be on a putlog. The blade of a putlog tube or adaptor end must be at least 75 mm long and 50 mm wide. In use, it must rest flat on the brickwork (not on edge) so that it has the maximum area of bearing surface. Putlogs are designed to resist bending stresses only, and should be able to bear a maximum distributed load of 4276 N over a span of 1.220 m. They cannot resist pulling strains – the ties do that.

### Outriggers or needles

These are horizontal load-bearing tubes or steel joists, cantilevered from suitable anchorage points and helping to support a working platform. They are sometimes set at a shallow angle, for example when used for suspended cradles and fan protections (see Fig. 5.8). Outriggers are also used for supporting: Cantilevers; Truss scaffolds; Suspended tubular scaffolds; Built-out working platforms. On cantilever and truss work, the outriggers must be fixed to the standards of the support scaffold. Outriggers should be kept off copings and sill where possible, otherwise suitable packings must be inserted between the outrigger and the

*Fig. 5.8* Scaffolding and fans used to protect adjacent buildings. *Note*: guard rails and toeboards

brickwork or masonry. For supporting suspended cradles, adequate back-weights must be fixed to the inboard end. Outrigger spacings must be strictly in accordance with the structural engineer's specifications. Materials used for outriggers must be completely free from defects as they are load-bearing members. All outrigger tubes must be fixed with load-bearing couplers.

### Guardrails and toeboards

All working platforms higher than 2 m above ground or floor level must be fitted with suitable guardrails and toeboards (Fig. 5.8) where there is any space of 150 mm or more through which a person could fall. Guardrails must be fixed to the insides of the standards with load-bearing couplers, not lower than 1 m nor higher than 1.2 m above the working platform. The open space between guardrail and toeboard must not be more than 0.9 m. Where a platform or stand is used by the public, an intermediate guardrail must be fitted to safeguard children and small persons, etc. Guardrails must always be carried round the end of a scaffold to make a 'stop end', and if the scaffold is erected in advance of the construction work then they must go all round. ~~Ladder scaffolds~~ ~~need not have a guardrail if a handhold is already incorporated.~~ On other scaffolds ~~where handrails cannot reasonably be fixed, safety belts must be used.~~ Toeboards are ordinary scaffold boards fixed to the insides of the standards in an upright position. They must be at least 150 mm high, and joints must be as near to a standard as possible. Toeboards should be fixed to the standards with proper toeboard clips, and they should be carried round the scaffold everywhere a guardrail is needed. Any toeboard removed temporarily for access or other purposes must be replaced as soon as possible.

Working platforms (Fig. 5.9)

These are governed by the Factories Act Construction (Working Places) Regulations, 1966. General access must not be allowed to any scaffold until it has been

*Fig. 5.9* An example of the use of scaffolding, fans, working platforms and hoardings on a demolition site in an urban area

completed. Any sections which are not finished must be blocked off to unauthorized persons. If any gap or opening is made in a working platform for any reason, then it must immediately be blocked off and suitable warning notices displayed. Where a ladder passes through any working platform, the opening must be as small as is practicable. Trestles *must not* be used on any working platform. Rubbish or unused materials must not be left on any working platform. Materials must not be stored beyond immediate reasonable requirements. Where loadings cannot be spread out evenly (as with bricklaying materials) then the heavier weights must be placed nearest the standards. Otherwise, any loading must be spread out as evenly as possible. If a working platform becomes covered with ice, snow, grease or any other slippery surface then action must be taken to reduce the hazard by sprinkling salt, sand, sawdust, etc. No heavy object must ever be allowed to fall on a working platform, or it may be necessary to make a complete check of all the members and fittings before the scaffold can be put back into use. If a working platform has a slope of 1 in 4 or steeper, then stepping laths must be fixed at suitable spacings with a barrow-run gap in the centre. The slope on a working platform must never be steeper than 1 in 1½. Everything loose must be removed from any working platform before it is dismantled. It is illegal to throw anything down from a scaffold or to allow anything to fall.

Buttress platform (Fig. 5.10)

This is used where it would be impossible to tie a scaffold to the building in any other way, such as with a gasholder. Buttresses are built in with the scaffold at a slope of 45 degrees – i.e. as far out as the height.

Ladders

Use and maintenance of ladders is governed by Regulations 31 and 32. The main points for use of ladders longer than 3 m are that they must be fixed at the top and must be secured to prevent undue swaying or sagging. Otherwise, a person must be stationed at the ladder base. *The following points apply to all ladders*, of any length: no ladder may be used with any missing or defective rungs; no ladder may be used with any rungs depending solely upon nails or spikes for support; all ladders must extend at least 1.5 m above the landing place or above the highest rung reached by the feet of the user. Ladders are generally used for light work of short duration and, of course, for access purposes.

*Single section*
'Standing' ladders are built with oblong stiles (sides), and oblong-, oval- or round-section rungs, and they are a maximum of about 7 m in height. They are fairly light in weight, and used mostly by painters and decorators, etc. 'Pole' ladders have the stiles made from half-round timber either sawn or cleft ('split'). The rungs may be either turned on a lathe, or hand-made. They are available

101

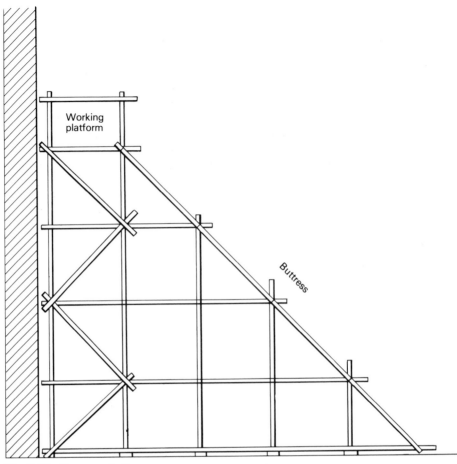

*Fig. 5.10*  Buttress platform

up to about 12 m in length, and are much heavier and stronger than the 'standing' ladders.

*Extending*
These are available in two or three sections, the total height being adjustable by sliding the sections apart. British Standard 1129:1966 specifies that: 'Two-section ladders may have a closed length of a maximum of 5 metres for extending by hand or maximum of 7 metres for extending by pulley ropes; three-section ladders may have a closed length of a maximum of 3 metres for extending by hand or maximum of 7 metres for extending by pulley ropes.' Extension ladders operated by ropes and pulleys can be put up more easily, and with less chance of damage, etc. They can be raised with one hand and held off with the other, to extend over openings or copings without snagging.

Scaffold loadings

The most important consideration is the 'slip load' on the scaffold fittings and the necessary safety factor.

British Standards require that scaffold fittings must be designed to withstand a load of 1270 kg before slipping. With a safety of 4 : 1, the maximum approved load would be only 315 kg, and this can be reached easily under normal work conditions. For example, one man, 120 bricks and a barrowload of mortar, all placed near one standard, would produce a total load of 353 kg, on the fitting. Six bags of cement and the man handling them would be even more.

Deliberate care is needed to avoid overloading scaffolds. Any loading over the theoretical slip load would be out of the question – even if the fitting held, the tube below would begin to deform. The consequences would depend on the lengths of tubing involved. That is why the test load laid down by British Standards must in no way be taken as applying to normal working conditions. It is meant only for testing materials to the point of failure.

The published British Standard slip load test figures are:

| | | |
|---|---|---|
| Right angle coupler | ⎱ | 12 455 N |
| Swivel coupler | ⎰ | |
| Sleeve coupler | – | 6227 N |
| Putlog coupler | – | 1245 N |

Various other considerations apply: fittings must not be greasy or oily, or frictional resistance will be lost; the correct length of spanner or podger must be used in the correct manner, to obtain the proper torque value without any overstressing of the screw threads. A reasonable torque value for fittings is obtained by applying 147 N to the end of a spanner or podger which is 225 mm long.

The fittings and the tubing must be in good condition, as any serious damage or deformity will be made worse by the loading and could lead to total failure.

Working platform loadings

There are four main kinds of loads affecting scaffolds:

1. Dead load: Weight of scaffold materials;
2. Wind load: Wind pressure × scaffold height;
3. Super load: Men, materials and equipment;
4. Live load: Movements of men and objects.

Typical examples of loadings per working platform are:

| | |
|---|---|
| Light independent | 716 N/m$^2$ |
| General independent | 1175 N/m$^2$ |
| Heavy duty tied | 2873 N/m$^2$ |
| Heavy duty independent | 1175 N/m$^2$ |
| Putlog scaffold | 2677 N/m$^2$ |
| Light birdcage | 716 N/m$^2$ |

*Table 5.1* Table of maximum recommended loads on scaffold and working platforms

| Type of scaffold | Spacing of standards (m) | Width of platform | | Platform area per bay (m²) | Permissible loading (N/m²) | Maximum load per bay (N) | No. of working platforms in use at one time | Example of maximum load per bay (see Note 2) |
| --- | --- | --- | --- | --- | --- | --- | --- | --- |
| | | No of 229 mm boards | Nominal width | | | | | |
| Putlog | 1.8 | 5 | 1.2 | 2.22 | 2697 | 5977 | 1 | 1 man mortar on spot board and 180 bricks |
| Putlog | 2.4 | 5 | 1.2 | 2.97 | 1765 | 5265 | 1 | 1 man mortar on spot board and 160 bricks |
| Light independent tied | 2.7 | 3 | 0.6 | 1.67 | 716 | 1200 | 1 | 1 man and hand tools paint or plaster |
| Light independent tied | 2.7 | 4 | 0.9 | 2.5 | 716 | 1801 | 1 | 2 men and hand tools paint or plaster |
| General purpose independent tied | 2.1 | 5 | 1.2 | 2.6 | 1765 | 4607 | 4 | 1 man mortar on spot board and 130 bricks |
| General purpose independent tied | 2.4 | 5 | 1.2 | 2.97 | 1422 | 4270 | 4 | 2 men and 2746 N materials |
| Heavy duty independent tied | 1.8 | 5 | 1.2 | 2.22 | 2844 | 6404 | | 1 man mortar on spot board and 200 bricks |
| Heavy duty independent tied | 1.8 | 6 | 1.37 | 2.5 | 2844 | 7205 | | 2 men and 5688 N of materials |
| Heavy duty independent tied | 1.8 | 5 | 1.2 | 2.22 | 1765 | 3949 | | 2 men and 2452 N of materials |

*Notes:* 1. Information as to the number of platforms that may be in use at any time is given in the approximate section of the Code.

2. Assumptions made: weight of a man = 747 N; weight of spot board and mortar = 311 N; weight of a brick = 27 N

3. If bricks weighing more than 27 N each are used, the total number of bricks per bay should be proportionally reduced.

4. Scaffolds are designed for uniform loading: point and impact loads should be avoided. If point and impact loads cannot be avoided then strengthening of the scaffold is required.

| Mobile tower | 1432 N/m$^2$ |
| Static tower | 1432 N/m$^2$ |

Loadings on hoist towers vary with the type of hoist.

Minimum permissible platform widths are as follows:

| Passageway only | 0.440 m |
| Footing only | 0.640 m |
| Men, materials, etc. | 0.870 m |
| Support higher platform | 1.070 m |
| Stonemasons' scaffold | 1.300 m |
| with higher platform | 1.500 m |
| Unguarded (no materials) | 0.870 m |

A putlog scaffold must be at least 1.150 m wide with a 100 mm gap from the wall for plumbing. The scaffold must always be erected in accordance with the Statutory Regulations and BS Codes of Practice, and to the design engineer's specifications.

The maximum recommended distributed loading on a scaffold or working platform is given in N/m$^2$ of platform area for each type of scaffold in the approximate section of the Scaffolding Code. In Table 5.1, these loadings are converted into maximum loads per bay according to the spacing of the standards and the width of the platform. Some examples of men and materials are given.

Loads on tubes

Safe working loads as below can be assumed for scaffold tubes of 48 mm outside diameter, made of 8-gauge steel or 7-gauge alloy, provided that the tubes are straight and true, and not damaged in any way. The permissible loads at *mid span* on tubes are shown in Table 5.2. If the load is *evenly* spread over the span,

*Table 5.2* Permissible mid-span working loads on 48 mm outside diameter tubes

| Free span of tube (m) | Steel tubing (kg) | Alloy tubing (kg) |
| --- | --- | --- |
| 0.305 | 1144 | 581 |
| 0.610 | 585 | 290 |
| 0.914 | 390 | 194 |
| 0.219 | 292 | 145 |
| 1.524 | 233 | 116 |
| 1.829 | 196 | 97 |
| 2.134 | 167 | 82 |
| 2.438 | 146 | 68 |
| 2.743 | 130 | 64 |
| 3.048 | 117 | 58 |
| 3.353 | 106 | — |
| 3.658 | 98 | — |

*Table 5.3*   Permissible end loads on standards and stryts

| Length of tube (m) | Steel tubing (tonnes) | Alloy tubing (tonnes) |
|---|---|---|
| 0.305 | 7.049 | 6.177 |
| 0.610 | 6.198 | 5.385 |
| 0.914 | 5.375 | 4.592 |
| 1.219 | 4.521 | 3.810 |
| 1.525 | 3.719 | 3.018 |
| 1.829 | 2.987 | 2.225 |
| 2.134 | 2.367 | 1.575 |
| 2.438 | 1.900 | 1.199 |
| 2.743 | 1.575 | 0.955 |

*double* calculations in Table 5.2. For loads on the *end of* a cantilever tube, *quarter* calculations in Table 5.2. For loads *evenly* spread over a cantilever tube *half* calculations in Table 5.2.

The *end loads* permissible on standards and struts are given in Table 5.3.

## Shoring

All types of shoring applied to a building or structure are temporary supports to comply with the Construction (General Provisions) Regulations 1961, section 50.[2] These regulations require that you take all practical precautions to safeguard persons from danger from the collapse of structures.

Examples of where shoring may be required are:

1.  As support to a wall which has or is likely to become dangerous due to subsidence (Fig. 5.11).
2.  To support a wall adjacent to deep excavations (see Fig. 3.4 on page 33).
3.  To support a wall adjacent to or connected with demolition (Fig. 5.12).
4.  To support sections of wall over an opening below caused by alterations or demolition (see Fig. 3.5 on page 34).
5.  To support a roof, floor or section of a building during replacement or removal of a lintel.

The illustrations of timber shoring and there construction are as Figs. 5.13 to 5.18, using a suitable softwood. Shoring using tubular scaffolding has already been shown under scaffolding and compares favourably with timber and is not prone to weather attack should the shoring be required to stay in position for a considerable time.

There are three types of shoring, each with its own separate function although a combination of any or all types is not uncommon and the use of a unsymmetric or bastard shore is sometimes necessary (Fig. 5.19).

106

*Fig. 5.11*   The use of timber in the construction of raking shores

*Fig. 5.12*   An example of the use of scaffolding to retain a building fascia after demolition but prior to redevelopment

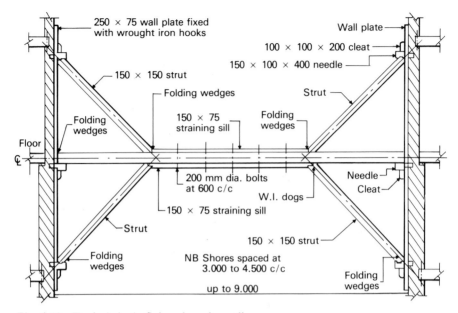

250 × 75 wall plate fixed with wrought iron hooks

Wall plate

100 × 100 × 200 cleat

150 × 100 × 400 needle

150 × 150 strut

Folding wedges

Strut

Folding wedges

Folding wedges

150 × 75 straining sill

Folding wedges

Floor

200 mm dia. bolts at 600 c/c

Needle

Cleat

W.I. dogs

150 × 75 straining sill

Strut

150 × 150 strut

Folding wedges

NB Shores spaced at 3.000 to 4.500 c/c

Folding wedges

up to 9.000

*Fig. 5.13*   Typical single flying shore in outline

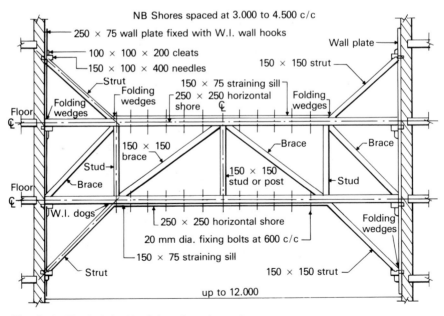

NB Shores spaced at 3.000 to 4.500 c/c

250 × 75 wall plate fixed with W.I. wall hooks

Wall plate

100 × 100 × 200 cleats

150 × 100 × 400 needles

150 × 150 strut

Strut

150 × 75 straining sill

Folding wedges

250 × 250 horizontal shore ℄

Folding wedges

Floor

Folding wedges

150 × 150 brace

Brace

Brace

Stud

150 × 150 stud or post

Stud

Floor

Brace

W.I. dogs

250 × 250 horizontal shore

Folding wedges

20 mm dia. fixing bolts at 600 c/c

150 × 75 straining sill

Strut

150 × 150 strut

up to 12.000

*Fig. 5.14*   Typical double flying shore in outline

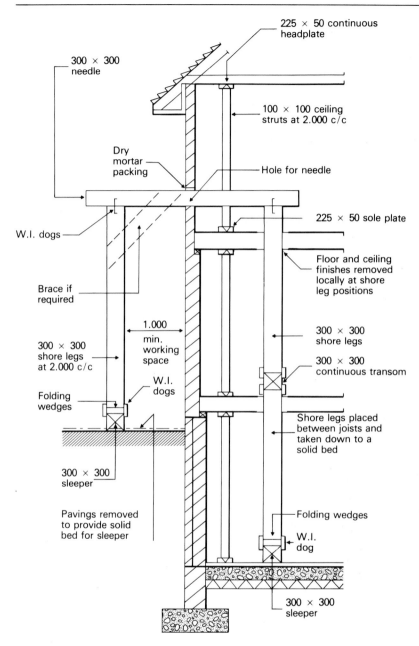

225 × 50 continuous headplate

300 × 300 needle

100 × 100 ceiling struts at 2.000 c/c

Dry mortar packing

Hole for needle

W.I. dogs

225 × 50 sole plate

Brace if required

Floor and ceiling finishes removed locally at shore leg positions

1.000 min. working space

300 × 300 shore legs

300 × 300 shore legs at 2.000 c/c

300 × 300 continuous transom

W.I. dogs

Folding wedges

Shore legs placed between joists and taken down to a solid bed

300 × 300 sleeper

Folding wedges

W.I. dog

Pavings removed to provide solid bed for sleeper

300 × 300 sleeper

Cross bracing, longitudinal bracing and hoardings to be fixed as necessary

*Fig. 5.15* Dead shoring in outline

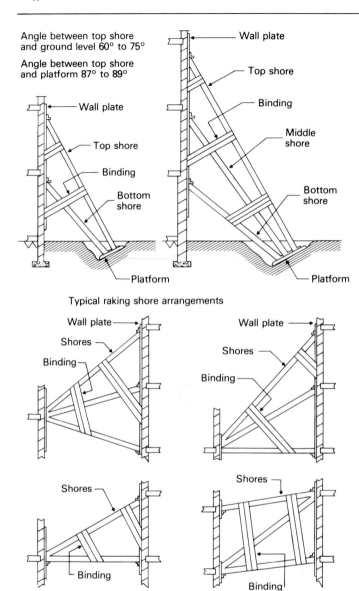

Angle between top shore
and ground level 60° to 75°

Angle between top shore
and platform 87° to 89°

Wall plate

Top shore

Binding

Bottom
shore

Wall plate

Top shore

Binding

Middle
shore

Bottom
shore

Platform

Platform

Typical raking shore arrangements

Wall plate

Shores

Binding

Wall plate

Shores

Binding

Shores

Binding

Shores

Binding

Unsymmetrical flying shore arrangements

*Fig. 5.16* Shoring arrangements in outline

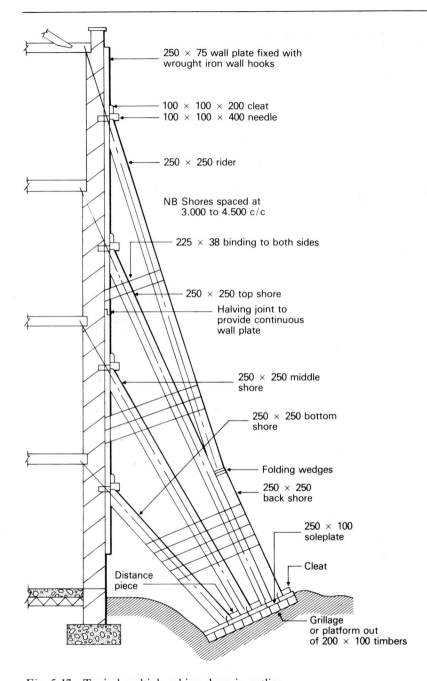

250 × 75 wall plate fixed with wrought iron wall hooks

100 × 100 × 200 cleat
100 × 100 × 400 needle

250 × 250 rider

NB Shores spaced at 3.000 to 4.500 c/c

225 × 38 binding to both sides

250 × 250 top shore
Halving joint to provide continuous wall plate

250 × 250 middle shore

250 × 250 bottom shore

Folding wedges
250 × 250 back shore

250 × 100 soleplate

Cleat

Distance piece

Grillage or platform out of 200 × 100 timbers

*Fig. 5.17* Typical multiple raking shore in outline

150 Important Ply Details

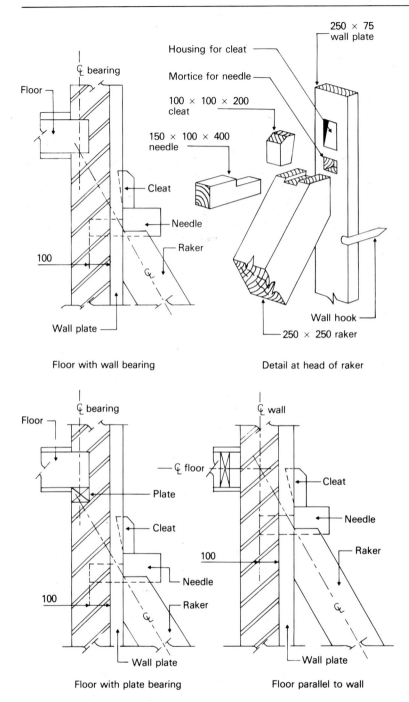

*Fig. 5.18* Raking shore in outline

*Fig. 5.19*   An example of the use of scaffold to construct raking, flying and dead shores for the retention of the facade of a listed building prior to redevelopment. *Note*: protective membrane covering retained facade to eliminate weather penetration

1.  *Raking shores* are used to transfer the wall and floor loading to the ground by means of rakers. These rakers must be correctly positioned to take wall and floor thrust should it occur. The centre line of each raker should intersect the centre line of the wall or floor bearing. It is not common to use this type of shoring above three storeys, with each floor having a separate raker. Should a four-storey building require shoring a 'rider' would be fitted as illustrated (see Fig. 5.17).
2.  *Flying shores* fulfil the same function as the raking shores and can be used between buildings, or in fact any two parallel surfaces. The use of timber shoring using this method becomes excessive over approximately 10 m, although tubular scaffolding is used over longer spans but may need central supports. This type of shoring allows clear working space or access to and from the area.
3.  *Dead shoring* is used to support dead loading from above which has a downward thrust and can be used to support a number of floors or similar types of construction. The use of timber or tubular scaffolding is equally suitable, although the patent adjustable prop (see Fig. 3.6 p. 35) is the ideal equipment for this type of shoring providing always the weight ratio is confirmed by a structural engineer.

Whatever type of shoring it is proposed to use, the material to be used in its construction must always be calculated by a competent engineer and the correct sequence followed for their erection and maintenance. Do not rely on 'rule of thumb' calculations to save cost as this method often results in substantial insurance claims against the contractor. Always ensure the shore base has a suitable

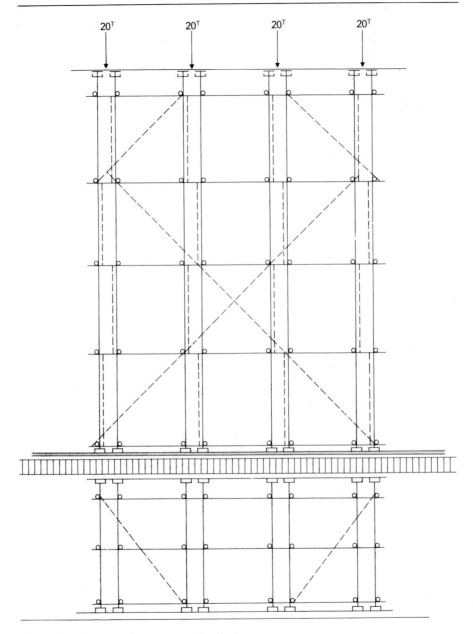

*Fig. 5.20*  Dead shoring (assumed loading)

load-bearing capacity and ensure the ground is stable, with no underground culverts or similar voids.

Once the shore has been erected initiate a periodic check by a competent person, and if the shoring encroaches on to the public footpaths or highway have it illuminated during hours of darkness and painted white up to a height of 2 m or to the requirements of the local authority.

## Vertical shoring

This is also known as 'dead' or 'needle' shoring (Figs. 5.20 and 5.21). It is used in underpinning operations, where the upper part of a building has to be held up while repairs or alterations are being done to the lower part or the foundations – also for supporting concrete formwork.

### Sequence of operations

All openings in the wall (windows, etc.) are strutted, to ensure that they do not become deformed by movements.

The roof and all the floors are supported by struts right down to the lowest level, to take as much weight as possible off the wall. The struts must all be exactly over the one below; each bearing on a continuous soleboard and each with a continuous headboard.

Horizontal members ('needles') are then passed through holes in the wall at the required intervals just above the level of the repair or alteration, depending on the length of brickwork or masonry which can be expected to be self-supporting. The needles will usually be of timber or steel joist. Each needle is carried on a pair of vertical timbers or tubes supported on continuous soleboards. The spacings between these shores will be governed by the load to be carried.

When they are in position and have been tightened against the needles, the weight of the upper part of the wall will be transferred to the ground. The wall below the needles can then be removed.

When the repair or alteration is complete and matured, the shoring is removed in easy stages in the following order: (1) needles; (2) window strutting; (3) floor struts. As a further precaution against mishap in tall or defective buildings, raking shores are employed in addition to the vertical shores (see 'Raking shores' on p. 117). They are placed close to the vertical shores or perhaps only near to the ends of the building, and are first to be placed and last removed.

### General design

This will be governed by the positions available for the needles. The needles must be placed so that they will transmit the loads to the shores. This may present difficulties, especially if the wall above has openings, such as windows.

The load-bearing ability of the ground underneath the shores must also be considered. It must be remembered that although a foundation may be able to

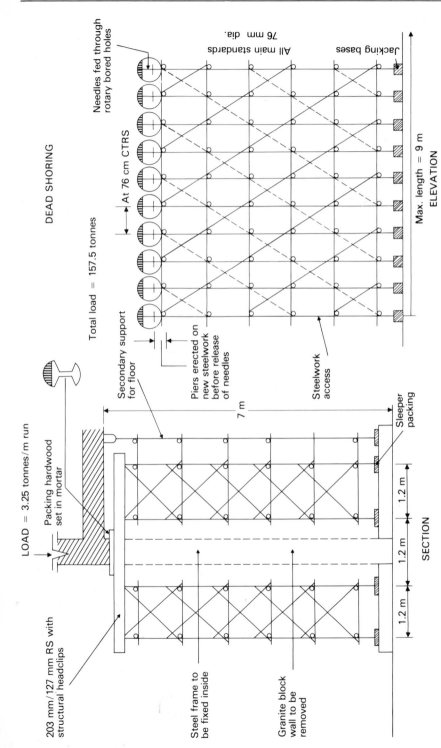

*Fig. 5.21* Dead shoring

take the load, significant settlement may still occur. With heavy shoring, it may be necessary to provide a concrete base at a suitable depth below ground level to prevent this from happening, as the consequences of settlement of the wall immediately above the shores (or the shoring structure itself) must obviously be avoided.

Other factors for consideration are:

(a)   Access for demolition purposes;
(b)   Working space for construction;
(c)   Space for new installations;
(d)   Access for new materials.

The methods of packing the needles to take the wall loads and of transferring the loads to the new structure must also be considered. Complete compliance with Building and Construction Regulations must be observed.

*Tubes and fittings*
For this kind of work, all couplings must be the load-bearing type, and all the fittings must be grouped tightly together.

The following considerations must be taken into account:

(a)   Direct loadings on the the struts;
(b)   Bending moments and shear forces on the needles;
(c)   The flexibility factors of the fittings.

Redistribution of loads due to needle deflections is also important.

The loadings on the shores are obtained from the following data:

(a)   Dead weight of the wall immediately above;
(b)   Dead loads on the floors immediately above;
(c)   Live loads on the floors immediately above;
(d)   Dead weight of the needles, headboards, etc.;
(e)   Extra live loads during construction work.

Raking shores

These are erected to provide a temporary means of holidng up a wall or building, and are often necessary while repairs or alterations are being carried out (Fig. 5.22). They are based on wooden soleplates or concrete pads firmly set on or in the ground, and butt against the building or wall on a 'needle' installed at a suitable point such as a floor level, with 'wall plates' spreading the pressure. The soleplates, concrete pads, needles and wallplates are normally supplied and installed by the customer or his main contractor.

The work may be in conjunction with the installation of vertical shores and can be complicated. All raking shores in tubular scaffolding materials must be erected in accordance with a structural engineer's designs and specifications. Ac-

117

*Fig. 5.22* The use of scaffolding as raking shores

cess scaffolds must be erected, to provide stagings for the scaffolders and the construction workers. The rakers and bracings will pass through these stagings, and it is important that they should be constructed in the same sorts of materials. Mixtures of scaffolding materials would lead to excessive difficulties in erection and removal.

The rakers (chords) are load-bearing tubes, set at the predetermined angle between the soleplates or concrete pads and the timber wallplates. It is essential that these tubes are positioned strictly in accordance with the structural engineer's designs and specifications. The best angle for rakers is 45 degrees (base equal to height), but space seldom allows fixing at this angle. The highest (longest) shore will usually be at 60 to 70 degrees (height equals one and a half times base).

The tubes will have to be cut accurately to the lengths required, and all ends must be cut dead square with no splits or other defects.

All couplers must be of the load-bearing type, and any sleeve or spigot couplers must be reinforced with splices.

The normal requirements apply to ledgers, puncheons, side and sway bracings, as set out previously.

In conclusion, before dismantling the staging, check all fittings for security, and get the site agent or general foreman to check and pass the finished job before handing over.

Figure 5.23 shows a completed raking shore in outline.

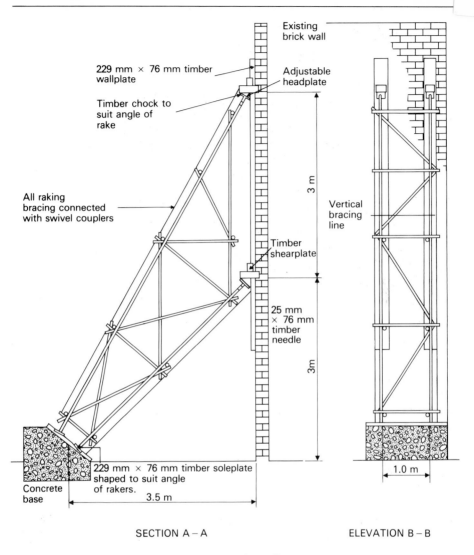

229 mm × 76 mm timber
wallplate

Existing
brick wall

Timber chock to
suit angle of
rake

Adjustable
headplate

All raking
bracing connected
with swivel couplers

Vertical
bracing
line

3 m

Timber
shearplate

25 mm
× 76 mm
timber
needle

3 m

229 mm × 76 mm timber soleplate
shaped to suit angle
of rakers.

Concrete
base

3.5 m

1.0 m

SECTION A – A                    ELEVATION B – B

*Fig. 5.23*   Typical example of a raking shore in outline

119

Flying shore

This is a horizontal box-shaped tubular structure fixed between two walls above ground level. It will often be placed between two houses remaining where an intermediate house is demolished (Fig. 5.24 and Fig. 3.8 on page 36). Points to look for before commencing erection are: access for placing materials; proper fixing of wall plates, needles, cleats, chocks; position for the proposed access tower. If erection will be from a temporary tower, the tower should be wider than the proposed flying shore. All tubing must be fixed with load-bearing clips. The ledgers should be fixed on top of the temporary tower, and should be truly horizontal. The tubes must be aligned with the chocks on the wallplates, with baseplates used on one side of the flying shore and adjustable baseplates on the other side. Puncheons should project 300 mm above and below the top and bottom ledgers, to allow for fixing bracing members. Four longer puncheons should be fixed, two at each end of the shore, to allow tie tubes to be fixed from the rakers to the puncheons. Transoms are fixed to the puncheons to give a box-beam effect, with projections of 300 mm on each side to catch the vertical bracing and rakers. The rakers are fitted with baseplates, and fixed from the chocks placed at the extremities of the wall plates, running to the ledgers. They should run at about 45 degrees, meeting the transoms at the second and third puncheons. The adjustable headplates can then be screwed up, transferring the weight of the flying shore to the timber wall plates. This is a temporary measure, and full adjustment will be made to the headplates later. The tubular beam is braced on all four sides, and diagonal bracings are fixed to each set of puncheons. Tie tubes are fixed from the long puncheons for strengthening. The adjustable headplates are tightened to the required amount by a key or a hammer. With a very long flying shore, it may be necessary to leave the tower in position, supporting the shoring.

## Mobile towers

These have wide application for light work of short duration at heights of up to about 12 m as on ceilings of large buildings, etc. allowing safe access to large areas. They should be used and may be moved only on surfaces which are sufficiently firm, level and smooth to maintain stability. Locking devices *must* be used to prevent any movement while a mobile tower is being used. They may be moved about *only* by application of force low down near the base away from the direction of movement. If necessary, the base should be ballasted for stability. In a building, the maximum permissible height is three and a half times the smallest base dimension. Out of doors, the maximum permissible height is only three times the smallest base dimension. Any mobile tower more than 10 m high must be adequately tied into the building before use. Where tying-in is not possible, a mobile tower over 10 m high must be anchored by one or more of

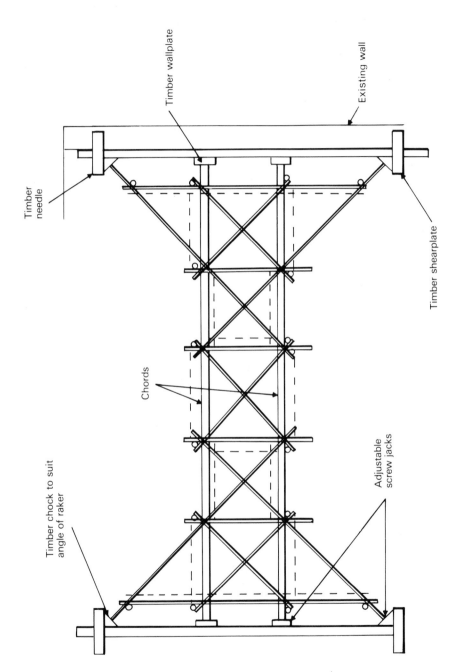

Timber wallplate

Existing wall

Timber needle

Timber shearplate

Chords

Adjustable screw jacks

Timber chock to suit angle of raker

*Fig. 5.24*   An example of a flying shore in outline

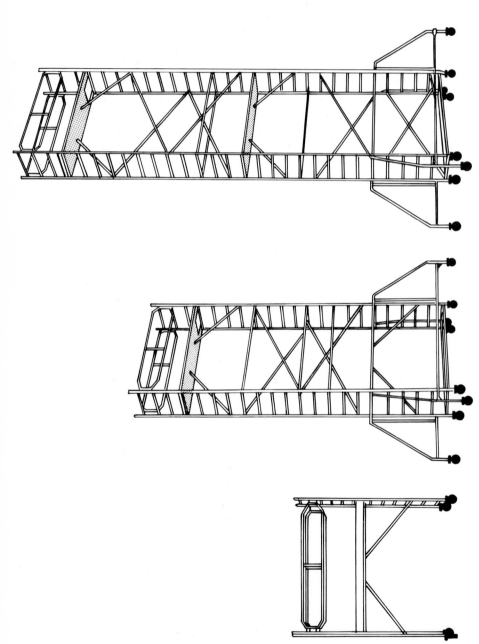

*Fig. 5.25* Examples of proprietary systems

the following methods: *guy wires* at 45 degrees from a high level; *physical anchoring* at the bottom corners; *adequate ballasting* at the base. Load-bearing couplers must be used through the construction of any mobile tower. There are two main types of mobile tower in general use (1) *tube and fittings* – conventional metal tubing, with adequate plan **and** diagonal bracing built into the design. With this type, the working platform size and height can be made to suit the job exactly, but there is the disadvantage of more labour and time needed for erecting, and the inherent danger of faults in design and/or workmanship. (2) proprietary systems (Fig. 5.25) – these have prefabricated pieces which slot together quickly and accurately, and there are various stock shapes and dimensions, with a range of weight-carrying capabilities. These system scaffolds are light and quickly erected, but they have a higher initial cost and their adaptability is limited.

## Ropes

### Fibre ropes

The term 'rope' is used for both fibre and wire ropes. The term 'cordage' applies to fibre ropes only. All ropes are constructed in the same way, with: several fibres twisted together to make a yarn; several yarns twisted together to make a strand; three or more strands twisted together into a rope. The way in which the strands are twisted together is called the **lay** of the rope, and it may be right-hand or left-hand, looking along the length of the rope from either end. The angle of lay between the direction of the strands and the centre line of the rope may be steep or shallow according to the amount of twist put in the strands. Steeper angles of lay make a rope more resistant to wear, but stiffer to handle.

There are three main types of rope lay:

#### Right-hand hawser lay

The fibres twist to the *right* to form the yarn;
The yarns twist to the *left* to form the strands;
The strands twist to the *right* to form the rope.

#### Left-hand hawser lay
The other way from the above.

#### Cable-laid rope
The consists of three hawser-laid ropes laid together the opposite way from the initial lays, and there are three main types of this in common use:

1. Three-strand plain or hawser laid, all at 37 degrees right-hand;
2. Four-strand shroud laid, all at 39 degrees right-hand;
3. Nine-strand cable or water laid: strands 37 degrees right-hand;
   ropes 31 degrees left-hand.

Commercially, the 'plain or hawser laid' ropes are also called 'shroud laid' by the makers and suppliers. The nine-strand cable laid are usually over 125 mm in circumference ('all round') or 40 mm diameter. The 'size' of any rope is always given as the length, and either the diameter **or** the circumference. Ropes are sometimes treated with tar to preserve them, but this makes them one-tenth heavier than plain ropes. Tar without any corrosive tendencies must be used. If plain rope is properly cared for and stored, then no undue deterioration will occur in ordinary use.

Natural fibre ropes

These are made from vegetable fibre obtained from various plants grown in different countries. Manila and sisal are most commonly used, and hemp and coir (coconut fibre) are also available. *Manila* is made from the long fibres of a tree grown in hot countries (particularly the Philippines), and this is the strongest of the natural fibre ropes. *Sisal* is made from the leaves of a cactus-like plant from semi-tropical countries. The fibres are shorter and less strong than manila. Natural fibre ropes are made up in coils of 220 m. Diameters (the measurement across the rope) are available from 7 to 150 mm, but 13, 19, and 25 mm are the most common. Coir fibre rope is about two-thirds the weight of the others. The following safety practices should be observed: *uncoil* by laying the coil flat with the inside end at the bottom. Pull the inside end up through the coil. *Take up slackness*, to avoid sudden snapping strains. *Pack up* sharp edges with wood, etc. to avoid chafing. *Parcel* any chafed parts with canvas daubed with tar and bound. *Reduce* strains on wetted cordages to two-thirds normal. *Dry out and air* all ropes before replacing them in store. *Slacken guys*, etc. in wet weather to allow for shrinkage.

*Manila*
This is a pale brown fibre, the one most commonly used. It stands exposure to the weather and damp better than hemp or sisal, and does not kink so readily. It is generally fairly soft and pliable. The best-quality manila is stronger than any other kind of natural fibre rope. British Standard 2053 identifies three standard grades:

| | |
|---|---|
| *Superior* | A blue thread in each of three strands. |
| *Grade I* | A blue thread in two of the strands. |
| *Grade II* | A blue thread in one strand. |

*Hemp*
Generally a greyish colour. Reddish brown from India. It is harder and less pliable than manila, and sometimes tarred to preserve it from the weather. Italian hemp is equal in strength to the best manila, but it is very expensive. From other countries it is equal in strength to a Grade I manila.

*Sisal*

A light creamy-coloured fibre. Coarse and rough to handle. Equal to a Grade II manila in strength.

*Cotton*

A white fibre from Egypt and the Americas. It is very strong when new, but loses strength and becomes hard and inelastic after it has been wetted.

*Coir*

This is the brown fibre from coconut husk, largely used for making mats and fenders, etc. It is much weaker than the other fibres, but it is also much lighter and will float in water.

*Spun yarn*

This is twisted yarns made from any sort of fibre, used for seizing and mousing, and by plumbers and water fitters. It is not 'laid' rope, so it comes apart easily.

Man-made fibre ropes

The first artificial fibre to be used for ropes was nylon. Further developments have now produced ropes made from Terylene, polyethylene, polypropylene and others. All of these materials have some characteristics in common, but each of them has some characteristics of its own. Comparisons between man-made and natural fibres show that the man-made fibres are stronger, less susceptible to chemical attacks, less able to absorb water and completely resistant to mildew and rot. They are all non-flammable, but they will melt if heated. Care must be taken to avoid undue friction by making sure that the correct size of thimble, sheave, etc. is used. Man-made fibre ropes cost five to six times as much as the natural fibre ropes, but if they are properly cared for they will last more than five or six times as long. Avoid unnecessary exposure to strong sunlight, heat or chemicals. If a rope becomes contaminated, wash it down thoroughly by hosing it with clean water, then let it dry naturally. Store man-made fibre ropes as for natural fibre ropes.

Effects of chemicals on ropes

Acid or alkaline chemicals can have various effects on man-made or natural fibre ropes. Depending on the rope material and the chemicals involved, the resultant effects can range from no loss in tensile strength to complete destruction of the rope. Many other factors have a bearing on the effect of chemicals on ropes: the strength of the acid or solution; length of time rope left unwashed after contamination; the temperature during the period of contamination; the exposure to light after contamination; degrading or admixture of chemicals involved, which can accelerate the attack with some ropes; water or acid hydrolysis which

*Table 5.4*  Effects of chemicals on rope materials

| Material | Attacked by | Resistant to |
|---|---|---|
| Nylon | Inorganic and certain organic acids. Also bleaching agents | Highly resistant to alkalis of all types, oils and organic solvents★ |
| Terylene | Alkalis | Highly resistant to acids (organic and inorganic). Virtually unaffected by bleaching agents, organic solvents and oils |
| Polyethylene | Some industrial solvents, particularly at high temperatures | Highly resistant to acids and alkalis. Unaffected by bleaching agents at normal temperatures and not affected by oils |
| Polypropene | Bleaching agents and some industrial solvents | Highly resistant to acids and alkalis. Not affected by oils |
| MANILA/ SISAL, etc. | All natural fibres are prone to attack by most chemicals **Avoid contamination** | |

★ While it is under test, no attack on nylon will be observed, but it is known that oxidizing oils accelerate deterioration of nylon on exposure to light. Oils, paints and other similar substances should be kept away from nylon rope.

can cause decomposition of fibres. Table 5.4 is a general guide regarding the effects of chemicals on different rope materials. If any rope in man-made fibre is suspected of contamination by chemicals, IMMEDIATE AND THOROUGH WASHING IN COLD WATER will considerably reduce the possibility of damage.

## Cradles

### Manually operated cradles

These are working platforms other than boatswains' chairs, suspended by fibre ropes and operated solely by hand, or by steel wire rope and operated by a manually powered machine. They are capable of being raised and lowered straight up and down, and also of being travelled across horizontally. The following terms are used:

1. *Suspension point* – where the suspension rope is connected to the cradle stirrup.
2. *Suspension rope* – the rope passing through the pulley block or suspension shackles, commonly called the 'fall rope'.
3. *Cradle* – the complete assembly, including the working platform, the

toeboards, guardrails and stirrups.

4. *Stirrups* – the end frames supporting the platform, and to which the blocks or lifting machines are attached.

There are many types of manually operated cradles available, constructed in metal, wood, glass fibre, etc. but generally two main types are distinguishable – *'one-man'* for light-duty work, *'two-man'* – for general duties. There are three distinct types of suspension:

1. *Travelling* – this indicates that the cradle can move across as well as straight up and down.
2. *Fixed* – this indicates that the cradle can move only up and down.
3. *Built-in* – these are cradles with permanent tracks built in to the structure. They are usually powered by electricity or air.

British Standard 2830: 1967 provides that: the *minimum width* of the platform should be no less than 432 mm; the *maximum length* of platform should be no more 3.200 m; the *minimum height* of the toeboard should be no less than 153 mm; the *maximum height* of the guardrail should be no more than 1.140 m; the *minimum height* of the guardrail should be no less than 914 mm. Exceptionally, if it would otherwise interfere with working, then the inside guardrail may be lowered to a height of only 762 mm. Also, if the operators have to sit down to work, then the inside guardrail and toeboard can be left off for the duration of the task requiring sitting, but under these circumstances safety devices such as safety belts or harnesses must be used by operatives, and the platform must be tied to the building to ensure that the inside edge of the platform remains within 305 mm of the face of the structure.

### Anchorages for suspended cradles

The main essential for the support of cradles and all other suspended scaffolds is that the anchorage is sufficient and strong enough to take the load. With built-in cradles the anchorage will normally be part of the permanent structure, but in other cases it will most commonly be an outrigger. Three main types of outrigger are used for suspended cradles: timber tube; timber poles; sectional steel. Timber poles are the traditional outriggers for light-duty work, such as industrial painting and cleaning of buildings. Larch and Norway spruce are the timbers mainly used, with a maximum length of 6.500 m and a natural taper. The thick butt end should be at least 115 mm in diameter, and this end must *always* be the overhang, to give the outrigger the maximum available strength. The thinner end should be not less than 65 mm in diameter. The projection (unsupported length) for a single outrigger should never be more than 450 mm. Timber poles should be tied down with a square lashing or box tie in 6 mm diameter wire rope, and the track should be tied to the outrigger with 9 mm diameter wire rope. Wire ropes should not be subjected to more than one-sixth of their breaking load, to ensure a margin of safety of 6 : 1.

At least three outriggers will be needed for each section of track, decided by the total weight to be carried. Each section of track should have an outrigger no more than about 450 mm from its end. Section steel outriggers are fixed the same as timber, with proper regard to protecting the ropes from acute bending strains around sharp corners. Timber packing pieces and hessian or other suitable cushioning material should be used to 'round off' the edges. All outriggers 'built-up' from tubular materials must be specially designed for the job by an engineer, and not left to on-the-spot judgment. The tubing must be in 8 gauge, preferably galvanized, and 50 mm diameter. All the fittings used must be load-bearing. For erecting a build-up on a roof, due consideration must be given to the roof covering and the condition of the roof. A person who is competent in roof structure work must make sure that the roof is capable of taking the total imposed weight. Care must be taken in placing the outriggers, especially when relying on a coping to take the weight at the fulcrum point. Copings are weaker than the main parts of a wall because of damp-proof courses and various aesthetic architectural features.

### Manual lifting devices

A large variety of hand-operated machines are available for raising and lowering cradles under control, but they are in two general types: 'drum' winch, with single or double arm; 'pumping' winch such at the **Tirfor**. They are all governed by the provisions of the Construction (Working Places) Regulations 1966, No. 94, which provides:

'(a) When the operating handle is released, a brake or similar device must arrest the machine from any further movement.
'(b) The machine must be adequately protected from the effects of weather, rain, dust, etc., likely to damage it.
'(c) When winches are used for suspended platforms, the fall rope must be long enough so that when the platform is at its lowest position (nearly down to the ground) there must still be at least two turns of the fall rope on the drum.
'(d) The length of the wire suspension rope (fall rope) must be clearly marked on the machine. The safe working load of a lifting machine for suspended platforms, etc., can be from 237 kg to 454 kg, according to the maker's specifications or company's requirement. For cradles up to but not more than 2 metres the safe working load is 227 kg. For cradles between 2 and 3 metres, the safe working load is 295 kg.'

The same safe working loads apply to the cradles themselves. In its design test, a cradle and the equipment involved must be capable of taking three times the safe working load spread evenly over the whole platform area. In its proof test, carried out at the maker's works, a cradle is hung from fixed hooks (with no blocks and tackle, machines or wire ropes) and it must be capable of taking an evenly spread out load one and a quarter times the safe working load.

## Safe practices

In the use of any **fibre** ropes, BS Code of Practice CP 97: Part 2: para. 1:3:5:2 recommends that where aggressive chemicals are being used (as in cleaning of buildings) then synthetic fibre ropes should be used in place of the natural fibre, provided that they have equal strength to the usual fibre rope and a suitable texture for adequate grip. It must also be remembered that synthetic fibres have less resistance to the effects of heat, which may be generated in the sheaves of the blocks or by direct friction. The *fall rope* should be in Superior Quality or Grade 1 manila, at least 57 mm in circumference. All ropes used for cradles must be inspected before every use, and a useful rule of thumb for their life span is between seventy and eighty working weeks according to conditions. Fibre ropes used for cradles must *not* have any splices. The maximum spacing for fibre rope falls is 3 m. Pulley blocks used for cradles must have a safe weight load (s.w.l.) of 227 kg. Counterweight calculation is the same as for boatswains' chairs, except that for cradles with two or more suspension points the safety factor used can be reduced to 3 : 1. *Do not forget* that the counterweight calculation is an assessment of each outrigger (not the total). Also, when two or more cra-

*Table 5.5*   Typical weights

|  | (*kg*) |
| --- | --- |
| 2 m cradle complete with stirrups | 61 |
| Rope (57 mm) – 150 m | 45 |
| Tirfoir wire rope | 7 |
| Strateline cradle winch | 26 |
| Sheave blocks, each | 3 |
| Jockey | 5 |
| Girder clip or hanging shackle | 5 |
| Travelling line | 2 |
| Stop end | 2 |
| Rolled steel joist – 3 m | 45 |
| Stirrup | 8 |
| Stabilizer | 14 |
| Platform – 3 m | 25 |
| Handrail | 6 |
| Toeboard | 6 |
| Tirfor T. 7 man cradle winch | 6 |
| Tirfor safety Blocstop | 2 |
| Barton runner | 6 |
| Barton hanging bracket | 6 |
| One man, normal build | 76 |
| Painters' tools and materials, per man | 2 |
| Impact loads, plus 10% weight of men and tools | 8 |

*Note*: Extra allowances must be assessed for any special or extra materials in the cradle or attached to it.

dles are suspended from one back build-up and there is any chance that the weight of both will be imposed on any one point in the track at the same time, then the backweight calculation must take this into account. 'Tying' is essential for stabilizing the cradle when in use. This can be done in several different ways: direct for the cradle; from the suspension ropes above the platform; from the 'underhang' of the suspension ropes. The tying point must be no more than 3 m from the platform in any direction. Only the *main* features of the structure must be used for anchorage points, *not* any of the attachments such as rainwater pipes or gutters. Raising and lowering should be done with both members of the team in unison, so that the cradle stays level at all times. If this cannot be achieved for any reason, then the slope of the cradle must *never* be more than 1 in 6.

*Table 5.6*  Example of loads (approximations will usually cancel each other out)

|  | *(kg)* |
|---|---:|
| *Small fixed cradle with one man* | |
| Cradle | 61 |
| Two falls of rope at 152 m | 90 |
| Four sheave blocks | 13 |
| One man | 76 |
| Tools and materials | 2 |
| Impacts at 10% of men, tools and materials | 8 |
|  | 250 |
| *Small fixed cradle with two men* | |
| Cradle | 61 |
| Two fall ropes at 152 m | 90 |
| Four sheave blocks | 13 |
| Two men | 153 |
| Tools and materials | 5 |
| Impacts | 15 |
|  | 337 |
| *Small travelling cradle and track (3 m) and two men* | |
| Cradle | 61 |
| Two fall ropes at 152 m | 90 |
| Two sheave blocks | 6 |
| Two jockeys | 9 |
| 3 m rolled aluminium joists (RAJ) | 45 |
| Girder clips or hanging shackles | 9 |
| Two travelling lines | 5 |
| Two stop ends | 5 |
| Two men | 153 |
| Tools and materials | 5 |
| Impacts | 16 |
|  | 404 |

*Table 5.7*  Inspection and examination intervals

| Reg. | Equipment | Inspect | Test and Exam. | Exam. only |
|------|-----------|---------|----------------|------------|
| 10 | Hoists for goods only | Weekly | Before first use and after re-erection or substantial alteration or repair | Every 6 months or more often |
| 34 and 40 | Excavators, draglines, piling frames, aerial cableways, overhead railways | Weekly | Not required | After any substantial alteration or repair or every 14 months |
| 34, 35 and 40 | Chains and lifting gear (except chains attached to excavator or dragline bucket) | — | Before first use and after lengthening, altering or welding | Every 6 months in normal use, or as often as necessary if use is occasional |

### Inspections and examinations

The Construction (Lifting Operations) Regulations require that inspections, examinations and tests must be carried out at the intervals laid out in Table 5.7.

### Factories Act 1961

The Act requires that every hoist or lift must be of good mechanical construction, and that: every hoistway must be efficiently protected by a substantial enclosure, and landing gates with efficient interlocking or other devices; the safe working load must be marked conspicuously on it; for hoists carrying persons (whether or not with goods) must be provided with additional safeguards such as devices to prevent overrunning. The requirements are somewhat less stringent for hoists built before 30 July 1973 (if any remain); also for hoists not connected to mechanical power, and for continuous hoists. Every opening or similar doorway used for hoisting or lowering goods must be fenced, and provided with a secure handhold on each side of the opening.

## Safety belts (Fig. 5.26)

Regulation 3B of the Construction (Working Places) Regulations requires that if due to the special nature of the work it is not practicable to erect a scaffold with safe working platforms and where it is also impracticable to install a safety net, then safety belts or harnesses **must** be used at working heights of 2.00 m or more.

British Standard 1397 describes four types of belts:

131

### Pole belts

These are used by line workers and other people who have to climb poles, etc. in circumstances where the load on the belt will be continuous. They must fit firmly around the wearer and at the same time be firmly secured around the structure. The design should permit the wearer to fall freely no more than 600 mm. Many applications of pole belts are feasible.

### General-purpose belts

Types 2 and 3, illustrated in Fig. 5.26, permit the wearer to drop a maximum of 600 mm and 1.800 m respectively. Where a 1.800 m drop is necessary, a proper harness is recommended. General-purpose belts consist of either a simple belt or a harness with shoulder straps. They are made of leather or webbing, and fitted with a metal 'D' ring, a length of rope and a safety clip/hook. Artificial fibre webbing is best for shock absorbing.

### Rescue harness

These are used in confined spaces such as in manholes or storage tanks where the worker may be overcome by fumes or noxious gases. They are so designed that an unconscious wearer would remain upright while being hauled to safety.

### Fitting

All types of safety belt or harness have adjustments so that they can be fitted accurately. This should be done with care, to ensure a firm, secure and comfortable fit.

All safety belts and harnesses must be clearly marked: BS 1397 and type number; name or trade mark of the manufacturer; the year of manufacture; maximum safe drop.

### Testing

A dummy weighing 136 kg is strapped in the belt or harness and allowed to fall freely to the extent of the line. Examine the belt, line and harness after the test for any sign of impending failure.

### Storage

All safety belts, harnesses, lines, etc. should be stored in a cool dry place such as in a cabinet where they will not be affected by strong sunlight. No part of the equipment should be under any strain or distortion.

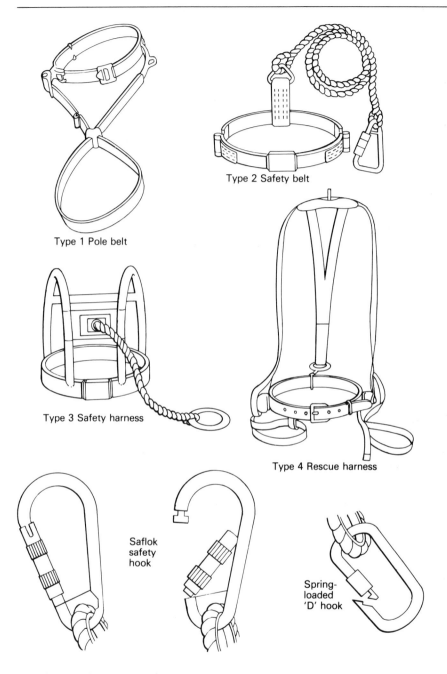

Type 1 Pole belt

Type 2 Safety belt

Type 3 Safety harness

Type 4 Rescue harness

Saflok safety hook

Spring-loaded 'D' hook

*Fig. 5.26*   Safety belts and harnesses

### Inspection

All belts and harnesses must be inspected regularly by a competent person and a record of the inspections kept. The following points should be checked: leather or webbing free from cracks, cuts, tears, abrasions, stretching or heat or corrosion damage; snap hook/rings faultless and not distorted; buckles free from stiffness and not distorted; no sign of wear or breaks in the stitching; ropes serviceable with no deterioration. Any equipment with defects should be taken out of service. Every person needing a safety belt or harness should keep it throughout the period of the contract, and should be personally responsible for examining it daily and carrying out any maintenance required.

### Maintenance

Artificial fibres need very little maintenance. Keep them clean and supple by washing in water. Leather equipment should be kept clean, and every three months should be serviced thoroughly by rubbing both sides with dubbing or neatsfoot oil and tallow until it is saturated. The dressing should be left to soak in and then any surplus wiped off.

### Fixing points

These must be even stronger than the safety devices. For scaffolding purposes the best fixing is usually a guideline of steel wire rope.

## Safety nets

Regulation No. 38 of the Construction (Working Places) Regulations requires that if, due to the special nature of the work, it is impracticable to erect a scaffold which complies with regulations regarding safe working platforms, then safety nets of suitable strength should be properly installed. It also requires that where it is not practicable to install a safety net, then safety belts or harnesses *must be used*. Personnel nets (Fig. 5.27) normally have a mesh size of 100 mm with square or diamond-shaped mesh. Fig. 5.28 shows the correct method of securing safety nets.

Debris nets normally have a mesh size of 19 mm, square or diamond shaped. They can be attached to personnel nets or used separately.

## Hoardings

There are two types of hoardings in common use today (1) permanent, and (2) temporary. Permanent hoardings are usually found on the perimeter of

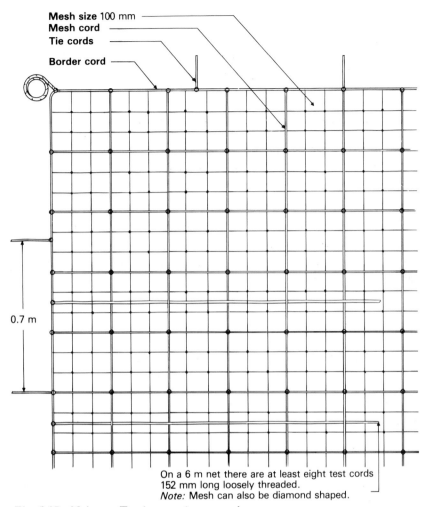

**Mesh size** 100 mm
**Mesh cord**
**Tie cords**
**Border cord**

0.7 m

On a 6 m net there are at least eight test cords
152 mm long loosely threaded.
*Note:* Mesh can also be diamond shaped.

*Fig. 5.27*  Nylon or Terylene cord personnel net

vacant sites and are used for advertising and bill posting. Temporary hoardings, those referred to in this book, are the protective screen around construction and demolition sites. Examples of this type of hoarding can be seen in Figs. 5.29 and 5.30.

Figure 5.29 is an illustration of a 2 m high plywood hoarding secured to a tubular steel scaffolding and illuminated with temporary lighting, leaving clear and free access for pedestrians on the public footpath and protected by fans from falling debris.

Figure 5.30 is an example of a full height hoarding projecting up to the eaves of the building being demolished. This illustration shows a walkway constructed under the hoarding and fitted with white-painted guardrails to allow the public

135

(a)

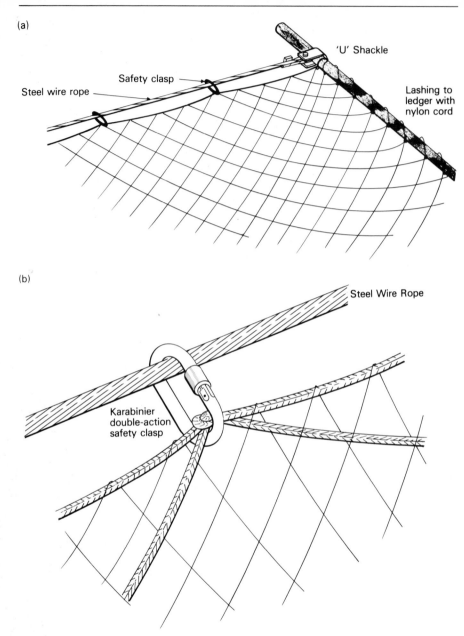

'U' Shackle

Safety clasp

Steel wire rope

Lashing to
ledger with
nylon cord

(b)

Steel Wire Rope

Karabinier
double-action
safety clasp

*Fig. 5.28*  Net fixing (a) shows a personnel net correctly secured (b) shows clasp attachment to steel wire rope in more detail

*Fig. 5.29*  (facing page) An example of plywood hoardings fitted to scaffolding and covered with a protective fan. *Note*: hoarding illuminated with red danger lights

*Fig. 5.30* Site shrouded with plywood hoarding with walkway underneath. *Note*: white-painted triangle to highlight danger to high-sided vehicles

to walk under and around the hoardings in one area without having to encroach on the highway. The return hoarding in this illustration is on a restricted width footpath, therefore protective balks have been laid in the road to protect the hoarding from vehicular traffic. The intersection has been painted white to highlight the danger to high-sided vehicles and danger notices posted to again warn the public of the work in progress.

Figure 5.31 shows illustrations and specifications for protective scaffolding fitted with close boarded hoardings in four different locations commonly found where demolition is taking place.

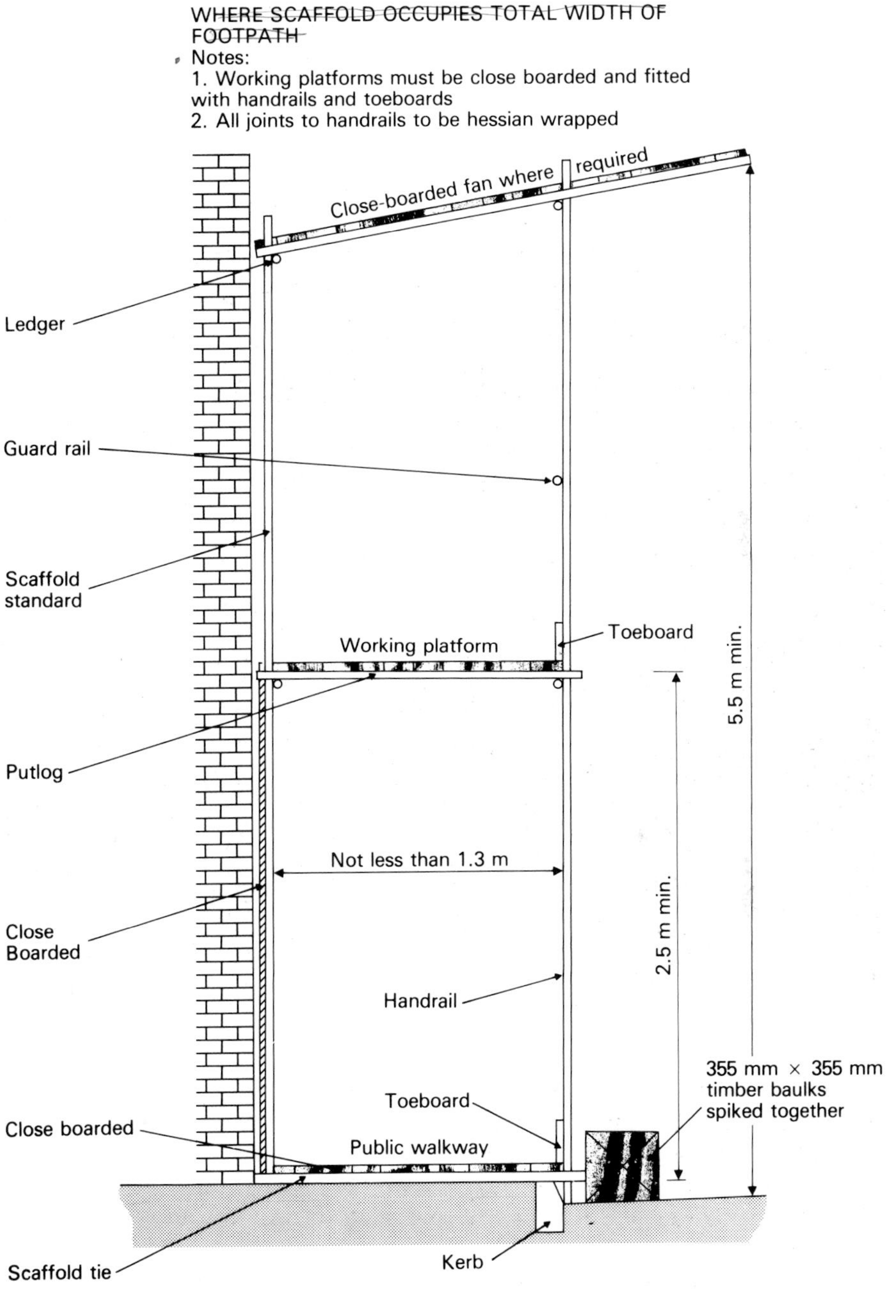

WHERE SCAFFOLD OCCUPIES TOTAL WIDTH OF
FOOTPATH
Notes:
1. Working platforms must be close boarded and fitted
with handrails and toeboards
2. All joints to handrails to be hessian wrapped

Close-boarded fan where required

Ledger

Guard rail

Scaffold
standard

Working platform

Toeboard

5.5 m min.

Putlog

Not less than 1.3 m

2.5 m min.

Close
Boarded

Handrail

355 mm × 355 mm
timber baulks
spiked together

Toeboard

Close boarded

Public walkway

Scaffold tie

Kerb

(a)

*Fig. 5.31*(a, b, c & d)   Examples of protective hoardings and fans over public walkways

NARROW PAVEMENT – 1.7 m
TOTAL WIDTH OF PAVEMENT

Notes:
1. Working platforms must be close boarded and
   fitted with handrails and toeboards
2. All joints to handrails to be hessian wrapped

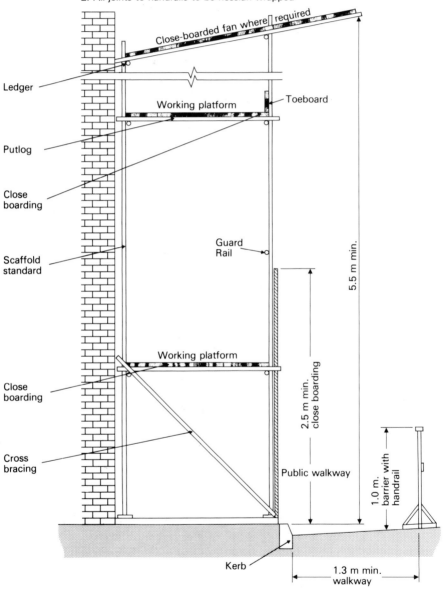

Close-boarded fan where required

Ledger

Working platform — Toeboard

Putlog

Close
boarding

Guard
Rail

Scaffold
standard

5.5 m min.

Working platform

Close
boarding

2.5 m min.
close boarding

Cross
bracing

Public walkway

1.0 m.
barrier with
handrail

Kerb

1.3 m min.
walkway

(b)

WIDE PAVEMENT – 1.3 m
CLEAR WIDTH OF PAVEMENT OUTSIDE HOARDING
Note:
Working platforms must be close boarded and
fitted with handrails and toeboards

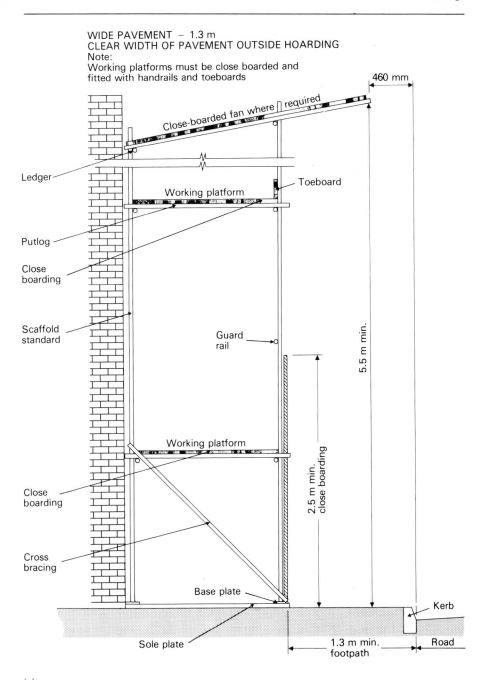

(c)

AVERAGE PAVEMENT WIDTH

Note:
1. Lighting will be provided where necessary at the discretion of engineer
2. All joints to handrails to be hessian wrapped

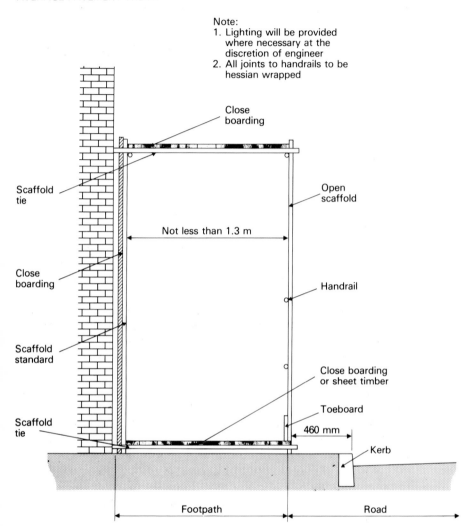

Close boarding

Scaffold tie

Open scaffold

Not less than 1.3 m

Close boarding

Handrail

Scaffold standard

Close boarding or sheet timber

Toeboard

Scaffold tie

460 mm

Kerb

Footpath

Road

(d)

## Chapter 6

# Health and safety

## Health and Safety at Work etc. Act 1974

Industrial accidents and diseases are as old as industry itself.[1] It is estimated today that there are four deaths daily through accidents at work and three more through prescribed industrial diseases. Around a century ago, there were calculations made that over 5000 people were dying annually in England and Wales alone due to injuries sustained at work – a figure that in terms of deaths during a prolonged military campaign or a full-scale war between nations would have been regarded as utterly catastrophic. And this was after the introduction of basic health and safety legislation, which began with the Health and Morals of Apprentices Act 1802, and was built up and extended, slowly but surely, throughout the nineteenth century (the first factory inspectors, for instance, were appointed in 1833).

The situation prior to 1802, then, is too horrific to imagine with any real clarity, and matters only improved very gradually through the efforts of a few enlightened individuals who pressed and agitated for social reform and the introduction of statutory obligations through the law of the land. In fact, the law and its requirements have, since 1802, been central to the question of workplace health and safety. Accordingly, a brief look at the legal position prior to the implementation of the Health and Safety at Work etc. Act 1974 will help to emphasize just how positive a contribution that particular Act (HASAWA) has made and will continue to make.

It can largely be said that our civil law is of two kinds: statute law created by an Act of Parliament (such as HASAWA itself) and case law which has developed slowly through the years via the hearing of cases relating to a wide variety of subjects, not only the question of health and safety at work in which we have a particular interest, to establish, among other things, a standard of duty which we, as citizens, owe one another. This latter, case law, is known more popularly as common law, although the term 'common law' in fact takes in the entire law of the land and extends to all laws including those set down by Parliament.

The basis of civil law in this country is the common law under which we all owe a common duty of care for the safety of others where our own actions or activities are concerned. What this basically means is that we are each responsible for our own wrongdoing, or 'tort' as the legal term is. The wrongdoing may involve our doing something we ought not to do or neglecting to do something we ought to have done but, either way, if we violate another person's right in the process, fail to fulfil our common duty of care and that person suffers damage or injury as a consequence, we are answerable at law to that person.

Common law is not written down in the sense that it is not on the Statute Book. It can only be interpreted by reference to case histories, the decisions of judges in previous civil court cases. By and large then, such law is judge-made, and judges have ruled that the law, and the common duty of care in particular, extends to employers in relation to the workers they employ. They have ruled that the employer's duty is to provide:

1. a safe place of work;
2. a safe plant, machinery and equipment;
3. safe work systems;
4. adequate supervision and instruction;
5. competent work-people;

but, along with this, and critically, that the level of care required is that which a 'reasonable' person would expect or apply in the circumstances of any cases as it arose, and that the possibility of accident, injury or ill-health should be foreseen 'as far as is reasonably practicable'. Naturally enough, it is around the interpretation of such words and phrases that the argument as to legal liability often revolves. The level of care appropriate in a particular case can be gauged by reference to statutory legislation such as the Factories Act, and in this way will be influenced by HASAWA.

The common duty of care is not normally enforceable by prosecution or the imposition of fines and penalties. It has grown up down the ages out of claims for compensation or damages that arise from a person's failure to observe his duty, whether through his own negligence or a conscious breach of statutory duty, and its main purpose is to give support to such claims.

Statute law has also evolved over the years, but by the passing of Acts of Parliament, repealing and replacing, amending or reinforcing existing legislation, and by the approval of subordinate regulations, statutory instruments, etc. statute law appears in written form and may be enforced by prosecution. If an employer fails to comply with his statutory duty under, for example, the Factories Act 1961, not only may he be liable for damages for any worker injured through his negligence, but he will also be open to prosecution in the criminal courts by a health and safety inspector where no injury, accident or ill-health has yet resulted. In this way, statute law in the health and safety field may be seen as playing a preventive role, compared to the remedial role of common law.

Prior to HASAWA, the two statutory provisions relating to health and safety at work that were of the greatest interest were the Factories Act 1961 and the Offices Shops and Railway Premises Act 1963.

The Factories Act 1961[2] is the most recent of a series of Acts bearing the

144

same title. It sets standards within the factory for:

- the cleanliness of working premises
- the prevention of overcrowding
- maintenance of a minimum temperature
- adequate ventilation; lighting and drainage
- sanitary accommodation
- the provision of welfare facilities: drinking water, washing facilities, seating, storage of clothing and first-aid arrangements
- the guarding and safe cleaning of dangerous machinery, and the training of young operatives
- the safe lifting of heavy weights
- the use of hoists or lifts, chains, ropes, lifting tackle, cranes, etc.
- the construction and maintenance of floors, steps, stairs, passages and gangways
- the provision of safe means of access to work and safe workplaces in general
- precautions against gassing, explosions of flammable dusts and gases, fire
- the construction and maintenance of air receivers, steam boilers and steam receivers
- work in underground rooms

as well as requiring notification of industrial poisoning or disease to the factory inspector and the Employment Medical Advisory Service, the notification of accidents and dangerous occurrences to the factory inspector and the keeping of records in a general register at the workplace; placing restrictions upon the employment of women and young people; giving powers of examination and inspection to factory inspectors, and of the medical examination of workers to Employment Medical advisers; and, finally, placing duties of safe conduct and behaviour on workers as well as employers.

The Offices, Shops and Railway Premises Act 1963 sets similar standards and lays down similar requirements to the Factories Act, but in the different working premises to which its title refers. Notification under the Offices, etc. Act is to local authority inspectors, who are empowered to enforce the law in the workplaces covered by the Act, instead of factory inspectors.

The Regulations laid down under the above Act provide for social security benefits to be paid to workers who have suffered from an accident arising out of and in the course of their employment. The Regulations are stringently applied and must be carefully and fully complied with for any benefit to be payable.

Each case is treated on its individual merits by an independent insurance officer who decides whether benefit is payable or not and notifies the Department of Health and Social Security (DHSS) of his decision. A worker denied industrial injuries benefit has the right of appeal to the Local Appeal Tribunal which consists of one member nominated by the trade unions, one by the employers' organization and a legally qualified chairman. Any such appeal must be made within twenty-one days. An appeal can be made against the decision of a

Local Appeal Tribunal on a point of law or a misrepresentation of material fact to the National Insurance Commissioner, but must be presented within three months of the tribunal's decision.

Certain medical conditions are catered for under the Regulations for prescribed industrial diseases. Most are contracted as a result of long-term exposure, and many years may elapse before a condition is diagnosed. Again, an insurance officer determines any claim on the basis of the medical board assessment of the extent of the disability. With a claim for benefit refused on the industrial history aspect of a case, there is a right of appeal to a Local Appeal Tribunal (within a time limit of ten days) and to the National Insurance Commissioner, as with claims for industrial injuries benefit. Where a claim is rejected on medical grounds, however, the right of appeal is to a Medical Appeal Tribunal. Claims for asbestosis, byssinosis and related dust diseases are dealt with by a special board called the Pneumoconiosis Medical Panel.

Despite the various legal provisions there was an estimated total time lost as a result of accidents and ill-health at work between June 1974 and June 1975 of 15.3 million man-days (about two and a half times the number lost through strikes); an estimated total annual cost of accidents and ill-health at work of £900 m. (at 1969 prices), with the government paying out over £200 m. each year directly in industrial injury benefits; and it was calculated that the average male manual worker had a one in ten chance of suffering severe injury or damage to his health during his working life.

During the 1960s and early 1970s the risk of accidents and ill-health at work was constantly on the increase, with hundreds of thousands of workers injured in industrial accidents and hundreds killed through either accidents or the contraction of industrial diseases at their workplace every year.

As we have seen in the previous paragraphs reform in the field of safety legislation, prior to the introduction of HASAWA, was long overdue.

(a) The Acts that covered health and safety were becoming increasingly out of date and inadequate to the needs of modern industry. Technological change and the widespread use of new machines, substances and work processes had created hazards existing laws were not geared to deal with, and, as they all referred in the main to a particular range of hazards, specific types of worker and places of work, they failed to extend any sort of protection to all those not covered by the Acts.

(b) Enforcement under the existing laws was lax, with too few powers given to health and safety inspectors, too few of the inspectors themselves appointed to see that the law was obeyed and penalties set at a derisory level.

(c) None of the laws encouraged the involvement of the workers they were supposedly designed to protect.

Clearly, then, a radical change in approach to the whole question of work and its hazards was called for and HASAWA, in supplying the legal framework to promote and foster better standards of health and safety at the workplace, was intended as just such an approach.

In view of the dangers inherent in many jobs today, the Act sets out to improve worker and management awareness, co-operation and effective action, by the pressure of enforcement on the one hand, and by the persuasive influence of recommended arrangements on the other.

Statutory workers' safety representatives and joint safety committees are seen as a powerful force in eliminating industrial accidents and diseases, and, with the proposed development of an integrated body of law and a unified inspectorate, the corner-stones of the Act are prevention and co-ordination.

The Act in no way replaces existing health and safety legislation. It supplements and operates alongside all previous laws – the Factories Act, the Offices, Shops and Railway Premises Act, etc. – and all relevant Acts and Regulations.[3] Their main provisions continue in force until substituted by an improved body[4] of law in the form of Regulations, Codes of Practice and Guidance Notes co-ordinated under HASAWA.

Regulations will be legal instruments drafted by the Health and Safety Commission and Executive after consultation with interested parties, and given over to the Secretary of State to lay before Parliament. They may be general in scope (e.g. dealing with environmental standards or the notification of accidents) or have a more specific application (e.g. concerning the use of abrasive wheels, or imposing industry or function-related requirements). There should be a considerable flow of Regulations, as they will have to fulfil at least three major roles:

1.  To replace with a systematic and co-ordinated body of legislation the chaos of old Acts and Regulations amassed over the years, as need arose or as pressure to improve standards had effected.
2.  To expand upon the general purposes of this Act with a body of rather more detailed requirements.
3.  To extend legal cover to areas as yet not protected by adequate health and safety legislation.

Regulations have the full force of law, but 'codes of practice' issued under them and the relevant Acts have a special quasi-legal status. They are not themselves legally enforceable, but may be used in court as evidence to indicate that the law has been broken, in much the same way as the Highway Code. Drawn up by the Commission, the Executive or by industry advisory committees, or in conjunction with such bodies as the British Standards Institution, Codes of Practice will:

(a)  Specify in greater detail, or a more amplified style than is practicable in the Regulations, precise technical, material or other standards to be kept up under the provisions of wider-ranging Acts and Regulations (Codes on *Lead*, *Noise*, etc.).
(b)  Explain what in particular circumstances would be regarded as satisfactory

compliance with the requirements of a general obligation (Codes on the *Appointment of Safety Representatives*, etc.)

Finally, 'Guidance Notes' will be issued by the Executive and the Commission, as those already drawn up on the establishment of safety committees. These Notes are the recommendations of the authority which drafts them and are not legally enforceable.

There are important differences then between these three 'levels of requirements' under HASAWA, and it is particularly crucial to bear this in mind when considering, to state a case in point, the provisions for the appointment and work of safety representatives and the setting-up of effective safety committees at the workplace. These are examined carefully in the next paragraph.

The whole gradual process of legislation renovation and replacement will take many years to complete. It will be the task of the Health and Safety Commission and Executive in consultation with both sides of industry. The appropriate trade union will have an opportunity to ensure that the present provisions are maintained where effective and improved upon where not.

The Act[5] does not specify precise legal requirements and name particular hazards as does, for example, the Factories Act 1961, and this is, perhaps surprisingly, one of its most positive features. In imposing broad general duties on employers, workers and others, HASAWA covers every hazard to health and safety at work regardless of its source – whether from unfenced machinery, unswept floors or inadequate training – and hence its strength. It aims to eliminate all kinds of hazards, to cover all places of work, and, by the following means, to protect everyone, not only workers, from the risks and dangers arising from work:

(a)   by securing the health, safety and welfare of persons as work;
(b)   by protecting the general public from hazards arising from work activities;
(c)   by regulating the acquisition, storage and use of all dangerous substances
(d)   by controlling pollution of the air by emissions from work premises.

These are the wide-ranging goals specified in section 1 of the Act.

People generally are protected by the Act where they face risks arising from the activities of men and women at work. Only employees themselves were covered by previous laws, but now customers in shops, passengers at stations, children at school and patients in hospital, to give but a few examples, are all given protection. This general cover, however, in no way detracts from the Act's promotion of workers' health and safety.

Only domestic servants in private households are excluded, although workers on Crown property – and this includes factories, airfields and docks that are part of the Armed Forces – find themselves in the exceptional position of being covered by all sections of the Act apart from those which give effect to legal enforcement – the issuing of notices and prosecution through the criminal courts by the relevant inspectorate. So for these workers the Act can only be enforced through persuasion and trade union pressure.

The general duties laid down by HASAWA are, by and large, those the neglect of which, under common law, would give rise to a claim for damages in the civil courts. Their restatement here, in statute law, makes a breach of them a criminal offence also, against which inspectors and other agents of enforcement may take legal action.

The overall duty of every employer is, as the Act states broadly (section 2) 'to ensure, so far as is reasonably practicable, the health, safety and welfare at work of all his employees', which includes, but does not stop at:

- the provision and maintenance of plant, work systems, workplaces, means of entry and exit, and a working environment that are safe and without risk to health, with adequate welfare facilities and arrangements.
- arrangements that are safe and without risk to health for the use, handling, storage, and transport of articles and substances.
- the provision of such information, instruction, training and supervision as is necessary to ensure the health and safety of his workers and 'to conduct his undertaking in such a way as to ensure' that the general public are not exposed to risks to their health and safety arising from work (section 3).

The employer must carry out these duties 'so far as is reasonably practicable'.

*Notes*: 'Reasonably practicable' is a narrower term than 'physically possible', and seems to imply that a computation must be made by the owner in which the quantum of risk is placed on one scale and the sacrifice involved in the measures necessary for averting the risk whether in money, time, or trouble) is placed in the other, and that if it be shown that there is a gross disproportion between them – the risk being insignificant in relation to the sacrifice – the defendants discharge the onus on them. The meaning in law of 'reasonably practicable' has been defined in this way and, accordingly, it involves the measuring of possible danger to safety or health against the overall cost of taking adequate precautions.

Qualifications of this kind, just as the vague and general terms in which the employers' general duties are couched, will always be open to abuse and sometimes provide a loophole for employers seeking to opt out of their responsibilities. But, just as the general, unspecific nature of the duties keeps their relevance and application as broad and far-reaching as possible with their more detailed implications to be filled out in better-defined and more precise regulations, such a qualification as 'reasonably practicable' also has its positive side.

Qualification certainly does not make the imposition of duties useless. In fact, if an inspector presses prosecution for an employer's neglect of his duties, it is the inspector who will lead with his own interpretation of what was 'reasonably practicable' under the circumstances. Significantly, too, the onus of proving that possible remedial measures in any instance were not 'reasonably practicable' lies squarely on the shoulders of the employer.

Additionally, these duties, despite their general nature and the 'reasonably practicable' proviso, are a plus in health and safety terms, as they in no way affect the specific duties placed upon employers by the Factories Act, etc.

The Act places some very far-reaching duties on employers without the 'so far as is reasonably practicable' proviso. These duties are:

(a)  To draw up, revise when necessary, and make available to all their workers a written statement of their health and safety policy (Appendix 1), a declaration of intent to provide the safest working conditions possible (which, once stated, employers should be made to put into practice), together with details of the organization and arrangements at the workplace made to give effect to that policy (what level of management holds responsibility for each aspect of health and safety, who are the appointed safety representatives, details of committee authority and membership, etc.) and the identification of the particular workplace hazards, referring the reader to more detailed information if necessary (section 2 (3)).

(b)  To consult with trade union appointed safety representatives from their workforce over arrangements to promote employer/worker co-operation in adopting and monitoring the effectiveness of measures to ensure health and safety at the place of work (section 2(6)).

(c)  To set up a safety committee to keep all health and safety measures under review if requested to do so by safety representatives at a particular undertaking (section 2(7)).

(d)  Not to charge their workers for any equipment provided or any work done for health and safety purposes under a statutory requirement (the fencing of transmission machinery, for instance, or the provision of protective clothing for women and young people employed in processes involving the use of a lead compound, under the Factories Act 1961) (section 9).

(e)  To provide the general public with information about their work activities where the public's health and safety might be at risk (section 3(3)).

The requirements concerning the setting-up of safety committees, consultation between employers and safety representatives and the employer's production of a safety policy are all of great importance and will be looked at for their implications later.

Workers' duties

These duties are phrased in general terms to ensure a broad rather than a precise application. By and large, they restate responsibilities that already exist under common law. Carrying no 'so far as is reasonably practicable' qualification, the duties are little more than sound common sense and are as follows. Workers are:

to take all reasonable care not to endanger themselves or others who might be affected by their work (section 7a)
to co-operate with their employer, works manager, etc. in complying with the law (section 7b)

not to intentionally or recklessly misuse anything provided in the interests of health and safety' (section 8)

Similar duties have existed under the operation of the Factories Act, but have only rarely been pressed against workers in the courts. Prosecutions occur annually at a very low level (there were eleven convictions in 1976, which resulted in an average fine of £69.50 per worker) and are usually for acts of extreme foolishness leading to the injury of a fellow worker rather than for a breach of workers' general duties. The number of prosecutions of workers should not increase under HASAWA, but it is as well to note that there is no longer a separate, lower level of fines for workers.

The 'co-operation' aspect is the only new element in the duty of workers, so trade unionists should be particularly careful about its application. While it will necessarily mean workers and employers getting together to discuss and put into action measures to ensure workplace health and safety through the machinery of safety representatives, committees, etc. it should not be used to hide the fact that inevitably conflicts of interest will arise between the two sides. These conflicts will only be resolved by negotiation, not by giving in to an employer quoting this duty of co-operation to railroad through solutions to safety problems which he has advised and are unsatisfactory from the point of view of the workforce. Such a view of 'co-operation' is contrary to the spirit and intentions of the Act, as well as to the duty of 'reasonable care' under section 7a.

All this does not mean that responsibility for health and safety is now a burden to be shared equally between worker and employer. Since the employer by the act of providing work creates the risks of employment, his is still the main responsibility. By the same token, the Act does not generally affect the position of claims for damages.

Duties also fall on:

- anyone in control of working premises, to ensure that the premises, any means of *entry to or exit from them*, and any plant or substance on them are safe and without risk to the health of workers, other than his own employees, who use those premises (section 4)

- anyone in control of working premises, to use the best practicable means for preventing the escape into the atmosphere of harmful or offensive substances, and for making harmless or inoffensive substances which do escape (section 5)

- the self-employed, to ensure that their work activities are safe and free from risks to health (section 3(2))

- designers, manufacturers, importers and suppliers of any article or substance for use at work, to ensure that it is safe when properly used, by prior testing, examination and research as necessary, and to provide adequate information about its safe usage (section 6)

- installers of machinery, etc. at the workplace to make sure that they have installed the article safely' (section 6(3)).

In each of these instances, except where the escape of substances into the atmosphere and where the provision of adequate information are concerned, the duties apply only 'so far as is reasonably practicable'.

Perhaps of greatest interest here is the duty on manufacturers, importers and suppliers to provide the employer with information on the article or substance he supplies – information on tests carried out and their results, information on the conditions necessary to ensure that the article or substance is safe when properly used. This information should be made available, in turn, by the employer to his workers and, in particular, to safety representatives.

Enforcement is the responsibility of the Health and Safety Executive (HSE) established under this Act. The Executive brings under one roof inspectors given powers under this and the various other existing Acts. Within it, the identities of the formerly separate inspectorates have been retained (Factories Inspectorate, Explosives Inspectorate, Nuclear Installations Inspectorate, etc.) but given a new co-operative force through a unified, co-ordinated overall approach. As a consequence, all factory inspectors operating under the HSE have the power to enforce the general provisions of this Act, the more specific requirements of the Factories Act and all related Regulations.

Local authorities, however, continue for the time being as the enforcement agency for certain areas of health and safety (e.g. fire escapes under the Factories Act) and for the non-industrial sector, where the workplace is covered by the Offices, Shops and Railway Premises Act 1963.

It follows that the success of the new legislation will continue to depend, in part, on the effectiveness of its inspectorate, and it will be vital to press for an enlarged body of inspectors. Particularly as, with the increased weight of legislation, around 8 million workers protected for the first time, and the inspectorate's policy of in-depth inspection of high-risk workplaces, it will be certainly no less important that workers are able to contact their local inspector easily for advice and action when necessary. Numbers have increased over recent years, but barely in proportion to the increased burden placed upon individual inspectors.

The Health and Safety Commission (HSC)

The Commission consists of representatives of both industry and the local authorities. Its members are all part-time, with the exception of its chairman. It takes over ultimate responsibility for policy development in the health and safety field from government departments, and must draw up and publish an annual report on its activities and on the overall effectiveness of health and safety legislation. More specifically, the Commission will:

(a)  draft Regulations and Codes to put before Parliament, replacing former safety legislation and expanding upon HASAWA (the Code of Practice on

*Time Off for Training of Safety Representatives*, for example);
(b)  conduct research into and provide information on all aspects of health and safety at work;
(c)  order an investigation into any 'accident, occurrence, situation or other matter' relevant to its purpose.

## The Health and Safety Executive (HSE)

The Executive is a separate statutory body appointed by the Commission to work under directions and guidance from the Commission itself. It is the enforcing authority for legal requirements and provides an advisory service to employers and trade unions, to management and workers. As explained, the major inspectorates have been integrated under the Executive, instead of working independently within different government departments.

In 1976, the Executive set out a detailed plan of its aims and objectives over the coming five years to provide as full a picture as possible of its future proposals. Its projects were arranged within seven main programmes according to subject:

1.  Projects relating to particular hazards, e.g. dust, noise and vibration, machinery, toxic substances, nuclear and other major hazards.
2.  Projects relating to a particular industry, e.g. construction, mines, quarries.
3.  Control of air pollution, including specific emission problems in various industries.
4.  General legislation not related to other programmes, e.g. sex discrimination, metrication, civil liability, etc.
5.  Research, including medical research, not related to other programmes, e.g. design and development of specialized breathing apparatus, alcoholism in industry, fluid mechanics, etc.
6.  Enforcement and inspection, including increased specialization and workload in the inspectorates, new organizational developments and responsibilities, etc.
7.  Implementation of HASAWA, including: general issues of policy, organization, planning and participation by industry, information and publicity services and ongoing work of general interest.

Under guidance from the Commission, local authorities will be empowered to enforce legislation in some areas of employment, including many protected for the first time under this Act. By and large, their inspectors will cover premises where, taken as a whole, the major work activity is non-industrial, with, of course, the exception of local authority premises themselves.

The HSC may also make agency agreements enabling government departments and other agencies to act on the Commission's behalf to enforce specialized sections of health and safety legislation (air pollution in Scotland is dealt with by HM Industrial Pollution Inspectorate for Scotland, for example).

The Employment Medical Advisory Service (EMAS)

The EMAS will act as the medical and research arm of the Commission, servicing and providing specialized advice to the Commission, the Executive and its unified Inspectorate. Otherwise, it will continue its former functions:

(a) Undertaking research and liaising with others researching into industrial medicine.
(b) Studying the medical requirements for different jobs, especially where the disabled are involved.
(c) Carrying out medical surveys and conducting periodic examinations to protect workers against hazardous substances and processes, at their employer's expense, on a compulsory basis in dangerous occupations where the law requires, voluntarily where not (examinations of workers normally take place during working hours in time paid for either by the employer or by compensation from the Department of Employment). Any Employment Medical adviser has the power to demand that an employer permit him to examine medically any worker whose health he believes to be endangered because of his work, at any reasonable time during working hours.
(d) Offering free advice to workers, trade unions and employers alike on general health and safety matters – the risks arising from dangerous substances, physically demanding work, stress, etc. – and to individuals, through their GPs, on any medical problems relating to their work.

(See also the section on EMAS on page 301, as a source of information.)

The factory inspector

Day-to-day enforcement under HASAWA will be, in the main, the responsibility of the factory inspector, and with the provisions in this Act of 'industrial relations' requirements (employers' policy statements, training duties, etc.), the role of the inspector will be increasingly that of prevention as well as cure, of adviser as well as a prosecutor.

Ideally, health and safety problems will be resolved at the workplace using the standard, established procedures. However, where a complaint is made by workers to an inspector, depending upon the gravity of the issue, he is likely to attempt to arbitrate. Naturally, such a resolution of matters failing, the question of the inspector carrying out his full duties and using his various powers of enforcement will inevitably arise.

The three duties most vital to the interests of work-people are:

1. Routine visits to workplaces.
2. The investigation of complaints.
3. Disclosure of information.

The factory inspector has the right and duty to pay periodical routine visits to all workplaces under his authority, with or without warning of his intentions, at his own discretion (the element of surprise is given positive encouragement by the Act). He may be accompanied during such an inspection by management and/or workers' representatives, by agreement between himself and the individuals concerned, although there is no legal right of accompaniment for workers or management. There is, however, a right for both employer and worker representatives to speak privately with the inspector visiting their workplace should they wish to do so.

All complaints regarding unsafe work practices, dangerous plant and machinery, etc. made to inspectors by safety representatives, should be investigated as speedily as possible – workload permitting, your local inspector should not put off dealing with a legitimate and pressing problem raised with him by an authorized safety representative.

An inspector must provide both workers and employers with adequate information about work matters affecting their health and safety at work, after visiting a workplace:

(a) Factual information about the premises or the work done there which the inspector has obtained at first hand, including the results of any atmospheric tests or analysis of samples taken, the conclusions of tests on plant and equipment or clinical examinations, in written or oral form depending on the seriousness or particular nature of his findings (this is known as a 'Report of Visit').

(b) Information about any action he has taken or intends to take, including details of legal proceedings to be initiated, copies of improvement or prohibition notices he has issued and his more general recommendations on matters of concern (a 'Notice of Action').

Additionally, your local inspector and area office should be a vital source of information on all matters of workplace health and safety, able to handle and provide advice and assistance on any queries you raise with them.

The only brake on an inspector's disclosure of information in any of these areas is that he must take into full account the confidential nature of any aspect of it and may not reveal information given by a third party without that party's consent.

The powers of the factory inspector relate directly to his duties and role as an enforcement officer:

- in the course of his duty, he may enter any premises at a reasonable hour, or at any time whatsoever should the danger of the situation in his opinion warrant it, taking with him:
  (a) a policeman if he believes he will be hindered or refused access;
  (b) any qualified person (e.g. specialist inspector) whose advise he might need;
  (c) any equipment or material required for use during the course of an inspection.
- he may carry out any relevant tests or examinations, take measurements, photographs, recordings, samples, etc. during an inspection.

155

- he may have any article or substance he considers likely to cause or to have caused danger to health and safety dismantled or tested, or taken away either for sufficient time to enable a more thorough investigation or for use in evidence if further proceedings are intended.
- he may seize and have rendered harmless, even by destruction, an article or substance he believes a cause of 'imminent danger of serious personal injury'.
- he may insist on access to and copies of books, records or documents relevant to his investigation, and the provision of facilities for and assistance in such an investigation.
- he has the right to question anyone he thinks fit for relevant information and to require them to sign a declaration of the truth of their answers (anyone questioned may insist on the presence of a third party of their choice).
- he may use any other power necessary to carry out his duties.

It is difficult, then, to imagine a situation where an employer could deny an inspector access, facilities and full co-operation.

Additionally and critically, HASAWA gives the inspector new, stronger powers of enforcement.

*Improvement notices*[5] (Fig. 6.1).  If an inspector believes someone to be contravening this Act or any related health and safety legislation in force at the time (e.g. the Factories Act), he may serve that person with an improvement notice, telling them to remedy the fault. Anyone served with such a notice may appeal to an industrial tribunal within three weeks. The notice must allow three weeks for carrying out any specified improvements and, where an appeal is made, the notice is temporarily suspended.

*Prohibition notices*[5] (Fig. 6.2):  If an inspector believes that work activities are being carried on that give rise to a risk of serious personal injury, he may serve a prohibition notice requiring that activity to stop either at once, if the danger is imminent, or within a specified time if not (deferred notice). A similar right of appeal applies here, but the notice may only be suspended if the tribunal so directs.

Similar powers to these existed before HASAWA, but were vested in the courts rather than the inspectorate and were not much used. To press the point, in 1973 there were only 200 cases where the use of powers was threatened and 37 where actual closure orders were obtained. By comparison, in 1976, under this Act, the Factory Inspectorate branch of the HSE issued 4123 improvement notices, 1451 immediate and 526 deferred prohibition notices, and, out of the total number issued (6100), only 43 appeal cases needed to be heard by tribunals. The facts and figures speak plainly in favour of arrangements under HASAWA.

Prosecution is the third weapon in the inspector's battery and can be used in the following situations:

(a)  in cases of non-compliance by employers with improvement and prohibition notices;

(b)  as an alternative or additional measure to the serving of notices;

(c)  as the appropriate action where there has been a breach of the general duties the Act imposes on employers, workers, etc.;

(d)  where other health and safety laws and regulations have been contravened (Factories Act, etc.);

(e)  where an inspector has been hindered in carrying out his duties.

With prosecutions sought in a magistrate's court, the maximum fine on summary conviction for most offences under the Act was, initially, a derisory £400, or less in real terms than the £300 maximum fine was when imposed by the Factories Act in 1961. However, commencement orders Nos. 1 and 5 of the Criminal Law Act 1977, when they came into force on 8 September 1977 and 17 July 1978 respectively, raised this maximum to £1000.

Prosecution for serious offences can be brought before the Crown court for a trial by jury. Here, on indictment, an unlimited fine may be imposed and/or, in a few restricted instances, up to two years' imprisonment (notably for failure to comply with a prohibition notice). When either improvement or prohibition notices have been issued and ignored, there is the additional possibility of a supplementary fine of £100 for every day of non-compliance. However, the HSE's policy on the question of when a particular offence will be prosecuted before a higher court, and when not, has not as yet been made public.

Overall, though, on the question of prosecution and fines as a form of deterrent, it has been particularly disappointing to note that, despite the possibility of larger corrective fines, the average level stood as recently as 1976 at the farcically low level of £95. It remains to be seen what the new £1000 maximum will do to this figure, but it seems inevitable that a ridiculously low figure will persist, posing few problems for the majority of employers.

If the reality of legal enforcement is disappointing when compared to its potential under the Act, HASAWA should still not be considered lacking in teeth. The Act not only gives greater powers to its inspectorate, but aims more nearly at the promotion of health and safety where it counts – at the workplace, through the efforts of workers themselves acting through their trade union.

Sections 2(4) and 2(6) are the relevant passages in the Act as far as this vital aspect of 'enforcement' is concerned, and they read as follows:

'Regulations made by the Secretary of State may provide for the appointment in prescribed cases by recognised trade unions . . . of safety representatives from amongst the employees, and those representatives shall represent the employees in consultation with the employers . . . and shall have such other functions as may be prescribed.'

and

'It shall be the duty of every employer to consult any such representatives with a view to the making and maintenance of arrangements which will enable him and his employees to co-operate effectively in promoting and developing measures to ensure

# IMPROVEMENT NOTICE

## HEALTH AND SAFETY EXECUTIVE
### Health and Safety at Work etc. Act 1974, Sections 21, 23, and 24

| | |
|---|---|
| *Name and address (See Section 46)* | To ................................................................ |
| | .......................................................... |
| *(a) Delete as necessary* | *(a)* Trading as .......................................... |
| | **I** *(b)* ........................................................ |
| *(b) Inspector's full name* | one of *(c)*.................................................... |
| *(c) Inspector's official designation* | of *(d)*......................................................... |
| | ............................................. Tel no. .................. |
| *(d) Official address* | hereby give you notice that I am of the opinion that at |
| | *(e)*................................................................ |
| *(e) Location of premises or place and activity* | you, as *(a)* an employer/a self employed person/a person wholly or partly in control of the premises. |
| *(f) Other specified capacity* | *(f)* ................................................................ |
| | *(a)*    are contravening/have contravened in circumstances that make it likely that the contravention will continue or be repeated |
| | ............................................................ |
| | ............................................................ |
| *(g) Provisions contravened* | *(g)*............................................................ |
| | ............................................................ |
| | The reasons for my said opinion are: – .................................... |
| | ............................................................ |
| | ............................................................ |
| | ............................................................ |
| | and I hereby require you to remedy the said contraventions or, as the case may be, the matters occasioning them by |
| *(h) Date* | *(h)*............................................................ |
| | *(a)* in the manner stated in the attached schedule which forms part of the notice. |
| | Signature.................................... Date .................. |
| | Being an inspector appointed by an instrument in writing made pursuant to Section 19 of the said Act and entitled to issue this notice. |
| | *(a)* An improvement notice is also being served on |
| | ............................................................ |
| **LP 1** | of............................................................ |
| | related to the matters contained in this notice. |

*Fig. 6.1* Improvement notice

Serial No. **I**

## NOTES

**1**   Failure to comply with an Improvement Notice is an offence as provided by Section 33 of this Act and renders the offender liable to a fine not exceeding £400 on summary conviction or to an unlimited fine on conviction on indictment and a further fine of not exceeding £50 per day if the offence is continued.

**2**   An Inspector has power to withdraw a notice or to extend the period specified in the notice before the end of the period specified in it. You should apply to the Inspector who has issued the notice if you wish him to consider this, but you must do so before the end of the period given in it. *(Such an application is not an appeal against this notice.)*

**3**   The issue of this Notice does not relieve you of any legal liability resting upon you for failure to comply with any provision of this or any other enactment, before or after the issue of this notice.

**4**   Your attention is drawn to the provision for appeal against this notice to an Industrial Tribunal. Details of the method of making an appeal are given below *(See also Section 24 of the Health and Safety at Work etc. Act 1974).*

(a)   Appeal can be entered against this notice to an Industrial Tribunal. The appeal should be sent to: —

(for England and Wales)      The Secretary of the Tribunals
Central Office of the Industrial Tribunals
93 Ebury Bridge Road LONDON SW1W 8RE

(for Scotland)      The Secretary of the Tribunals
Central Office of the Industrial Tribunals
Saint Andrew House
141 West Nile Street GLASGOW G1 2RU

(b)   The appeal must be commenced by sending in writing to the Secretary of the Tribunals a notice containing the following particulars: —

(1)   The name of the appellant and his address for the service of documents;

(2)   The date of the notice or notices appealed against and the address of the premises or place concerned;

(3)   The name and address *(as shown on the notice)* of the respondent;

(4)   Particulars of the requirements or directions appealed against;

and      (5)   The grounds of the appeal.

A form which may be used for appeal is attached.

(c) Time limit for appeal

A notice of appeal must be sent to the Secretary of the Tribunals within 21 days from the date of service on the appellant of the notice or notices appealed against, or within such further period as the tribunal considers reasonable in a case where it is satisfied that it was not reasonably practicable for the notice of appeal to be presented within the period of 21 days. If posted, the appeal should be sent by recorded delivery.

(d)   The entering of an appeal suspends the Improvement Notice until the appeal has been determined, but does not automatically alter the date given in this notice by which the matters contained in it must be remedied.

(e)   The rules for the hearing of an appeal are given in:

The Industrial Tribunals (Improvement and Prohibition Notices Appeals) (SI 1974 No. 1925) for England and Wales.

and      The Industrial Tribunals (Improvement and Prohibition Notices Appeals) (SI 1974 No. 1926) for Scotland.

159

# PROHIBITION NOTICE

## HEALTH AND SAFETY EXECUTIVE
**Health and Safety at Work etc. Act 1974, Sections 22 — 24**

*Name and*    To . . . . . . . . . . . . . . . . . . . . . . . . . . . . . . . . . . . . . . . . . . . . . . . . . . . . . . . . . . .
*address (See*
*Section 46)*    . . . . . . . . . . . . . . . . . . . . . . . . . . . . . . . . . . . . . . . . . . . . . . . . . . . . . . . . . . . . . . .

*(a) Delete as*    *(a)* Trading as . . . . . . . . . . . . . . . . . . . . . . . . . . . . . . . . . . . . . . . . . . . . . . . .
    *necessary*
               **I** *(b)* . . . . . . . . . . . . . . . . . . . . . . . . . . . . . . . . . . . . . . . . . . . . . . . . . . . . . . . . . .
*(b) Inspector's*
    *full name*    one of *(c)* . . . . . . . . . . . . . . . . . . . . . . . . . . . . . . . . . . . . . . . . . . . . . . . . . .

*(c) Inspector's*   of *(d)* . . . . . . . . . . . . . . . . . . . . . . . . . . . . . . . . . . . . . . . . . . . . . . . . . . . . . . .
    *official*
    *designation*   . . . . . . . . . . . . . . . . . . . . . . . . . . . . . . . . . . . . . . . . . . . Tel no. . . . . . . . . . . .

*(d) Official*     hereby give you notice that I am of the opinion that the following activities,
    *address*
               namely: . . . . . . . . . . . . . . . . . . . . . . . . . . . . . . . . . . . . . . . . . . . . . . . . . . . . . . . . .

               . . . . . . . . . . . . . . . . . . . . . . . . . . . . . . . . . . . . . . . . . . . . . . . . . . . . . . . . . . . . . . .

               . . . . . . . . . . . . . . . . . . . . . . . . . . . . . . . . . . . . . . . . . . . . . . . . . . . . . . . . . . . . . . .

               which are *(a)* being carried on by you / about to be carried on by you / under your control
*(e) Location*
   *of activity*    at *(e)* . . . . . . . . . . . . . . . . . . . . . . . . . . . . . . . . . . . . . . . . . . . . . . . . . . . . . . .

               involve, or will involve *(a)* a risk / an imminent risk, of serious personal injury
               I am further of the opinion that the said matters involve contraventions of the following
               statutory provisions: -

               . . . . . . . . . . . . . . . . . . . . . . . . . . . . . . . . . . . . . . . . . . . . . . . . . . . . . . . . . . . . . . .

               . . . . . . . . . . . . . . . . . . . . . . . . . . . . . . . . . . . . . . . . . . . . . . . . . . . . . . . . . . . . . . .

               . . . . . . . . . . . . . . . . . . . . . . . . . . . . . . . . . . . . . . . . . . . . . . . . . . . . . . . . . . . . . . .

               because . . . . . . . . . . . . . . . . . . . . . . . . . . . . . . . . . . . . . . . . . . . . . . . . . . . . . . . . . .

               . . . . . . . . . . . . . . . . . . . . . . . . . . . . . . . . . . . . . . . . . . . . . . . . . . . . . . . . . . . . . . .

               . . . . . . . . . . . . . . . . . . . . . . . . . . . . . . . . . . . . . . . . . . . . . . . . . . . . . . . . . . . . . . .

               and I hereby direct that the said activities shall not be carried on by you or under your
               control *(a)* immediately / after
*(f) Date*       *(f)* . . . . . . . . . . . . . . . . . . . . . . . . . . . . . . . . . . . . . . . . . . . . . . . . . . . . . . . . . . . . . .

               unless the said contraventions and matters included in the schedule, which forms part of this
               notice, have been remedied

               Signature . . . . . . . . . . . . . . . . . . . . . . . Date . . . . . . . . . . . . . . . . . . . . . . . . . . . . . . . .

**LP 2**        being an inspector appointed by an instrument in writing made pursuant to Section 19 of
               the said Act and entitled to issue this notice

*Fig. 6.2*   Prohibition notice

Serial No. **P**

NOTES

**1** Failure to comply with an Prohibition Notice is an offence as provided by Section 33 of this Act and renders the offender liable to a fine not exceeding £400 on summary conviction or to an unlimited fine or to imprisonment for a term not exceeding two years or both on conviction on indictment and a further fine of not exceeding £50 per day if the offence is continued.

**2** An Inspector has power to withdraw a notice or to extend the period specified in the notice before the end of the period specified in it. You should apply to the Inspector who has issued the notice if you wish him to consider this, but you must do so before the end of the period given in it. *(Such an application is not an appeal against this notice.)*

**3** The issue of this Notice does not relieve you of any legal liability resting upon you for failure to comply with any provision of this or any other enactment, before or after the issue of this notice.

**4** Your attention is drawn to the provision for appeal against this notice to an Industrial Tribunal. Details of the method of making an appeal are given below *(See also Section 24 of the Health and Safety at Work etc. Act 1974).*

(a) Appeal can be entered against this notice to an Industrial Tribunal. The appeal should be sent to: –

(for England and Wales)  The Secretary of the Tribunals
Central Office of the Industrial Tribunals
93 Ebury Bridge Road LONDON SW1W 8RE

(for Scotland)  The Secretary of the Tribunals
Central Office of the Industrial Tribunals
Saint Andrew House
141 West Nile Street GLASGOW G1 2RU

(b) The appeal must be commenced by sending in writing to the Secretary of the Tribunals a notice containing the following particulars: –

(1) The name of the appellant and his address for the service of documents;

(2) The date of the notice or notices appealed against and the address of the premises or place concerned;

(3) The name and address *(as shown on the notice)* of the respondent;

(4) Particulars of the requirements or directions appealed against;

and  (5) The grounds of the appeal.

A form which may be used for appeal is attached

(c) Time limit for appeal

A notice of appeal must be sent to the Secretary of the Tribunals with 21 days from the date of service on the appellant of the notice or notices appealed against, or within such further period as the tribunal considers reasonable in a case where it is satisfied that it was not reasonably practicable for the notice of appeal to be presented within the period of 21 days. If posted the appeal should be sent by recorded delivery.

(d) The entering of an appeal does not have the effect of suspending this notice.
Application can be made for the suspension of the notice to the Secretary of the Tribunals, but the notice continues in force until a Tribunal otherwise directs. An application for suspension of the notice must be in writing and must set out: –

(a) The case number of the appeal, if known, or particulars sufficient to identify it and

(b) The grounds on which the application is made. It may accompany the appeal.

(e) The rules for the hearing of an appeal are given in:

The Industrial Tribunals (Improvement and Prohibition Notices Appeals) Regulations 1974 (SI 1974 No. 1925) for England and Wales

and  The Industrial Tribunals (Improvement and Prohibition Notices Appeals) (Scotland) Regulations 1974 (SI 1974 No. 1926) for Scotland

the health and safety at work of the employees, and in checking the effectiveness of such measures.'

A summary of offences and penalties contained within sections 33 to 42 inclusive

*Note*: This summary is an outline of the Act only. Interpretation of the various parts of the Act will be tested and case law established as a result of experience and legal remedies.

The offences for which imprisonment can be imposed are:

1. Failure to comply with a prohibition notice (section 22).
2. Disclosure of information (sections 27(4) and 28).
3. Failure to comply with any part of the Explosives Regulations.
4. Failure to comply with or obtain a licence issued by the Health and Safety Executive (section 33(4)).

**It is an offence**
(a) to fail to discharge a duty contained in sections 2 to 7.
  – Penalty★
(b) Contravene sections 8 or 9.
  – Penalty★
(c) Contravene any Health and Safety Regulations ... any requirement or prohibition (here applied in widest sense) imposed under regulations ... or attached to any licence, approval or exemption granted.
  – Penalty†
(d) Contravene any requirements laid down under 'Power of the Commission to direct Investigations and Inquiries' (section 14) i.e. wilful obstruction of a person exercising these powers.
  – Penalty†
(e) Contravene requirements imposed by an inspector under sections 20 and 25 i.e. 'Powers of Inspectors' and 'Power to deal with Cause of Imminent Danger'.
  – Penalty† or ★
(f) Prevent any person from appearing before or answering an inspector in pursuance of his powers.
  – Penalty†
(g) Contravene terms imposed by improvement or prohibition notices.
  – Penalty★
(h) Intentionally obstruct an inspector in the course of his duties.
  – Penalty†
(i) (j) Contravene any requirement in respect of the obtaining or disclosing of information to Commission, enforcing authorities etc. (sections 27 and 28).
  – Penalty★
(k) To make an intentional false statement in respect of furnishing information required under the relevant statutory provisions or obtaining the issue of a document by falsification.

(l) Intentionally make a false entry in any book or document required under the relevant statutory provisions.
   – Penalty*
(m) With intent to deceive, forge, and/or use, or be in possession of a so produced document specified under the relevant statutory provisions.
   – Penalty*
(n) To falsely pretend to be an inspector.
   – Penalty*
(o) To fail to comply with a court order requiring . . . 'cause of Offence to be remedied, or in some cases, forfeiture' (section 42).
   – Penalty*

*Penalties*
Penalty * (and includes for an offence under any of the existing statutory provisions) . . . shall be liable . . .
(a) On summary conviction, to a fine not exceeding £1000
(b) On conviction on indictment . . . to imprisonment for a term not exceeding two years, or a fine, or both . . .

Penalty[†] . . . On summary conviction liable to a fine not exceeding £1000

It should be noted that among the offences qualifying for the greater potential severity of conviction on indictment is, possession, acquisition, etc. of an explosive article or substance in contravention of statutory provisions.
And
Contravention of any requirement or Prohibition imposed by a prohibition Notice
This statement has been underlined, for if there is evidence of a continuation of the offence after conviction there will be a further liability of a fine of £50 for each day the contravention is continued. *Note*: The Criminal Law Act 1977, sections 15 and 30 and schedules 1 and 11 increased this fine to £100.

*Section 36 – Offences due to fault of other person*
It is important to note that this section enables the inspector to launch a prosecution against any person who is at fault. There can be dual liability. Foremen, supervisors, safety officers and other employees can be prosecuted under this section in addition to, or instead of, the employer.

   (1) 'Where the commission by any person of an offence under any of the relevant statutory provisions is due to the act or default of some other person, that other person shall be guilty of the offence, and a person may be charged with and convicted of the offence by virtue of this sub-section whether or not proceedings are taken against the first-mentioned person.'

*Section 37 – Offences by bodies corporate*
   (1) Where an offence under any of the relevant statutory provisions committed by a body corporate is proved to have been committed with the con-

163

sent or connivance of, or to have been attributable to any neglect on the part of, any director, manager, secretary or other similar officer of the body corporate or a person who was purporting to act in any such capacity, he as well as the body corporate shall be guilty of that offence and shall be liable to be proceeded against and punished accordingly.

(2) Where the affairs of a body corporate are managed by its members, the preceding subsection shall apply in relation to the acts and defaults of a member in connection with his functions of management as if he were a director of the body corporate.

## Safety and general precautions

Demolition contracts are frequently lost to firms who undercut on pricing with the sole purpose of making little or no attempt to comply with statutory and other safety legislation. The methods of work and approach to safety of these contractors is evidence enough of their lack of interest and knowledge, thereby taking unfair advantage of safety-conscious companies.

The standards of the more competent and safety-conscious companies will compare with their counterparts in any other industry, and yet the whole industry is tarnished by the unruly elements who still obtain contracts.

The only way to improve safety standards is for 'Authority' to penalize those responsible for cutting corners, including the clients who encourage this action. The one sure way to achieve this would be to increase the monetary penalty and impose closure notices on sites where accidents occur, so that investigations are initiated. Delays cost money, both to contractor and client, therefore both may exercise more care knowing this could happen.

The operation of safety on demolition or any site may cost money, but accidents also cost money, far more than safety. The company as well as the operatives benefit from safe sites, and the operation of a company safety policy (Appendix 1), but the incentive must come from the top. In any company, if the management is enthusiastic about a safety scheme, it spreads throughout the workforce. You may get one who does not want to comply, in which case he is best asked to comply in no uncertain terms or move on. If the company management do not show any incentive then I regret the same attitude will permeate through the entire workforce.

All too often we hear operatives state that the wearing of protective helmets, 'hard hats', make them perspire or gives them headaches. That is all too easy an excuse for not wearing them. A protective helmet can be likened to a new pair of boots, 'they feel odd for a time until you get used to wearing them and then they fit comfortably'. An operative would not discard his boots after a few minutes because they were stiff, so why discard his helmet which could save his life.

The use of scaffolding, working platforms, fans and safety measures are covered adequately in chapters 5 and 8; therefore, it is sufficient at this stage to reiterate that properly constructed scaffolds, etc. are an essential part of safety and procedures in the demolition industry.

We are aware that safety and safe working practices are covered by the HASAWA and that the HSE is the officially responsible body. The Inspectorate of the HSE is often under-staffed and hard pressed to cover all sites at all times, which is fully understood by all, including government, and often the reason for abuse by unscrupulous contractors, and yet it is proposed to make a 6 per cent cut in the Executive's budget in 1983/84 after already suffering a 3 per cent reduction in 1979/80. This will be a severe blow to the already hard-pressed Inspectorate.

In May 1979 the HSE issued a report[6] of the sub-committee of the Joint Advisory Committee on Safety and Health in the Construction Industry entitled *Safety in Demolition Work*, the content of which has been covered in chapters 5 and 6, but for convenience the twenty-two main recommendations of that Committee and various accident reports and legal requirements are set out below under their relevant headings.

### Main recommendations of the committee

1. Information on accidents in demolition work should be improved (para. 2).

2. There is a need to present the law relating to demolition, and guidance on its meaning, in a single publication (para. 10).

3. A survey of the physical characteristics of the buildings should be mandatory and a written record of the survey should be kept available for inspection (paras 11 and 12).

4. A duty should be laid on the client when inviting tenders for a contract to supply the contractor with all the information available to the client about potential hazards involving the property to be demolished or dismantled (para. 12).

5. A contractor should be under a duty not to start work until he has a certificate from the gas and electricity authorities that all known supplies have been cut off from the site except those required for the execution of the work (para. 13).

6. The Department of the Environment should issue advice to local authorities having control over space around demolition sites, urging them to separate the public from the demolition work to the maximum possible extent (para. 14).

7. The present statutory duty to notify the commencement of demolition work should be reviewed with the object of reducing the present six-week limit to three weeks. Extra staff to inspect a proportion of these smaller sites should be made available by the Factory Inspectorate (para. 15).

165

8. A formal training scheme on a regioinal basis should be established for the demolition industry. Priority should be given to training those who are in immediate control of demolition work, and there should be, among other things, a standardized training programme and a record of training as described in paras 19, 21 and Appendix 4.

9. The requirements relating to supervision and competency in Regulations 39 and 41 of the Construction (General Provisions) Regulations 1961 should be strengthened by requiring a higher standard of supervision of the demolition of structures, particularly where there is a risk of a collapse that might endanger life; and by requiring that those exercising supervision shall have received training in the correct techniques of demolition, the prevention of accidents and the precautions against risks to health (para. 25).

10. Greater thought should be given to the planning of each phase of demolition work, and employers, when choosing a method of work at the planning stage, should keep to the order of preference listed in the report in para. 29.

11. Safety helmets should be worn by everyone on a demolition site (para. 35).

12. The person responsible for carrying out the statutory weekly inspection of a lifting appliance used for balling should be trained to identify defects resulting from balling (para. 38).

13. The attention of the Health and Safety Commission (HSC) is drawn to the Committee's views on the licensing of plant drivers and operators. It is suggested that the Commission might wish to consider initiating a study of this problem (para. 41).

14. When 'hot work' is to be undertaken in the demolition or dismantling of plant containing explosive or flammable substances the demolition contractor should invariably institute a written permit-to-work system. Consideration should be given to whether the law governing this type of process should be strengthened (para. 42).

15. Closer control over the competency of men responsible for the storage and use of explosives in demolition work should be exercised by means of certificates of competence associated with defined standards of training (para. 43).

16. A suitable procedure should be instituted so that new buildings which are either:
    (a) post-tensioned structures; or
    (b) unbonded stressed structures; or
    (c) structures which are progressively stressed as construction proceeds and further dead load added;
    could be readily identified. The plans of such buildings deposited with loc-

al authorities should be used to provide information in connection with the appraisal of the building's structural characteristics prior to demolition (para. 46).

17. In any revision of the law relating to the inspection of scaffolding used in demolition work, suitably stringent inspection requirements should be applied (para. 47).

18. In dealing with the risks arising from the presence of asbestos dust on demolition sites the Committee recommends that the Advisory Committee on Asbestos should consider the following proposals:
    (a) that before work starts on a site the sample analysis of 'lagging' asbestos should be obligatory;
    (b) that stronger measures should be taken to ensure that there is strict control of the removal of asbestos in demolition; one possibility which should be considered is that of changing the present requirements in Regulation 6 of the Asbestos Regulations 1969, about notification of processes involving crocidolite, by extending their application to the removal of lagging containing any form of asbestos;
    (c) that the possibility of some form of licensing of contractors who undertake work involving the extensive removal of asbestos should be considered;
    (d) that research should be initiated into the risks produced by, and the control of, asbestos dust; and
    (e) that a long-term medical survey of sufficient numbers of demolition workers to establish the incidence of asbestosis or other medical conditions caused by asbestos should be undertaken (paras. 55 to 59).

19. A 'check list' should be prepared for supervisors giving brief guidance on the actions and precautions to be taken when asbestos is found to be present on a site (para. 60).

20. Men whose work exposes them to lead fumes should be medically supervised, and a man offering himself for employment should only be accepted after undergoing a pre-employment medical assessment in relation to lead (para. 61).

21. An advisory publication for the demolition industry on health hazards in demolition work should be prepared (para. 63).

22. Private clients should follow the lead given by the government by letting contracts only to firms who are members of the DDIR (para. 66).

Several other recommendations are made in the report concerning, for example: (a) the factors to be taken into account in the preparation of legislation for demolition work (para. 10); (b) the use of 'aerial' platforms (para. 30 (a)); (c) anchorage points for safety belts and harnesses (para. 30 (b)); (d) lifting appliances used for balling operations (para. 39).

Analysis of accidents

The normal procedure of the HSE in developing policies to reduce accidents is, firstly, to gather and analyse information, including statistical data; secondly, to attempt to identify the characteristics of events which cause accidents; and, finally, to devise remedies which will eliminate or reduce the chance of the events in question happening. This technique obviously depends on the ability precisely to identify the 'hazardous event' and to link it with some specific circumstance within a limited field of activity, for example, with some particular aspects of a machine or its operation. The successful use of this method is particularly well illustrated by the analysis of hazards and the remedial action which was undertaken to deal with accidents at power presses used in engineering work and which resulted in the Power Presses Regulations 1965. Risk analysis of this sort is, however, much more difficult in demolition where the pattern of

*Table 6.1*  Reported accidents during the demolition of buildings and all reported accidents at building operations,[7] 1969–75.

| Year | Demolition of buildings | | All building operations | |
|------|------|------|------|------|
| | *Fatal.* | *Total reported.* | *Fatal.* | *Total reported.* |
| 1969 | 21 | 809 | 174 | 34 982 |
| 1970 | 19 | 687 | 138 | 30 938 |
| 1971 | 15 | 580 | 144 | 26 683 |
| 1972 | 14 | 718 | 132 | 27 524 |
| 1973 | 15 | 663 | 148 | 27 991 |
| 1974 | 16 | 614 | 113 | 25 831 |
| 1975 | 16 | 559 | 121 | 26 555 |
| Total | 116 | 4630 | 970 | 200 504* |

* see footnote to Table 6.3 p. 169.

*Table 6.2*  Reported demolition accidents related to the type of building involved[7]* (fatalities in brackets)

| | *1970* | *1971* | *1972* | *1973* | *1974* | *1975* |
|------|------|------|------|------|------|------|
| Industrial building | 278 ( 8) | 220 ( 6) | 284 ( 6) | 234 ( 8) | 265 ( 8) | 204 ( 7) |
| Commercial and public building | 164 ( 9) | 153 ( 4) | 177 ( 3) | 206 ( 5) | 141 ( 4) | 146 ( 6) |
| Blocks of flats | 7 (—) | 13 ( 1) | 14 ( 1) | 14 ( 1) | 8 (—) | 14 (—) |
| Dwelling-houses | 133 (—) | 98 ( 2) | 136 ( 1) | 129 ( 1) | 131 ( 1) | 103 ( 3) |
| Other building operations | 105 ( 2) | 96 ( 1) | 107 ( 3) | 80 (—) | 69 ( 3) | 92 (—) |
| Total reported accidents | 687 (19) | 580 (15) | 718 (14) | 663 (15) | 614 (16) | 559 (16) |

* see footnote to Table 6.3 on p. 169.

*Table 6.3* Analysis of reports of fifty fatal accidents to men employed in demolition[7]*

| | | |
|---|---:|---:|
| *Collapse of part of building* | | 18 |
| Meaning collapse not expected by workmen involved or a deliberate collapse commenced before every person is in a safe position | | |
| *Material falling* | | 4 |
| Meaning (a) part of a building, after being prised off, falls on to a person | 2 | |
| (b) part of a building, being thrown down catching on clothing pulling man down | 2 | |
| *Men falling from a height* | | 17 |
| Meaning (a) from a working position or means of access | 9 | |
| (b) through fragile roof covering or through roofs when stripping sheets | 4 | |
| (c) through openings in floors | 4 | |
| *Plant accidents* | | 7 |
| Meaning negligence in use of or alteration of plant such as vehicles or cranes | | |
| *Miscellaneous or cause not known* | | 4 |
| Total | | 50 |

*Table 6.4* Analysis of reports of fifty fatal accidents to men employed in demolition:[7] age distribution of the deceased

| Age | Number of men killed |
|---|---|
| Up to and including 19 | 3 |
| 20–29 | 14 |
| 30–39 | 11 |
| 40–49 | 11 |
| 50–59 | 4 |
| 60–64 | 4 |
| 65 plus | — |
| Age not known | 3 |
| Total | 50 |

events giving rise to a particular hazard can be very complex and the formulation of safeguards correspondingly more difficult. This difficulty should be borne in mind in any consideration of the statistics and conclusions set out in Tables 6.1, 6.2, 6.3, 6.4 and 6.5.

* The figures in Tables 6.1, 6.2 and 6.3 relate to accidents which (i) are required to be reported under the Factories Act 1961 (i.e. any accident which disables a man for more than three days from earning full wages at the work at which he was employed) and (ii) occurred at 'building operations' as defined in section 176 of the Factories Act 1961. They do not include accidents to self-employed men. The figures of fatal accidents are thought to be accurate within close limits, but those showing total reported accidents should be used with caution because it is suspected that many accidents (possibly up to 50%) are not reported. *Note*: The number of accidents considered is small and conclusions drawn from them need to be used with care.

*Table 6.5* Number of men employed, number of sites and duration of contracts in 1973

| Number of men employed at each site | Number of sites and duration of contract | | | |
|---|---|---|---|---|
| | Less than 4 weeks | 4 to 26 weeks | More than 26 weeks | Total |
| 5 men or less | 711 | 513 | 9 | 1233 |
| 6 men or more | 57 | 325 | 58 | 440 |
| Total | 768 | 838 | 67 | 1673 |

Legal requirements: the Factories Act

On 1 March 1962 the Safety, Health and Welfare Regulations 1948 (Statutory Instrument No. 1145) which included reference to demolition work was revoked in favour of the Construction (General Provisions) Regulations 1961 (Statutory Instrument No. 1580).

The Construction Regulations sub-divide demolition work into four sections:

1. The application of the Regulations.
2. The supervision of demolition work.
3. Fire and flooding.
4. Precautions to be observed in connection with demolition.

## Accidents – cause and remedy

Up to 31st December 1980 accident reporting required two forms to be completed:

1. From B1.510 the *Accident Book*[8] in accordance with the Social Security Act 1975 (Fig. 6.3)
2. Form F36 the *General Register*[9] in accordance with the Factories Act 1961 (Fig. 6.4)

*The Accident Book – B1.510*
A copy of this book must be on each site and all accidents (major or minor) entered in by a competent person in charge of that site. If the accident requires the person injured to remain away from work for more than three days it becomes a *reportable accident* and the person in charge on that site must report to his superior and have the accident entered into the General Register.

*General Register – F36*
The General Register is usually kept in the company office and again administered by a competent person. Once an entry is made in the General Register the

**Form BI 510**

Consecutive Number assigned to this Book } ....................

For mines, quarries and factories and for other business premises on or about which ten or more employed earners are normally employed at the same time.

## SOCIAL SECURITY ACT, 1975

# ACCIDENT BOOK

**In the form approved by the Secretary of State for Social Services**

**To be kept in a place readily accessible at all reasonable times to any injured employee and any person *bona fide* acting on his behalf.**

Name and Address of the works or premises to which this Book relates. } ..........................................................

..........................................................................

..........................................................................

Name of Occupier or Employer..........................................................

**An entry of an accident in this book does not relieve the occupier of any obligations he may have under the Factories, or Mines and Quarries, or Offices, Shops and Railway Premises Acts, to notify accidents to the appropriate enforcing authority, nor of the obligation under the Factories Act to enter accidents in the General Register.**

*Fig. 6.3* Form B1 510 (Accident Book)

DEPARTMENT OF EMPLOYMENT
FACTORIES ACT 1961
Form prescribed by the Secretary of State for Employment

GENERAL REGISTER
For Building Operations and Work
of Engineering Construction

Important – Reporting of Accidents

Every fatal accident and every accident which disables a worker for more than three days from earning full wages at the work at which he was employed (whether or not he continues to receive full wages), must be reported forthwith to HM Inspector of Factories for the District in the prescribed form (form F43B) (copies of which have been inserted at the back of this Register) and entered in Part 3 of this Register. The report (on form F43) must be sent whether or not particulars of the accident have been sent to the Department of Health and Social Security.

Cases of Poisoning and Disease

Certain cases of poisoning or disease must also be notified forthwith and particulars must be entered in Part 4. This applies even if a worker is disabled for less than three days.

Period covered by this Register

.................... to ....................

This Register must be kept available for inspection by HM Inspectors of Factories and Employment Medical Advisers for two years or other prescribed period after the date of the last entry therein.

INDEX

| | page |
|---|---|
| Part 1 General | 1 |
| Part 2 Young persons | 2 |
| Part 3 Accidents | 6 |
| Part 4 Cases of poisoning and disease | 10 |

*Fig. 6.4* Form F36 (General Register)

Factories Act 1961, section 80 requires the company to notify the Factory Inspectorate on form F 43B (Fig. 6.5). This allows a link up, because the injured party has also had to report the accident to the DHSS, and any industrial injury claim can be finalized.

The 1st January 1981 brought the inception of the Notification of Accidents and Dangerous Occurrences Regulations 1980.[10]

These regulations laid down new rules governing the notification of accidents to authorities and meant contractors had to change their recording and reporting system.

The notification of accidents which resulted in operatives being absent from work for more than three days would now be notified on the revised form (Fig. 6.6) to the DHSS who would pass copies of the report to the HSE. In general, if accidents are costed at all then, not surprisingly, it is the most serious accidents which are considered first. In other words, those accidents causing the most serious injuries are those which result in the highest cost to an employer. The reason is that if an employee is seriously injured, there is a strong possibility that he or she will make a claim in common law that the employer has been negligent towards them. This in turn is likely to result in payments to compensate the employee for the effect of the injuries. In addition to the cost of common law settlements, it is quite possible that the employer may be fined for an associated breach of statute law, such as the Factories Act.[11] Thus an injury resulting from, say, a defective machine guard could result in the injured employee claiming compensation, and a prosecution under section 14 of the Factories Act arising from action by the Factory Inspectorate.

It is worth noting that the cost of meeting legal claims is on the increase, both in quantity and in the size of individual awards. This arises to a large extent from the growing willingness and ability of employee groups such as trade unions to represent their members in legal proceedings against the employer. Perhaps the clearest index of this increase is the cost of settling claims under Employers' Liability insurance. For example, the average settlement cost for a claim relating to a minor injury causing four weeks off work has risen from about £60 in 1970 to around £200. For total disablement, typical figures show a rise from £35,000 to £125,000. It should be emphasized that these figures exclude loss of earnings to the time of settlement and this often represents a substantial addition to the claim.

Insurance

The Employers' Liability (Compulsory Insurance) Act 1969 places a duty on employers (unless they are exempt) to take out and maintain approved insurance policies with authorized insurers against liability for bodily injury or disease sustained by their employees in the course of their employment. The Act also applies to employment on offshore installations as defined in regulations made under the Mineral Workings (Offshore Installations) Act 1971.

173

A notice in this form should be sent (immediately the accident or dangerous occurrence becomes reportable) to HM Inspector of Factories. (*See instructions overleaf.*)
NOTE:—If the accident is fatal HM Inspector should be informed immediately by telephone.

DEPARTMENT OF EMPLOYMENT

**FACTORIES ACT 1961, section 80**

(as extended by SR & O 1947 No. 31)

Prescribed form of written notice of

**ACCIDENT OR DANGEROUS OCCURRENCE**

occurring in the carrying on of a Building

Operation or Work of Engineering Construction

**F 43B**

**FOR OFFICIAL USE**

District and date of receipt.

1  (a)  Person (or company or firm) undertaking Building Operation or Work of Engineering Construction:
Name
Registered office or address
   (b)  Actual employer of injured person (if other than above):
Name
Address
   (c)  Trade of actual employer of injured person (*tick item which applies*):

| | | |
|---|---|---|
| Asphalt/tar sprayers ............ | Electrical contractors ............ | Plant hiring contractors ........ |
| Builders (General) ............ | Flooring contractors............ | Plasterers ............ |
| Building and civil engineering contractors ........ | Glaziers ............ | Plumbers ............ |
| Civil engineering contractors ............ | Heating and ventilation contractors ............ | Reinforced concrete contractors ............ |
| Constructional engineers............ | Joiners and carpenters............ | Roofers ............ |
| Demolition contractors ............ | Painters and decorators............ | Scaffolding contractors ............ |

Other trade (*specify*) ............

2  **SITE** where accident or dangerous occurrence happened:
   (a)  Address (and telephone number) of site
   (b)  Exact place on site

3  **NATURE OF WORK** carried on at:
   (a)  **Building Operations** (*tick items which apply*)
       (i)  Construction ............
       (ii)  Maintenance ............       of
       (iii)  Demolition ............

       (iv)  Industrial building ............
       (v)  Commercial or public building ............
       (vi)  Dwellings over 3 storeys ............
       (vii)  Dwellings of 3 storeys or less............
       (viii)  Other............

   (b)  **Work of Engineering Construction** (*specify type*)

4  **INJURED PERSON**
   (a)  Full name (*surname first*)                    Sex        Age
   (b)  Address
   (c)  Occupation (*tick item which applies*):

| Bricklayer | Carpenter/Joiner | Painter | Plasterer | Plumber | Scaffolder |
|---|---|---|---|---|---|
| Steel erector | Demolition worker | Steeplejack | | Slater/Tiler/Other roofing worker | |

Labourer (*specify trade where labourer worked for a tradesman*)

Other occupation (*specify*)

*Note:* Semi-skilled men or apprentices should be classified under the appropriate occupation.

5  **ACCIDENT or DANGEROUS OCCURRENCE**
   (a)  Date............................ Time............................
   (b)  Full details of how the accident or dangerous occurrence happened. If a fall of person or materials, plant, etc., state height of fall. (*If necessary continue overleaf.*)
   (c)  State exactly what injured person was doing at the time.
   (d)  If machinery was involved, state:
       (i)  Name and type of machine concerned (inc. cranes)
       (ii)  Part of machine involved
       (iii)  Whether in motion by mechanical power at the time

6  **INJURIES AND DISABLEMENT**
   (a)  Nature and extent of injury (e.g. fracture of leg, laceration of arm, scalded foot, scratch on hand followed by sepsis).
   (b)  Was injured person disabled for more than three days from earning full wages at the work at which he was employed?
   (c)  Was the accident fatal?

7  Has accident (or dangerous occurrence) been entered in the General Register?
Signature of Contractor, Employer, or Agent                    Date

| |
|---|
| MR Group |
| Ref. to |
| M of T, etc. |
| 1  Serial No. |
| 2  MWBG |
| 3  Age Group |
| 4  F, NF, DO |
| 4(a) |
| 4(b) |
| 5  Process |
| 6  SIC |
| 7(a)  Causation |
| 7(b) |
| 7(c) |
| 7(d) |
| 7(e) |
| 7(f) |
| 7(g) |
| 7(h) |
| 7(j) |
| 7(k) |
| 7(l) |
| 8  Occupation |
| 9  Injury Nature \| Site |
| 10 Trade of employer |
| 11 |
| 12 |
| 13 |

(*Please see overleaf*)

*Fig. 6.5*   Form F43B (Accident or dangerous occurrence)

How the accident or dangerous occurrence happened (contd.).  *(See 5(b) overleaf)*

## Instructions

1   Where there occurs on a Building Operation or Work of Engineering Construction:

(a) an accident causing loss of life to a person employed therein; or

(b) an accident which disables any person employed therein for more than three days from earning full wages at the work at which he was employed; or

(c) a dangerous occurrence of the kind named below, which is not reportable under (a) or (b) above as an accident:

    (i) bursting of a revolving vessel, wheel, grindstone or grinding wheel moved by mechanical power;

    (ii) collapse or failure of a crane, derrick, winch, hoist, or other appliance used in raising or lowering persons or goods, or any part thereof (except the breakage of chain or rope slings), or the overturning of a crane;

    (iii) explosion or fire causing damage to the structure of any room or place in which persons are employed, or to any machine or plant contained therein, and resulting in the complete suspension of ordinary work in such room or place or stoppage of machinery or plant for not less than five hours, where such explosion or fire is due to (i) the ignition of dust, gas, or vapour, or (ii) the ignition of celluloid or substances composed wholly or in part of celluloid;

    (iv) electrical short circuit or failure of electrical machinery, plant, or apparatus attended by explosion or fire or causing structural damage thereto, and involving its stoppage or disuse for not less than five hours;

    (v) explosion or fire affecting any room in which persons are employed and causing complete suspension of ordinary work therein for not less than twenty-four hours;

    (vi) explosion of a receiver or container used for the storage at a pressure greater than atmospheric pressure of any gas or gases (including air) or any liquid or solid resulting from the compression of gas.

whether causing personal injury or disablement or not

the person undertaking the Operation or Work must forthwith send notice thereof on this Form to HM Inspector for the District.

2   If an accident notified as above as causing disablement results in the death of the person disabled, the person undertaking the Operation or Work must send to HM Inspector for the District notice of the death as soon as it comes to his knowledge.

3   Some accidents to persons employed in public docks, dock warehouses, railway warehouses or railway factories (including repairing sheds) are notifiable both to HM Inspectors of Factories and to the Department of the Environment. By arrangement between the Departments, such accidents need not be separately notified to the Department of the Environment, but should be notified on this Form to HM District Inspector of Factories, who will forward the notices to the Department concerned (see, however, paras 4 and 5 below).

4   Boiler explosions must also be notified by the occupier directly to the Department of Trade and Industry, Marine Safety Division, Sunley House, 90–93, High Holborn, London WC1V 6LP, whether causing personal injury or not.

5   An explosion of explosives, or a fire (whether causing personal injury or not) in a factory, magazine or store (other than Crown premises) in which explosives are made or kept, and any accident which occasions loss of life or personal injury due to explosion or fire of petroleum spirit on licensed premises or in connection with any ship or vehicle, must be notified to HM Chief Inspector of Explosives, Home Office, Horseferry House, Dean Ryle Street, London SW1A 2AP.

**Health and Safety Executive**
Health and Safety at Work etc Act, 1974
Notification of Accidents and Dangerous Occurrences Regulations, 1980

## Report of an accident and/or dangerous occurrence and injuries sustained

*Please read the notes on pages 1 and 2 before completing this form.*

**Part I Administrative**

1 Person or organisation reporting the accident/dangerous occurrence

Name _____

Address _____

_____

_____Postcode _____

Nature of undertaking _____

Signature of person
making this report _____

Date _____

Name (*block capitals*) _____

Position in organisation _____

(where applicable)

Tel. No.                    Ext.

2 Place of accident/dangerous occurrence if different from 1 (for construction sites give name of main contractor)

Name _____

Address _____

_____

_____Postcode _____

Tel No _____ Ext _____

Name of site manager or other person in charge (*block capitals*)

Address (*if not as above*) _____

_____

_____

_____ Postcode _____

Tel. no.                    Ext.

**Part II General report of the incident**

1 Date _____ 2 Time _____*am/pm

3 Precise place, e.g. South Warehouse, No 2 Machine Shop, canteen kitchen

_____

4 Was there a dangerous occurrence as defined in    yes ☐ no ☐
the regulations?

If yes, state type _____

5 Number of (a) deaths __(b) major injuries __

6 Give a full account of the accident/dangerous occurrence, explaining so far as possible how it happened and how those killed or hurt received their injuries. Give name and type of any plant, equipment, machinery or vehicle involved and note whether it was in motion.

**F2508**                    **delete as appropriate*                    Part III — overleaf

*Fig. 6.6*   Form F2508 (Report of an accident and/or dangerous occurrence and injuries

**Part III Details of injured/deceased person(s)**
*This part should be completed for each person for whom a direct report is required – those included at 5(a) and (b) of Part II (see notes). Space is provided for two persons; if more is needed attach further copies of the form as continuation sheets (number the cases consecutively).*

*(At questions 3, 4, 8 and 9 tick the appropriate box ✓ )*

| | |
|---|---|
| Case number _____ | Case number _____ |
| 1 Surname _____ | 1 Surname _____ |
| 2 Forename(s) _____ | 2 Forename(s) _____ |
| 3 Was he/she:<br>at work as an employee? ☐ | 3 Was he/she:<br>at work as an employee? ☐ |
| at work self-employed? ☐ | at work self-employed? ☐ |
| not at work, but injured as a result<br>of work activity? ☐ | not at work, but injured as a result<br>of work activity? ☐ |
| 4 Male ☐          Female ☐ | 4 Male ☐          Female ☐ |
| 5 Age last birthday _____ | 5 Age last birthday _____ |
| 6 Address _____ | 6 Address _____ |
| _____Postcode _____ | _____Postcode _____ |
| 7 Occupation (*for employees and self-employed persons only*) e.g. carpenter, electrician | 7 Occupation (*for employees and self-employed persons only*) e.g. carpenter, electrician |
| 8 Was the injury fatal?  yes ☐  no ☐ | 8 Was the injury fatal?  yes ☐  no ☐ |
| 9 Was he/she treated in hospital for more than 24 hours?<br>          yes ☐  no ☐ | 9 Was he/she treated in hospital for more than 24 hours?<br>          yes ☐  no ☐ |
| 10 Nature and site of injury (e.g. compound fracture of left leg, loss of right eye, amputation of right hand) | 10 Nature and site of injury (e.g. compound fracture of left leg, loss of right eye, amputation of right hand) |
| 11 What was he/she doing at the time of the incident? If he/she fell, how far? | 11 What was he/she doing at the time of the incident? If he/she fell, how far? |

Signature _____  Date _____

Name (*block capitals*) _____

on behalf of (organisation) _____

177

A contract of insurance is based on information given by employers when negotiating a policy. If the information is not accurate, or the questions have not been properly answered, the policy may not cover all the employer's business activities, or it may be treated as void. In such circumstances employers may be liable for prosecution under the Act, so they are advised to ensure that the policy covers all aspects of their business, and to give prior notice to the insurers of all changes of circumstances which may affect the policy.

Insurers must issue a certificate of insurance to employers who take out or renew insurance policies and employers are required to display the certificate, or a copy, at each place of business, for the information of the employees. In the case of offshore installations, they must keep a copy on the installation and produce it at all reasonable times if requested by an employee.

An employer must be insured for at least £2 m. in respect of claims arising out of any one occurrence.

For the purposes of the Act, the term business includes a trade or profession, or any activity carried on by a body of people, whether or not they are incorporated. Many activities that might not normally be considered as business, but where staff are employed, e.g. in sports or social clubs, will come within this definition.

*Exempt employers*
1. Any local authority (other than a parish council).
2. Any joint board or committee whose members include representatives of any such local authority.
3. Any police authority.
4. Any nationalized industry and its subsidiaries.
5. Certain bodies financed out of public funds (these are defined in the Exemption Regulations.)[12]
6. Employers of crews on offshore installations, ships and hovercraft if they are covered instead with a mutual insurance association of shipowners or shipowners and others.

An approved policy is a policy that is not subject to prohibited conditions. These are certain conditions, specified in the General Regulations[13], which would, if not complied with by the insured employer, allow the insurer to repudiate a claim under the policy. There is, however, no objection to conditions that enable the insurer, in specified circumstances, to reclaim from the insured employer the amount of any compensation (including incidental costs and expenses) paid by the insurer to the injured employee.

Insurer

A person or body of persons lawfully carrying on a class of insurance business in Great Britain under Part II of the Companies Act 1967 as amended by the Insurance Companies Act 1974, or in Northern Ireland, under the Insurance Companies Act (Northern Ireland) 1968, and issuing the policy of employers' liability insurance in the course of that business. A list of authorized insurers is given in the *Insurance Business Annual Report* published by the Department of Trade and available through HMSO.

Defined in the Act as 'an individual who has entered into or works under a contract of service or apprenticeship with an employer, whether by way of manual labour, clerical work, or otherwise, whether such contract is expressed or implied, oral or in writing' and they may be full-time or part-time.

1. People who are not 'employees' as defined in the Act (e.g. independent contractors who are not the employees of the people engaging them).
2. People employed in any activity that is not a business as defined in the Act, e.g. a domestic servant.
3. People whose employer is related to them as their husband, wife, father, mother, grandfather, grandmother, stepfather, son, daughter, grandson, granddaughter, stepson, stepdaughter, brother, sister, half-brother or half-sister.
4. People who are not ordinarily resident in Great Britain and who are working here for fewer than fourteen consecutive days.

*Note*: In the case of offshore installations, people not normally resident in the United Kingdom who work on an installation for more than seven days are not exempt.

The insurer will issue, in addition to the policy document, a certificate to indicate that the policy satisfies the requirements of the Act. The dates of commencement and expiry of the policy are shown on the certificate. The certificate must be issued to the employer within thirty days of a contract of insurance being entered into, and similarly at each renewal.

The employer must display the current certificate of insurance at each place of business for the information of employees. The certificate must be removed from display by the employer at the end of the period of insurance cover or when the policy is cancelled. In the case of offshore installations, the certificate or copies must be kept there and produced at all reasonable times when requested by an employee.

An authorized inspector can require an employer to send the current certificate, or a copy, to him for inspection. Employers must also produce the current policy, or a copy. Reasonable notice of this requirement for inspection, either at the place of business or at the registered office of the company, will be given. In the case of offshore installations 'authorized inspectors' means an inspector appointed under the Mineral Working (Offshore Installations) Act 1971.

For every day on which an employer is not insured in accordance with the Act, he will be liable on summary conviction to a fine not exceeding £200. Where the offence has been committed with the consent or connivance of, or facilitated by the neglect of, any official of the company, that person is liable for prosecution as well as the company.

Additionally, in the case of offshore installations, the concession owner and the owner of the installations are liable on summary conviction to a fine not exceeding £200 per day where the employer is not insured.

An employer will be liable on summary conviction to a fine not exceeding £50 if he fails to comply with the following requirements:

(a)  to display the certificate or a copy (or in the case of offshore installations, to keep a copy of the certificate on the installations);

(b)  to send the certificate or a copy to an authorized inspector when required to do so;

(c)  to produce the certificate or a copy on demand to an authorized inspector;

(d)  to allow the policy to be inspected by an authorized inspector. Additionally, in the case of offshore installations, the concession owner and the owner of the installations will be liable on summary conviction to a fine not exceeding £50 where an employer fails to comply with any of the above requirements.

The Act does not grant an employee an automatic right to compensation. The purpose of the Act is to ensure that, when an employee succeeds in a claim, his employer is insured and can pay the compensation that is due.

### The Act and Regulations currently in force

- The Employers' Liability (Compulsory Insurance) Act 1969
- The Employers' Liability (Compulsory Insurance) General Regulations 1971 (SI 1971 No. 1117)
- The Employers' Liability (Compulsory Insurance) Exemption Regulations 1971 (SI 1971 No. 1933)
- The Employers' Liability (Compulsory Insurance) (Amendment) Regulations 1974 (SI 1974 No. 208)
- The Employers' Liability (Compulsory Insurance) (Amendment) Regulations 1975 (SI No. 194)
- The Offshore Installations (Application of the Employers' Liability (Compulsory Insurance) Act 1969) Regulations 1975 (SI 1975 No. 1289)
- The Employers' Liability (Compulsory Insurance) (Offshore Installations) Regulations 1975 (SI 1975 No. 1443)

### Accident reports[14]

These are seldom good reading, but they occur all too often. The following two reports are actual happenings and may have been eliminated if proper safety precautions had been followed. One is a report as entered in the Accident Book and the other is a post-mortem report. The locations, dates and names have been erased for obvious reasons, although the facts are as occurred.

*Both accidents were fatal.*

### *Report as entered in Accident Book*

On Friday . . . . . . I was assisting . . . . . . the site foreman to dismantle three overhead pipes running across the road on site. These pipes ran from a pipe gantry that runs parallel to the road then cuts across to a concrete pillar, and are fixed to that by hanging brackets.

I positioned myself with the crane so as after . . . . . . had fixed on the brother chains I could hook on and support the pipes while he released them. After the chains were on and I had taken up the slack he moved across to the concrete pillar side. He stood on the opposite side of the pillar to which he intended to cut the pipes and reached over and cut the two largest of them. He then started to cut the smallest of the three, but when liquid started to flow out of it he had to stop, and decided to blow the bolts on the flange instead. He completed this, then cut through the underslung bracket that held it. He then turned off his gun and stepped over the top of the concrete pillar and sat down on the same, placing one foot on the small pipe and the other on the pipe that leads down to the large water tank that is near the concrete pillar. Then he stood up with one hand on the concrete pillar and the other hand holding the cutting gun. His left foot was standing on the smaller pipe which to me still remained firm and he gave a push with his right foot on the largest pipe that runs down the pillar to see if it moved. It did not move at that time. Then with his hand still resting on the top of the pillar he took a small step forward on to the large pipe at which time there must have been same movement as that is when he lost his balance. As he fell he tried to grab hold of this pipe pulling it down at an angle, but was unable to get a grip and fell to the ground.

I saw him land on his shoulders and back. I turned to jump out of the crane and as I did so I looked towards him and saw him striking the ground the second time but with his head hitting the kerb that runs around the large water tank. At the time of the collision to the best of my knowledge he was still wearing his helmet, goggles and gloves.

I ran across to him and spoke to him, when he did not answer I put my hand on his shoulder and rolled him over towards me so as I could see his face. I saw blood rushing from his nose and mouth and a dent in his head by his left temple. I jumped up and called to . . . . . . another of our men to call an ambulance. I saw the fluid coming down from one of the pipes which at that time I wasn't sure was water, and as it was running towards him I dragged him a couple of feet to one side without lifting him.

The ambulance arrived a short time afterwards and I went with him, firstly to . . . . . . Hospital where he received a quick examination, and then we were transferred to . . . . . . Hospital. I spoke to a doctor at . . . . . . who told me he had a skull fracture and they were taking him down for a scan and x-rays.

Signed in Accident Book

. . . . . . . . . . . . . . .

## Post-mortem report

*To: HM Coroner*
*Report* of post-mortem examination upon the body of . . . . . . aged 27 years, of . . . . . . who was found to be dead on arrival at the Royal Infirmary . . . . . . at 9.05.a.m. Wednesday . . . . . .
*Post-mortem* examination was made by me in the Mortuary of . . . . . . General Hospital at 10.00.a.m. Thursday . . . . . .

### External appearances

The body was that of a strongly built, young, adult male. The lips and nail-beds were deeply cyanosed. The following recent external injuries were seen:

| | |
|---|---|
| *Head and Neck*: | **Abrasions to forehead and face;** laceration above right eye, 2 cm; laceration above left eye, 2 cm; **laceration right nostril, 3 cm;** laceration to chin, 2 cm; |
| *Chest*: | Abrasions to front of chest; small bruise on back. |
| *Left Arm*: | Abrasions to left forearm and hand; laceration of left armpit, 14 cm. |
| *Right Arm*: | Abrasions to right forearm and hand. |
| *Right Leg*: | Abrasions to right hip and thigh. |
| *Left Leg*: | Abrasions to left knee; laceration to left ankle, 6 cm; open fracture of left ankle. |

*Internal appearances*

| | |
|---|---|
| *Head and neck*: | Both cheek bones were fractured and there were multiple fractures of the bones of the base of the skull.<br><br>The Brain showed extensive sub-arachnoid haemorrhage mainly on the underside of the left temporal and occipital lobes.<br><br>There was also superficial damage to the cortex and white matter of the left temporal and occipital lobes.<br><br>The left lateral ventricle was filled with blood.<br><br>A few small softenings were also found internally in the substance of the left cerebral hemisphere.<br><br>The Mouth and Pharynx showed bruising.<br><br>The Larynx contained blood.<br><br>The Thyroid Gland appeared normal. |
| *Chest*: | The Right Clavicle was dislocated at the sternoclavicular joint.<br><br>The Left Clavicle was fractured near its lateral end.<br><br>Multiple rib fractures were present. On the left side the first and second ribs were fractured anteriorly and the 3rd, 4th, 5th and 6th ribs posteriorly. On the right side the 1st, 4th and 5th ribs anteriorly were fractured and the 9th rib posteriorly. A fracture dislocation of the spine was present affecting the 10th dorsal vertebra.<br><br>The chest wall, particularly at the back, showed well-marked bruising. About 300 ml of blood-stained fluid was present on the left side.<br><br>The air passages contained fresh blood.<br><br>The upper and lower lobes of the left lung showed lacerations posteriorly and were partly collapsed. The Right Lung appeared normal.<br><br>The Heart weighed 335 g. The chambers, valves, coronary arteries and great vessels appeared normal. |
| *Abdomen*: | The abdominal and pelvic organs showed no abnormality. |

*Summary*:
In my opinion death was due to: *Multiple injuries*
There was no evidence of any disease present.

(Signed) . . . . .                                    (Signed) . . . . . .

### The principle of accident prevention

There are legal and economic grounds for providing a safe place of work and a safe system of work. To honour these obligations it is necessary to implement an active programme of accident prevention. In order to formulate this programme it is necessary to define an acceptable meaning of the words 'safety' and 'accidents'.

*Industrial safety*

The control of men, machines, materials and methods to provide a working environment in which people will not be injured, or property damaged.

*Accident*

An accident is an unplanned, uncontrolled and undesirable event or sudden mishap which interrupts an activity or function.

From this definition it will be seen that injury to people or damage to property is not an accident, but evidence to show that an accident has occurred.

*Reportable accidents – all industries*
The total number of 'Reportable Accidents' in 1974, in the last year for which figures are available (HM Chief Inspector of Factories, *Annual Report*) show that 256,930 people lost more than three days from work as a result of industrial injury and that 479 of these injuries were fatal.

*Heinrich theory*

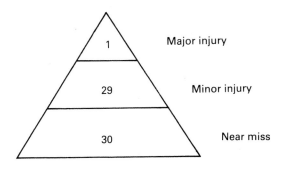

183

In preventing accidents it is important to recognize the potential hazards and take the appropriate action. This period of hazard recognition may take the form of one of the various types of safety audit.

As a preliminary guide to the recognition of hazard potential the phrase 'most safe places' may be of use:

*M for Machinery* Sources of mechanical power, operating plant, transmission machinery, guarding and the use of internal transport and road transport within the company.

*O for Openings* Pits, sumps, shafts, ducts, drains and stairways.

*S for Stacks* Stored materials, raw and processed. Pallets, stillages, bales, sacks, boxes and cartons.

*T for Tools* All types of tools including hammers, chisels, screwdrivers, spanners, and saws and portable electric tools, drills, saws, planers, etc.

*S for Structure* Floors, walls, ceilings, aisles, gangways, passageways, platforms, ramps and roads.

*A for Atmosphere* Dust, gases, fumes and sprays.

*F for Fire* Fire evacuation procedures, assembly points, check lists, extinguishers, hoses, sprinklers, fire points and fire exits.

*E for Electricity* Wires, cables, switches, electric motors and lighting. It would also include other services, gas, steam, compressed air, etc.

*P for Pressure Vessels* Boilers, calorifiers, compressors, etc.

*L for Ladder* Steps, trestles, scaffolds and other means of access.

*A for Attire* Personal protective clothing, hats, helmets, goggles, ear defenders, masks and respirators, overalls and footwear.

*C for Cranes* Hoists, derricks, escalators, conveyors, ropes, chains, hooks, slings and eye bolts.

*E for Explosives* Flammable liquids, liquefied petroleum gases, poisons, radioactive materials and other known dangerous substances.

*S for Signals* Warning lights, radios, telephones, signs, posters, buzzers and bells.

On recognition of the hazard the procedure must be to implement one or more of the following actions:

- Eliminate
- Reduce or substitute
- Isolate
- Control
- Issue personal protection
- Discipline

Investigating accidents

*Why investigate?*
Reasons for carrying out an investigation include:

1. Finding the causes so that similar accidents can be prevented by making improvements to, for example housekeeping, training, equipment and supervision.
2. Being able to publicize information on the accident to make others aware of what went wrong and how to put it right. Or, in certain situations, to reassure people about the possibility of recurrence.
3. Revealing the frequency pattern of certain types of accident indicative of special action to prevent recurrence.
4. Determining and recording *facts* which might have a bearing on any legal action connected with the accident.

*What to investigate*
As a general guide only, because individual sites may wish to give emphasis to particular factors; the following cover the most usual incidents which initiate investigations:

1. All lost-time accidents.
2. Injuries of a certain type on which information may be being gathered.
3. Any unusual accident which might reveal unsuspected hazards although only slight personal injuries were caused.
4. All dangerous occurrences. This should cover incidents which affect 'things' as well as people. For example a 'near miss' which does not cause an injury but which wrecks a machine is as much of an accident as if it had had fatal results. It is always necessary to investigate the *cause* rather than the effect which may appear insignificant.

*When to investigate*
Immediate investigations should determine:

1. Where and when the accident happened.
2. The conditions prevailing at the time, e.g. lighting, housekeeping, guarding, etc.

3. If there were any eye-witnesses.
4. The basic *facts*, e.g. measurements, etc. if appropriate. A photograph or sketch of the incident and 'location marks' would be helpful.

It is vital to hold an on-the-spot investigation while the incident is fresh in the mind of witnesses and the evidence is undisturbed by essential clearance.

### How to investigate

There are all manner of investigatory techniques from the rudimentary to the sophisticated. Certain **basic questions** require to be asked, particularly in immediate investigations and these include:

1. Did the job require a permit to work or some other form of clearance (verbal or written)?
2. Was the permit or authority to proceed correctly given?
3. Was there good access to the place of work?
4. Was there a 'safe place of work'?
5. Were safe methods of work used? What instructions were given either verbal or written? Were they understandable? Were they followed?
6. Was proper supervision exercised?
7. Was the man trained and reasonably experienced in the work?
8. Did the man's action, either before or at the time of the accident, contribute to what took place?

These are some of the questions which amplify the main guidelines for accident investigation, viz.:

(a) What were the unsafe conditions which prevailed?
(b) What were the contributory unsafe acts?
(c) To what extent were people responsible?

Developing accident investigation technique to the next stage, a comprehensive format can be designed to help with the systematic consideration of all the factors surrounding the accident. One such example to use is shown in Figs. 6.7, 6.8 and 6.9 under the separate headings of: The person; The equipment; The system.

An accident is an accident whether or not anyone is injured.
If a man slips the result may be that he:

1. recovers his balance;
2. falls and twists an ankle;
3. cuts his arm;
4. fractures his skull and it proves fatal;

Although these four results differ widely and only one man is seriously injured, these are identical accidents. It is the *accident itself* not the result of the accident, which should determine the *need to investigate* and take *corrective action*.

*Fig. 6.7* (facing page) An aid to accident investigation – the person

AN AID TO ACCIDENT INVESTIGATION I
THE PERSON

*Direct causes: personal*

Operating without authority
Ignoring instructions
Using unsuitable equipment
Not using personal protective equipment
Adopting unsafe position, posture
Making safety devices inoperative
Distracted attention, not concentrating
Unauthorized plant modification

*Reasons for unsafe acts*

| | |
|---|---|
| HUMAN FAILING | reasonable, unreasonable |
| IMPROPER ATTITUDE | reckless, lazy, impatient, absentminded |
| LACK OF KNOWLEDGE OR SKILL | not informed, not trained, inexperienced |
| PHYSICALLY UNSUITED | poor hearing, poor eyesight, too old, slow reaction |

*Persons injured, involved*

Age and experience
Previous accident record
Home background
Supervisor's influence

*Remedies*

1. Instruction, persuasion, appeal
   Improved training, improved written instructions, ensure they are read

2. Personal adjustment
   Better selection of individuals
   Better placement of individuals

3. Discipline (a last resort)
   Admonishing
   Entering on record
   Transferring to other work
   Suspending

187

AN AID TO ACCIDENT INVESTIGATION II
THE EQUIPMENT

*Direct causes: mechanical, physical, chemical*

| | |
|---|---|
| Defective condition | rough, sharp, slippery, corroded, cracked, leaking |
| Unsafe arrangement | unstable stacking, obstructed aisles, overloading |
| Unsafe methods | poor housekeeping, bad planning, faulty isolation, wrong tools |
| Inadequate ventilation | |
| Inadequate machinery guarding | |
| Unauthorized plant modification | |
| Unsatisfactory environment | bad light, poor ventilation, dust emission, high noise level, too hot, too cold |

*The machine 'process' or place*

| | |
|---|---|
| Legal infringements | guarding, handrail, access |
| Maintenance | inadequate, shortage of spare parts |
| Previous accidents | lack of information, lessons not learned |
| Operating instructions | difficult to follow, not followed |
| Inspection | inadequate, cursory, infrequent, not effective |
| Supply position | high stocks, high demand, communications with supplier, out-of-spec material inadequate, short of resources |
| Responsibilities | not clearly defined |

*Remedies*

1. Physical changes
   Better maintenance
   Better inspection
   Better housekeeping

2. Instruction, persuasion, appeal
   Improved procedures
   Better supervision
   More safety publicity

*Fig. 6.8* An aid to accident investigation – the equipment

AN AID TO ACCIDENT INVESTIGATION III
THE SYSTEM (DESIGN, CONSTRUCTION, PROCESS)

| *Direct causes* | |
|---|---|
| Design | not complying with modern standards, poor access for process and maintenance, underdesigned for output and stocks. |
| Construction | poor inspection, damaged materials, faulty interpretation of design instructions, precommissioning studies badly done, parts not complete at start-up |
| Hazardous chemical properties | corrosive, explosive, flammable, irritant, toxic, radioactive, delayed medical effects |
| Hazardous physical properties | all forms of potential energy (steam, power, pressures, vacuum, gravity) |

*Remedies*

Improved design
Better methods
Hazard and operability study
Introduce modification

*Fig. 6.9*   An aid to accident investigation – the system

Defective tools

Tools become lethal weapons when allowed to get in a dilapidated condition. Figure 6.10(a) shows a hammer with a loose wedge which can result in the hammer head flying off its shaft. Using a spanner with strained jaws or of the incorrect size (Fig. 6.10(b)) can result in the spanner slipping off the bolt-head or nut. Mushroom heads on chisels can cause severe eye injury from flying metal and hand injury because of a slipping hammer (see Fig. 6.10(c)).

If possible grind off the burrs; if not replace with new tool.

189

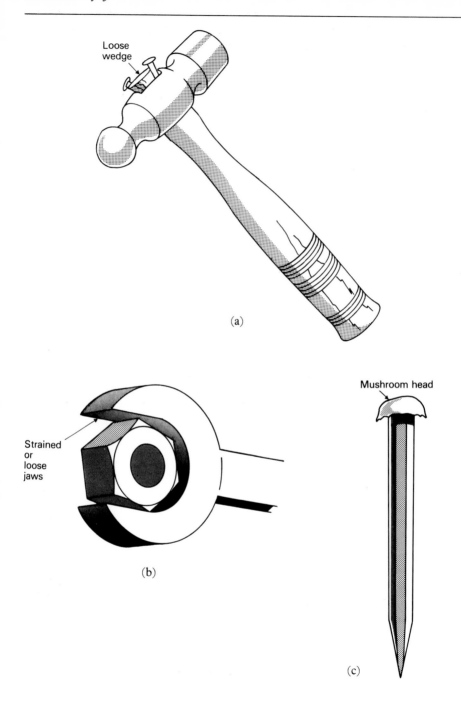

*Fig. 6.10(a)* Hammer with a loose wedge; (b) spanner with strained jaws; (c) mushroom head on chisel

Tables 6.6, 6.7 and 6.8 show the breakdown of the type of accidents, fatal and reported, that occurred in various industries.

*Table 6.6* Comparative fatal accident rates in various industries and occupations[15]

|  | No. of deaths/ 100 million, man hours |
| --- | --- |
| Chemical industry | 3.5 |
| All manufacturing industry | 4 |
| Steel industry | 8 |
| Fishing industry | 35 |
| Coal mining | 40 |
| Railway shunters | 45 |
| Construction industry | 67 |
| Air-crew | 250 |
| Staying at home | 1 |
| Travelling by bus | 3 |
| Travelling by train | 5 |
| Travelling by car | 57 |
| Cycling | 96 |

*Table 6.7* Summary of reported accidents[16]

|  | Fatal | Total |
| --- | --- | --- |
| Machinery (power and non-power) | 62 | 34 537 |
| Rail transport | 5 | 578 |
| Transport other than rail | 65 | 16 091 |
| Falls of persons | 49 | 33 631 |
| *Other, viz:* |  |  |
| Stepping on or striking against persons or objects | 1 | 8 932 |
| Handling goods | 3 | 62 073 |
| Struck by falling objects | 27 | 13 356 |
| Fires and explosion of combustibles | 13 | 664 |
| Explosions of pressure vessels | 36 | 784 |
| Due to electricity | 12 | 881 |
| Poisoning and gassing | 6 | 329 |
| Use of hand tools | — | 13 562 |
| Not otherwise specified | 11 | 23 583 |

Hands, feet and body

- *Gloves, footwear and other protective clothing* must be in good condition and free from defects.
- Use only *gloves* specified for the job. Do not use discarded gloves. Take care of them.

Table 6.8 Construction processes: further analysis of persons or materials from heights 1974–75[17]

| Accident classification | Falls of persons | | | | | Falls of materials | | | |
|---|---|---|---|---|---|---|---|---|---|
| | Number of fatal accidents | | Total number of reported accidents | | 1975 | Number of fatal accidents | | Total number of reported accidents | |
| | | | | | Falls of 2 metres or less / Falls of over 2 metres | | | | |
| | 1974 | 1975 | All falls 1974 | All falls 1975 | Falls of 2 metres or less | Falls of over 2 metres | 1974 | 1975 | 1974 | 1975 |
| From scaffolds | 19 | 16 | 1359 | 1356 | 743 | 613 | 1 | 3 | 256 | 229 |
| From ladders or stepladders | 12 | 9 | 1525 | 1503 | 862 | 641 | — | — | 12 | 37 |
| Through openings in floors or walls, or from or down stairways | 3 | 6 | 806 | 814 | 656 | 158 | — | — | 9 | 23 |
| Through fragile roofing materials | 14 | 14 | 255 | 257 | 40 | 217 | — | — | 6 | 8 |
| From sloping roofs | 4 | 6 | 194 | 169 | 34 | 135 | — | — | 28 | 28 |
| Into excavations | — | — | 385 | 391 | 336 | 55 | — | 1 | 37 | 37 |
| From other working places gangways or runs | 15 | 12 | 608 | 516 | 254 | 262 | 9 | 7 | 283 | 290 |
| Other falls from heights* | 9 | 4 | 896 | 914 | 680 | 234 | 2 | 5 | 1012 | 894 |
| Total falls from heights | 76 | 67 | 6028 | 5920 | 3605 | 2315 | 12 | 16 | 1643 | 1616 |

* Including falls from hoists or into hoistways and into water.

- Use *special gloves* when handling sharp-edged materials such as sheet metal.
- *Barrier creams* are needed for some operations. Wash before applying.
- Use *cleaning agents* for removing grease and dirt. Do not use chemicals or abrasives unless supplied. At meal times and before finishing work, *wash hands*.
- Take special care when working with *machinery*. Beware of loose clothing, e.g. ties, loose overalls, etc.
- Do not use *compressed air* for cleaning down plant or clothing.
- A *'Hard hat'* will protect your head from the danger of falling materials.
- Toes are very susceptible to injury – wear safety boots.
- In cold weather, wear *warm clothing*.

Handling of chemicals

A few general rules:
- When dealing with dangerous materials you must wear prescribed protective clothing in good condition.
- All containers should be clearly marked: there should be no doubt about their identification.
- Never touch chemicals you are not sure about.
- When transferring chemicals from one container to another take care that the receptacle is clean and in good condition.
- Chemical containers must not be used other than for the specified purpose. To do so may cause serious injury.
- Observe and carry out any special rules for cleaning floors. Cleanliness is an important factor in health and safety.

Your eyes have to last you all your life

You cannot get replacements!

- *Goggles* and other forms of protection guard your eyes against injurious heat/light rays; fumes, liquids, gases, etc.
- If you should get any *chemical* in your *eye* irrigate copiously with wash-bottle or in clean water. Then report to first-aider for treatment.
- When *welding* do not look at arc without wearing the correct dark-coloured goggles or mask.
- When *grinding or chipping* wear eye protection provided for the job.
- When *chipping* do not let chips fly; others may not be protected – erect a screen if possible.
- *Wear* your eye protection. Goggles or other protection on your forehead or in your pocket is OUT.
- When breaking any *joint, pipeline or plant equipment*, take care – there may be pressure or residues in a line.
- When clearing a *blockage* stand clear of any opening.

Protection of Eyes Regulations 1974 (Summary)[18]

*Employed persons eye protectors*

1. Blasting, etc. of concrete by abrasive materials propelled by compressed air.
2. Cleaning of buildings by abrasive material propelled by compressed air.
3. Cleaning by means of high-pressure water jets.
4. Striking of masonry nails by means of hand- or power-driven portable tool.
5. Any work involved with hand-held cartridge-operated tools.
6. Chipping of metal, chipping, cutting, etc. of rivets, bolts, etc. from structure of plant using either hand or power tools (portable).
7. Chipping or scurfing of paint, rust, etc. from metals, etc. by hand or power tools (portable)
8. Use of power-driven high-speed metal cutting saw or abrasive cutting-off wheel.
9. Pouring or skimming of molten metal in foundries.
10. Work at molten salt bath when molten salt surface is exposed.
11. Work involved with plant which contains (or has contained) acids, alkalis and other dangerous corrosive substances.
12. Handling in open vessels of acids, alkalis and other dangerous corrosive substances.
13. Driving in of bolts, pins, etc. to structures by hand or power tools (portable).
14. Injection by pressure of liquids or solids into structures, etc.
15. Breaking up of metals by hammer or tup.
16. Breaking, cutting, dressing, drilling, etc. by hand or power tool (portable) of glass, hard plastics, concrete, stone, bricks, etc.
17. Use of compressed air in removing swarf, dust, etc.
18. Work at furnace containing molten metal and pouring, skimming of molten metal in places other than foundries.
19. Processes in foundries where hot sand may be thrown off.
20. Work in the manufacture of wire and wire rope.
21. Coiling wire, etc.
22. Cutting of wire or metal strapping under tension.
23. Manufacture or processing of glass or handling of cullet.

## Chapter 7

# Demolition training

## Construction Industry Training Board

The Construction Industry Training Board (CITB) was constituted in 1964 following the passing of the 1964 Industrial Training Act.[1] The purpose of the Act was to make better provision for the training of persons over compulsory school age. To help achieve this, the Act gave the Secretary of State the power to set up individual training boards for different industries.

Further legislation affecting training came into being in 1973 when the Employment and Training Act was passed. This provided government funds to pay the administrative costs of boards and to assist with the provision of grants in key areas of training.

Some 38 500 firms are on the CITB register, representing 1 000 000 employees. They cover building, civil engineering services, mechanical engineering services and a large range of specialist firms.The principal objectives of the CITB are to serve industry by:

1.  Improving the *quality* of training.
2.  Improving the *facilities* available for training.
3.  Helping to provide *enough* trained people.

The CITB is appointed by the Secretary of State and consists of 10 employer members, 10 employee members, 7 representatives from the education service, a chairman and a deputy chairman. There are also 4 government assessors serving on the CITB. The 7 administrative areas of the CITB are illustrated in Fig. 7.1.

Five industrial committees – building, specialist building, civil engineering, electrical engineering services, mechanical engineering services – provide extensive consultation with industry, and recommend training and levy/grant policies for their sectors. These committees appoint subcommittees and working parties to deal with special aspects of their work.

The Health and Safety at Work etc. Act 1974[2] requires every employer to provide information, instruction and the training necessary to ensure the health, safety and welfare at work of his employees, to help employers fulfil this duty.

Shetland Island Area

Orkney Island Area

Western Isles
Island Area

Stornoway

Portree

Inverness

Highlands Region    Grampian Region

Aberdeen

**1**

Tayside Region

Oban    Perth    Dundee

Central
Region    Fife Region

Stirling

Glasgow    Edinburgh

Greenock    Lothian Region

Paisley    Motherwell

Lanark    Peebles

Berwick on Tweed

Strathclyde
Region    Borders
Region

Ayr

Dumfries and Galloway
Region    Northumberland

Dumfries

Wigtown    Newcastle upon Tyne

Kirkcudbright    Sunderland

Carlisle    Tyne and Wear

Cumbria    Durham    Cleveland

Kendal    Darlington    Middlesbrough

**2**

North Yorkshire    Scarborough

Lancaster    Harrogate    York

**3**

Lancashire    West    Leeds
Yorkshire    Humberside

Greater Manchester    Huddersfield    Hull

Merseyside    Oldham    South    Grimsby
Manchester    Yorkshire

Liverpool    Sheffield

Denbigh    Cheshire    Derbyshire    Lincolnshire

Clwyd    Stoke-on-Trent    Nottingham

Gwynedd    Wrexham    Staffordshire

**4**    Nottinghamshire

West Midlands    Leicestershire    Kings Lynn

Powys    Salop    Leicester    Norfolk

Wolverhampton    Cambridge    Norwich
-shire

Birmingham    **6**

Herefordshire    Warwick-    Northampton    Ely
and    shire    Northamptonshire    Suffolk

Dyfed    Worcestershire    Bedford    Bedford
-shire

Hereford    Hertfordshire

West    Gloucestershire    Essex
Glamorgan    Gwent

Mid    Oxford
South    -shire    Greater
London

Swansea    Cardiff    Bristol    Berkshire

Avon    Bath    **5**    **7**

Wiltshire    Basingstoke    Maidstone

Somerset    Surrey    Kent

Taunton    Hampshire    West    East
Sussex    Sussex

Devon    Yeovil    Dorset    Southampton    Brighton

Exeter    Dorchester    Isle of Wight

Cornwall

Bircham Newton Training Centre (BNTC)

The centre was set up in 1966 by the CITB to provide training in civil engineering skills for the construction industry and it is now one of the most advanced residential training centres in the country. It is also the largest plant training centre in the world. By mid-1977 over 31 400 trainees had completed training at BNTC. The centre's facilities include approximately 243 hectares of outdoor and indoor training area, large hangars, lecture rooms, a restaurant, cinema, social club, sports amenities and over 500 bedrooms.

*Training*
The centre offers more than eighty different courses lasting from three to six weeks, but the usual period is two weeks.

The courses cover the following areas:

- *plant* – earth-moving, cranes, roadworks, rough-terrain forklifts;
- *construction* – bar-bending and steel-fixing, kerblaying, drainlaying, timbering, small plant, manual handling, gas distribution, painting, plastering;
- *management* – supervisory, safety officers, graduate engineers practical training, work study.

In addition BNTC puts on special courses designed to meet the needs of individual companies. The centre's instructors also run in-company courses in many parts of the country.

Merton Training Centre

The centre was set up in 1974, it is mainly a scaffolding training centre, but courses in specialist building skills are also available. Number of trainees – 4358 by mid-1977. The centre's facilities include 1 hectare of land, good outdoor and indoor training areas, special training devices, lecture rooms and a canteen. The centre is non-residential, but lodgings are arranged in the neighbourhood if required.

*Training*
The centre offers the following courses:

- scaffolding;
- safety courses;
- specialist building skills (standard scheme of training) – ceiling fixing, built-up felt roofing, roof sheeting, flooring.

The centre's instructors frequently run in-company courses.

*Fig. 7.1*   (facing page) The seven administrative areas of the CITB

Glasgow Training Centre

The centre was set up in 1975 to provide training facilities for construction firms in Scotland and the north of England. It had trained 1122 people by mid-1977. Facilities include outdoor and indoor training areas, lecture rooms and a canteen. The centre is non-residential, but accommodation is available in the neighbourhood.

The CITB assists industry to improve its training through a grants scheme which is published each year for a training year running from 1 August to 31 July of the following year. Grants are paid to encourage employers to ensure that their trainees are properly trained including, where appropriate, attendance at courses of further education. Specific grants are available for approved courses run by independent organizations, safety courses, in-company courses, the development of learning programmes, research, group training, etc. Under the present scheme top priority is given to encouraging first-year, off-the-job, craft training.

The CITB also attaches great importance to continuation training and to the administration of training, i.e. group training schemes, and the training of training staff (company and group training officers and instructors).

In addition to funds provided from government sources, the CITB is financed by an annual levy which is calculated on the number of employees in the firm. The rate per employee varies according to the occupation of the employee. For labour-only workers, employers are levied at 1 per cent of all payments made to subcontractors under labour-only agreements. There is no levy on trainees. The levy is mainly used to pay grants to employers who carry out approved training.

The annual levy is collected in December and any grants payable are deducted from the levy due. Some firms receive money from the Board at this time, as their grant is greater than their levy. Small firms with an annual payroll (including labour-only payments) of less than £15 000 are excluded from paying the levy. They are not, therefore, normally eligible to claim grants. However, small firms can claim certain government-funded grants. All firms paying the levy receive a rebate of £20 off the levy assessed.

Before the formation of the CITB, much of the organized training undertaken on a major scale was for apprentices only. Today, training opportunities are much wider. On average more than 120,000 adults and school-leavers are trained for the construction industry each year with CITB help. Training, aided by CITB grants, is undertaken at company or CITB training centres, educational establishments or through on-the-job training schemes.

Management and supervisory courses are developed based on surveys of training needs, and training recommendations have been published. These are geared to meet the special requirements of small, medium and large firms. Training recommendations and technical modules, which are training programmes designed for a specific aspect of the subject, have been produced to cover all sections within the technician and technologist groups.

In 1968, in co-operation with a variety of technical colleges throughout the country, the CITB mounted courses based on a new pattern of training for operative skills. The object was to create a more flexible labour force – speeding up the training process, increasing productivity and improving safety.

These courses were followed in 1972 by a pilot training awards scheme for school-leavers. This scheme, designed to help provide more apprentices for industry, gave six months' basic training off-site at a technical college in a variety of crafts – carpentry and joinery, bricklaying, plastering, painting and decorating, plumbing, heating and ventilating, and electrical installation. The CITB paid the college fees and a fixed award each week to help the trainees with travelling and subsistence, and, at the end of the course, placed the boys in firms as apprentices.

The boys were pleased because they were learning a craft and could earn while they trained. The employers liked the scheme because it gave them an apprentice who was productive from the first day he went on a site.

As from the 1974/75 training year, new standard off-site training schemes, based on the awards scheme, were introduced for the building crafts. Similar schemes were brought in for the engineering services. A major change is that the trainees are now employed by firms before starting their training instead of being sponsored, initially, by the CITB. However, some awards are still given by the CITB to school-leavers who cannot find an employer immediately.

Employers are sought for these trainees during their off-site training.

In their first year, the trainees on these new schemes spend about six months under intensive basic training in off-site conditions, either at a technical college, CITB training centre or a company's own training centre.

In the first year, 6700 young new entrants to the construction industry were trained under these CITB off-site schemes. In the following year 1975/76, this figure rose to 8400 and the target for 1976/77 is for about 9500 trainees.

Firms too small to employ their own training officer are encouraged to form group training associations. They share a training officer and the CITB provides financial assistance with the running costs of the group. There are 139 groups covering firms in general building, painting and decorating, civil engineering, plant, roofing, scaffolding, steeplejacking, electrical engineering services and mechanical engineering services. They include about 2500 firms with over 160 000 employees. The CITB has set up a National Consultative Committee on Group Training which includes representatives from groups in each region of the country.

The CITB under the chairmanship of Leslie C. Kemp (Fig. 7.2) and with the co-operation of the NFDC – London and Southern Counties Region launched a 'Demolition Training Scheme' on 30 November 1978.[3] Mr Kemp who has been associated with the demolition and dismantling industry for a number of years and who sits on a number of committees dealing with demolition and allied work and who in fact was on the drafting committee for the Code of Practice – CP94:1971 – has long been an advocate of training, not only in the demolition industry but all construction and civil engineering.

*Fig. 7.2* Mr L. C. Kemp, CBE – Founder Chairman of the Demolition Training Group, Founder Joint Registrar of the Demolition Register and Chairman of the CITB

The Demolition Industry Group Training Association (London and Southern Counties) as it is called, is the first-ever training group formulated specifically for demolition companies. The CITB in fact do run a number of courses for machine operators, burners, timbering, scaffolders, etc. which are all directly associated with the demolition industry to a larger or smaller degree.

The setting up of the Group Training Association marked the recognition by the industry of the need to move away its image as being rough, tough and largely unskilled.[4]

The industry now accepts the need for training in the use of more sophisticated equipment and specialized tools and machinery to equip itself for the task of demolition beyond the 1980s into the twenty-first century.

These problems have been adequately highlighted in previous chapters, but include high-rise city centre developments almost certainly containing tensioned structures, industrial complexes such as petro-chemical works and radioactive structures such as nuclear power facilities with all their modern new designs and changes in the technology of their construction. Last, but by far the most important item, coupled with all the new training, is the need to improve safety on sites to ensure that not only are the operatives better trained but that supervisors at all levels are more safety conscious.

Demolition and dismantling, along with all other sections of the building and civil engineering industry, has a shortage of skilled labour; therefore the need for training is vital.[5] The industry does not lend itself to being an ideal training module because of the nature of the work, although a limited number of schemes are being operated on less complicated sites made available by certain London boroughs.

One of the first tasks of the group training officer along with the CITB staff, was to devise a series of training modules aimed mainly at the supervisory side of the industry to form a firm base from which to build.

The training of demolition operatives can be a lengthy and expensive task. The very nature of the work involved, as has been previously stated, needs considerable knowledge of other sections of the building and civil engineering industry, and therefore must include training in the following:

1. General demolition activities.
2. Knowledge of the legal aspects associated with demolition.
3. Knowledge and understanding of the WRA.
4. Knowledge of Statutory Regulations in respect of demolition.
5. Training in site safety and organization.
6. Elementary knowledge of construction.
7. Methods – CP.94:1971.
8. Method study (demolition procedures).
9. Care of plant and equipment (not mechanical).
10. Use and maintenance of equipment such as hoists, winches, etc.
11. The value of certain components.
12. Hazards of certain materials (asbestos and toxic waste).
13. Elementary shoring, hoarding and scaffolding.
14. Plant operators – effective use and maintenance of machines.

Once training had been completed the operative could then be issued with a certificate of competence similar to that issued in the scheme in operation for the scaffolding operative.

## Chapter 8

# Plant and equipment used in demolition

The technological changes in the demolition industry has increased the demand for more sophisticated plant and equipment.[1] The use of such equipment and the safety of operation depends upon the effectiveness of a smooth partnership between the manufacturers, the contractors and the operatives.

There is always a potential danger in the incorrect use of a machine or item of equipment.[2] The manufacturer cannot be held responsible for incorrect use of a machine on work for which it is not designed or protected. The contractor, under section 2 of the Health and Safety at Work Act, must ensure:

1.  The machine must only be used for the purpose for which it is designed and manufactured.
2.  The machine is properly maintained.
3.  The operator is properly trained to operate the machine.
4.  The machine is tested and certified at proper intervals by a suitably qualified independent person.

When mishaps occur it is almost invariably due to neglect or misuse on the part of the operator rather than an actual malfunction on the part of the machine.[3] Fortunately, all mishaps are not accidents although they are potential accidents, and given the correct circumstances, especially in the incorrect use of a machine, often prove fatal.

Whenever a demolition operative has to reach above his own height to work, whatever the reason, he has to think about plant and equipment whether it be a crane to lift or a working platform for access. The specification and capability of this equipment has to be understood, otherwise, for example with the crane, it could become overloaded and dangerous. The machines, plant and equipment illustrated in this chapter are just a few of the many in daily use in the demolition and dismantling industry today.

Fig. 8.1 shows a typical small tipper lorry in common use in the early 1940s and did not develop much over the next decade, whereas the illustrations in Figs. 8.2 and 8.3 clearly show the development in technology in the lorries of the 1980s. Figure 8.2 shows an articulated lorry with a metal body used to transport bulk material such as scrap metal from site direct to steelworks to be reprocessed back into the economy. Figure 8.3 illustrates the latest development

*Fig. 8.1*   Typical tipper lorry in use when the NFDC was founded

*Fig. 8.2*   Turbo-charged articulated tractor unit fitted with bulk-carrying metal body

by Leyland trucks. Although this is a rigid-bodied design used extensively throughout the construction industry, it is ideal for clearing material from large demolition sites.

The roll-on/roll-off truck shown in Fig. 8.4 shows how versatile this type of vehicle can be. With countless containers one tractor unit can service a number of different sites in one day, thereby eliminating wasted site waiting time.

*Fig. 8.3*   The new breed of British truck in use on demolition sites today

*Fig. 8.4*   Roll-on/roll-off truck depositing skip on site for collection of scrap metal

A relatively new innovation in the demolition of the interior of blast-furnaces/ and soaking pits is the Slageater, as illustrated in Figs. 8.5, 8.6 and 8.7. Once in position this equipment allows all work to be carried on and controlled by remote control from outside the furnace.

The plant and equipment shown in Fig. 8.8 would usually only be found on large demolition sites. The use of (1) a fixed derrick would not normally be used unless the equipment was already on site as part of the demolition contract and required dismantling on completion of the work. Items (2) tracked crane, and (3) mobile rubber-wheeled crane, are in common use on most demolition sites today, either removing components as the demolition progresses, used for balling masonry and concrete and loading and unloading materials on to (4) site tipper lorries. The final piece of equipment in this illustration (5) the compressor,

*Fig. 8.5*   Assembly of slageater prior to demolition

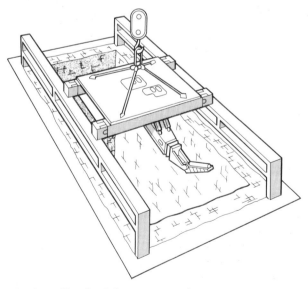

*Fig. 8.6*   Sketch of slageater over pit

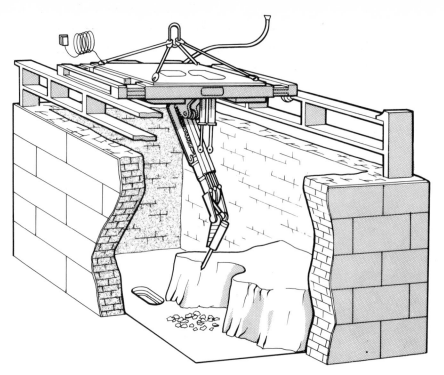

*Fig. 8.7*   Cut out showing working application in section

*Fig. 8.8*   Typical large demolition site with 1) fixed derrick, 2) tracked crane, 3) mobile rubber wheeled crane, 4) tipper lorry and 5) compressor in use

is vital to any demolition contractor as a means of supplying compressed air for air-powered tools such as concrete breakers.

The hydraulic excavator is one of the most versatile pieces of equipment to be developed this century. Figures 8.9 to 8.15 show the benefits of using this type of equipment on any demolition site. The safety features built into this machine and its numerous attachments go a long way to providing more safety for the operatives and the general public, quicker demolition without risking the operative in dangerous situations, and help establish a less labour-intensive site. A good example of all-round cab protection is shown in Fig. 8.14.

The loading shovel (Figs. 8.16 to 8.18) is another example of modern technology developed primarily as an earth-moving piece of equipment and adapted as essential hardware for demolition contractors. This equipment with its numerous attachments is necessary to clear the bulk rubbish and hardcore created by demolition. The use of this type of equipment has become necessary for speedy clearance of our redevelopment areas to allow new development to commence as quickly as possible.

The hydraulic breaker (Figs. 8.19 and 8.20) indicates the numerous advantages and working applications this type of attachment can have, and with the ever increasing need to eliminate heavy and dangerous tasks for the operative, this type of development is essential.

*Fig. 8.9*  Hydraulic excavator fitted with demolition arm

*Fig. 8.10* Drop ball attachment fitted to a hydraulic excavator

*Fig. 8.11* Track-laying hydraulic excavator fitted with tooth grapple

*Fig. 8.12* (facing page) Demolition arm in use

*Fig. 8.13*  Arm grapple fitted to hydraulic excavator

*Fig. 8.14*  All-round cab protection for the operator

*Fig. 8.15*   Two sizes of hydraulic excavator

*Fig. 8.16*   Rubber-wheeled loading shovel

211

*Fig. 8.17* Loading shovel with bucket

*Fig. 8.18* Track-laying loading shovel fitted with grab bucket

*Fig. 8.19* Breaker in use (mounted on hydraulic excavator)

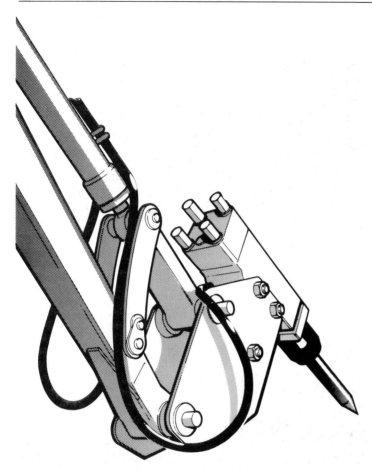

*Fig. 8.20*  Close-up of breaker

The mobile working platform (Figs. 8.21 to 8.24) has been developed as a safe and speedy means of access to difficult, almost impossible, locations where otherwise a permanent scaffold would be necessary. The mobility of these hydraulic platforms allow a number of locations to be worked by one team. One example would be the cutting of the base of a metal roof truss. One side of the structure could be cut first, then the hydraulic platform could be swung to the other side and the second cut made within minutes, thereby eliminating the need for a scaffold or, more commonly, men climbing on to the structure without adequate safety precautions. Figure 8.21 illustrates the advantage of such platforms as a means of rescue of salvage during a collapse.

Finally, the crane (Fig. 8.25) can be used as a lifting, dragline, grabbing or pile-driving piece of equipment. The most frequent use of this plant is when a drop-ball attachment is fitted. The range and working angles of this machine are illustrated in Fig. 8.26.

*Fig. 8.21* Hydraulic working platform being used to render scaffold safe that has collapsed due to overloading

*Fig. 8.22* Lightweight hydraulic working platform used to gain access to underside of bridge

*Fig. 8.23*   Trailer-mounted hydraulic working platform

*Fig. 8.24*   Lorry-mounted hydraulic platform used as a safe working platform to strip roof

215

*Fig. 8.25* The use of a crane to operate a demolition ball

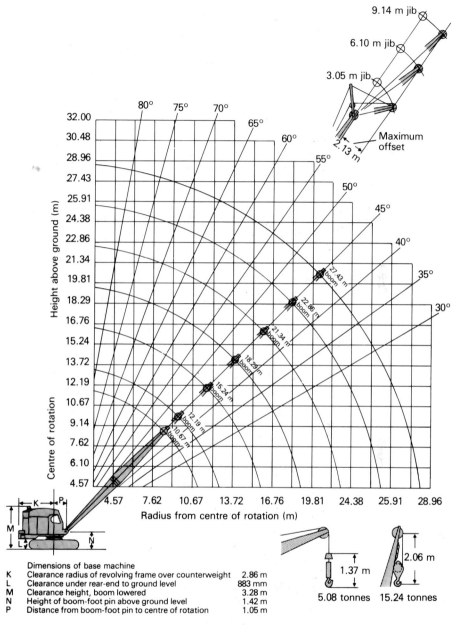

Dimensions of base machine
K   Clearance radius of revolving frame over counterweight   2.86 m
L   Clearance under rear-end to ground level   883 mm
M   Clearance height, boom lowered   3.28 m
N   Height of boom-foot pin above ground level   1.42 m
P   Distance from boom-foot pin to centre of rotation   1.05 m

*Fig. 8.26*   Range and working angles of a lifting crane

217

## Chapter 9

# Category of companies

Numerous suggested figures have been discussed during the last decade as to how many bona-fide contractors there are in the demolition and dismantling industry, and how many operatives they employ.

Official figures discussed before the formation of the DDIR in 1974 indicated there was less than 300 contractors who, in turn, employed approximately 6000 operatives. As with all statistics, figures can be manipulated to fit into circumstances, therefore it is impossible to give anything approaching an accurate calculation.

At the present time something like 200 contractors are members of the NFDC and yet 700 plus were registered on the DDIR.[1] The 200 membership of the NFDC has not altered substantially during the last decade. However, the membership has changed, new members taking over from contractors who for one reason or another fall by the wayside as in all industry.

When the DDIR was formed in 1974 the government of the day along with the industry looked at membership at no more than 300–350; this figure has now been surpassed and still all contractors who carry out demolition have not been accounted for. The latest calculations show there could be as many as 1000 contractors in the UK who carry out works of demolition as a major part of their workload, and these 1000 contractors could employ upwards of 15 000 operatives who, although not employed full-time as demolition operatives, should be employed under the DICB WRA or a similar agreement accepted by the industry.

Somewhere in the region of 8000 full-time operatives may be employed by bona-fide contractors. That is to say, contractors who employ full-time trained demolition operatives including machine operators, drivers and fitters solely on demolition and dismantling. To these figures must be added those members working in constructional engineering, scrap processing, explosives engineering and steeplejacks who all undertake work involving demolition and dismantling and who are an important part of the overall industry. Then comes those contractors who for one reason or another are not members of any related federation, or sometimes indeed no federation at all, who wish to remain independent but who play an ever increasing role in the overall picture within the industry. When it is considered that of the 1000 or so contractors calculated to represent

218

the industry only approximately 500 are members of one of the representative federations, it is apparent that a body of the standing of the DDIR is still required to check and control the industry as a whole.

Demolition and dismantling work is carried out by the following types of contractors.

1. Pure demolition/dismantling contractors.
2. Dismantling contractors whose main activity is in the scrap-processing and associated industries.
3. Construction engineers who carry out demolition or dismantling prior to renewal of components, etc.
4. Builders and civil engineers.
5. Specialist contractors, i.e. steeplejacks, explosives engineers.
6. Small general contractors, plant hire companies, etc. although it must be stressed that in most cases these are usually controlled by one or other of the above categories of contractor.

The difficulty of employment of labour among the contractors who carry out demolition and dismantling was, in the past, not too great a problem as there had been no effective method of control, but during the life of the DDIR, this problem was highlighted.

Although the numerous WRAs which are associated or directly connected to the demolition/dismantling/construction/civil engineering/steeplejack industry are similar on a number of counts there are significant differentials when the industry considers specialist employment, and because of this the DDIR accepted the criteria of only three agreements to form the basis of registration, namely:

1. The Demolition Industry Conciliation Board.
2. The British Scrap Federation.
3. The Master Steeplejacks.

At the present time others associated with the industry are being considered and may be accepted under certain conditions.

The wide range in size of contractors in the industry from a working partnership of two men up to multinational contractors who employ hundreds of operatives, makes the problem of control more difficult, especially when the labour force can fluctuate from week to week mostly on a casual basis. That is to say they are in the direct employ of the contractor sometimes only for as long as the contract lasts.

As the DDIR controlled the industry by regular inspections it was possible to give a fair analysis of the type and size of contractors who were engaged in the industry. These figures would need very careful analysis to give an accurate job category of all operatives employed, especially those employed by contractors whose activities are not solely demolition.

An example of the above situation was considered by the DDIR with a large constructional engineering contractor in Scotland, who employed in excess of 4000 operatives throughout the UK on works of refurbishing power stations and similar establishments who by the very nature of such work had to remove worn-out components, machines, equipment and in some cases steel-framed buildings. No one can dispute that they were expert in their field of installing the new equipment, etc. and by the very nature of their training they had to know how to remove the defective part which then became dismantling. This is not to say that the operative is a dismantling or a demolition operative, and in most cases he would not thank you for being classed as one, yet in the true sense of the word the man is doing that class of work and should be controlled as such. Only possibly 100 men out of the 4000 would ever be employed to carry out this work.[2] Not necessarily the same men would be employed on each job and some of these in any case would be general labourers; therefore, you can understand the problem of associated WRAs.

As the main demolition industry has always been associated with family businesses it is not uncommon to find small contractors who do not employ anyone from outside the family, but in latter years often the small company is made up of partners who in the past have worked together as a gang and finally decided to go legitimate and form a company either as a working partnership, a legal partnership or a limited company. It is possible for a man to be a sole trader, although in my opinion this can only be applied to contractors similar to an explosives engineer or similar type of specialization.

An analysis of contractors in the industry at the last full yearly inspection of the DDIR[1] is as follows:

| *Contractors* | *Number of operatives* |
|---|---|
| +  10 | More than 101 |
| 450 | 10 and under |
| 150 | 11 to 25 |
| 50 | 26 to 50 |
| 22 | 51 to 100 |

Of these only two are known to have in excess of 3000 operatives although not all employed in demolition.

The official negotiating bodies for the different sections of the industry have different category of employee to cover the respective operation to be carried out. The Demolition Industry Conciliation Board represents the majority of employees in the demolition industry. This is considered more fully in Appendix 4 and covers all the respective operations required in the industry including supervision of plant operators, drivers and fitters – trades which are not readily associated with the demolition industry.

With the exception of the categories listed above, the main activity can now be divided into three main categories: Topman; Burner, General labourer, although in latter years the category of Stripper appears and that of Mattockman is almost a thing of the past. There are numerous variations of the above categories, i.e. topman burner or ground burner, general labourer and general labourer/equipment operator. It must not be assumed because the industry is dirty and knocks buildings down that no craft structure exists. In fact the only way a general labourer can progress in the trade is by serving an apprenticeship like any other industry, learning and progressing gradually through to become a 'topman' the craftsman who by experience is competent to carry out any operation at any height (except the operation of mechanical plant). Before the advent of the latest mechanical equipment the industry was very labour-intensive, and in some areas still is, but like all industry today labour costs have risen, and the labour market has diminished, therefore the contractor has been forced by necessity to look for alternative means which has brought the development and adaptation of mechanical equipment as specified in Chapter 8. The need to clear sites more quickly has forced the industry to look to manufacturers to develop machines with more power, more height, more reach and more sophistication to carry out the contract at greater speed, using as little labour as possible. When labour was cheap and the safety requirements were not as closely observed the site could be flooded with labour (at most times casual labour) with no thought for the conditions under which the men had to work. With present legislation, both for the employment of labour and the statutory requirements, the abuse of labour is not now common although men are still told to carry out almost impossible tasks on some contracts.

The manual operation is not, and will never become, a thing of the past as the very nature of the work involves the salvage of material. Therefore, certain works involving the demolition of intricate items must be carried out by individual operators usually working for hours to salvage a special item which the contractor can resell and recover some of the costs on the contract.

The whole of the building and civil engineering industry[3] is renowned for being a casual industry and the demolition and dismantling section is no exception. Therefore, the control of an itinerant, casual labour force has been the problem for years, even to the extent that attempts to improve conditions for the operatives have been rejected by the operatives themselves. In fact the attitude in a number of cases throughout the industry has been 'if in doubt don't trust it, reject it' making it difficult for management as well as trade unions to progress. Coupled with the fact of dangerous conditions – which by the very nature of the work are always present – the problems of casual, often untrained, labour is a sound recipe for the high accident rate in the industry as a whole.

There are a number of different categories under which a contractor can be placed: as a specialist in a particular field, or covering the whole spectrum of the industry. The best example of this can be found in the booklet issued by the NFDC which lists twelve separate categories, the first of these being the location followed by general demolition, site clearance and excavation, shoring, demolition of mass and reinforced concrete, chimney demolition, machinery dismantling, explosives, plant hire, supply of hardcore, removal of dangerous structures and sale of recovered material.

Some contractors who cover all aspects of demolition also give a nationwide service, although this service is usually restricted to a few large contractors who demolish power stations, cooling towers or very large structures and who have a permanent large labour force, although when working away from their main base would employ a percentage of local labour, but always maintaining a nucleus of permanent staff and supervision.

The industry has one category with which it would like to dissociate and with which it has been bedevilled for a number of years. This category is classed as the 'Lump' and in real terms is no category at all. The lump has brought the industry into dispute with a number of statutory bodies for various contraventions. The payment of a lump sum for a particular job brought about the name – often the payment was in cash with no control of the payment of taxes or little consideration of how the demolition would be carried out.

As could be expected this method of employment soon attracted the notice of the Inland Revenue and the HSE, therefore, more and more legislation has been introduced to try to control this method.

It must be made clear that not all labour-only subcontractors operate in such a way. There are some bona-fide subcontractors who do employ labour in the direct employ of the company and who pay the correct rates and conditions of the industry, but the ever increasing number of **casual** operators must be controlled. These operators do not usually consider the safety of the operative who they take on for a 'job' on a casual basis, nor do they consider the general public who may be at risk from their operatives.

The introduction of the 714 Tax Exemption Certificate has been one of the attempts to control the abuse in the industry, and several attempts have been made with legislation, but it must be emphasized that for every **casual operator** who works in the industry there is a so-called bona-fide contractor or client who employs them, therefore, the onus must be on the controlling bodies of the industry along with government departments and trade unions to put their own house in order.

## Chapter 10

# Conclusions[1]

The demolition and dismantling industry has, since its inception, faced a variety of problems, some of its own making and some created by outside bodies, but mainly those inherent in the industry as detailed throughout the preceding chapters.

All problems can be solved and all buildings can be demolished, but all parties require a far greater understanding of the complex nature of the industry and the people who operate within it.

One problem, as with the whole of the building and civil engineering industry, is the lack of skilled labour and the almost nomadic existence of the largely casual labour force. This problem can only be overcome by training and giving the labour force a secure future by decasualization of the whole industry. The introduction of the first of what is hoped will be many training groups is a step in the right direction.

The designer, architect, planner and client must be made more aware of the important role of the demolition contractor and technology must be developed accordingly.

The almost obsessive practice of giving the contract to the lowest tenderer without the client first checking the competence of the company submitting that tender must be overcome, by legislation if necessary. This and total compliance with the Fair Wages Enactment of Parliament – October 1946 – would be the only fair and realistic means of assessment of tender figures or quotations. To eliminate unfair and unrealistic tendering would also eliminate the unsavoury element within the industry.

The accident statistics appear to indicate that accidents occur when trying to cut corners or when inexperienced labour is being used. The main reason for this type of work is mainly because an unrealistic tender has been submitted to start the chain reaction of disaster.

The bulk of the demolition and dismantling contracts are controlled by local authorities and other statutory bodies, therefore the need to have more competent supervision by these bodies is of prime importance. Local authorities should be more understanding in their approach to all aspects of the demolition and dismantling industry and be more ready to assist rather than restrict. Equally, the industry must also be more co-operative and put more effort into progressing into the twenty-first century and to take note of what was stated at the end of Chapter 9: 'For every bad demolition contractor or operative there is a bad client who employs them.' This practice must be stamped out from *within* as well as outside the industry either by co-operation or legislation.

At present, new buildings containing tensioned structures are not included in a register and no longer use the special plaque advocated by the NFDC. There is a need for this procedure to be readopted for all buildings containing potentially dangerous components and not just those with tensioned structures. The government and all other statutory bodies involved in the planning and approving plans of buildings, whether they be simple dwelling-houses, complicated tensioned structures or nuclear facilities, owe future generations the inheritance of an agency who have been allowed to collate and record the details of such structures. This will enable contractors to identify any inherent hazards when the time comes for such buildings to be demolished. As has been previously stated, the DDIR would have been an ideal type of agency for such matters. With the introduction of such processes as microfilm, silicon chip technology and computers to collect and store information, it would not have been a difficult task.

# Specimen written company safety policy

The criminal law obliges employers to draw up, publish and circulate policies to identify arrangements for safety and safety responsibilities. These policies must be discussed with safety representatives and be reviewed from time to time.

This requirement came into being in 1974 and yet it is estimated that as many as 40 per cent of all employing organizations still have no safety policy and could therefore face criminal prosecution.

A large number of organizations who have prepared one would find it inadequate should an accident occur and are therefore themselves in breach of the criminal law.

The safety policy document is an ongoing one and *must* be updated on a regular basis to comply with the law.

The example in this appendix should not be taken as a document that could be copied for every company. A safety policy is individual to that company for which it is written and must include individual characteristics of such an organization although the example does give adequate guidelines for one to be prepared.

Remember, a safety policy prepared today may need to be updated next month.

The company's health and safety policy requires the company managing director to publish a statement of the organization and arrangements for implementing that policy. The statement which follows sets out the organization and arrangements. Part 1 refers to the responsibilities of the management of the company and each of its divisions and details the responsibilities of the works/construction management organization. Part 2 states the various arrangements we have to fulfil the policy.

## Company safety policy

As an employee you are required to read this statement in conjunction with the statement of the company's health and safety policy. Each of us has a part to play in making this an effective policy and we must all accept the responsibility and challenge that it presents. With your commitment and support we can make safer and healthier working a reality throughout the company.

Managing Director
Date . . . . . .

Part 1: Organization

1. *Managing Director*
   The Managing Director of the company is accountable to the company's Chairman for implementing the health and safety policy.

2. *Executive directors*
   The Deputy Managing Director and the directors of each division (Manufacturing, Contracting, Building) are accountable to the Managing Director for implementing the health and safety policy in each unit, Works or Site, and in particular have to:
   (a) prepare and publish details of the organization and arrangements for implementing the policy – this statement is published to meet this requirement;
   (b) establish an effective service at each level to advise management on matters concerning accident control and other health and safety matters, and ensure that the standards of the service are maintained;
   (c) establish and maintain training programmes for all levels of management in the policy and programmes for accident control and also for specific job training of all employees in safe methods of work;
   (d) establish a system which will ensure that accident control is integrated in the design and operations of new plant or equipment or when methods are being revised;
   (e) set objectives annually with the aim of improving health and safety at work and review performance against these objectives;
   (f) establish joint consultative machinery to discuss health and safety matters and arrange the training of joint committee members to help ensure that consultation is effective;
   (g) see that adequate arrangements are established and maintained for the health and safety of all their employees;
   (h) establish an effective system for ensuring that remedial recommendations, following major accidents, are implemented.

3. *Functional directors*

   (*i*) *Director – Personnel and Administration*   The Director – Personnel and Administration is accountable to the Managing Director for fulfilling the following responsibilities:
   (a) implementing the company's health and safety policy as it affects all employees under his direct control;

226

(b) monitoring the implementation of the company's health and safety policy across the company;

(c) establishing and maintaining an effective and comprehensive service on health and safety matters which is co-ordinated across the company;

(d) developing and maintaining realistic accident-control indices on a uniform basis in line with company policy for monitoring and controlling performances at all levels and for the setting of company accident-control objectives;

(e) ensuring that the implementation of company policy forms an integral part of the programmes and general activities of the personnel function in the company;

(f) producing and publishing company documents giving information and guidance on matters of health and safety policy, on regulations and approved codes of practice and the company/procedures and codes on health and safety.

(ii) *Other directors* Where appropriate, other directors will have responsibility for the implementation of the company's health and safety policy as it effects all employees within their departments and for its incorporation into any programme on objectives for which they are responsible.

4. *General managers*

Each General Manager, or equivalent where appropriate, is responsible to the appropriate executive director for the implementation of the health and safety policy in his departments. In particular, he has to:

(a) ensure that his departmental managers are familiar with the policy, implement it, and draw upon the advisory services on health and safety which have been established;

(b) ensure that training programmes are established and maintained for all levels of management regarding health and safety and that job training in safe and healthy methods of work is carried out;

(c) ensure that accident control is integrated in the design and operations of new plant or equipment for his departments and when methods are revised;

(d) set objectives annually within his departments with the aim of improving health and safety at work and review performance against these objectives;

(e) establish joint consultative machinery to discuss health and safety matters and to arrange for the training of joint committee members to help ensure that consultation is effective;

(f) ensure that all Standing Instructions and agreed procedures are adhered to.

(g) ensure that relevant information is made available to customers on health and safety hazards which may be associated with the company;

(h) establish effective communication links to discuss the health and safety

227

programmes at all levels within his departments;
(i)  ensure that plant and departmental inspections are carried out at regular intervals;
(j)  establish a major disaster plan for the Works backed up by local full-time emergency service organizations;
(k)  maintain records on the safety performance of his staff.

5.   *Other managers*

*5.1   Manager in charge of accident prevention*   Each Manager in charge of accident prevention is required by his respective General Manager, or equivalent where appropriate to:
(a)  implement the company's health and safety policy as it affects all employees under his direct control;
(b)  monitor the implementation of the company policy in the Works and Sites;
(c)  develop and maintain realistic accident-control indices on a uniform basis and in line with company policy for monitoring and controlling performance at all levels and for the setting of Works/Sites accident-control objectives;
(d)  ensure provision and or availability of documents giving information and guidance on matters of health and safety including information on regulations and approved codes of practice as well as Company/Division/Works and Sites procedures and codes on health and safety;

*5.2   Departmental managers*   (Works Manager, Demolition Manager, Dismantling Managers and Contracts Managers, etc.)
Each Departmental Manager is responsible for the implementation of the health and safety policy in his department. In particular, he has to:
(a)  ensure that all his managers, supervisory staff and other employees are familiar with the health and safety policy, implement it and draw upon the established advisory services;
(b)  ensure that tenders take account of safe methods of work and suitable health and welfare facilities;
(c)  establish and maintain safe and healthy working conditions, procedures and systems of work;
(d)  determine at the planning stage of contracts as far as possible the most suitable plant, methods of working, lighting, known hazards, fire precautions, allocation of responsibilities, welfare and protective clothing;
(e)  ensure that contractors on the Works and subcontractors on Site projects are familiar with the health and safety policy and implement the procedures and arrangements necessary for ensuring the health and safety of their employees and other people. At the contract stage arrangements will be made to establish responsibility for the safety, health and welfare of all sub-contractors and a policy of co-ordination

between main contractors, sub-contractors and any other contractors working on the same site;

(f) ensure that induction and training programmes are established and maintained for all employees regarding health and safety and that specific job training in safe methods of work is carried out;

(g) ensure that accident control is integrated in the design and operation of new plant or equipment for his department and when methods are revised;

(h) make regular inspections of Works and Sites and take corrective action where required;

(i) set objectives annually within his department with the aim of improving health and safety at work and review performance against these objectives;

(j) establish joint consultative machinery to discuss health and safety matters and arrange for the training of joint committee members to help ensure that consultation is effective;

(k) approve all safe working procedures and ensure they are implemented by establishing a checking system at departmental supervisors level.

*5.3 Departmental supervisors* – Works (superintendents, and other supervisory staff)

The responsibility of each Supervisor within his area of control includes the following:

(a) implementing the policy,

(b) participating in the formulation of and ensuring that safe and healthy procedures are laid down, understood and implemented;

(c) providing personal protective clothing/equipment where required and taking steps to see their operatives fulfil their obligations to use it;

(d) the job induction of new starters;

(e) the inspection of means of access and places of work to ensure that safe conditions prevail;

(f) correcting defects within his capability and reporting those which require specialist attention;

(g) investigation and reporting of accidents and taking action to prevent recurrence;

(h) taking action to prevent the repetition of accidents arising from similar causes;

(i) ensuring that the appropriate statutory requirements are implemented;

(j) ensuring that mechanically operated plant is free from patent defect, mechanically sound and the operator is competent;

(k) bringing to the notice of all employees:

   (i) that they must take reasonable care for their own health and safety and those of any other person who may by affected by their work;

   (ii) that they must not intentionally or recklessly interfere with or misuse anything provided in the interests of health, safety and welfare; and

(iii) that they must report at once any defects in plant or equipment and unsafe conditions or put the matter right, if this is possible, without endangering themselves.

*5.4   Other managers and supervisors – Sites* (including Project/Asst., Project/Area managers/agents/engineers/general foremen and other supervisory site staff). The person in charge of the site is responsible for implementing the health and safety policy. His supporting supervisory staff must ensure that it is implemented in the areas or operations under their direct control. In particular each Manager and Supervisor is required to:

(a) ensure all employees are familiar with the health and safety policy, implement it and draw upon the advisory services on health and safety which have been established in the company;

(b) ensure that safe and healthy procedures are followed;

(c) ensure that job induction and training of all employees in safe methods of work is carried out;

(d) ensure joint consultative machinery is established to discuss health and safety matters and to arrange for the training of joint committee members to help ensure that consultation is effective;

(e) implement within the company's area of responsibility the specific accident-prevention arrangements made at the contract stage with sub-contractors and other contractors working on the same site/premises. While each contractor has the primary responsibility for the health and safety of his own employees, sub-contractors must be made familiar with the health and safety policy and implement the procedures and arrangements necessary for ensuring the health and safety of their employees and other people. There must be close liaison to ensure that they work to statutory requirements;

(f) ensure that sufficient protective clothing/equipment/devices are available and used when necessary. Set a personal example by using these when necessary;

(g) satisfy himself, so far as reasonably practicable, that mechanically operated plant is free from patent defect and mechanically sound and that copies of the current test certificates and thorough examination reports are examined and retained before the item of plant is used;

(h) verify that the operator of plant, hired or otherwise, has been thoroughly trained and is competent and experienced to drive the item of plant to which he is to be allocated;

(i) ensure that crane-makers' operating manuals are on site for each crane, hired or otherwise, and that supervisors in charge of crane operations and the operator are conversant with the main features relating to safe use, including its limitations and the effect of ground conditions/slopes on its safe working loads;

(j) ensure that the Construction Regulations and other statutory requirements are observed on site. That all registers, records and reports are in order and that the 'competent person' appointed has sufficient knowledge of plant and machinery to evaluate all aspects of its safe operation;

(k) ensure that all sites are left in a safe condition to eliminate as far as is reasonably practicable, risk to the general public, particularly children;

(l) ensure that all machinery and plant at the end of the day cannot be started by unauthorized persons;

(m) regularly inspect means of access and places of work to ensure that safe conditions prevail.

(n) correct defects within his capability and report those which require specialist attention;

(o) investigate, complete reports of accidents and take action to prevent recurrence;

(p) bring to the notice of those employees for whom he is responsible:
  (i) that they must take reasonable care for their own health and safety and those of any other person who may be affected by their work;
  (ii) that they must not intentionally or recklessly interfere with or misuse anything provided in the interests of health, safety and welfare; and
  (iii) that they must report at once any defects in plant or equipment and unsafe conditions or put the latter right, if this is possible, without endangering themselves.

6.  *Functional managers*
Where appropriate, other functional managers will have responsibility for the implementation of the company's health and safety policy as it affects all employees within their departments and for its incorporation into any programmes or objectives for which they are responsible.

7.  (a) *Health and safety advisory and emergency services – Works*
The company has medical and safety specialist facilities and also draws on the services of the regional medical officers and industrial hygienists. The task of these services is to advise both management and other employees on health and safety matters. However, as line management are responsible for the health and safety of those under their control employees should always discuss health and safety matters with their immediate supervisor in the first instance.

Fire-fighting, ambulance and emergency services are available. Works management will have effective liaison with these local authority, fire, ambulance and police services to call upon their resources if necessary.

The fire and ambulance emergency telephone number should be available and conspicuous instructions posted of the action to be taken in the event of an emergency.

The location and telephone numbers of the medical and safety staff are given in the Works telephone directory or posted in conspicuous locations for easy reference.

(*b*) *Health and safety advisory and emergency services – Sites*
First-aid boxes and fire-fighting appliances should be available on all Sites. The location and services available will be publicized on Site.

Part 2: Arrangements for implementing the policy

The hazards associated with the company's operations are those normally encountered in the operations which form the company's business, for example:

- Handling, transportation of material by cranes, stacking and the associated slinging operations.
- Storage and use of highly flammable substances.
- Chipping, cutting etc. of material.
- Falling objects.
- Misuse of mobile cranes.
- Unsuitable means of access.

The aim is to eliminate, control or guard against such hazards. This can only be achieved by management at all levels having total commitment to its preparation and implementation and a workforce that is equally committed to following it at all times.

The following pages give a good indication of the arrangements made to eliminate, control or guard against such hazards.

1. *Planning and design of plant and equipment*
   If plant is designed with health and safety uppermost in the minds of the designers, the chances of its unsafe operation are greatly reduced. It is the company policy to use all available resources including technical, safety medical and plant operators, to ensure this ideal is achieved, and thereby avoid building in potential risks to health and safety.

   Similarly, management is responsible for the establishment of continuing inspections of all plant and equipment to ensure it is maintained in a safe and proper state.

2. *Safe working procedures*
   Experience has shown that many accidents are caused by a lack of safe working procedures or non-adherence to an established procedure.

   As such, the safe way of carrying out all jobs within the Works and Sites will be analysed. They will identify the hazards inherent to or associated with the work performed and set out to eliminate or minimize these hazards. The procedures may take the form of an overall Company/

Branch/Works/Sites policy – e.g. safe working procedures for the mainte-nance of cranes or an individual occupation in a particular department.

Management must co-ordinate and instruct employees in their use, and employees must follow the rules at all times. Action will be forthcominng on any employees not adhering to the correct procedures.

Any change in practice will result in the revision of the safe working procedure.

3. *Training and information on health and safety*
An essential part of the company programme for health and safety is train-ing of all employees so that they can recognize the hazards and know the safe working methods and the precautions to take, enabling them to work safely. This training will be given in off-the-job courses run in conjunction with the Training Department at the various training centres or on the job by line management assisted by safety, medical and training staff as re-quired. Suitable courses will continue to be arranged with the co-operation of the medical, training safety services.

In addition to training for the job, from time to time it may be neces-sary to provide information on new developments in health and safety de-tails of new health and safety legislation; the findings of research into par-ticular types of work are examples. This information will be provided to employees affected through the normal joint consultative channels, notice boards, as well as through the day-to-day communication between man-agement, staff, shop floor workers and site personnel.

4. *Instruction and supervision*
Each employee and new recruit will be given instructions as to the health and safety risks that may be associated with the job he has to do and he will be instructed in the safe working methods and procedures to follow to ensure the health and safety of himself and others.

On particular sites, for example on a client's Works where continuous production processes are being undertaken, employees and new recruits are to be advised of the hazards in their working area and the steps that have and must be taken to ensure their health and safety.

The various processes and operations that are undertaken in the Works and on sites will be supervised by the Management with the co-operation of all other employees so that any risks to health and safety are eliminated or controlled.

On appointment, all supervisory staff shall, before commencing their normal work, or in extenuating circumstances as soon as possible there-after, spend such time as is necessary with the appropriate safety adviser who will instruct them on their responsibilities and on statutory and com-pany requirements with regard to safety.

5. *Accident reporting and investigation*
The measures taken to ensure health and safety at work do not completely

233

eliminate every hazard and prevent all accidents and injuries. Accidents that do occur, whether or not they cause injury, need to be investigated to establish the causes so that action can be taken to prevent a recurrence. Injured persons must always obtain medical treatment. Having been treated at the nearest surgery a copy of a brief report on the injury is made out by the injured person's foreman who in turn should investigate the accident.

When treatment is obtained on a site the injury and treatment must be recorded in the appropriate register and reported by the injured person to his supervisor who has to investigate the accident.

The Foreman/Supervisor must take immediate action where possible to prevent a recurrence and report the details on the appropriate form without delay.

Accident investigations are not witch hunts; they are carried out so that both management and employees can take action to prevent further accidents. Employees are instructed in the interest of their own and other people's health and safety to report accidents and hazardous situations to their management.

6. *Joint Consultation*

(i) *Joint Health and Safety Advisory committees* A joint Health and Safety Advisory Committee will function at each works of the company. It will be jointly representative of the management and trade unions representing persons employed in the Works. As far as possible meetings will be held on a monthly basis and chaired by a member of senior management. The same procedure will apply on Sites wherever it is practicable to do so.

Committees, essentially advisory in character, will keep under review all matters affecting the health and safety of persons employed and endeavour to promote safer working conditions and adherence to the company's health and safety policy within the Works or Site.

Where, on Sites, items discussed for attention may not be specific to company employees but general to other contractors, such items will be referred by the management to the client. In its proceedings such a committee will not infringe the normal negotiating procedures.

To help make these joint consultative committees as effective as possible all members of such committees will attend a training course on joint consultation with special reference to health and safety.

(ii) *Safety representatives* Safety representatives will be appointed from the workforce. A person appointed as a Safety Representative will serve for a period but may be reappointed for further terms.

Each Safety Representative will be responsible for discussing any health and safety matters relevant to the section of a department he covers with the appropriate management or with the Safety Adviser or

Medical Department. He may refer unresolved matters to the Joint Health and Safety Advisory Committee.

(*iii*) *Informal consultation* Informal consultation between management and employees on a day-to-day basis is an essential part of the arrangements for ensuring health and safety. Many of the health and safety matters can and must be dealt with through this more immediate and personal involvement by those people affected. All employees are encouraged to discuss fully health and safety matters appertaining to their work and workplace with their supervisors, managers, safety advisers and medical staff as appropriate.

7. *Routine works/Sites inspections*
   Routine inspections will be carried out by members of Works/Site management and the workers' Safety Representative to a predetermined programme.

8. *Identification and rectification of hazards*
   Hazards observed during routine inspections, day-to-day surveillance or as reported by employees will be recorded and their rectification put in hand and progressed on a systematic basis by Works/Site management.

9. *Protective clothing/equipment/devices*
   To safeguard all employees from injury or hazard the protective clothing provided must be worn and equipment and devices used as necessary to provide maximum protection and, where appropriate, in order to conform to statutory requirements.

10. *Health and safety contacts*
    It is the responsibility of all managers and supervisors to maintain an effective contact with employees under their direct control. Essentially, this must ensure that the correct methods are being followed, protective equipment is being worn and all employees are continually aware of the ongoing need to comply with the overall health and safety programme.

11. *Housekeeping*
    It is the responsibility of all employees to maintain a high standard of housekeeping throughout the workplace. In addition, there are housekeeping inspections at intervals throughout the year, and management will establish routine inspections in all departments.

12. *Information*
    The company requires each Branch/Works/Site to provide adequate information to all employees on all relevant health and safety matters through joint consultation, informal discussions, use of notice boards,

235

issuing of minutes, safe working procedures, safety rules, publicity campaigns, films, etc.

Specific requirements

In addition to the responsibilities listed previously for general managers and their need for supervision of this document the following specific requirements apply:

1. *Central plant organization – General Manager and supervision*
   (a) Ensure that all its plant sent to Sites is safe and fully efficient, is guarded and equipped with agreed safety devices and examined and tested in accordance with the Construction Regulations.
   (b) Ensure that all repair maintenance work required and carried out on the plant is done in a proper manner, and that emergency repairs are dealt with properly and expeditiously.
   (c) When plant, either belonging to Central Plant Organization (CPO) or a plant hire firm, is damaged or contributory to personal injury or dangerous occurrence, assist in establishing the root cause, whether mechanical or operator failure, etc. Advise on the remedial action required, carry out repairs in respect of hired plant and check that these have been carried out and, after test, pronounce it in safe working order before re-use.
   (d) Assist with the arrangements for training supervisors and operators in basic and detailed safe use of plant.
   (d) Introduce and maintain a disciplinary procedure on plant hire firms who fail to supply or maintain, in a safe and efficient condition, plant on hire to the company or in the event of their supplying incompetent operators.

2. *Building services – General Manager and supervision*
   While not having extensive duties as an employer, building services have all the duties of a main contractor in control of premises, which involve ensuring that the premises are safe and co-ordinating the activities of subcontractors. This entails safety meetings of all contractors' representatives and ensuring that contractural documentation stipulates adherence to company rules, Standing Instructions, guidance, codes of practice, Health and Safety at Work Act and other statutory requirements and to the health and safety policy of the company.

In the undernoted smaller Branch/Works where the management/supervisory structure differs from that of the larger Works the following will apply:

3. *Senior line managers (financial and administrative, production/technical/contracts/and commercial managers):*

(a) have the responsibilities outlined in sections 4 and 5.2 in Part 1;

(b) because the number of employees engaged is small and the duration of work on any Site is short managers will have collective representation on the Works Joint Health and Safety Advisory Committee.

4. *Works and workshop managers*

A Works Manager has the responsibilities outlined in Section 4 in Part 1.

A Workshop Manager has the responsibilities outlined in Section 5.2 in Part 1.

The names of all company accident-prevention managers, safety officers and safety advisers must be detailed in an appendix to the Policy.

All safety equipment must be listed, its issue recorded and a signature obtained for its issue.

All employees should sign that they have read and understand the company's policy for health and safety.

# Specimen specification for demolition

THE
## NATIONAL FEDERATION OF DEMOLITION CONTRACTORS
(Limited by Guarantee)

# SPECIFICATION FOR DEMOLITION AND ASSOCIATED WORKS IN THE CLEARANCE OF EXISTING BUILDINGS AND STRUCTURES

SECRETARY
NATIONAL FEDERATION OF DEMOLITION CONTRACTORS
COWDRAY HOUSE
PORTUGAL STREET
LONDON
WC2A 2HH

Copyright

Issued 1976

Introduction

The following specification for demolition and associated works has been produced to meet an expressed need, and in order that this document should be most widely applicable it is recommended that the National Federation of Demolition Contractors own Form of Direct Contract be used in the contract that will follow tendering.

The accompanying practice notes which are designed to complement the clauses and conditions of the specification combine by way of explanation and reference to Acts of Parliament, existing Law, Codes of Practice and the general conditions of the Form of Direct Contract issued by the National Federation of Demolition Contractors to provide the background and substance required to produce a specification which will clearly define the areas of responsibility, the code of conduct in executing the works and the true extent of the contract operation.

The specification appears on the right-hand side on the numbered pages of this document with practice notes and references placed on the left-hand side in juxtaposition with the specification items to which they refer.

September, 1976.

Drafting committee

R. E. Willment.    M.A., M.I.C.E., F.I.D.E.    (Chairman)
W. F. Brand.       B.Sc., F.I.D.E.
S. L. Hunt.        F.F.B., F.R.S.A.
R. W. Walker.

. . . .

The Employer (principal party to the contract) or his professional representative will enter the full name, or corporate title and address of the Employer and indicate also the same relevant details for the professional advisers who will represent the interests of the Employer in the execution of the works.

1.00   The Employer should give the postal address of the property to be demolished and supply a plan clearly defining the boundaries.

2.00   No two demolition sites are identical and if the text of this section of the specification, together with any further revisions or amendments does not convey a true and accurate account of the expected works a completely new section should be written which will leave no room for doubt in the parties' minds as to the full extent of the works.

The following subject headings are offered as guidance.

(a) Brief details of construction of building(s) to be demolished.
(b) Demarcation lines.
(c) Outbuildings.
(d) Boundary walls and fences.
(e) Retaining walls.
(f) Hardstandings and pavings.
(g) Trees and shrubs.
(h) Part wall works (weather-proofing, etc.).
(j) Shoring – permanent (whether tubular scaffold or timber).
(k) Hoarding – permanent (detailed specification required – gates, etc.).
(l) Final site levels (it is important that the Employer specifies clearly the levels to which the buildings are to be demolished, including any external walls retained as boundaries).
(m) Treatment of wells.
(n) Alternative means of escape for adjoiners in the event of fire.

3.00

3.01   The keys should be made available for collection and the site of works accessible for inspection for the whole period up to the date of submission of tender to allow for tenderers other commitments.

3.02   (a) The Employer to notify the existence of public service and other installations (Contract Condition 2c).

(b) It is the duty of the Employer 'to give to persons (not being his employees) who may be affected by the way in which he conducts his undertaking the prescribed information about such aspects of the way in which he conducts his undertaking as might affect their health or safety'.

(c) Where the Employer is aware of asbestos, and most particularly, blue asbestos (crocidolite) existing within the structures which is not readily apparent to the Contractor as he inspects the premises, he should notify the facts to the Contractor at enquiry stage to allow the Contractor to include in his estimate the costs he will encounter in the special tasks necessary to dispose of the material according to the requirements of the Asbestos Regulations 1969.

(d) In circumstances where neither party could have foreseen the presence of asbestos and the Contractor is required to carry out its removal, the costs incurred in neutralizing the material, carting off site and disposing of it at a registered tip, including any incidental costs and/or expenses resulting from delay, to be valued by the Contractor, including his overheads and profit, and allowed as an addition to the contract sum.

| | | |
|---|---|---|
| *Preambles* | | Employer ........................................................................................ |
| | | ................................................................................................ |
| | | ................................................................................................ |
| | | ................................................................................................ |
| | | ................................................................................................ |
| | | ................................................................................................ |
| | | 19...... |

*Description of the works*

.1.00 The works included in this specification comprise the demolition and clearance of the properties known as ..........................................................

.................................................................................................

............ as clearly detailed on the accompanying sketch plan of the site and defined herein.

*Scope of the works*

2.00 The buildings must be taken down to the level of the upper side of the respective existing ground floor slabs unless otherwise specified, and the whole of the materials arising from the demolition work must be removed from site. The aforesaid subject to the following revisions, or exclusions.

(a) ..........................................................................................

.............................................................................................

(b) ..........................................................................................

.............................................................................................

(c) ..........................................................................................

.............................................................................................

(d) ..........................................................................................

.............................................................................................

(e) ..........................................................................................

.............................................................................................

(f) ..........................................................................................

.............................................................................................

*Inspection of the site*

3.00 The site of the works at ....................................................................
can be viewed at any time between ............................... and
.......................: by appointment made with ...................................
............................ Telephone No: ...............................

*Keys for Access*

3.01 The keys to the property are in the hands of ..............................................
............................ Telephone No: ...............................
to whom application should be made.

*Contractor to inspect*

3.02 The Contractor shall examine the drawings and inspect the site and its surroundings and shall be deemed to have made himself thoroughly acquainted with the conditions under which he will work, the nature of the construction of the buildings, all local and existing conditions, means of access, parking and unloading regulations, working and storage space, facilities generally, and all other matters which might affect his tender as no claim for additional payment on the grounds of lack of knowledge will be entertained.

4.00 The drawings, which should form part of the contract will clearly convey the true boundaries of the demolition works, any further areas available for use by the Contractor and should accurately define the line of cut where buildings are severed from other structures, or parts of the structure. The drawings should also indicate, where necessary the following:

(a) Line for erection of permanent hoarding.

(b) Identification of walls to remain as boundaries.

(c) Wells for treatment, or protection.

(d) Trees to be preserved.

(e) Public Utilities or other services or installations within the site or closely affected by the works.

5.00  (a) The Employer's responsibilities written into the Conditions of the Form of Direct Contract include:

2(b) Make the site available.

2(c) Report Public Service and other installations.

4(c) Allow reasonable extension for varied work.

5(a) Instruct expenditure of provisional sums.

8    Give all notices, etc.

9    Accept completed works.

10   Damage by trespassers.

11   Costs arising from delay.

16   Loss or damage caused by the Employer, or third parties.

17   Cost of shoring, or other works not included in the contract sum.

18 Accommodation for storage of materials retained by Employer.

20 Payments.

21 Retention money.

22 Loss or damage by fire, or otherwise, not due to the Contractor's negligence.

23 Indemnities.

24 Insurance.

25 /

26 Determination.

27 Arbitration.

28 Fluctuations.

(Form of Direct Contract).

(b) The estimate will be fixed price, valid for six months, subsequent to which fluctuations will apply (Contract Condition 28).

(c) Where the scope of works and the value of credits would suggest a payment, or offer, by the Contractor the specification should describe the method of settlement.

5.01  (a) The provision of a firm date of possession will allow the Contractor to take proper account of fluctuations in price of labour and materials, etc. thus to present an estimate reflecting true costs at the time of execution of the works (Agreement – Clause 4).

(b) The Employer will establish the limits of indemnity in respect of the liabilities of the Contractor to allow the Contractor to assess the cost of premium to be included in his estimate.

5.02 Dayworks required to be executed during periods out of normal hour working will merit supplementary payments to recover non-productive overtime costs, etc. or calculated at premium rates as laid down in the Schedule of Daywork Charges produced by the National Federation of Demolition Contractors.

| | | |
|---|---|---|
| *Drawings* | 4.00 | The following separate drawings will accompany this specification and are issued to assist the Contractor in preparing his tender. |

*No.*                             *Title*

..............................................    ..............................................

..............................................    ..............................................

..............................................    ..............................................

..............................................    ..............................................

..............................................    ..............................................

| | | |
|---|---|---|
| *Contract Particulars* | 5.00 | The form of contract will be the Agreement and Conditions of the Form of Direct Contract (revised 1974) issued by the National Federation of Demolition Contractors. |
| *The agreement* | 5.01 | The Agreement to be signed by the parties to the contract will be completed as follows: |

Clause 4. Date for possession.

..........................................................................................................

Clause 5. Date for completion.

..........................................................................................................

Clause 6. (1) Liquidated and Ascertained Damages.

..........................................................................................................

             (2) Early completion bonus (*a*

..........................................................................................................

Clause 7. (1) Insurance under Condition 24 in the sum of:

..............................................................................(Employers)

             (2) Insurance under Condition 24 in the sum of:

..............................................................................(Contractors)

| | | |
|---|---|---|
| *Daywork* | 5.02 | Where the Employer issues an instruction requiring a variation which is not of a similar character, or executed under similar conditions to the work as aforesaid and where the work cannot properly be measured and valued, the Contractor shall be allowed payment on daywork basis at the following rates founded on the guide lines set out in the National Federation of Demolition Contractors Schedule of Daywork Charges current as date of tender. |

   (a) *Labour*                        *Rate per hour* (*normal time*)

Foreman.                  ..........................................

Topman.                    ..........................................

Mattockman.             ..........................................

Cleaner, Sorter, Improver.    ..........................................

General Labourer.          ..........................................

..........................................    ..........................................

..........................................    ..........................................

   (b) *Materials*
       – as defined, plus addition for
         profit.                  ...............................................%

   (c) *Plant*
       – as defined, plust addition for
         profit.                  ...............................................%

6.00    (a) Where the Employer has prior knowledge of arrangements which will confine elements of the Contractors working to periods outside normal working hours, whether by party wall awards or as a result of negotiation, he should apprise the Contractor of the facts at estimating stage (Contract Condition 3c).

    (b) Immediately the Contractor is given possession of the site he shall thereupon begin the works forthwith and regularly and diligently proceed with the same and shall complete the works within the stated period, subject to the provisions laid down in the contract regarding reasonable extension of time for delay, as defined (Contract Condition 3).

    (c) The Control of Pollution Act 1974 does not set the standards of acceptable noise levels. This is established by Local Authorities in the light of local needs, practical possibilities and existing ambient noise levels. The Employer should take the initiative prior to tender by obtaining from the local council the consent required under the Act. The Contractor, who will be working within the limitations set by the Code of Practice, BS 5228 will thereby be in a position to base his price on acceptable work methods and plant, determined by the consent which should accompany the tender enquiry.

6.01    The Code of Practice formulates the discipline to which demolition must conform if it is to be carried out with safety and to a proper standard of workmanship.

6.02    (a) Under the terms of the Conditions of Contract the Employer warrants to give proper notice to the relevant authorities and to pay any fees or charges payable by law in respect of works or service disconnections or, in the absence of such arrangement to reimburse the Contractor as an addition to the contract sum (Contract Condition 8).

    (b) When the Law of Scotland varies from English Law, the Law of Scotland shall be deemed to apply to this contract. Technical terms of English Law which are used in the contract documents shall be construed according to their nearest equivalent in the Law of Scotland, and where any reference is made to any statutory enactment which does not extend to Scotland, it shall be read as a reference to the corresponding provision (if any) in any statutory enactment relating to Scotland.

6.03    The Employer will insure against his own liabilities for loss or damage, etc. according to the terms of the Conditions of Contract (Contract Conditions 22, 23 and 24).

6.04    The Contractor's work will be limited to sealing off the sewer or drain within the confines of the site (Public Health Act 1961 – Section 29 and also Contract Condition 8).

6.05    Permanent shoring, if required by the Employer to be left on completion of the works is to be measured separately and valued at the rate given by the Contractor in the appropriate item of the Schedule of Prices and Rates (Contract Condition 17).

6.06    The Contractor will obtain all necessary licences from the local authority, pay deposits, or fees, and meet subsequent costs of remedial work (Contract Condition 14).

6.07    Where the necessary information is not available from the Employer, the Contractor will consult with the Public Utilities and other authorities to determine the location of services before excavation footpaths and forming crossovers (Contract Condition 2d).

| | | |
|---|---|---|
| *Workmanship* | 6.00 | Demolition is to be carried out in such a manner and at such times as to cause as little inconvenience as possible to either adjoining owners, occupiers, the public or the Employer. Rubbish is to be sprinkled with water to minimize the risk of dust rising and suitable precautions are to be taken to avoid unnecessary noise and vibration. The Contractor will follow the recommendations of the Code of Practice, BS 5228–Noise Control on Construction and Demolition Sites. |
| *Code of practice* | 6.01 | The Contractor is to carry out the works of demolition and site clearance in accordance with the recommendation of the British Standard Code of Practice (CP94) 1971, incorporating amendments. |
| *Statutory requirements, regulations, etc.* | 6.02 | The Contractor is to comply with all relevant Acts, by-laws, regulations, instruments and Codes of Practice relating to demolition and the consequential works. |
| *Damage and reinstatement* | 6.03 | All demolition, as hereinafter described, is to be carried out without damage to the adjoining properties and if such damage occurs in the carrying out of the works due to the Contractor's negligence the Contractor shall make good at his own expense. |
| *Drains* | 6.04 | The Contractor shall search for and disconnect at the limit of the site, all disused drain connections which shall be sealed in a proper manner. |
| *Temporary works* | 6.05 | It will be the Contractor's responsibility to provide, erect and maintain during the progress of the works, all necessary temporary shoring, propping, etc. |
| *Temporary roads, etc.* | 6.06 | The Contractor is to provide, maintain and alter from time to time as may be required all necessary temporary roadways, crossings, gantries, etc. for access to the site, and for the works, and shall clear away when no longer required and make good all works disturbed and pay all charges. |
| *Footpaths* | 6.07 | The Contractor will be responsible and is to include in his tender for upholding the adjoining roads and footpaths, etc. with the mains and services thereunder immediately he takes possession of the site and until completion of the contract and he is to hold the Employer indemnified against all and every claim which may be brought against him for loss and/or damage of any description which may be caused to the adjacent roads and footpaths with the mains and services thereunder by reason of the negligence of the Contractor. |

6.08    (a) Permanent hoardings, if required by the Employer to be left on site at completion of the works, are to be measured separately and valued at top rates given by the Contractor in the appropriate item of the Schedule of Prices and Rates.

    (b) Where licences exist for permanent works left on completion, the cost of deposits rendered to the local authority to be met by the Employer and recovered by him on removal of the structure.

6.09    (a) The extent of these works would be varied by the 'Scope of Works' as in the instance of vault filling, packing of voids, filling basement areas, etc.

    (b) Where the occupants quit the property, to which this specification refers at a date subsequent to inspection by the Contractor and inordinate amounts of debris are left on site by them, the Contractor will be entitled to have this valued as an addition should he be required to remove it.

7.00

7.01    (a) Where the Employer is himself an employer in the construction industry, within the meaning of the Act, he will require the Contractor who is to execute the demolition works, prior to signing the contract, to satisfy the Employer that he is either a Limited Company, or has a Certificate of Exemption from the Inland Revenue. In turn, the Contractor will have a like duty to satisfy himself as to the exemption status of his sub-contractor (Finance Act 1971, sections 29–31 and Schedule 5).

    (b) The Contractor shall keep a competent foreman on the site at all times during working hours (Contract Condition 2a).

7.02    (a) The Contractor and his sub-contractors would be liable for and be deemed to be properly covered by policies of insurance for claims under the Fatal Accident Act, National Insurance Act 1946 (Industrial Injuries), Workmen's Compensation Act and insurance acts or statutes including any liability at Common Law within the framework of the relevant clauses of the Conditions of Contract (Contract Condition 23 and 24).

    (b) The Employer's attention is drawn to his responsibility to indemnify the Contractor and arrange suitable insurance to cover his liability under the contract (Contract Condition 22–24).

| | | |
|---|---|---|
| *Protection*<br>*of works*<br>*and persons* | 6.08 | The order of the work will be at the Contractor's discretion but he is to ensure that all measures for the protection of the public and adjoining owners and occupiers by way of fans, temporary hoardings, barriers, footways, etc. have been erected before any major demolition works commence and he shall obtain the required consents and pay all fees and charges in connection therewith. |
| *Clearing*<br>*up* | 6.09 | The Contractor shall remove all rubbish, materials arising from the demolitions and incidental works, leave existing cellars, inspection pits, manholes, and basements, etc. free and completely clear and the whole of the site clean and tidy on completion to the satisfaction of the Employer. |
| *Generally* | 7.00 | The Contractor is to allow in his estimate such sum as he considers necessary to comply with the various clauses of the Conditions of Contract. |
| *Contractors*<br>*obligations* | 7.01 | The Contractors estimate shall include for his obligations hereunder stated: |

(a) All costs of labour, including National Insurance, pensions, holidays, rates of wages and other emoluments and expenses payable by the Contractor in accordance with the rules, decisions and agreements laid down by the Demolition Industry Conciliation Board, and by relevant Acts of Parliament.

(b) All safety, health and welfare measures and amenities, as laid down in current Regulations where applicable to this contract and shall maintain all safety measures and provide suitable and adequate temporary mess, shelter and sanitary accommodation and first aid equipment as required during the progress of the works and clear away and make good all work disturbed on completion.

(c) All necessary access and protective scaffolds, fans, gantries, screens, etc. for the proper protection and security of the works and of the public, the adjoining owners and the Employer and the Contractor will be held responsible for the design, erection and safety of them.

(d) All necessary temporary lighting and power for the works, water for welfare facilities, and for use in operations to minimize the spread of dust, plant, tools, vehicles and haulage, necessary for the proper execution of the works.

(e) All the necessary steps to ensure the security of the site including watching, lighting, and safeguarding of the works, protection of property and persons.

| | | |
|---|---|---|
| *Indemnities*<br>*and*<br>*insurance* | 7.02 | (a) The Contractor shall be required to maintain the necessary insurances to meet his obligations under the relevant clauses of the Contract Conditions. He shall be liable for and shall indemnify the Employer against any expense, liability, loss, claim or proceeding in respect of personal injury or death, injury or damage to any property real or personal in so far as such injury, death or damage arises out of or in the course of, or by reason of the carrying out of the works, and provided always that the same is due to any negligence, omission or default of the Contractor, his servant or agents or of his sub-contractor, his servants or agents. When called upon, the Contractor shall produce for inspection, documentary evidence that the required insurances are properly maintained. |

(b) Should the Contractor, or his sub-contractor, make default in insuring or in continuing or in causing to insure as required, the Employer may himself insure against any risk with respect to which the default shall have occurred and may deduct a sum or sums equivalent to the amount paid or payable in respect of premiums from any money due or to become due to the Contractor.

7.03

7.04 The refundable cost of overtime working sanctioned by the Employer will be as laid down in the Demolition Industry Conciliation Board's working rule agreement, with special reference to hours constituting the normal working week and premium hours for overtime working. In addition, the Contractor is entitled to reimbursement of the extra expense in labour on-costs for Employers Liability and Public Liability insurances, abnormal travelling expenses, etc.

7.05

7.06 The Employer's rights will be restricted by reason of safety and he will defer to the Contractor in aspects governing his well-being on site. (Health and Safety at Work etc. Act 1974).

8.00  (a) Unless otherwise stated, the whole of the resulting materials, debris, etc., will become the Contractor's property and will be taken off site by him. The Employer should specify in detail which materials he intends to retain for his own use if the removal of his materials is intended to take place at some time after inspection of the site by the Contractor at time of tender. This will prevent misunderstandings in regard to the Contractor's estimate of credits taken into his reckoning in arriving at the net cost of the contract works (Contract Condition 12(a)i).

(b) Articles of archaeological interest which may be found on site are to be handed over to the Employer (Contract Condition 12(a)ii).

8.01

8.02 In addition to the ancillary site works listed under specification item 8.02, the Employer may find it necessary to seek prices, or establish provisional or prime cost sums for one or more of the following categories which he cannot properly quantify at time of tender.
(a) Remedial work to party walls.
(b) Bricking-in openings.
(c) Filling vaults.
(d) Providing alternative means of eascape for adjoiners in the event of fire.
(e) Work by specialists (e.g. removal of transformers by Electricity Authority, etc.)

| | | |
|---|---|---|
| *Workmen* | 7.03 | The Contractor is to confine his workmen to the actual site of the works. If the contract demands that workmen must enter upon adjoining property the necessary permission must first be obtained by the Contractor. |
| *Overtime working* | 7.04 | No overtime will be paid for unless specifically ordered in writing by the Employer or his authorized representative. Where so ordered, the net difference between plain time and overtime rates will be refunded to the Contractor only on the time worked in excess of normal working week allowed for in the tender. The Contractor will be required to submit for approval, time sheets or similar records to verify the additional payment. |
| *Advertising* | 7.05 | Advertising rights on hoardings will be reserved to the Employer but the Contractor will be permitted to erect name boards in reasonably prominent positions. |
| *Access to authorized persons* | 7.06 | The Employer and his authorized representative are to have free access to the site at all times during the progress of the works. |
| *Schedule of prices and rates* | 8.00 | The Contractor is to allow in his prices for the cost of demolition, the value of credits derived from the materials which will accrue to him and include for removing from site all rubbish and debris, etc. resulting from the demolition works. He shall include also any costs, fees, charges or other expense stated, or implied by the requirements of the specification. |

*Demolitions*   8.01   Demolition of ..................................................................................
including clearance of materials,
etc. as specified.                                                                £.
*Less* value of credits derived
from the works, which become
the Contractor's property.                                                  £.
Net cost of contract works.                                       _____

*Ancillary works, etc.*   8.02   Ancillary site works (all provisional).
(a) Permanent hoardings – as
      specified (Spec. 2.00k)
      .................... metres @ ......... metre            £.
(b) Hoarding gates – as specified.
      (Spec. 2.00k)
      .................... No. (single/double leaf)
      @ ............................ each.                           £.
(c) Permanent shoring – as specified
      (Spec. 2.00j)
      .................... metre 3 @ .................... metre 3     £.
(d) Weatherproofing – as specified
      (Spec. 2.00h)

(e) ................................................................................

      ................................................................................

(f) ................................................................................

      ................................................................................

*Provisional and contingency sums*   8.03   Contingencies – provisional sum.                            £.

CARRIED TO FORM OF TENDER £.
                                                          ═══════════

# FORM OF TENDER
Demolition and Site Works
at

.......................................

for

.......................................

To: ...................................

...................................

I/We the undersigned do hereby tender and undertake to provide all materials, labour, plant and implements of every description necessary for the proper demolition and completion of the works in strict conformity with the drawings and specification.

For the sum of ...............................................................

...............................................................£

which sum includes all provisional and contingency sums mentioned in the specification. (Exclusive of VAT)

I/We hereby undertake if this tender is accepted to complete the works within .............. weeks from commencement. Your written acceptance of our tender shall constitute a binding contract between us pending the preparation and execution of an agreement embodying the conditions and terms of the Form of Direct Contract.

As witness my/our hand(s) this ........................... day of ........................... 19..........

Signature ...............................................................

In the capacity of ...............................................................
Duly authorized to sign tenders on behalf of:

...............................................................

Address ...............................................................

...............................................................

Telephone Number ...............................................................
I/We understand that tenders are prepared at our own expense and the Employer is not bound to accept the lowest, or any tender.

# Specimen form of direct contract

THE

## NATIONAL FEDERATION OF DEMOLITION CONTRACTORS

(LIMITED BY GUARANTEE)

# FORM OF

# DIRECT CONTRACT

**COPYRIGHT**

ORIGINALLY ISSUED 1960
REVISED EDITION 1974

# THE NATIONAL FEDERATION OF DEMOLITION CONTRACTORS

## **FORM OF DIRECT CONTRACT**

𝕬𝖓 𝕬𝖌𝖗𝖊𝖊𝖒𝖊𝖓𝖙 made this                              day of                              19

BETWEEN ................................................................................................................................

of [whose registered office is at]................................................................................................

..................................................... in the County of..............................................(hereinafter

called "the Employer") of the one part and ............................................................................

of [whose registered office is at]................................................................................................

.........................................................................................................................(hereinafter

called "the Contractor") of the other part WHEREBY it is agreed as follows:—

NOTE:—
Delete in each
case what does
not apply.

1.  For the consideration hereinafter mentioned the Contractor will upon and subject to the Conditions annexed hereto undertake execute carry out and complete the Works shown in or on the [Enquiry] [Specification/s] [Schedule/s] [Plan/s] [Drawing/s] [Design/s] [Bill/s of Quantity] [the Work Specified in the [estimate] [tender] of the Contractor dated..........................................19..........] signed by or on behalf of the parties hereto for the purpose of identification.

2.  The Employer will by way of consideration pay to the Contractor the sum of................................ ...........................................................(£                              ) together with such additional monies (if any) as shall be payable hereunder at the times and in the manner specified in the Conditions annexed hereto

3.  The lands and other places available to the Contractor in connection with the Works shall be

..................................................................................................................................................

..................................................................................................................................................

..................................................................................................................................................

4.  The said lands and other places shall be handed over to the Contractor for commencement of the Works on..............................................................19.......... and the works shall be commenced [by Agreement] [on that date].

5.  The date for completion of the Works shall (subject as provided by the said Conditions) be the ...........................................................19.......... [as agreed]

6.  (1) If the Works shall not be completed by the time (including all proper extensions) required by this Contract (as affected by the due application of the said Conditions) it is hereby agreed that the damage suffered by the Employer by reason thereof shall be quantified at £........................................ [a day] [a week]

(2)   If and so far as the Works shall be completed prior to the time (including all proper extensions) required by this Contract (as affected by the due application of the said Conditions) it is hereby agreed that an "early completion bonus" of £................................................................................ per day shall be paid by the Employer to the Contractor in addition to all other sums payable hereunder.

7. (1)   The insurances to be obtained by the Employer under Condition 24 of the said Conditions shall be taken out and maintained in the sum of £................................................................................

(2)   The insurances to be obtained by the Contractor under the said Condition 24 shall be taken out and maintained in the sum of £................................................................................

8.   Condition 28 of the said Conditions shall be applied differentially on the footing that the Works are subdivided into the undermentioned Phases and that the work upon such Phases respectively is to commence on the dates shown opposite them.

[Works shown in Tender as Phase I]:   Phase I ...........................................................................................19...............
[Works shown in Tender as Phase II]:   Phase II...........................................................................................19...............

[Signed by] [The Common Seal of]
the above named Employer [was hereunto
affixed] in the presence of:—

[Signed by] [The Common Seal of]
the above named Contractor [was hereunto
affixed] in the presence of:—

NOTE:—(1) The above attestation clauses must be completed to meet the particular case.

(2) If the Employer is a Local Government Authority the Contract must be sealed by the Authority.

(3) Where the Contract is executed under seal it must be stamped 50p.

253

# CONDITIONS

### 1. Definitions

(*a*) In these Conditions the following expressions shall have the meanings assigned to them respectively below:—

    (i) "The Employer" shall mean the party of the first part and shall include any person for the time being appointed by the Employer to act as his duly appointed Agent for the purposes of the Contract.

    (ii) "The Contractor" shall mean the party of the second part.

    (iii) "The Contract" shall mean as well as this document all documents mentioned in Clause 1 above as signed by or on behalf of the parties.

    (iv) "The Contract sum" shall mean the amount mentioned in Clause 2 above.

    (v) "The Works" shall mean the works to be performed by the Contractor in accordance with the Contract.

    (vi) "The Site" shall mean the buildings or lands or other places allocated to the Contractor within the boundaries described in the Contract.

(*b*) The Contract sum is calculated upon the footing:—

    that no requirements as to working overtime or on night shifts are imposed by the Employer (except, if at all, as otherwise expressly stated in the Contract).

    Any such requirement by the Employer as aforesaid shall entitle the Contractor to such increment to the Contract Sum as shall be appropriate.

### 2. Execution of Works

(*a*) The Contractor shall provide everything necessary for the proper execution of the Works in accordance with the accepted trade practices of the Demolition Industry including supervision by a competent foreman and shall execute and complete the Works subject to and in accordance with the Contract to the reasonable satisfaction of the Employer.

(*b*) The Employer shall be solely responsible for the Site being and remaining available to the Contractor for the period requisite for the performance of the Contract.

(*c*) The Employer shall notify the Contractor of all public service and other installations upon, adjacent or subjacent to the site and of the exact location thereof and the safety of all such installations so notified shall be the responsibility of the Contractor. Damage to public service and other installations not so notified by the Employer occurring in the execution of the Works and not attributable to the negligence of the Contractor shall be at the risk of the Employer and the Contractor shall be entitled to be indemnified against all claims in respect thereof.

(*d*) The Contractor shall be entitled to add to the Contract sum and recover from the Employer the cost of meeting the reasonable requirements of all public service undertakings as to the execution or recovery of the cost of works for the protection and storage pending removal of equipment of theirs on the Site and for the proper sealing off diversion or severance upon or outside the Site of installations serving or passing over under or through the Site *PROVIDED* that no such addition shall be made hereunder for work expressly comprised in the Works or for expenses provided for under Condition 8.

### 3. Progress of Works and Completion

(*a*) The Works shall be commenced upon the date specified in the Contract or, if no date is specified, upon a date to be agreed in writing between the parties.

(*b*) The Works shall be executed diligently and be completed by the due date for completion specified in the Contract or, if no date is specified, within a reasonable time; subject in either case as undermentioned.

(*c*) The Contractor shall be entitled to such extensions of time for the performance of the Works as may be reasonable for any delay in the execution thereof not attributable to the default of the Contractor, howsoever caused.

### 4. Variations, Alterations, Additions and Omissions

(*a*) The Employer shall have power by notice in writing to order the Contractor to alter, amend, omit, add to or otherwise vary the Works provided that no such variation shall except with the consent of the Contractor be such as will together with any variations already ordered involve a nett decrease in the Contract sum.

(*b*) Except where the value of variations so ordered is expressly agreed between the parties the said value shall be determined by reference to the work involved.

(*c*) The provisions of these Conditions shall, *mutatis mutandis*, apply to all alterations, additions, omissions, or other variations ordered hereunder as they apply to the Works but, without prejudice to the generality of the foregoing, a reasonable additional time shall be allowed for all extra work authorised hereunder unless expressly otherwise agreed.

### 5. Provisional Sums and Sub-Contracts

(*a*) The Contractor shall not do any work in connection with any provisional sums set out in the Contract without instructions from the Employer but those instructions shall not be unreasonably withheld or delayed.

(*b*) The Contractor shall be entitled at his discretion to sub-contract any part or parts of the Works which in the opinion of the Contractor ought to be delegated to specialists.

### 6. Fair Wages

The Contractor shall in the execution of the Contract observe and perform the conditions of the Working Rule Agreement for the time being in force and issued by authority of the Demolition Industry Conciliation Board.

### 7. Construction Regulations [and Code of Practice]

The Contractor shall comply with the Construction Regulations currently in force as applicable to the Demolition Industry [and shall, so far as practicable, observe the recommendations of British Standard Code of Practice 94 (1971) as amended].

### 8. Local and Other Authorities' Notices and Fees

The Employer warrants and undertakes that he has or will in due time give all notices and comply with the requirements of any Acts of Parliament, Regulations and/or Bye-Laws of any Local Authority, National or Public Service Utility Company or Authority affected by the Works or from whose system any installations on the site will be disconnected and in particular that he has obtained every licence permission or authority required for the execution of the Works and that he will pay the fees or charges payable by law under such Acts Regulations and/or Bye-Laws in respect of the Works or any disconnections aforesaid or will reimburse the Contractor any amounts expended by the Contractor for any of such purposes as an addition to the consideration payable to the Contractor hereunder unless expressly allowed for in the Contract sum.

### 9. Fencing, Watching, Lighting and Protection of Works

(*a*) The Contractor shall as from the date upon which the Site is handed over to the Contractor and until the site shall be taken back by the Employer be responsible for and take reasonable and proper steps for protecting the Site and for providing and maintaining any necessary temporary fencing and barriers hoarding or fans for the safety of the Public. The Contractor shall notify the Employer in writing so soon as the Works have been completed and the site is ready to be taken back and the Employer shall within seven days of such notification formally take back the Site and shall in default of so doing be deemed to have taken the Site back at the expiration of the seven days.

(*b*) It is expressly declared and agreed that no liability for safety measures on the Site shall attach to the Contractor before the handing over of the Site to him or after handing back of the Site takes place or is deemed hereunder to take place and that the Contractor shall be entitled to indemnity by the Employer in respect of any claims arising directly or indirectly from alleged liability of the Contractor prior to the handing over of the Site to him or after handing back taking or being deemed to take place.

### 10. Trespass

The Contractor shall take all reasonable precautions to prevent trespass on the Site, but unless in default hereunder, shall be under no liability for and shall be indemnified by the Employer against all third party claims or claims by the Employer for damage by trespassers.

### 11. Precautions to Prevent Nuisance

The Contractor shall take reasonable precautions to prevent a nuisance or inconvenience to the owners tenants or occupiers of other properties and to the public generally. This provision shall not preclude the Contractor from carrying out the work in accordance with the accepted trade practices of the Demolition Industry and if for any reason he shall be precluded from or delayed in completing the Works in accordance with such practices any additional cost to the Contractor shall be borne by the Employer.

### 12. Ownership of Materials Recovered

(*a*) All materials severed from the Site by demolition or clearance shall become the property of the Contractor and shall be removed from the Site during the Contract period there being excepted from this provision:—

(i) all items required to be recovered for the Employer as specified in the Contract which excepted items unless otherwise provided by the Contract shall be left on the Site, and

(ii) any ancient relics discovered on the Site which shall be handed over by the Contractor to the Employer against the receipt of the Employer therefor.

(*b*) The Contractor shall be entitled to use materials recovered from the site other than those to be recovered for the Employer for temporary works.

### 13. Facilities for Other Works

The Contractor shall have sole control of the Site during the Contract period but will, without liability for the safety of such persons, by prior arrangement with the Employer allow reasonable facilities for the execution upon the Site by other persons of work not included in the Contract provided that the same shall not impede the progress of the Works, add to the cost thereof, be contrary to any regulations or be in the opinion of the Contractor prejudicial to the safety, health or welfare of such other persons.

### 14. Carting over Footway

Where the Contractor shall be responsible for the protection of any public footpaths and for making good any damage to such footpaths and for any expense incurred in reinstating the same he shall discharge the cost of such protection making good and reinstating.

### 15. Precautions against Fire Risks

(*a*) The Contractor shall take all reasonable precautions to prevent loss or damage from fire on the Site and to minimise the amount of any such loss or damage.

(*b*) The Contractor shall comply with any statutory regulations governing the storage or use of explosives petrol or other material brought on to the Site.

### 16. Damage to Plant and Material

The Contractor shall be responsible for all loss or damage to his own plant and tools brought on to the Site for the execution of the Works unless caused by the Employer or third parties on the Site at the request of the Employer or their respective servants or agents.

### 17. Damage to Adjoining Property

The Contractor shall take reasonable and proper precautions to avoid damage to any adjoining premises during the execution of the Works and where shoring and/or works to adjoining premises or the making good of the same is necessary in the opinion of the Contractor or the District Surveyor or other Local Authority such work shall if not expressly provided for in the Contract sum be carried out by the Contractor at the cost of the Employer at the agreed rates provided in the Contract and to the satisfaction of the Local Authority and/or District Surveyor and to the reasonable satisfaction of the Employer.

### 18. Provision of Storage Facilities

The Employer shall free of charge to the Contractor provide safe and proper accommodation on the site to the reasonable requirements of the Contractor for the storage of all materials and other items required to be recovered for the Employer and from the time such materials and items are deposited at the accommodation so to be provided they shall be at the sole risk in all respect of the Employer.

### 19. Vesting of Materials

All plant, materials and equipment of any kind whatsoever which are brought onto the Site by the Contractor but are not intended by the Contractor for incorporation in the Works shall remain the property of the Contractor in any event.

### 20. Payment

(*a*) At periods not more frequent than once monthly the Contractor may make application to the Employer stating the total value of work done including the value of work (if any) carried out in accordance with variation orders and materials properly delivered to the site for incorporation in the Works. Within fourteen days of receipt of such application the Employer shall pay to the Contractor the full amount so stated less only the amount of any instalments previously paid and the amount which may be retained by the Employer in accordance with sub-clause (*b*) of this condition.

(*b*) The Employer shall be entitled to retain until such times as are specified in Condition 21 hereof ten per cent of the value so stated of the aforesaid work and materials.

### 21. Release of Retention Money

The Employer shall within fourteen days of the date of notification by the Contractor under condition 9 hereof of completion of the Works release to the Contractor all sums retained by the Employer under condition 20 (*b*) hereof and shall within seven days of the delivery of final accounts discharge such accounts in full.

257

### 22. Loss and Damage to Work and Materials (a) By Fire (b) Otherwise

(*a*)  The Works (including materials and goods of the Contractor intended to be incorporated in the Works) and all structures property and things belonging to the Employer which may be adjacent thereto including materials and items required to be recovered for the Employer shall

   (i) as regards any loss or damage by fire be at the sole risk of the Employer unless such fire be caused by the negligence of the Contractor or those for whose actions he is responsible

   (ii) as regards loss or damage otherwise than by fire be at the sole risk of the Employer unless such loss or damage be caused by the negligence of the Contractor or those for whose actions he is responsible.

(*b*)  Loss or damage by fire (or otherwise) to adjacent premises shall, as between the Contractor and the Employer, be at the sole risk of the Employer unless such loss or damage be caused by the negligence of the Contractor or those for whose actions he is responsible.

(*c*)  The Employer shall indemnify the Contractor in respect of any loss or damage which is at the Employer's risk as aforesaid (including in particular but without derogating from the generality of this indemnity claims by reason of the exposure of party walls) and shall pay to the Contractor the cost of replacing materials intended to be incorporated in the Works and of reinstating completed and uncompleted work intended to be incorporated in the Works as though the same were an addition ordered under condition 4 hereof.

### 23. Indemnities

(*a*)  The Contractor shall save as provided in condition 22 hereof indemnify the Employer against:

   (i) any claim in respect of personal injury to or the death of any person in the employment of the Contractor provided that such claim does not arise from the negligence of the Employer, his servants or agents or any other Contractors engaged by or on behalf of the Employer; and

   (ii) any claim in respect of injury to person or property arising from negligence on the part of the Contractor or his workmen or from breach of statutory duty by the Contractor.

(*b*)  Subject to aforesaid the Employer shall indemnify the Contractor against any claim in respect of injury to person or property due to the execution of the Works.

(*c*)  In the event of any claim against which an indemnity is hereby given being made against either party then the party giving the indemnity shall have the right to have the conduct of any proceedings arising therefrom. Nevertheless the party giving the indemnity shall be relieved of his obligation if the party indemnified shall by himself his servants or agents admit liability or make any payment in connection with such claim without the express authority of the party giving the indemnity.

### 24. Insurance

The Employer and the Contractor shall respectively at their own expense insure against their several liabilities as defined in conditions 22 and 23 hereof in such sums as shall be provided by the Contract and in default of any provision therein then in such sums as shall be reasonable and each party shall upon the request of the other at any time produce for inspection the relevant policy or policies of insurance and the receipts for premiums paid.

### 25. Determination by Employer

(*a*)  If the Contractor shall make default in any of the following respects, viz:

   (i) If without reasonable cause he wholly suspends the Works before completion; or

   (ii) if he fails to proceed with the Works with reasonable diligence;

then if such default shall continue for ten days after notice by registered post specifying the default has been given to him by the Employer, the Employer may without prejudice to any other rights or remedies thereupon by written notice by registered post determine the employment of the Contractor under this Contract provided that such notice shall not be given unreasonably or vexatiously and shall be void if the Employer is at the time of either of the said notices in breach of this Contract.

(*b*) If the Contractor shall commit an act of bankruptcy or shall make or enter into any deed of arrangement or composition with his creditors or being a Company enter into liquidation whether compulsory or voluntary (except for purposes of reconstruction or amalgamation) or suffer or allow any execution whether legal or equitable to be levied on his property or obtained against him then the Employer may without prejudice to any other rights or remedies by written notice by registered post forthwith determine the employment of the Contractor under this Contract.

(*c*) If the employment of the Contractor shall be determined under this condition then the Employer shall only be liable for:

(i) the value of any work actually and properly executed and not paid for at the date of such determination such value to be calculated in accordance with condition 4 hereof and

(ii) the value of any unfixed materials and goods delivered upon the Site for use in the Works and for no other sums whatsoever and the Employer shall have the right to recover or deduct from or set off against any amount due from the Employer hereunder the amount of damages suffered and/or of loss and expense incurred by him by reason of the failure of the Contractor to complete this Contract.

### 26. Determination by Contractor

(*a*) If the Employer shall at any time fail to make payment in accordance in all respects with condition 20 hereof, or if he shall commit an act of bankruptcy or make or enter into any deed of arrangement or composition with his creditors or being a Company enter into liquidation whether compulsory or voluntary (except for the purposes of reconstruction or amalgamation) or suffer or allow any execution whether legal or equitable to be levied on his property or obtained against him, or if the whole or substantially the whole of the execution of the Works shall be delayed for more than four weeks by circumstances outside the Contractor's control, the Contractor may without prejudice to any other rights or remedies thereupon by written notice by registered post to the Employer determine the employment of the Contractor under this Contract.

(*b*) Upon such determination without prejudice to the accrued rights of either party the respective rights and liabilities of the parties shall be as follows:

(i) The Contractor shall with all reasonable care and despatch and subject to the provisions of sub-clause (ii) of this clause of this Condition remove from the Site all his property;

(ii) The Contractor shall be paid by the Employer (less only the amount of instalments previously paid):

(*a*) The value of all work completed at the date of such determination, such value to be calculated in accordance with condition 4 hereof:

(*b*) The value of work begun and executed but not completed at the date of such determination, such value to be calculated in accordance with condition 4 hereof;

(*c*) The value of any unfixed materials and goods delivered upon the Site for use in the Works the property in which has passed to the Employer;

(*d*) The cost of materials or goods properly ordered for the works for which the Contractor shall have paid or of which he is legally bound to accept delivery which materials and goods shall on payment by the Employer of the cost in full become the property of the Employer;

(*e*) The reasonable cost of the Contractor's removal including the cost of removing his equipment, plant, machinery, stores, goods and materials;

(*f*) Any loss or damage caused to the Contractor by such determination.

Provided that in addition to all other remedies the Contractor upon such determination may take possession of all materials which may have become the property of the Contractor under this Contract.

259

(*c*)  In the case of such delay as is mentioned in clause (*a*) of this Condition the Contractor may at his option give written notice to the Employer by registered post that in lieu of determining his employment under the Contract he proposes to claim in addition to the Contract sum such sum as will compensate him for any extra expense caused to him by the said delay. Within 14 days of receipt of such notice the Employer may by counter notice by registered post to the Contractor require that the Contractor determine his employment under the Contract, in which case the Contractor's said employment shall be deemed to be determined on the day following the posting of such notice and the rights and liabilities of the parties shall be governed by clause (*b*) of this Condition. And if no such counter notice by the Employer is given there shall be added to the Contract sum such sum as will fairly and properly compensate the Contractor for such extra expense as aforesaid.

### 27.  Arbitration

In case any dispute or difference shall arise between the Employer and the Contractor either during the progress or after Completion or abandonment of the Works as to the construction of the Contract or as to any matter or thing arising thereunder or in connection therewith either party may forthwith give to the other notice in writing of such dispute or difference and the same shall be and is hereby referred to the arbitration and final decision of a single Arbitrator to be agreed upon by the parties or failing agreement within 30 days of such notice to be appointed at the request of either party by the President for the time being of The National Federation of Demolition Contractors Limited. The award of such Arbitrator shall be final and binding upon the parties.

## SUPPLEMENTARY CONDITION

### 28.  Fluctuations

(1)  In this Condition the expression "the Costing Date" means:

   (*a*)  where this Contract results from acceptance of a Tender by the Contractor, the date of such Tender

   (*b*)  in any other case, the date of this Contract.

(2)  Where more than six months elapses between the Costing Date and commencement of the Works then there shall be added to the Contract Sum the aggregate increase (if any) and deducted from the Contract sum the aggregate decrease (if any) arising from:

   (i)  any increase or decrease between the Costing Date and the dates when relevant expense is incurred by the Contractor in performance of this Contract in

   (*a*)  the market prices and rates for materials and goods

   (*b*)  the cost of transport

   (*c*)  the cost of labour due to any change in the working conditions and/or rates of wages allowances or other expenses recognised by the Demolition Industry Conciliation Board (including the cost of Employer's Liability insurance, National Insurance, Third Party insurance and Holidays with Pay stamps).

   (*d*)  the cost of any part or parts of the Works duly sub-contracted due to the like or similar circumstances.

   (ii)  there shall also be added to the Contract Sum any additional cost to the Contractor resulting from legislation, Government Order, Regulation or Direction subsequent to the Costing Date.

(3)  If and where expressly so provided by this Contract the provisions of this Clause shall be applied, *mutatis mutandis*, differentially as regards the date of commencement of different phases of the Works there specified.

(4)  The value of any additions to or deductions from the Contract sum which fall to be made under this Condition shall be allowed for in the computation of the value of work done for the purpose of all applications and payment from time to time made under Condition 20 hereof.

*Dated*........................................................ 19..............

# Contract

BETWEEN

........................................................................................

........................................................................................

AND

........................................................................................

........................................................................................

*Issued by*

## THE NATIONAL FEDERATION OF
## DEMOLITION CONTRACTORS

(LIMITED BY GUARANTEE)

**LEICESTER**

Revised Edition 1974

*Copyright*

Jordan & Sons Limited, Jordan House, 47 Brunswick Place, London N1 6EE

261

# Specimen working rule agreement

## THE DEMOLITION INDUSTRY CONCILIATION BOARD

COWDRAY HOUSE
6 PORTUGAL STREET
LONDON WC2A 2HH

*Employers' Secretary:*
A. B. Feldman, Esq., M.A., B.A.I.
The National Federation of
  Demolition Contractors
Cowdray House
6 Portugal Street
London WC2A 2HH

*Operatives' Secretary:*
G. P. Henderson, Esq.
Transport & General
  Workers Union
Transport House
Smith Square
London SW1P 3JB

# Constitution of the Board

### AND

# Working Rule Agreement

FOR THE DEMOLITION & DISMANTLING INDUSTRY
IN ENGLAND, WALES & SCOTLAND

*Revised Edition*
30th June 1980

1980

# INDEX

1

This Agreement supersedes all earlier Agreements and is between THE NATIONAL FEDERATION OF DEMOLITION CONTRACTORS LIMITED and THE UNIONS NAMED IN THE CONSTITUTION OF THE DEMOLITION INDUSTRY CONCILIATION BOARD SET OUT BELOW and provides that there shall be constituted a Joint Board in which shall be vested responsibility for the interpretation of the Agreement and for the settlement of disputes or differences arising out of its operation.

𝔑𝔬𝔴 𝔦𝔱 𝔦𝔰 𝔞𝔤𝔯𝔢𝔢𝔡 by the Parties to this Agreement as follows:

## PART A
## CONSTITUTION OF THE DEMOLITION INDUSTRY CONCILIATION BOARD

1. THE DEMOLITION INDUSTRY CONCILIATION BOARD shall consist of representatives of

   *(a)* THE NATIONAL FEDERATION OF DEMOLITION CONTRACTORS LIMITED; and,

   *(b)* TRANSPORT AND GENERAL WORKERS UNION; and,

   *(c)* GENERAL AND MUNICIPAL WORKERS UNION; and,

   *(d)* UNION OF CONSTRUCTION, ALLIED TRADES AND TECHNICIANS.

   The Employers' Side shall consist of three representatives together with a Secretary.

   The Operatives' Side shall consist of three representatives together with a Secretary.

   Each Side shall appoint its own representatives and may arrange for the appointment of substitutes where necessary.

2. CHAIRMAN AND VICE-CHAIRMAN
   A Chairman and Vice-Chairman shall be elected by the Board.

3. MEETINGS
   Meetings of the Board shall be held in London or at such other place as the occasion may require and shall, on representation by either of the parties, be convened by the Joint Secretaries. In any event, an annual meeting shall be held in London not later than the 15th March in each year.

2

4. VOTING

Ordinary voting shall be done by show of hands but shall be by ballot upon request of either Side. Any decision, to be binding, must be carried by a majority of votes on each Side of those present and voting. The Secretaries shall be entitled to vote.

5. INFORMATION AND/OR EVIDENCE

The Board shall have power to call for information and hear evidence of any question which may arise for adjudication or settlement.

6. SUB-COMMITTEES

The Board may appoint such sub-committees as are necessary in its opinion for the transaction of its business.

7. JURISDICTION AND EXTENT

The Board's jurisdiction and interests shall extend to all matters relative to the industry, including questions of health, safety and welfare, as well as to terms and conditions of employment.

8. HONOUR CLAUSE

This agreement, although not legally enforceable, has been entered into freely and voluntarily and is intended to be binding in honour as between the parties. The parties therefore undertake to take all such steps as are reasonably practicable to prevent any persons covered by it from acting in breach of its provisions.

## PART B
## PREVENTION OR SETTLEMENT OF DISPUTES

1. The parties to the Agreement agree that in the event of any dispute or difference arising between their respective memberships or any of them, every means of effecting an amicable settlement shall be exhausted before resorting to direct action.

2. Either or both of the parties to any difference or dispute which arises out of the operation of the Agreement may request that the difference or dispute be considered by a Demolition Industry National Disputes Commission or Panel as appropriate.

3. Such a request shall be made in writing to the appropriate Joint Secretary and on such reference being properly made it shall be the duty of the Joint Secretaries to confer and (if the matter is incapable of settlement by them jointly) to convene as soon as possible a Disputes Panel or a Demolition Industry National Disputes Commission for the purpose of considering the difference or dispute.

4. Decisions of a Disputes Panel or of a Demolition Industry National Disputes Commission shall be final and binding upon both parties.

3

5. In no event shall such a decision form a precedent in any other difference or dispute outside the demolition or dismantling industry.

6. Nothing in the foregoing arrangements shall be construed as conferring upon the said Panels or Commissions the right to take decisions on matters of general rulings on the Working Rule Agreement.

7. Disputes Panels shall consist of a Chairman appointed *ad hoc* together with the Joint Secretaries and shall consider individual employment grievances and disputes arising between employers and employees.

8. Demolition Industry National Disputes Commissions shall be composed of three representatives from each Side together with the Joint Secretaries appointed *ad hoc*, and shall:—

*(a)* Hold an enquiry without delay in the place where the dispute is occurring or about to occur or elsewhere as may be deemed most expedient.

*(b)* Take evidence from the parties concerned and otherwise enquire into the cause and nature of the dispute.

*(c)* Make such report and recommendations as the Commission may think fit to the respective national governing bodies as to the settlement of such dispute.

*(d)* Give such directions as the Commission may think fit as to preventing a stoppage of work or, in the event of a stoppage having taken place, as to providing for a resumption of work pending consideration of the report and recommendations under *(c)* aforesaid by the respective national governing bodies and ratification or otherwise by them.

9. The expenses of those appointed to serve on Disputes Panels and Commissions shall be paid by their respective organisations.

10. Reports by Disputes Panels and Commissions shall be laid before the respective national governing bodies of each side as soon as practicable after they have been received and be dealt with promptly in one of the following ways:—

*(i)* The recommendations may be approved and in that case communications shall be exchanged between the national governing bodies intimating that they will give effect thereto.

*(ii)* The recommendations may be disapproved wholly or partly in which case communications shall be exchanged between the national governing bodies as to further steps which shall be taken in regard to the dispute or difference.

4

*Signed on behalf of the Employers' Side*
> *For* THE NATIONAL FEDERATION OF DEMOLITION CONTRACTORS LIMITED.
>> R. E. WILLMENT, *President*
>> A. B. FELDMAN, *Secretary*

*Signed on behalf of the Operatives' Side*
> *For* TRANSPORT & GENERAL WORKERS UNION
>> G. E. HENDERSON, *National Secretary*

> *For* GENERAL & MUNICIPAL WORKERS UNION
>> F. EARL, *National Officer*

> *For* UNION OF CONSTRUCTION, ALLIED TRADES & TECHNICIANS
>> L. WOOD, *General Secretary*

*Dated this* 30*th day of June* 1980.

---

## WORKING RULE AGREEMENT

THIS AGREEMENT REGULATES the Wages, Hours and Working Conditions for operatives employed on demolition and dismantling work in England, Wales, and Scotland

## DECLARATION OF INTENT

It is the purpose of the parties hereto that all operatives:

(1) Shall be in the direct employment of a demolition or dismantling contractor or sub-contractor and working in accordance with the conditions laid down in this Agreement;

(2) shall be employed at the rates of wages and under the conditions laid down herein.

## 1. WAGES—GENERAL

*(a)* The rates of wages for demolition and dismantling operatives shall be those prescribed from time to time by the Demolition Industry Conciliation Board (hereinafter called "the Board").

*(b)* For the purposes of this Agreement, operatives employed within the 32 Inner and Outer Boroughs of London shall be paid at London Rates. Grade A rates shall be paid to all operatives outside the defined London area.

5

(c) The guaranteed minimum weekly earnings of demolition and dismantling industry operatives shall comprise:—
   (i) The current weekly standard rates of wages (hereinafter called "the plain time rate") and:
   (ii) A guaranteed minimum attendance payment (GMA) at the rates fixed and promulgated by the Board from time to time.

(d) The payweek shall be from midnight Sunday to midnight Sunday, but it shall be permissible for wages to be made up to Friday nights.

(e) The pay day shall be Thursday, but where a day or days of recognised public or winter holiday occur in a pay week, wages may be paid on a suitable alternative day in that week.

(f) Where an Annual Holiday occurs, the wages in respect of the payweek immediately preceding such holiday shall be paid on the Thursday in the payweek immediately succeeding such holiday.

(g) Payments made under these Rules for Christmas Day, Boxing Day and New Year's Day shall be made on the pay day in the first full working week immediately succeeding the winter holiday.

## 2. PLAIN TIME RATES

### (a) General Operatives

As and from 30th June 1980 the plain time hourly rates shall be as follows:—

| Category of Operatives | London | Grade A |
|---|---|---|
| General Labourer | 155p | 153p |
| Cleaner Sorter or Improver | 158p | 156p |
| Mattockman | 166p | 164p |
| Burner Groundman | 166p | 164p |
| Shorer's mate assisting in preparation and erection of shoring (timber) | 166p | 164p |
| Shorer (Timber) | 182½p | 180½p |
| Topman capable of carrying out and fully skilled in all operations in connection with demolition work | 182½p | 180½p |
| Burner Topman | 182½p | 180½p |

6

### (b)  Watchmen

*(i)*   Remuneration shall be at a rate per shift calculated at eight times the appropriate rate for labourers, plus the guaranteed minimum attendance payment.

The night shift rate shall be as the day shift rate plus 25%.

The rate per shift for watchmen is as follows:—

|         | Day    | Night  |
|---------|--------|--------|
| Grade A | £13.84 | £17.30 |
| London  | £14.00 | £17.50 |

*(ii)*  A Watchman's shift during the day is the period during which a day gang would be working. During the night the shift is from the normal time of operatives leaving work until the time of starting next day. Saturday afternoons until ordinary week-day time of leaving off is to be arranged by the employer and paid at not less than half the rate for a shift.

### (c)  Young Labourers

Young labourers shall be paid the following proportion of the current labourers' plain time rate:-

At 16 years of age     50% of the current rate.
At 17 years of age     75% of the current rate.
At 18 years of age and over the full current rate.

Young labourers shall be paid the same proportion of the guaranteed minimum attendance payment as their basic wage rate bears to the labourers' rate.

### (d)  Mechanical Plant Operators

These operatives shall be paid the basic plain time rate for labourers together with the following plus rates:—

| Category | Hourly Plus Rate |
|----------|------------------|
| *Power-Driven Tools*<br>Operative using power-driven tools as breakers, percussive drills, picks and spades, rammers, punching and tamping machines | 7p |
| *Compressors*<br>Mobile or portable Air Compressor, Operator of | 8p |

7

| Category | Hourly Plus Rate |
|---|---|
| *Mobile Cranes* Self-propelled Mobile Crane on road wheels or caterpillar tracks including lorry mounted: capacity up to and including 2 tons (or metric tonnes), Driver of | 16p |
| Capacity over 2 tons (or metric tonnes) and up to and including 6 tons (or metric tonnes), Driver of | 23p |
| Capacity over 6 tons (or metric tonnes) and up to and including 20 tons (or metric tonnes), Driver of | 31p |
| Capacity over 20 tons (or metric tonnes) and up to and including 50 tons (or metric tonnes), Driver of | 35p |
| Capacity over 50 tons (or metric tonnes), Driver of | 44p |
| *Dumpers* Dumper up to and including 1 cu. yd. (or up to and including 0.8 cu. metres) struck capacity, Driver of | 10p |
| Dumper over 1 cu. yd. and up to and including 5 cu. yds. (or over 0.8 cu. metres and up to and including 3.85 cu. metres) struck capacity, Driver of | 16p |
| *Excavators* Excavator with rated bucket capacity up to and including $^3/_8$ cu. yd. (or up to and including 0.3 cu. metres), Driver of | 15p |
| Excavator with rated bucket capacity over $^3/_8$ cu. yd. and up to and including $^3/_4$ cu. yd. (or over 0.3 cu. metres and up to and including 0.6 cu. metres), Driver of | 23p |
| Excavator with rated bucket capacity over $^3/_4$ cu. yd. and up to and including 2 cu. yds. (or over 0.6 cu. metres and up to and including 1.6 cu. metres), Driver of | 30p |
| Excavator with rated bucket capacity over 2 cu. yds. and up to and including 5 cu. yds. (or over 1.6 cu. metres and up to and including 3.8 cu. metres), Driver of | 35p |
| Operative attending Cranes or Excavators (Banksman) | 7p |

8

| Category | Hourly Plus Rate |
|---|---|
| *Front-end Shovels* | |
| Front-end Shovel capacity up to and including 1 cu. yd. (or up to and including 0.8 cu. metres), Operator of | 15p |
| Front-end Shovel capacity over 1 cu. yd. and up to and including 3 cu. yds. (or over 0.8 cu. metres and up to and including 2.3 cu. metres), Operator of | 23p |
| Front-end Shovel capacity over 3 cu. yds. and up to and including 8 cu. yds. (or over 2.3 cu. metres and up to and including 6.1 cu. metres), Operator of | 31p |

**(e)  Lorry Drivers**

Drivers of lorries shall be paid the following hourly rates:

| | | | |
|---|---|---|---|
| Class 1 | ............ £2.03 | Class 3 | ............ £1.75 |
| Class 2 | ............ £1.89 | Class 4 | ............ £1.68 |

**(f)  Plant Drivers and Preparatory and Finishing Work**

Drivers of plant are to be paid at ordinary hourly rates half an hour before and half and hour after ordinary time if required for preparatory or finishing work, such as refuelling, firing up, oiling round, getting out, starting up, banking down, checking over, cleaning out and parking the machine.

**(g)  Servicing at Weekends**

A shift of eight hours at ordinary rates is to be paid to one operative for diesel and petrol excavator, tractor, greasing, changing oil and general servicing, if required to be done on Sunday and a shift of five hours at ordinary rates to be paid to one operative if required to be done out of working hours on Saturday.

**(h)  Exceptionally Rigorous Conditions**

Operatives engaged in conditions on any site which are obnoxious or rigorous to a degree in excess of that normally encountered in the demolition and dismantling industry shall be paid 5p an hour extra. (This includes "boot money".)

**(i)  Foremen and Fitters**

The rates of wages of foremen and fitters shall continue to be dealt with between individual employers and their foremen and fitters in

9

accordance with their long-standing practice; provided always that such employees shall be entitled to holidays with pay in accordance with Rule 7 hereof.

### 3. GUARANTEED MINIMUM ATTENDANCE PAYMENT

(1)  As from commencement of employment all operatives shall be entitled to receive a weekly guaranteed minimum attendance payment (GMA) of £8.00 subject to the following conditions:—

*(a)* The payment will be made weekly where the operative has met the conditions of availability for work prescribed in Rule 12 hereof.

*(b)* There has been no action during normal working hours by or on behalf of the operative or operatives preventing, interrupting or otherwise interfering with full production.

*(c)* The entitlement of an operative to the guaranteed minimum attendance payment shall be reduced proportionately for any part of normal working hours for which he has not been available for work due to authorised absence within the meaning of Rule 12.

*(d)* Young labourers shall be paid the same proportion of the guaranteed minimum attendance payment as their basic wage rates bears to the labourer's rate.

*(e)* An operative shall not be entitled to his guaranteed minimum attendance payment or any proportionate reduction thereof if he has not been available for work due to unauthorised absence within the meaning of Rule 12.

*(f)* Payment of the guaranteed minimum attendance payment shall not be affected by the occurrence during a payweek of a day or days of public holiday for which payment is due under these Rules and, where the payweek includes no normal working day to which the guaranteed payment can apply, a like appropriate proportion of it shall be paid in respect of each day of public holiday.

*(g)* The sum payable under the foregoing provisions shall be set off against all other bonus payments or extra payments other than those prescribed in these Rules. It shall in no case be additional to them.

### 4. OVERTIME

(A)  *(i)* Overtime shall be calculated from Monday to Friday inclusive after the 40 hours of guaranteed working week have been worked.

10

*(ii)* Overtime shall not count until full time for the normal working week has been made: this provision shall not apply unless the loss of time is through the operative's own fault.

*(iii)* Overtime shall be paid at the rate of time-and-a-half for the first three hours on each of the following days:

Monday, Tuesday, Wednesday, Thursday and Friday, subject to 4 (A) (i) above. Thereafter until starting time next morning, double time is payable.

Saturday: time-and-a-half from starting time until 4.00 p.m. afterwards and until starting time on Monday, double time is payable.

*(iv)* Where, in any locality, any such day is generally worked and another day is, or other days are recognised as a general holiday, one such other day shall be deemed a holiday for the purpose of this paragraph in lieu of overtime payment for the holiday hereinbefore prescribed.

(B)   (1) **England and Wales**

All time worked in England and Wales during normal working hours and until starting time the following morning on Good Friday, Easter Monday, the May Day Bank Holiday, the Spring Bank Holiday, the Summer Bank Holiday, and Christmas Day, Boxing Day (or, where the latter occurs on a Sunday, the 27th December) and New Year's Day (or where the latter occurs on a Sunday, the 2nd January), provided that such holidays are recognised as holidays by the Demolition Industry Conciliation Board, shall be paid for at double time.

(2) **Scotland**

All time worked in Scotland during normal working hours and until starting time the following morning on New Year's Day (or, where this occurs on a Sunday, the 2nd January) the second day of the year (excluding Sunday), the Monday at the Spring Holiday, a Monday in May, the Friday immediately preceding the Annual Summer Local Trades Holiday, the Friday and Monday at the Autumn Holiday. Christmas Day and Boxing Day shall be paid for at double time.

## .5.   SHIFT WORK

It shall be permissible for the Industry to work on shifts. Where regular shift working is in operation, the following shall apply:—

Day shift—Ordinary plain time rate

Night shift—+30p an hour

## 6.   HOLIDAY PERIODS—RESTRICTED WORKING HOURS

Subject always to the general over-riding principles of this Agreement, where on the night immediately prior to, or immediately following, a public or other recognised holiday, work cannot proceed, provided that the operative would otherwise have been available for work, he shall be

11

paid in respect of that payweek(and excluding any overtime earnings) at his plain time rate for the hours so lost, so far as they fall short of 40 hours.

## 7. ANNUAL HOLIDAYS WITH PAY

Holidays with Pay for operatives in the demolition and dismantling industry shall be met by affixing the appropriate stamps weekly to the operatives' cards as provided for in the Agreement for Holidays with Pay Scheme dated 28th October 1942, between the National Federation of Building Trades Employers, the National Federation of Building Trades Operatives, the Federation of Civil Engineering Contractors and the Operatives Panel of the Civil Engineering Construction Conciliation Board, or any amendments of that Agreement from time to time.

Interpretation of that Agreement and settlement of disputes arising therefrom shall be dealt with in accordance with the procedure laid down in a separate Agreement of the parties dated 5th April 1943.

The application of that Agreement shall be subject to the following provisions:—
1. The Winter, Easter (Spring) and Summer Holidays shall be granted as decided by the Board annually in accordance with the following intention:
   (*i*) That the Winter Holiday shall be seven working days taken in conjunction with Christmas Day, Boxing day and New Year's Day, to give a Winter Holiday of two calendar weeks.
   (*ii*) That Easter (Spring) Holiday shall be four working days immediately following Easter Monday (or the appropriate Spring Holiday Monday in Scotland), to give an Easter (Spring) Holiday of one calendar week.
   (*iii*) That the Summer Holiday shall be two calendar weeks, not necessarily consecutive, to be granted in the "summer period" i.e. between 1st April and 30th September. Except by mutual agreement, neither week is to be taken in conjunction with the Easter (Spring) Holiday.
2. Notwithstanding the conditions prescribed in that Agreement in regard to the provision weekly by the employer of holiday credit stamps, the employer shall not be required to stamp the operative's holiday card when the operative without good cause is available for work for less than a minimum period of three normal days in a pay week.

## 8. PUBLIC HOLIDAYS

### (*a*) England and Wales

Christmas Day, Boxing Day, New Year's Day, Good Friday, Easter Monday, the Spring Bank Holiday and the Summer Bank Holiday shall

12

be recognised as holidays in England and Wales, provided that such days are generally recognised as holidays in the locality in which the work is being done. Where, in any locality, any such day is generally worked and another day is, or other days are, recognised as a general holiday, then not less than one such other day shall be recognised as a holiday.

### *(b)* **Scotland**

In Scotland, Monday at the Spring Holiday, a Monday in May, the Friday immediately preceding the Annual Summer Local Trades Holiday, Friday and Monday at the Autumn Holiday, Christmas Day, Boxing Day and New Year's Day shall be recognised as public holidays.

## 9. PAYMENT FOR PUBLIC HOLIDAYS

*(i)* Payment for days of public holiday recognised as aforesaid, shall be made by the employer to an operative in his employment at the time of each such holiday, of the equivalent of 8 hours at ordinary rate on the pay day in respect of the pay week in which such holiday occurs, provided that:—

*(a)* An operative who has completed 6 normal working days in employment, but who is no longer in the employment of the employer on such a public holiday shall, nevertheless, be entitled to payment in respect of such holiday if he was in the employer's employment at any time during the pay week immediately preceding the pay week in which the holiday falls, but the employment was terminated by the employer (otherwise than for misconduct) before the holiday occurred. Payment shall be made on termination of employment.

*(b)* An operative who is required to work on such a public holiday, or is on annual holiday on the occasion of such a public holiday, has the option, by arrangement with the employer, of an alternative day of holiday as soon thereafter as is mutually convenient, in which case the payment prescribed by this Rule shall be made in respect of such alternative day instead of the public holiday. When the employment is terminated before such alternative day occurs, the operative shall receive such payment on the termination of employment.

*(c)* The operative presents himself and remains available for work within the meaning of Rule 12(a) hereof or provides satisfactory evidence of incapacity for work on the normal working day immediately following the day or days of public holiday.

*(ii)* For the purposes of Rule 3 (Guaranteed Minimum Attendance payment) an operative is deemed to be available on the above public holidays.

13

## 10. MEAL INTERVALS

Mutually agreed arrangements shall be made for the taking of meals. The interval or intervals for meals, for which no payment shall be due, shall not exceed a total period of one hour.

## 11. TRAVELLING AND SUBSISTENCE ALLOWANCE

When an operative is taken on at the job, or elsewhere than at the job on the understanding that his engagement commences on arrival at the job, he shall not be entitled to payment of travelling or subsistence allowance. In all other cases the following provisions shall apply:—

### (1) KEY-MEN

The question of payment of such allowances to key-men shall continue to be dealt with between individual employers and their key-men in accordance with their long-standing practice.

### (2) OTHER OPERATIVES

*Daily Travel*

Daily travelling allowances on the following scales for distances travelled in excess of three miles each way daily from a convenient centre to the job:

*(i) Transport Provided Free by Employers*

Where, at the option of the employer, an operative travels by transport provided free by the employer:

First 3 miles each way—Nil.

Exceeding 3 miles each way—11p per mile for each mile or part of a mile in excess of 3 miles, one way.

The cost of providing free transport by employers under this Rule in addition to the appropriate monetary allowance, shall be deemed to be a payment of travelling allowances to operatives within the meaning of the Rule.

*(ii) Public Transport*

Where an operative travels by public transport:

First 3 miles each way—Nil.

Exceeding 3 miles each way—24p per mile for each mile or part of a mile in excess of 3 miles, one way.

### (3) CONDITIONS AFFECTING DAILY TRAVEL

*(i) Convenient Centre*

The convenient centre shall be a railway station, bus station or other similar place in the area in which an operative is living.

*(ii) Measurement of Distances*

All distances shall be measured in a straight line from the booking-on centre at the job to the convenient centre in the area in which the operative is living. Where special physical conditions such as a river or a

14

mountain range make the operation of such straight line measurement inequitable, the distance shall be measured in a straight line from the job to the nearest crossing place, then in a straight line across the crossing place, and then in a straight line to the convenient centre in the area in which the operative is living. Where an operative is entitled to daily travelling payments, he shall only be paid in respect of the distance in excess of 3 miles one way.

*(iii) Limit of Payment*

Whether transport is provided free by the employer or whether public transport is used, the sum payable to operatives in respect of daily travelling allowance (at the rate of 11p per mile in the former case and 24p per mile in the latter) shall not exceed £5.40 per head per day (excluding the cost of provision of free transport in the former case).

*(iv) Operatives in respect of Periodic Leave and /or Subsistence Allowances*

To qualify for daily travelling allowances in addition to periodic leave and/or subsistence allowances an operative must show he is living as near to the job as there is accommodation (being a camp or other accommodation) available.

*(v) Normal Working Hours*

Time spent daily travelling is not to be reckoned as part of the normal working hours.

*Periodic Travel*

Periodic travelling allowances are as follows:

*(i)* Fares shall be paid or, at the option of the employer, an operative may be conveyed—

- *(a)* from a convenient centre to the job at commencement of his employment on the job;
- *(b)* from the job to the convenient centre on termination of his employment on the job by his employers;
- *(c)* to and from the job at the following periodic leave intervals: Jobs up to 80 miles (in a straight line) from the convenient centre—6 weeks.

Jobs over 80 miles (in a straight line) from the convenient centre—an interval fixed by mutual arrangement between the employer and the operative before the operative goes to the job.

*(ii) Payment for time spent travelling between the convenient centre and the job:*
- *(a)* At commencement of his employment at the job, provided that an operative shall not be entitled to such payment if, within one month from the date of commencement of his employment on the job, he discharges himself voluntarily or is discharged for misconduct;

15

(b) on termination of his employment on the job by his employer, provided that he is not discharged for misconduct;

(c) in returning to the job (i.e. one way only) after periodic leave provided that he returns to the job at the time specified by his employer and provided also that operative shall not be entitled to such payment, if, within one month from the date of his return to the job, he discharges himself voluntarily or is discharged for misconduct.

## (4) Conditions Affecting Periodic Travel

### (i) Convenient Centre

The convenient centre shall be a railway station, bus station or other similar suitable place in the area in which an operative is living.

### (ii) Measurement of Distance

All distances shall be measured in a straight line from the booking on centre at the job to the convenient centre in the area in which the operative is living.

Where an operative is entitled to periodic travelling-time payments, he shall only be paid in respect of the journey one way.

### (iii) Payment of Fares

Where in the case of periodic leave employers do not exercise the option to provide free transport, the obligation to pay fares may, at the employers' option, be discharged by the provision of a free railway or bus ticket or travel voucher or the rail fare.

## (5) Travelling-Time Payments

(A) Time spent in periodic travelling is not to be reckoned as part of the normal working hours.

(B) Periodic travelling-time payments shall in no case exceed payment for 8 hours per journey.

(C) Periodic travelling-time payments shall in all cases be at plain time rates to the nearest quarter of an hour.

## (6) Subsistence Allowances

Subsistence allowances shall be paid at the rate of £7.00 per night to an operative necessarily living away from the place in which he normally resides.

Subsistence allowances shall not be paid in respect of any day on which an operative absents himself from work except that subsistence allowance shall be paid by an employer to an operative in his employment in respect of any such day covered by a Medical Certificate during which:

(i) the operative is absent from work due to sickness or industrial injury, and

16

*(ii)* he continues to live in the accommodation the occupation of which entitled him to subsistence allowance immediately prior to the sickness or industrial injury;

and provided that the employer receives from the operative, within 3 working days from (and including) the day on which the absence due to sickness or industrial injury first occurs, and at such intervals thereafter as the employer may require, a Medical Certificate relating to the sickness or industrial injury.

## 12. GUARANTEED WEEKLY WAGES—AVAILABILITY FOR WORK

### *(a)* Availability for Work
'Available for Work' means that:

(1) Unless otherwise specifically instructed by the employer or his representative each operative shall present himself for work each weekday at the usual starting time of the shop, job or site and shall there remain for work throughout normal working hours. Decisions as to when, during the normal working hours, work is to be carried out, interrupted on account of weather conditions or otherwise and resumed, and as to whether some or all of the operatives shall work at any particular time shall be made by the employer or his representatives and shall be implicitly observed.

(2) If in the shop or on the job or site, work is not available for an operative in his own occupation, he shall hold himself ready and willing to perform work in any other suitable demolition or dismantling industry occupation or at any other job, site or shop where work is available.

(3) In cases where abnormal weather conditions interrupt work over a period, suitable arrangements, appropriate to the circumstances of each case, may be made by the employer by which operatives shall register or establish that they are available for work on each day.

### *(b)* Guaranteed Weekly Wage

(1) GENERAL
An operative shall be guaranteed payment of his guaranteed minimum weekly earnings comprising the current weekly standard basic rates of wages and the guaranteed minimum attendance payment for the full normal working hours of each complete payweek of the period of employment, whether work is or is not provided by the employer and regardless of temporary stoppages through inclement weather or other causes beyond the control of the parties.

17

This guarantee is subject to the following conditions:

    *(a)* That throughout the normal working hours of the payweek the operative is available for work as defined above.

    *(b)* The guarantee does not apply to weeks of Annual Holiday or to Winter Holiday or Easter/Spring Holiday.

    *(c)* The guarantee is reduced proportionately for any pay-week in which:

        *(i)* the operative is engaged after the commencement of the pay-week;

        *(ii)* the operative's employment terminates before the end of the pay-week;

        *(iii)* the operative is absent for part of the pay-week due to certified sickness or injury; or

        *(iv)* the operative is absent for one or more days of Winter, Easter/Spring, Public or recognised holiday.

    *(d)* That where on a job or in a shop collective action is taken by any operatives employed under this agreement, the employer shall at all times use his best endeavours to provide continuity of work for those operatives who are not involved in the dispute and who remain available for work. If, because of the industrial action taken, the employer cannot provide such continuity of work, the provisions of the rule relating to guaranteed time payments shall be suspended until normal working is restored.

(2) Loss of Guarantee

An operative who has not been available for work within the meaning of the preceding paragraph shall not be entitled to the weekly guarantee but shall be entitled only to payment of the appropriate proportion of his guaranteed minimum weekly earnings as defined in clause 12 (b) (1) above for half the number of any hours during which, although available for work, he has been prevented from working by inclement weather or other cause beyond the control of the parties.

(3) Temporary Lay-Off

Where work is temporarily stopped or is not provided by the employer and a payweek during which the operative actually works is followed by a complete payweek during which, although remaining available for work, he is prevented from performing actual work, he shall be paid for that payweek his guaranteed mimimum weekly earnings as defined in clause 12(b) (1) above. Thereafter and while the stoppage of work continues and the operative is similarly prevented from actually working, he may be required by the employer to register as an unemployed person, in which event the provisions of this Agreement relating to continuity of employment during temporary stoppage of work shall apply to him.

18

## (4) DISPUTES

Disputes arising under this Rule shall, in the event of no decision by the Board, and in that event only, be referred by the Board to the Advisory, Conciliation and Arbitration Service for adjudication.

## 13. CONDITIONS OF SERVICE AND TERMINATION OF EMPLOYMENT

*(a)* The employment of all operatives in the demolition and dismantling industry shall be upon the following conditions which shall be equally binding upon both employer and operative.

*(b)* At the discretion of the employer an operative may be transferred at any time during the period of his employment from one job to another.

*(c)* The contract of employment shall be deemed a contract from hour to hour and that payments other than as prescribed in this Agreement shall be for time actually worked.

*(d)* In cases of misconduct an operative may be summarily discharged at any time.

*(e)* On termination of the particular operation for which the operative has been engaged, or when work is stopped on the instructions of a recognised competent authority, employment may be terminated at two hours' notice expiring at the end of any day.

*(Note:* In the case of stoppage of work by a recognised competent authority, the provisions of rule 13(e) do not apply to operatives who have been in the continuous employment of the employer for 4 weeks or more. Such operatives must be given the notice to which they are entitled under the Employment Protection (Consolidation) Act 1978).

*(f)* The notice that an employer shall give to an operative is as set out in sub-paras (1) to (7) below.

The notice that an operative shall give to an employer is as set out in sub-paras (1) and (2) below, but an operative with 4 weeks' continuous employment or more is required to give one week's notice.

| | | |
|---|---|---|
| 1. | During the first six normal working days of employment. | Two hour's notice to expire at the end of normal working hours on any day. |
| 2. | After the first six normal working days but less than four weeks. | One clear day's notice to expire at the end of normal working hours on a Friday. |
| 3. | Four week's continuous employment or more but less than two years. | One week's notice. |
| 4. | Two years' continuous employment or more. | Two weeks' notice. |

19

5.  Three years' continuous employ-    Three weeks' notice.
    ment or more but less than four
    years.
6.  Four years' continuous employ-    Four weeks' notice.
    ment or more but less than five
    years.
7.  Five years' continuous employ-    Five weeks' notice.
    ment or more but less than six
    years.

Thereafter, one week's notice for each additional year of service up to a maximum of 12 weeks' notice after 12 years' service.

(*Note:*   After 4 weeks' continuous employment minimum periods of notice are prescribed by the Employment Protection (Consolidation) Act, 1978, and the provisions of the Act are incorporated in the fore-going).

*(g)* **Termination of employment by mutual consent, etc.**
The employment may be terminated at anytime either:—
   (1)  by mutual consent (which should be expressed in writing), or
   (2)  by the payments, in lieu of the prescribed period of notice, of the amount to which the operative would have been entitled under paragraph 2 of Schedule 3 of the Employ-ment Protection (Consolidation) Act 1978 if notice had been given.

*(h)* **Continuity of Employment**
*Temporary stoppage of work.*
Where there has been a temporary stoppage of work (e.g. through inclement weather), and an operative who has been temporarily laid-off under these Rules, is re-started by the employer, the employment shall, for the purposes of paragraph (f) of this rule, be deemed to have been continuous.

*POINTS OF GUIDANCE*
The following procedure for dismissals should be observed as may be appropriate:
1.  Before other action is taken over any alleged failure by an operative with regard to conduct (subject to para. 4 below) or workmanship the operative should be given a verbal warning by his immediate supervisor, preferably before a witness.
2.  If further warning is necessary, it should be given in writing. Where a shop steward is involved, a copy of the written warning should be sent to the appropriate full-time official of the union concerned.
3.  If the operative persists in the actions which led to his being warned under this procedure, and is dismissed, the reason for his dismissal shall be clearly stated in writing.

20

4. Dismissal without previous warning should be reserved for cases of gross misconduct.
5. Employers are recommended to utilise the grievance procedure and conciliation facilities of the Board, as provided for in Part B of the Constitution and the Appendix to these Rules.

   This procedure shall not apply during the first six normal working days of employment except that an operative shall in all cases be notified of the reason for his dismissal.

## 14. TRAVELLING AND EMERGENCY WORK INSTRUCTED BY EMPLOYER

If an operative at his employer's place of business is sent from there, or if employed on a job, from that job to the site of other work for the purpose of doing any work, or, not being at work is called from his home at a time not within normal working hours, for the purposes of carrying out emergency work, he shall be allowed travelling expenses and time, at ordinary rates, occupied in travelling one journey each way for the job.

Normal working hours for the purpose of this paragraph shall include night work hours where the operative is for the time being employed on night work.

## 15. PAYMENT FOR ABSENCE DUE TO SICKNESS OR INJURY

*(i) Amount of Payment*

An operative who during employment with an employer is absent from work on account of sickness or injury shall subject as herein provided be paid £4.20 per working day, subject to the conditions laid down in paras (iii) to (vii) below. Saturday shall be treated as a working day whether or not a five day week is in operation.

*(ii) Medical Certificates*

The whole period of absence from work shall be covered by a certificate or certificates of incapacity for work given by a Registered Medical Practitioner, to the satisfaction of the employer.

*(iii) Qualification*

An operative shall not be entitled to payment under this Rule unless in the period of eight calendar weeks ending with the calendar week immediately prior to that in which the absence from work starts, four or more weekly credit stamps (not including "S" stamps affixed under the Annual Holidays Agreement) have been affixed to his Annual Holiday card(s).

*(iv)* No payment shall be due:—

    *(a)* for the first three working days of each period of absence;

    *(b)* for Sundays, public holidays and days of annual or winter holiday granted in accordance with the provisions of the Holidays With Pay Agreement;

21

    *(c)* for incapacity arising directly or indirectly from insurrection or future war, attempted suicide or self-inflicted injury, the operative's own misconduct, any gainful occupation outside working hours, participation as a professional in sports or games, and in the case of women operatives for incapacity arising from pregnancy.

## *(v) Limit of payment*

For an operative who holds an Annual Holidays card current from the beginning of an Accounting Period for the Annual Holidays Scheme, the maximum number of days of absence for which there shall be entitlement to payment during that Accounting Period shall be 48 days, including days of absence for which payment has been made by previous employers.

*(vi)* For a new entrant to the industry, including an operative who on entering an employment is unable to produce an Annual Holidays card, the foregoing maximum during the current Accounting Period shall be reduced by four days for each calendar month which has elapsed between the beginning of the Accounting Period and the date of entry into employment. In such a case the employer on issuing the Annual Holidays card shall cancel the appropriate number of spaces in the boxes which are provided on the card for keeping a record of days of paid absence: see para *(vii)*.

## *(vii) Record of Absence*

A record of days of absence for which payment has been made under this Rule in any one Accounting Period shall be kept by each employer on the Annual Holidays card current at the time by cancelling the appropriate number of spaces in the boxes provided on the card for that purpose.

*(viii)* Where any period of sickness shall continue beyond twelve days then subject to the provisions of this Rule the employer shall be under no obligation to make payment to an operative who is entitled to receive Supplementary Sick Pay under the National Health Insurance Acts at the rate of £4.20 per day or more and shall only be under an obligation to an operative entitled to receive less than £4.20 per day to pay to the operative the difference between the amount of his daily Supplementary Sick Pay and £4.20 any such payments not to exceed the total of 48 days specified in *(v)* above.

## 16. DEATH BENEFIT SCHEME

*(a)* An operative is entitled to be provided by his employer with death benefit cover of £3,500 in accordance with the conditions laid down in the Building and Civil Engineering Death Benefit Scheme, which is published separately.

*(b)* Cover is to be provided by payment of a surcharge on the value of the weekly credit stamps under the Annual Holidays Scheme.

22

*Guidance Note*

Since the entitlement to the death benefit cover is a provision of the Working Rule Agreement, it follows that it constitutes part of the terms and conditions of employment of demolition and dismantling operatives. An employer, therefore, who fails to observe the Building and Civil Engineering Death Benefit Scheme shall himself be liable for the benefit in the event of the death of an operative in circumstances covered by the rules of the scheme.

## 17.  HEALTH & SAFETY AT WORK

*(a)* It is the responsibility of the employer to ensure, so far as is reasonably practicable the health and safety at work of his employees. It is equally the responsibility of all employees to take care for their own health and safety at work as well as the health and safety of others who may be affected by their activities.

*(b)* As from 1st April 1975 it is the legal duty of all Employers (other than those with less than five employees) to prepare and periodically revise a written statement of the employer's policy for health and safety at work, and to bring that policy (and any revision of it) to the notice of all employees. The employer must also have an organisation and arrangements for giving effect to that policy.

*(c)* The Board attach the greatest importance to this requirement and to the implementation of the spirit as well as the letter of the law and recommend the following as a basis for the policy statement of employers in the demolition and dismantling industry:—

"This company believes that it has a responsibility, so far as lies within its power to do so, to prevent injuries to its employees. To this end every reasonable effort will be made to provide safe and healthful working conditions, to prevent fire and other damage, etc. To achieve this the active co-operation of all employees is essential. Everyone is expected to work in such a way that accidents to themselves and others are avoided. The company will make available safety training, participate in joint consultation, provide such personal protective clothing and equipment as may be prescribed by the D.I.C.B. or required by law, and check and inspect its safety organisation. Complete details of the company's safety programme are available and may be consulted on request. Employees are under a legal duty to co-operate with Management in safety, health and welfare matters. This is the law".

*(d)* The Board draws particular attention to the health hazards involved when working with asbestos and all Employers are reminded of the obligations imposed by the Asbestos Regulations 1969 and of the recommendations of the voluntary codes of practice issued by the Asbestosis Research Council, which should be followed.

23

## 18.   WELFARE CONDITIONS

It shall be the responsibility of the employer to provide proper welfare facilities on site, namely:

*(a)*   Shelter from inclement weather.
*(b)*   Accommodation for clothing.
*(c)*   Accommodation and provision for meals.
*(d)*   Provision of drinking water.
*(e)*   Sanitary conveniences.
*(f)*   First aid facilities.
*(g)*   Washing facilities.

N.B.:   The attention of all employers is drawn to the provisions of the Construction (Health and Welfare) Regulations 1966, which have the force of law, subject to any amendments brought into operation under the terms of the Health & Safety at Work etc. Act 1974, and any subsequent legislation.

## 19.   INTERPRETATION OF AGREEMENT

The Demolition Industry Conciliation Board shall be responsible for interpretation of this Agreement and settlement of disputes or differences arising out of the operation of the Agreement.

## 20.   DETERMINATION OF AGREEMENT

This Agreement may be terminated at any time by agreement of the parties or by either party giving to the other six months' notice of termination in writing to expire on the 31st March in any year.

## 21.   EMPLOYING AUTHORITIES

It is the decision of the Board in respect of the foregoing Agreement that it shall be circulated to all Employing Authorities advising them that the terms and conditions of this Agreement should be applied to all demolition and dismantling work in order to comply with the "Fair Wages" Resolution of the House of Commons, 1946, and other subsequent Resolutions or legislation.

The foregoing Agreement is deemed to be operative immediately.

Dated this 30th day of June 1980.

24

*Signed on behalf of the Employers' Side*
   *For* THE NATIONAL FEDERATION OF DEMOLITION
   CONTRACTORS LIMITED.
               R. E. WILLMENT, *President*
               A. B. FELDMAN, *Secretary*

*Signed on behalf of the Operatives' Side*
   *For* TRANSPORT & GENERAL WORKERS UNION
               G. E. HENDERSON, *National Secretary*

   *For* GENERAL & MUNICIPAL WORKERS UNION
               F. EARL, *National Officer*

   *For* UNION OF CONSTRUCTION, ALLIED TRADES &
   TECHNICIANS
               L. WOOD, *General Secretary*

25

# *APPENDIX*

## GRIEVANCE PROCEDURE

### Grievance Procedure

### 1. Individual Cases.

An individual operative having an issue or grievance shall in the first instance raise it verbally with his immediate supervisor and every effort should be made to reach a settlement at this level.

Failing settlement the issue or grievance may then be taken up with the site or works manager, agent or general foreman, or other person designated by management for that purpose. At this stage the operative may be accompanied by his union representative. If the problem cannot be resolved it should be referred to the Joint Secretaries for conciliation.

### 2. Collective Cases.

Where the issue or grievance affects a group of operatives they should refer the matter to their union representative who may proceed to take it up with the site manager, agent or general foreman, or other person designated by management for that purpose. Where the issue or grievance affects the members of more than one union the convenor steward shall deal with the matter in similar fashion.

### 3. Further Steps—Disputes or Differences.

In either case where the issue or grievance arises between members of the bodies affiliated to the Board, or any of them, and it cannot be resolved through the procedure laid down in paragraphs 1 and 2 above then it shall be the duty of the union representative to report the facts to the Operatives' Joint Secretary.

In the event that management and the full-time regional trade union officer are unable to resolve the difficulty it shall be the responsibility of both sides to progress the matter at National level. In the meantime there shall be no stoppage of work, restriction of hours worked, or reduction in output and the union representative shall see that this requirement is carried out. In all instances it shall be the responsibility of both the union and/or the convenor steward and of management to communicate decisions to the operatives concerned. In the case of management having an issue or grievance the matter should immediately be referred to the Joint Secretaries, as provided for in Part B of the Board's Constitution.

26

# Demolition safety check list

## A. Before work starts

1. Has a competent practical man been appointed to inspect the structure carefully (houses, flats, factories, etc.)?
   Has a competent technical man been appointed to inspect carefully: gas works, docks, mines, reinforced concrete structures, etc.?
2. Have plans been obtained from the local authority?
3. Has local authority permission been obtained for use of the demolition ball or other machinery?
4. **Is permission required for street closure or traffic diversion?**
5. Have all public services been located – gas, water, electricity, sewers, telephones? Have diversions been arranged as necessary?
6. Has the load-bearing capacity of floors to be used as working platforms been checked?
7. Have all shoring, scaffolds, lighting, danger notices, etc. been arranged?
8. Is sufficient protective clothing and equipment available?
9. Has a competent supervisor been nominated in writing?
10. Has a safe method been planned?

## B. During the contract

1. Is site properly enclosed and are fans erected?
2. Have danger notices been erected? Is all access to the public barred?
3. Are only physically fit men at work?
4. Is there sufficient shoring to prevent premature structural collapse or damage to adjacent property?
5. Are all ladders, cranes, cables and other equipment in good order?
6. Are any floors in danger of being overloaded?
7. Is all protective clothing and equipment being used?
8. Are all personnel (except crane operator and signalman) clear of the danger area when the ball is in use?
9. Are all crane windows properly protected?
10. Is sufficient watering taking place to keep down dust?

# Acts and regulations

*Legislation specially applicable to demolition work*

Clean Air Act 1956
Explosives Act 1875 and 1923
Factories Acts 1961
Construction Regulations 1961 and 1966
Highways Act 1959
Noise Abatement Act 1960
Town and Country Planning Act 1947
Water Act 1945
Electricity Regulations 1908 and 1944
Public Health Act 1936 and 1961
Public Health (London) Act 1936
Public Utilities Street Works Act 1950
Greater London Council (General Powers) Act 1966
London Building Acts (Amendment) 1939
Building (Scotland) Act 1959
Building Operations (Scotland) Regulations 1963
Building (Scotland) Act 1959 (Procedure) Regulations 1964
Building (Scotland) (Forms) Regulations 1964.

*Existing Acts and Regulations still operative along with HASAWA 1974.*

| | | |
|---|---|---|
| 1875 c. 17. | The Explosives Act 1875 | The whole Act except ss. 30 to 32, 80 and 116 to 121 |
| 1882 c. 22. | The Boiler Explosions Act 1882 | The whole Act |
| 1890 c. 35. | The Boiler Explosions Act 1890 | The whole Act . |
| 1906 c. 14. | The Alkali etc. Works Regulation Act 1906 | The whole Act |
| 1901 c. 43. | The Revenue Act 1909 | Section 11. |
| 1919 c. 23. | The Anthrax Prevention Act 1919 | The whole Act |
| 1920 c. 65 | The Employment of Women, Young Persons, and Children Act 1920 | The whole Act |
| 1922 c. 35. | The Celluloid and Cinematograph Film Act 1922 | The whole Act |

| | | |
|---|---|---|
| 1923 c. 17. | The Explosives Act 1923 | The whole Act |
| 1926 c. 43. | The Public Health (Smoke Abatement Act) 1926 | The whole Act |
| 1928 c. 32. | The Petroleum (Consolidation) Act 1928 | The whole Act |
| 1936 c. 22. | The Hours of Employment (Conventions) Act 1936 | The whole Act |
| 1936 c. 27. | The Petroleum (Transfer of Licences) Act 1936 | The whole Act |
| 1937 c. 45. | The Hydrogen Cyanide (Fumigation) Act 1937 | The whole Act |
| 1945 c. 19. | The Ministry of Fuel and Power Act 1945 | Section 1(1) so far as it relates to maintaining and improving the safety, health and welfare of persons employed in or about mines and quarries in Great Britain |
| 1946 c. 59. | The Coal Industry Nationalisation Act 1946 | Section 42(1) and (2) |
| 1948 c. 37. | The Radioactive Substances Act 1948 | Section 5(1) (a) |
| 1951 c. 21. | The Alkali, etc. Works Regulation (Scotland) Act 1951 | The whole act |
| 1951 c. 58. | The Fireworks Act 1951 | Sections 4 and 7 |
| 1952 c. 60. | The Agriculture (Poisonous Substances) Act 1952 | The whole Act |
| 1953 c. 47. | The Emergency Laws (Miscellaneous Provisions) Act 1953 | Section 3 |
| 1954 c. 70 | The Mines and Quarries Act 1954 | The whole Act except s. 151 |
| 1956 c. 49. | The Agriculture (Safety Health and Welfare Provisions) Act 1956 | The whole Act |
| 1961 c. 34. | The Factories Act 1961 | The whole Act except s. 135 |
| 1961 c. 64. | The Public Health Act 1961 | Section 73 |
| 1962 c. 58. | The Pipe-lines Act 1962 | Sections 20 to 26, 33, 34 and 42, Schedule 5 |
| 1963 c. 41. | The Office Shops and Railway Premises Act 1963 | The whole Act |
| 1965 c. 57. | The Nuclear Installations Act 1965 | Sections 1, 3 to 6, 22 and 24, Schedule 2 |
| 1969 c. 10. | The Mines and Quarries (Tips) Act 1969 | Sections 1 to 10 |
| 1971 c. 20. | The Mines Management Act 1971 | The whole Act |
| 1972 c. 28. | The Employment Medical Advisory Service Act 1972 | The whole Act except ss. 1 and 6 and Schedule 1 |

## Current legal and administrative controls in the workplace

| Relevant legislation, etc. | General remarks | Summary of the relevant provisions |
|---|---|---|
| Asbestos Regulations 1969 | Asbestos is defined in the Regs. Places/Process to which Regs apply is stated. HSE Guidance Note gives hygiene standards as follows:<br><br>0.2 fibres/ml measure over 10 minute period } for crocidolite<br>2 fibres/ml averaged over 4 hours<br>12 fibres/ml averaged over 10 minutes } for other types of asbestos<br><br>Exposure to all types of asbestos dust should be reduced to the minimum that is reasonably practicable. | 1. 28 days' written notice to HMFI before processes involving crocidolite begun.<br>2. Exhaust ventilation equipment to be provided, examined and maintained.<br>3. Where 2 impracticable RPE★ and protective clothing are required.<br>4. Workplaces to be kept clean and free from dust using dustless method (RPE required where this method impracticable)<br>5. Dust and waste to be stored in suitable receptacles.<br>6. Changing/storage facilities and cleaning to be provided for RPE and protective clothing.<br>7. Employment of persons under 18 prohibited in process, as using asbestos or for cleaning described in 6.<br>8. Certain requirements apply on cleanliness and cleaning systems in new buildings where Regs will apply.<br><br>★ RPE – Respiratory Protective Equipment. |
| Mines & Quarries Act 1954 | Section 74 applies to Mines and s. 12 to Quarries. These sections primarily apply to risks from dusts other than asbestos but can be applied to any operation where asbestos dust is given off. | 1. Mine managers have to see that dust of such a character or quantity as to be likely to be injurious to the persons employed is minimized and that any dust that enters the air is trapped or dispersed harmlessly. Any accumulation of dust should be cleared up, removed or treated to make it safe.<br>2. Quarry managers have a similar responsibility to 1 and a general duty to protect employees against the inhalation of dust. |

| | | |
|---|---|---|
| Health & Safety at Work etc. Act 1974 | Although there is no special mention of asbestos or health risks from dusts in the Act, ss. 2, 3, 4 and 6 require employers, manufacturers, etc. to ensure the absence of risks to health so far as reasonably practicable. This obliges an employer, etc. to do better than the standards if the necessary steps are reasonably practicable. The employer can choose the method for achieving the objective providing his obligation is fulfilled. | 1. Employers, etc. have a duty for the health* of:<br>(1) their employees for the absence of risk to health in connection with use, handling, storage and transport of articles or substances.<br>(2) persons other than their employees who:<br>(a) may be exposed to risk from the employer's work operations: or<br>(b) may use premises owned by the employer, etc. as a place of work.<br>The owner has to see that the means of access or egress to the premises or any plant used there are without risks to health.<br>2. Manufacturers, designers, importers and suppliers of substances for use at work have to ensure* generally that these substances are and remain safe when put to their intended use.<br>3. Manufacturers, etc. should also inform purchasers about any conditions which have to be observed to ensure safety during use and carry out or sponsor research for discovery*, minimization and elimination of any health risk the substance may give rise to.<br>4. There is also a duty for the best practicable means to prevent the emission into the atmosphere from prescribed premises of noxious or offensive substances and to render such substances as may be emitted as harmless and inoffensive.<br>* As far as reasonably practicable. |
| Social Security (Industrial Injuries) (Prescribed Diseases) Regs 1975 | Reg. 51 requires persons engaged in certain specified occupations involving risk of asbestosis to submit themselves for medical examinations. | 1. Before employing a new worker an employer must arrange for the worker to be medically examined usually by informing his local Pneumoconiosis Medical Panel.<br>2. The first exam should be carried out within 2 months of the date the employee first starts and then further exams every 2 years. |

Abrasive Wheels Regs 1970
Asbestos Regs 1969
Blasting (Casting and Other Articles) Special Regs 1949
Chemical Works Regs 1922
Chromium Plating Regs 1931
Clayworks (Welfare) Special Regs 1948
Construction (Health and Welfare) Regs 1966
Construction (General Provisions) Regs 1961
Construction (Lifting Operations) Regs 1961
Construction (Working Places) Regs 1966
Docks Regs 1934
Electricity (Factories Act) Special Regs 1908 and 1944
Foundries (Protective Footwear and Gaiters) Regs 1971
Grinding of Cutlery and Edge Tools Regs 1925 and 1950
Grinding of Metals (Miscellaneous Industries) Special Regs 1925 and 1950
Highly Flammable Liquids and Liquefied Petroleum Gases Regs 1972
Petroleum Gases Regs 1972
Horizontal Milling Machine Regs 1928
Ionising Radiations (Sealed Sources) Regs 1969
Ionising Radiations (Unsealed Radioactive Sources) Regs 1968
Iron and Steel Foundries Regs 1953
Lead Paint Regs 1927
Locomotive and Wagons (Used on lines) Regs 1906
Non-Ferrous Metals(Melting and Founding) Regs 1962
Pottery (Health and Welfare) Special Regs 1950
Power Presses Regs 1965
Protection of Eyes Regs 1974
Safety Representatives and Safety Committees Regs 1976
Shipbuilding and Shiprepairing Regs 1906
Woodworking Machinery Special Regs 1974

## Factories Act 1961

This Act consolidates the Factories Acts of 1937, 1948 and 1959, and affects building operations and works of engineering construction. Building operations and works of engineering construction are defined in s. 176 of the 1961 Act. Definition of a work of engineering construction is extended by the Engineering Construction (Extension of Definition) Regulations 1960, and by the Engineering Construction (Extension of Definition No. 2) Regulations 1968.

These operations and works may also be subject to some Special Regulations, such as:

| | | | |
|---|---|---|---|
| Abrasive Wheels, 1970 | S I 1970: | No. | 535 |
| Construction (General Provs.) | S I 1961: | No. | 1580 |
| Construction (Lifting Opns) | S I 1961: | No. | 1581 |
| Construction (Working Places) | S I 1966: | No. | 94 |
| Construction (Health & Welfare) | S I 1966: | No. | 95 |
| Compressed Air Special Regs | S I 1958: | No. | 61 |
| Compressed Air (Amdmt.) Regs | S I 1960: | No. | 1307 |
| Diving Operations Special Regs | S I 1960: | No. | 688 |
| Electricity Special Regs | S R 1908: | No. | 1312 |

| | | |
|---|---|---|
| Electricity Special Regs | S R 1944: | No. 739 |
| Woodworking Machinery Sp. Regs | S R 1922: | No. 1196 |
| Woodworking Machinery Sp. Regs | S R 1927: | No. 207 |
| Woodworking (Amendment of Scope) | S R 1945: | No. 1227 |
| Lead Paint Regulations | S R 1927: | No. 847 |
| Ionising Radiations Regs | S I 1969: | No. 808 |
| Asbestos Regulations | S I 1969: | No. 690 |

Certain official forms are prescribed for use in connection with building operations and works of engineering construction, and it is important to ensure compliance with the legal requirements. Full information for this can be obtained from HM Inspector of Factories.

## Registers and certificates

These should be kept on site or in the company offices:

| | | | |
|---|---|---|---|
| General Register | | F. | 36 |
| Specific Registers for Reports on: | | | |
| Inspection of Scaffolds | (Part 1A) | F. | 91 |
| Excavations, Shafts, Tunnels, etc. | (Part 1B) | F. | 91 |
| Weekly Inspection of Lifting Gear | (Part 1C) | F. | 91 |
| Derrick Crane Anchorage Tests | (Part 1D) | F. | 91 |
| Automatic Safe Load Indicator Tests | (Part 1E) | F. | 91 |
| Passenger Hoists Tests | (Part 1F) | F. | 91 |
| Examination of Lifting Gear After Repair | (Part 2G) | F. | 91 |
| Six-monthly Examination of Hoists | (Part 2H) | F. | 91 |
| Examination of Ropes, Chains, Lifting Gear | (Part 2J) | F. | 91 |
| Heat Treatment of Chains and Lifting Gear | (Part 2K) | F. | 91 |
| Certificate of Test and Examination Hoists | | F. | 75 |
| Crab, Winch, Pulley Block or Gin Wheel | | F. | 80 |
| Test and Examination of Wire Rope Before First Use | | F. | 87 |
| Certificate of Test and Examination of Crane | | F. | 96 |
| Test and Examination of Chains and Lifting Gear | | F. | 97 |
| Register of Persons Employed Painting Buildings | | F. | 92 |
| Abrasive Wheels Regulations Register | | F. | 2346 |
| Abrasive Wheels Regulations Cautionary Placard | | F. | 2347 |
| Abrasive Wheels Regulations Wheel Speeds Notice | | F. | 2350 |
| Abrasive Wheels Speeds Notice for Occupier | | F. | 2351 |
| Lead Paint Regulations Instructions Leaflet | | F. | 394 |
| Work in Compressed Air Workers' Transfer Record | | F. | 750 |
| Health Register | | F. | 751 |
| Lock Attendants' Register | | F. | 752 |
| Man-Lock Notice | | F. | 753 |
| Advisory Leaflet for Workers | | F. | 754 |
| 'Fragile Roof Coverings' Warning Notice | | F. | 901 |
| Register of Drivers' Fitness | | F. | 2015 |

## Notifications

These are for sending to factory inspectors and others:

Notice of Building Operations or Works of Engineering Construction
Lasting More Than Six Weeks      F. 10
Notice of Accident, Death Following an Accident Already Reported, or
Other Dangerous Occurrence      F. 43B
Notice of Poisoning or Disease      F. 41

## Pamphlets and booklets, etc.

| | |
|---|---|
| Memorandum on the Electricity Regulations | No. 928 |
| Abrasive Wheels, Safety in Installation and Use | No. 264 |
| List of Factory Inspectorates | No. F 243A |
| Safety in the Use of Abrasive Wheels booklet | No. 4 |
| General Site Safety Practice | No. 6A |
| Safety in Construction Work: Roofing booklet | No. 6B |
| Safety in Construction Work: Excavations booklet | No. 6C |
| Safety in Construction Work: Scaffolding booklet | No. 6D |
| Safety in Construction Work: System Building | No. 6F |
| Ionising Radiations Precautions for Users | No. 13 |
| Asbestos Health Precautions in Industry | No. 14 |
| Safety in Stacking Materials | No. 4 |
| Overhead Power Lines Accidents | No. 6 |
| Falls from Ladders | No. 9 |
| Crane Accidents on Construction Sites | No. 10 |

## Technical data notes

| | |
|---|---|
| Standards for Asbestos Dust Concentrations | No. 13 |
| Repair and Demolition of Large Storage Tanks | No. 18 |
| Metrication of Construction Regulations | No. 22 |
| Use of Working Platforms on Fork Lift Trucks | No. 23 |
| Erecting and Dismantling Tower Cranes | No. 26 |

## Construction (Working Places) Regulations 1966 (S I 94)

This is the code of regulations dealing with the safety of working places and the
means of getting to them and away from them (means of access and egress):

| | | |
|---|---|---|
| Reg. 9 | – | Construction of a Scaffold |
| Reg. 13 | – | Standards, Ledgers and Putlogs |
| Reg. 15 | – | Stability of Scaffolds |
| Reg. 16 | – | Slung Scaffolds |
| Reg. 17 | – | Cantilever Jibs, Figures and Brackets |
| Reg. 20 | – | Boatswains' Chairs |
| Reg. 21 | – | Trestle Scaffolds |
| Reg. 22 | – | Inspection of Scaffolds |
| Regs 24–26 | – | Working Platforms |
| Reg. 28 | – | Guardrails and Toeboards |
| Reg. 31–32 | – | Ladders |

Reg. 35    – Work on Sloping Roofs
Reg. 36    – Work On or Near Fragile Materials
Reg. 38    – Safety Nets and Belts

## Construction (General Provisions) Regs 1961 (S I 1580)

This code of regulations deals with a variety of subjects

Reg. 5 & 6   – Appointment of Safety Supervisors;
Reg. 8–14   – Excavations, Shafts and Tunnels;
Reg. 15–18   – Cofferdams and Caissons;
Reg. 19   – Use of Explosives;
Reg. 20–22   – Dangerous or Unhealthy Atmospheres;
Reg. 23–24   – Work On or Near to Water;
Reg. 25–37   – Use of Transport;
Reg. 38–41   – Demolition Work;
Reg. 42–43   – Guarding of Machinery;
Reg. 44   – Use of Electricity;
Reg. 46   – Protection from Falling Materials;
Reg. 48   – Damage from Projecting Nails;
Reg. 52   – Protection of Eyes;
Reg. 55   – Lifting Excessive Weights.

## Construction (Lifting Operations) Regs 1961 (S I 1581)

This code of regulations deals with the use on site of lifting appliances and lifting gear, etc.:

Regs 10–33   – Erection, Stability, Maintenance and Inspections, S.W.L.S, Signalling, etc.;
Regs 34–41   – Chains, Ropes, etc. Construction, Testing, Examination, S.W.L., etc.;
Regs 42–46   – Hoists, Enclosure, Gates, Tests, etc.;
Regs 47–49   – Carrying Persons and Securing Loads.

## Construction (Health and Welfare Regs) 1966 (S I 95)

This code of regulations requires the provision of certain facilities for the site personnel:

Reg. 4 – First Aid Boxes;
Reg. 6 – Contents of First Aid Boxes;
Reg. 7 – Training in First Aid Treatment;
Reg. 8 – Provision of Ambulances;
Reg. 9 – First Aid Rooms;
Reg. 11 – Provision of Mess Rooms;
Reg. 12 – Washing Facilities;
Reg. 13 – Sanitary Conveniences;

Reg. 15 – Protective Clothing.

## Compressed Air Working Places 1958 and 1960

These regulations should be studied thoroughly by supervisors on contracts for work in compressed air:

Reg. 16 – Advisory Leaflet for Every Worker;
Reg. 19 – Workers' Warning Label for Wearing;
Reg. 20 – Notification of Work to Hospitals.

## Further references

British Standard Specifications

| BSS | 15 | Mild Steel |
|-----|-----|-----|
| BSS | 153 | Steel Bridges |
| BSS | 449 | Structural Steel |
| BSS | 1129 | Timber Ladders, Steps, Trestles and Stagings |
| BSS | 2037 | Aluminium Ladders, Steps and Trestles |
| BSS | 1139 | Specifications for Metal Scaffolding |
| BSS | 2052 | Ropes – Coir; Hemp; Manila; Sisal |
| BSS | 1692 | Gin Blocks for Fibre Ropes |
| BSS | 1839 | London Pattern Pulley Blocks |
| BSS | 2830 | Suspended Safety Chairs and Cradles |
| BSS | 462 | Bulldog Grips |
| BSS | 1775 | Steel Tube |
| BSS | 1474 | Aluminium Tube |
| BSS | 2483 | Timber Scaffolding Boards |
| BSS | 3913 | Industrial Safety Nets |
| BSS | 1397 | Safety Belts and Harnesses |
| BSS | 2095 | Safety Helmets (Light) |
| BSS | 2826 | Safety Helmets (Heavy) |
| BSS | 2092 | Industrial Eye Protectors |
| BSS | 679 | Filter for Use during Welding and similar Industrial Operations |
| BSS | 1542 | Equipment for Eyes, Face and Neck protection Against Radiation |

*Quarries Explosives Regulations 1959 (SI 2259)* – though not applicable to the Construction Industry as such, contain much useful information in a general way on the use of explosives.

Also, the BS Handbook No. 4 *Lifting Tackle*, Parts 1 and 2.

British Standard Codes of Practice

CP3     *Design of Buildings*
CP97    Pt 1 – *Common Scaffolds in Steel*
CP97    Pt 2 – *Suspended Scaffolds*
CP112        – *Timber in Buildings*

# Useful addresses

**Health and Safety Executive; Chief Factory Inspector; Chief Employment Medical Adviser**: Baynards House, Chepstow Place, Westbourne Grove, London W2 4TY. Tel: (01) 229-3456

**EMAS/Factory Inspectorate Laboratory**: 401 Edgware Road, Cricklewood, London NW2. Tel: (01) 450-8911

**Industrial Health and Safety Centre**: 97 Horseferry Road, Westminster, London SW1. Tel: (01) 828-9255

**Royal Society for the Prevention of Accidents (ROSPA)**: Cannon House, The Priory Queensway, Birmingham B4 6BS. Tel: (021) 233-2461

**British Safety Council**: 62 Chancellors Road, London W6. Tel: (01) 741-1231

**Socialist Medical Association**: 9 Poland Street, London W1V 3DG. Tel: (01) 439-3395

**British Society for Social Responsibility in Science (Work Hazards Group)** (address as above). Tel: (01) 437-2728

**TUC Medical Adviser** Trades Union Congress, Congress House, Great Russell Street, London WC1B 3LS. Tel: (01) 636-4030

**TUC Centenary Institute of Occupational Health**: Keppel Street, Gower Street, London WC1 Tel: (01) 580-2386

**British Standards Institution:** Collect Sales: 2 Park Street London W1A 2BS. Tel: (01) 629-9000. Postal Sales: 101 Pentonville Road, London N1. Tel: (01) 837-8801

**Industry Training Boards –**
  (i) Construction: 1st Floor, Radnor House, 1272 London Road, Norbury, London SW16. Tel: (01) 764-5060
  (ii) Chemical and Allied Products: Staines House, 158/162 High Street, Staines, Middlesex. Tel: Staines 51366

**Industrial Advisory Committees –**
  (i) Construction: – various (many still to be formed): Mr A. J. Hinksman (Secretary), Mr A. D. Sill (Chairman), London South Area Office (HSE), 1 Long Lane, Southwark, London SE1 4PG. Tel: (01) 407-8911

*Area offices of the Health and Safety Executive as at April 1980*

1 **South West** (Avon, Cornwall, Devon, Gloucestershire, Somerset, Isles of Scilly) Inter City House, Victoria Street, Bristol BS1 6AN. Tel: 0272 290681

2 **South** (Berkshire, Dorset, Hampshire, Isle of Wight, Wiltshire)
Priestley House, Priestley Road, Basingstoke RG24 9NW. Tel: 0256 3181

3 **South East** (Kent, Surrey, East Sussex, West Sussex)
Paymaster General's Building, Russell Way, Crawley, West Sussex RH10 1UH. Tel: 0293 511671

4 **London NW** (Barnet, Brent, Camden, City of London, Enfield, Hammersmith, Harrow, Hillingdon, Hounslow, Kensington and Chelsea, City of Westminster)
Chancel House, Neasden Lane, London NW10 2UD. Tel: 01-459 8844

5 **London NE** (Barking, Hackney, Haringey, Havering, Islington, Newham, Redbridge, Tower Hamlets, Waltham Forest)
Royal London House, 18 Finsbury Square, London EC2 1DH. Tel: 01-638 2841

6 **London South** (Bexley, Bromley, Croydon, Greenwich, Kingston upon Thames, Lambeth, Lewisham, Merton, Richmond upon Thames, Southwark, Sutton, Wandsworth)
1 Long Lane, London SE1 4PG. Tel: 01-407 8911

7 **East Anglia** (Essex except parts of Essex covered by Area 5, Norfolk, Suffolk)
39 Baddow Road, Chelmsford, Essex CM2 OHL. Tel: 0245 84661

8 **Northern and Home Counties** (Bedfordshire, Buckinghamshire, Cambridgeshire, Hertfordshire)
King House, George Street West, Luton LU1 2DD. Tel: 0582 34121

9 **East Midlands** (Leicestershire, Northamptonshire, Oxfordshire, Warwickshire)
Belgrave House, 1 Greyfriars, Northampton NN1 2LQ. Tel: 0604 21233

10 **West Midlands** (West Midlands)
McLaren Building, 2 Masshouse Circus, Queensway, Birmingham B4 7NP. Tel: 021-236 5080

11 **Wales** (Clwyd, Dyfed, Gwent, Gwynedd, Mid Glamorgan, Powys, South Glamorgan, West Glamorgan)
Brunel House, 2 Fitzalan Road, Cardiff CF2 1SH. Tel: 0222 497777

12 **Marches** (Hereford and Worcester, Salop, Staffordshire)
2 Hassell Street, Newcastle-under-Lyme, Staffs ST5 1DT. Tel: 0782 625324

13 **North Midlands** (Derbyshire, Lincolnshire, Nottingham)
Birkbeck House, Trinity Square, Nottingham NG1 4AU. Tel: 0602 40712

14 **South Yorkshire** (Humberside, South Yorkshire)
Sovereign House, 40 Silver Street, Sheffield S1 2ES. Tel: 0742 739081

15 **West and North Yorks** (North Yorkshire, West Yorkshire)
8 St Pauls Street, Leeds LS1 2LE. Tel: 0532 446191

16 **Greater Manchester** (Greater Manchester)
Quay House, Quay Street, Manchester M3 3JB. Tel: 061-381 7111

17 **Merseyside** (Greater Merseyside)
The Triad, Stanley Road, Bootle L20 3PG. Tel: 051-922 7211

18 **North West** (Cumbria, Lancashire)
Victoria House, Ormskirk Road, Preston PR1 1HH. Tel: 0772 59321

19 **North East** (Cleveland, Durham, Northumberland, Tyne and Wear)
Government Buildings, Kenton Bar, Newcastle upon Tyne NE1 2YX. Tel: 0632 869811

20 **Scotland East** (Borders, Central, Fife, Grampian, Highland, Lothian, Tayside and the island areas of Orkney and Shetland)
Meadowbank House, 153 London Road, Edinburgh EH8 7AU. Tel: 031-661 6171

**21 Scotland West** (Dumfries, and Galloway, Strathclyde, and the Western Islands)
314 St Vincent Street, Glasgow G3 8XG. Tel: 041-204 2646

Communications should be addressed to the Area Executive of the area concerned.

## Employment Medical Advisory Service – EMAS regional organization

**Northern** (Metropolitan County of Tyne and Wear, Cleveland, Cumbria, Durham, Northumberland)
Government Buildings, Kenton Bar, Newcastle upon Tyne NE1 2YN. Tel. 0632 863411
**Eastern and South East Midlands** Bedfordshire, Buckinghamshire, Cambridgeshire, Essex, Hertfordshire, Leicestershire, Norfolk, Northamptonshire, Oxfordshire, Suffolk, Warwickshire)
4 Dunstable Road, Luton, Beds LU1 1DX. Tel. 0582 415722
**South Western** (Avon, Berkshire, Cornwall, Devon, Dorset, Gloucestershire, Hampshire, Isle of Wight, Somerset, Wiltshire)
Beacon Tower, Fishponds Road, Bristol BS16 3HA. Tel. 0272 659573
**West Midlands** (Metropolitan County of West Midlands, Wolverhampton, Coventry, Hereford and Worcester, Salop, Staffordshire)
1 McLaren Buildings, 2 Masshouse Circus, Queensway, Birmingham B4 7NP. Tel. 021 236 5080
**Scotland** (Scotland)
Meadowbank House, London Road, Edinburgh EH8 7AU. Tel. 031 661 6171
**North Eastern** (Metropolitan Counties of South Yorkshire and West Yorkshire, Derbyshire, Humberside, Lincolnshire, North Yorkshire, Nottingham)
8 St Paul's Street, Leeds LS1 2LE. Tel. 0532 446191
**London and South Eastern** (Greater London, Kent, Surrey, East Sussex, West Sussex)
Atlantic House, Farringdon Street, London EC4 A 4BA. Tel. 01 583 5020
**Wales** (Wales)
St David's House, Wood Street, Cardiff CF1 1PB. Tel. 0222 43984
**Northern Western** (Metropolitan Counties of Greater Manchester, and Merseyside, Cheshire, Lancashire)
Quay House, Quay Street, Manchester M3 3JE. Tel. 061 831 7111

## Her Majesty's Stationery Office government bookshops

**London** 49 High Holborn WC1V 6HB (callers only); P O Box 569 SE1 9NH (trade and London area mail order)
**Cardiff** 41 The Hayes CF1 1JW
**Bristol** Southey House, Wine Street BS1 2BQ
**Belfast** 80 Chichester Street BT1 4JY
**Edinburgh** 13a Castle Street EH2 3AR
**Manchester** Brazennose Street M60 8AS
**Birmingham** 258 Broad Street B1 2HE

## *CITB offices*

**Headquarters** Radnor House, 1272 London Road, London SW16 4EL. Tel. 01-764 5060

**Information Services** Glen House, Stag Place, London SW1E 5AL. Tel: 01-834 2181, 01-834 2195, 01-834 2169

**Scotland** 3-4 Claremont Terrace, Glasgow G3 7XR. Tel: 041-332 3323

**North East Region** Jesmond House, Victoria Avenue, Harrogate, Yorks HG1 4QG Tel: 0423-68322. Counties served: Cleveland, Durham, Humberside, Northumberland, North Yorkshire, South Yorkshire, Tyne and Wear, West Yorkshire.

**North West Region** Federation House, Hope Street, Liverpool, L19HL. Tel: 051-709 8489. Counties served: Cheshire, Clwyd, Cumbria, Greater Manchester, Gwynedd, High Peak of Derbyshire, Lancashire, Merseyside.

**Midland Region** 9 North Street, Rugby, CV21 2AB. Tel: 0788-65546/2738/71909. Counties served: Derbyshire (excluding High Peak), Hereford and Worcester, Leicestershire, Lincolnshire, Northamptonshire, Nottinghamshire, Salop, Staffordshire, Warwickshire, West Midlands

**West and Wales Region** 18/19 Belmont, Bath BA1 5DZ. Tel: 0225-316695. Counties served: Avon, Cornwall, Devon, Dorset (excluding Poole), Dyfed, Gloucestershire, Gwent, Mid Glamorgan, Powys, Somerset, South Glamorgan, West Glamorgan, Wiltshire

**Eastern Region** 56 Park Street, Luton, Beds, LU1 3JD. Tel: 0582-27462. Counties served: Bedfordshire, Berkshire, Buckinghamshire, Cambridgeshire, Essex, Hertfordshire, Norfolk, Oxfordshire, Suffolk

**London and South East Region** Glen House, Stag Place, London, SW1E 5AL. Tel: 01-828 7384/8. Counties served: East Sussex, Greater London, Hampshire (and Poole, Dorset), Isle of Wight, Kent, Surrey, West Sussex

## *National Training Centres*

**Bircham Newton Training Centre**, Bircham Newton, Nr King's Lynn, Norfolk. Tel: Syderstone 291

**Civil Engineering College**, Bircham Newton, Nr King's Lynn, Norfolk. Tel: Syderstone 291

**Merton Training Centre**, Littler's Close, Runnymede, Merton, SW19 2TE. Tel: 01-542 0696

**Glasgow Training Centre**, 2 Edison Street, Hillington, Glasgow GS2 4XN. Tel: 041-882 6455/6

# Health hazards

## *Lead[1]*

### Introduction

In the past, HSE reports highlighted the problems of lead poisoning within the demolition industry. Recent information shows that the industry still has a long way to go in prevention of lead absorption.

The following notes are intended as an information guide to the problem of lead, preventative measures and legislation which will be applicable to the demolition industry.

### Types of lead

Chemically there are basically two types of lead:

1. Inorganic lead – found in paint.
2. Organic lead – additive used in petrol.

The commonest type in demolition is – **inorganic**.

Normally, the higher lead levels in paint are found on older-type structures e.g. railway stations, bridges.

### Medical aspects of lead absorption

Lead when taken into the body system enters the bloodstream. The route of entry to the system for inorganic lead is by inhalation or ingestion. Organic lead is absorbed through skin tissues. Lead absorbed into the bloodstream results in a measurable blood lead level. There are medically laid down limits which are listed as follows:

| Test | A<br>Normal | B<br>Acceptable | C<br>Excessive | D<br>Dangerous |
|------|-------------|-----------------|----------------|----------------|
| Blood Lead | $<1.9 \mu$ mol/l<br>($<40 \mu$ g/100 ml) | $<3.9 \mu$ mol/l<br>($<80 \mu$ g/100 ml) | $3.9-4.9 \mu$ mol/l<br>($80-100 \mu$ g/100 ml) | $>4.9 \mu$ mol/l<br>($>100 \mu$ g/100 ml) |

Specific reaction of individuals to lead absorption cannot be generalized. Experience shows that even a very high blood level does not necessarily constitute lead poisoning. Low haemoglobin, together with urine lead levels coupled with clinical physical symptoms should be taken into account by a doctor before prescribing 'lead poisoning'. Supervisors and foremen should be familiar with levels quoted and the units of measurement. A basic understanding is necessary in order to discuss the problem of lead with visiting factory inspectors and/or doctors.

Notification of lead poisoning

Should a member of your workforce suffer from lead poisoning then your company has a legal duty to notify the HSE. Notification is made to the Factory Inspectorate and Employment Medical Advisory Service on a form F41.

Prevention of lead poisoning

The potential lead risk should be evaluated.

(*a*)  *Tests* – with flame cutting of lead-painted structures, lead is given off as particulate dust suspended in air. Atmospheric tests should be carried out, and the results will indicate whether respiratory protection is needed and of what type.

(*b*)  *Threshold Limit Value (TLV)* – for lead is $0-15$ mg/m$^3$ of air. Levels of lead in air above the TLV necessitate the wearing of adequate respiratory protection or some form of extraction equipment to reduce the lead level.

(**c**)  *Respirators* – these range from ori-nasal dust respirators to full air-line equipment. Various types have differing protection values in relation to the TLV. Only British Standards equipment as approved by the HSE should be used.

(*d*)  *Personal hygiene* – a high level is required. Adequate washing facilities are essential and ideally showers should be available.

(*e*)  *Medical examinations* – the workforce engaged in work where there is a lead risk should have regular medical examinations.

Legislation

Previously there had been an absence of statutory law in relation to lead work within the demolition industry. This situation altered when the new regulations 'Lead at Work' became effective. Previously the enforcing authorities utilized the recommendations as set out in the Guidance Note – Lead Health Precautions. This Guidance Note has been used in the formulation of regulations and a Code of Practice entitled the *Control of Lead at Work*. Published as a consultative document during 1978, comments were invited from industry, and final document was published towards the end of 1980.

When the new regulations became effective it placed the demolition industry under statutory lead legislation for the first time. The requirements of the regulations are extensive and will have a considerable effect on the industry.

### Lead compounds, etc.

Every contractor who employs any persons on a site in a process in which lead compound or other poisonous substance is used, must provide the facilities required as the case may be, and must include nail brushes: the troughs, basins, buckets or washbasins so provided must be on the scale of one for every five persons so employed. All washing facilities provided under this regulation must be conveniently accessible to the accommodation afforded for taking meals, and must be kept in a clean and orderly condition.

For the purpose of definition 'lead compound' means any material containing lead which, when treated in the manner prescribed by rules made under section 132 of the Factories Act 1961, yields to an aqueous solution of hydrochloric acid a quantity of soluble lead compound exceeding (when calculated as lead monoxide) 5 per cent of the dry weight of the portion taken for analysis.

### Conclusion

The Regulations may seem far-reaching, but in most cases are merely an extension with more statutory powers of what should exist at present.

Trade federations within the industry made comments to the HSE on various aspects. The Regulations are aimed at bringing all lead activities within the whole of industry under one set of Regulations instead of the previous fragmented situation.

As with any regulations one can argue that we are different and, therefore, a special case. In purely practical terms it is envisaged that certain parts of the Regulations may be relaxed or made non-applicable to the demolition industry. However, it is certain that the bulk will apply and the industry should be prepared for their implementation.


## Hazards affecting eyes, ears, skin and lungs[1]

### Legal obligation

Under the Health and Safety At Work Act 1974, section 2(2c) an employer has a duty: for the provision of such information, instruction, training and supervision as is necessary to ensure, so far as is reasonably practicable, the health and safety at work of his employees.

Parts of the body at risk

1. The Skin – cancer and dermatitis.
2. The Lungs – fumes, dust and gases.
3. The Eyes – flying particles and intense light.
4. The Ears – noise.
5. Body Organs – poisons.

*The skin*

(a) *Cancer.*  Can affect the whole body, but normally enters the body via the lungs or skin.

Any substance which causes cancer is known as a **carcinogen**. The best-known carcinogens are tar, shale oil and cigarette smoke.

Skin cancer can be caused by long periods in contact with mineral oils, paraffins, tars and arsenic, X-rays, ultra-violet light.

(b) *Dermatitis.*  The most common industrial disease is an inflammation of the skin. The disease can be caused by tens of thousands of chemicals and apparently harmless substances – what may cause dermatitis to one person may not cause it in another.

There are three kinds of risk:

1. Primary irritants – chemicals that are harmful in their own right. Most dermatitis is caused by this type of substance.
2. Substances that remove the oil from the skin – solvents, thinners, etc.
3. You become allergic to a particular substance.

Protective measures:

(a) Protective clothing – gloves and overalls.
(b) Barrier creams.
(c) Skin cleansers.
(d) Personal hygiene.

*The Lungs*

*Dust*  On entering the lungs this can be very dangerous. If the dust contains concentrations of various chemicals it can destroy the tissues of the lungs. Pneumoconiosis is the name given to a group of lung diseases caused by dust containing poisonous substances, e.g. asbestosis.

*Nuisance dust*  This is comprised of particles which are a nuisance rather than harmful. In general, have little history of causing adverse effects.

*Fumes*  When minute particles reach the lungs, they may dissolve in the natural fluids residing there and be distributed around the body via other organs. Exposure to fumes containing metal particles could lead to metal poisoning, e.g. lead poisoning.

*Poisonous gases*    There are two main groups:

1.  Irritants, which have a strong, unpleasant smell, e.g. ammonia.
2.  Gases that are easy to inhale, such as carbon monoxide, this gas kills more people than any other.

Protective measures:

(a)  Harmful dusts – appropriate dust respirator.
(b)  Nuisance dust – spraying with water, in bad conditions appropriate dust respirator.
(c)  Fumes – appropriate dust respirator.
(d)  Gases – stringent safety measures and self-contained breathing apparatus.

*The eyes*

The Protection of Eyes Regulations 1974 govern the requirements for the protection of the eyes in an industrial environment.

Employers must provide eye protection for certain processes and the following requirements must be complied with:

(a)  Suitable for the person for whose use they are provided.
(b)  Made to an approved standard.
(c)  Contain particulars to indicate their purpose.
(d)  Replaced when defective or lost.

Persons provided with eye protection must:

(a)  Use it at all times.
(b)  Take reasonable care of it.
(c)  Report when eye protection is defective or lost.

Eye protection must be used when:

(a)  Working with hand-held cartridge-operated tool.
(b)  Cold cutting with hand tools or power tools.
(c)  Demolishing plant, etc. that has contained a dangerous substance.
(d)  Abrasive cutting.
(e)  Breaking, cutting or drilling with a hand tool or power tool.
(f)  Cutting of material with flame-cutting equipment.

*The ears*

At present there are no statutory regulations concerning noise control.

A Code of Practice has been published, which covers:

(a)  Methods of controlling noise exposure.

(b)  Limits of noise exposure.

(c)  Ear protection.

*Effect of noise*  (a)  Interferes with working efficiency by hindering communication.

(b)  Violent noise can rupture the eardrum.

(c)  Deafness can also be caused by continual exposure to noise. This sort of damage is often slow to develop and may take years of exposure to noise before the effects become serious.

*Noise level*  Hearing protectors should be worn by people exposed for eight hours to a noise level exceeding 90 dB.

Method of controlling noise levels:

1.  Exhaust systems – provided with effective silencers.

2.  Machines, etc. – provided with sound-insulating enclosures.

3.  Inspection and maintenance – regular inspection and maintenance by a competent person.

*Body organs*

*Poisoning*  This is caused by substances that circulate in the bloodstream and attack organs other than your lungs or skin – even if they have obtained access by those routes.

The organs most likely to be attacked are:

(a)  The blood itself.

(b)  The liver.

(c)  The kidneys.

(d)  The brain and nervous system.

*Hazard data sheets*  These are a good method of providing relevant information of a particular dangerous substance.

The sheet will contain such information as:

1.  The threshold limit value.

2.  Hazards encountered.

3.  What precautions to take.

4.  If the substance produces acute or chronic poisoning effects.

## Threshold Limit Value (TLV)

A means of expressing acceptable concentration of a particular substance.

It is defined as 'the level to which it is believed that nearly all workers may be repeatedly exposed day after day without adverse effect'.

Exposure time is assumed to be eight hours a day and forty hours a week.

TLV values are measured in parts per million (p.p.m.) or number of milligrams per cubic metre $(mg/m^3)$.

## Asbestos $(MgSiO_4)$

TLV : Crysotile – 2.0 fibres per c.c. of air
: Amosite – 2.0 fibres per c.c. of air
: Tremolite – 2.0 fibres per c.c. of air
: Crocodilite – 0.2 fibres per c.c. of air

**First aid measures**: None called for.

*General data*

Grade III Material

Asbestos: (meaning unconsumable) is a collective term applied to a group of silicate materials of different chemical composition but exhibiting valuable physical properties. It is a mineral containing fibres of variable length and is capable of being spun into yarn and woven into textiles.

Its principal qualities are that it is:

1. Resistant to fire and heat.
2. Has low heat conductivity.
3. Has high electrical resistance.
4. Is inert to chemical reaction.

*Uses and varieties*

1. Serpentine or chrysotile asbestos constitutes 90% of world production and is a magnesium silicate with very short fibres.
2. The Amphibole Group consists of amosite, crocidolite and tremolite.
(a) Amosite contains iron and is a dirty brown colour. The fibres are several inches long and are of poor spinning quality. It is used for heat-resistant blocks and for asbestos sheeting used in buildings.
(b) Crocidolite or blue asbestos has been used extensively for its resistance to chemical reaction.
(c) Tremolite is white and has very long fibres often over a metre in length. It is mainly used for lagging of boilers and steam pipes.

The main uses of asbestos are:

1. Gaskets, joints and brake linings.
2. Heat protective clothing usually rigidly bonded and carrying a low risk of release of asbestos into the atmosphere.
3. Lagging material for steam pipes and boilers.
4. Refractory asbestos for its heat- and fire-resistant properties on steel and

blast furnaces and vacuum degassing vessels.

*Hazards* (by inhalation)

1. Asbestosis – a fibrosis (solidification) of lung tissue.
2. Lung cancer.
3. Mesothelioma (a malignant tumour) of the lining of the chest and abdominal cavities (pleura and peritoneum). This disease has a unique association with crocidolite or blue asbestos and has led to the banning of the use of blue asbestos in this country.

These diseases are liable to arise in the asbestos-using industries such as the steel industry due to the dust which arises during cutting, sawing of sheets or dismantling of asbestos lagging materials.

*Precautions*

Have become very rigid in recent years and are covered by the Asbestos Regulations 1969. Those recommended in the British Steel Corporation are:

1. Substitute materials should be used where possible.
2. The enclosure of the process where possible.
3. By the use of local exhaust ventilation to reduce atmospheric contamination below the threshold limit value (monitoring the atmosphere is mandatory and will be enforced by the Factory Inspectorate). Hygiene Laboratory testing.
4. By wetting the process where possible.
5. By the provision of respirators. The Asbestos Regulations demand in addition:
(a) If the dust concentration is up to 40 fibres per c.c. of air – a half face respirator.
(b) If the dust concentration is up to 200 fibres per c.c. of air – a pressure-fed respirator.
(c) Over 200 fibres per c.c. of air – a fresh-air-line respirator must be supplied and used.

Other precautions demanded by the Regulations include:

(a) The provision of overalls.
(b) Special changing facilities.
(c) Laundering of protective clothing to be done on the works or by special arrangement.
(d) No young persons (under 18 years of age) to be employed in the area.

*Acute poisoning*
There is none.

*Chronic poisoning*
The three varieties of disease produced by inhaling asbestos fibres are long term and require up to 20 years' exposure or longer before symptoms become manifest. Symptoms:

1. Shortness of breath.
2. Cough with sputum.
3. Loss of weight and general debility.

*Treatment*
By prevention of exposure to asbestos dust by:

(a) Substitution.
(b) Regular monitoring of the area by the Hygiene Laboratory.
(c) Provision of adequate exhaust ventilation or air-line respirators.
(d) Routine radiography of personnel exposed to the hazard.

*Factories Act references and regulations*
Section (4); s. (30); s. (58); s. (59); s. (63); s. (82).

- Asbestos Regulations 1969.
- Technical data Note No. 13 DEP.
- Asbestosis is a prescribed disease under the National Insurance (Industrial Injuries) Act.
- The Factory Inspectorate require to be notified before any work is undertaken in stripping old lagging which may contain crocidolite.
- Ministry of Labour HM Factory Inspectorate, *Problems Arising From the Use of Asbestos*, HM Stationery Office, 1967.

*Organizations able to provide air monitoring and analytical services*
The following health laboratories have facilities for counting asbestos fibres:
**TUC Centenary Institute of Occupational Health**, London School of Hygiene and Tropical Medicine, Keppel Street, London WC1E 7HT.
**National Occupational Hygiene Service Ltd**, 12 Brook Road, Fallowfield, Manchester M14 6UH.
**North of England Industrial Health Service**, 20 Claremont Place, Newcastle upon Tyne NE2 4AA.
**Department of Social and Occupational Medicine**, Welsh National School of Medicine, Heath Park, Cardiff CF4 4XN.
**Institute of Occupational Medicine**, Roxburgh Place, Edinburgh EH8 9SU.
**Scottish Occupational Health Laboratory Service Ltd**, 9 Dudhope Terrace, Dundee DD3 6HG.

Primary manufacturers of asbestos products may be able to supply a service where their products are involved and, in particular, assistance may be obtained from the following:

**TAC Construction Materials Ltd**, Trafford Park, Manchester M17 1RU.
**Cape Universal Ltd**, Cowley Bridge Works, Iver, Nr. Uxbridge.
**Industrial Health Unit**, BBA Ltd, Cleckheaton, Yorks.

*Insulating materials and finishes which may contain asbestos*
Usually applied dry:
    Moulded asbestos – 100% asbestos
    Moulded calcium silicate
    Moulded 85% magnesia
    Moulded high-temperature insulation blocks
    Asbestos reinforced building boards
    Asbestos cloth
    Asbestos rope
    Asbestos millboard
Usually applied wet:
    85% magnesia plastic
    Calcium silicate plastic
    Asbestos plastic
    High-temperature plastic
    Asbestos spray
    Hard-setting non-conducting compositions
    Self-setting cements
    Bituminous armouring coatings
    Bituminous mastics
    Polymeric mastics
    Polymeric mastics
    Metal joint sealers or caulking compounds
*Note*: When sampling for asbestos content of existing systems, samples should
    be taken throughout the total insulation thickness.

*Mobile asbestos decontamination unit specification* (shown in Fig. 4.29)
A three-compartment unit with a 'dirty' area at one end, a shower compartment
in the centre and a 'clean' area at the other end. The 'dirty' area and 'clean' area
each to have bench seating and five numbered lockers for the storage of
clothing.

The personnel using the unit should enter the 'dirty' area through the outside
door, either two or three persons at any one time, and remove the major part of
the dust from their clothing by means of the Nilfisk GS 80 vacuum with absolute filter to BS 2989/65.

Sodium Flame Test at 99.997 per cent efficiency extracting particle size down
to 0.3 $\mu$m.

The personnel should then remove their clothing and place this in sealed
plastic bags for removal at a later stage, while still retaining their face mask in
position. There is a 'through the wall' fan and filter in the 'dirty' area which
would provide a negative purge on the shower area into the 'dirty' area and, in

the 'clean' area into the shower area. To the outlet fan in the 'dirty' area, there would be fitted a Volkes absolute filter which gives 0.003 per cent penetration against a Sodium Flame Test, BS 3928. This filter is suitable for 100 per cent relative humidity and will operate by removing particles down to 0.01 $\mu$m. The absolute filter is protected by a disposable pre-filter, 50 mm thick resin bonded fibre filament and the air is drawn through both filters by a backward-inclined fan providing 0.13 m$^3$/s at 1425 r.p.m. utilizing a 1119 W single-phase motor with external weatherproof cover.

The personnel, once they have removed their clothing, will then pass through a sliding door into the shower compartment and immediately before stepping into the shower, they should remove their face mask and place this into a container. Once they have showered, they should go through the further sliding door into the 'clean' area where they will change into everyday clothing from the lockers provided. The sliding doors are interlocked to avoid both doors being opened.

Figures A8.1, A8.2, A8.3 and Tables A8.1, A8.4, A8.5, and A8.6 show the distribution, usage and varieties of asbestos and asbestos related products in the UK. Tables A8.2 and A8.3 show the world production and UK imports of asbestos and Fig. A8.4 shows a typical asbestos dust extractor.

*The Asbestos Research Council*
Secretary to the Council, P.O. Box 40, Rochdale, Lancashire, Tel: Rochdale 47422
Environmental Control Committee, Secretary, P.O. Box 18, Cleckheaton, West Yorkshire. BD19 3UJ Tel: Cleckheaton 875711

*Table A8.1* Asbestos fibres usage in the UK (thousands of tonnes)

|  | 1970 | 1973 | 1976 |
|---|---|---|---|
| 1. Asbestos cement products for building (including (5)) | 52.5 | 55.6 | 42.9 |
| 2. Fire-resistant insulation boards | 18.5 | 22.5 | 14.5 |
| 3. Other insulation products (including spray) | 4.0 | 4.0 | 0.4 |
| 4. Floor tiles and coverings | 20.5 | 16.2 | 15.8 |
| 5. Asbestos cement pipes (included under (1)) |  | 9.0 | 8.1 |
| 6. Friction materials | 15.0 | 17.0 | 15.7 |
| 7. Jointings and packings | 9.0 | 11.4 | 10.0 |
| 8. Textiles products not included in (6) and (7) | 9.0 | 8.3 | 6.3 |
| 9. Fillers and reinforcements (felts, millboard paper, underseals, mastics, adhesives, etc) | 21.5 | 25.7 | 28.4 |
| 10. Moulded plastics and battery cases | 4.5 | 2.8 | 1.2 |
| Totals | 154.5 | 172.5 | 143.3 |

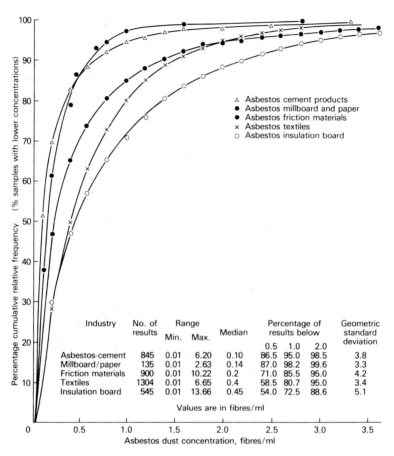

The chart legend:
- △ Asbestos cement products
- ● Asbestos millboard and paper
- ● Asbestos friction materials
- × Asbestos textiles
- ○ Asbestos insulation board

| Industry | No. of results | Range Min. | Range Max. | Median | Percentage of results below 0.5 | 1.0 | 2.0 | Geometric standard deviation |
|---|---|---|---|---|---|---|---|---|
| Asbestos-cement | 845 | 0.01 | 6.20 | 0.10 | 86.5 | 95.0 | 98.5 | 3.8 |
| Millboard/paper | 135 | 0.01 | 2.63 | 0.14 | 87.0 | 98.2 | 99.6 | 3.3 |
| Friction materials | 900 | 0.01 | 10.22 | 0.2 | 71.0 | 85.5 | 95.0 | 4.2 |
| Textiles | 1304 | 0.01 | 6.65 | 0.4 | 58.5 | 80.7 | 95.0 | 3.4 |
| Insulation board | 545 | 0.01 | 13.66 | 0.45 | 54.0 | 72.5 | 88.6 | 5.1 |

Values are in fibres/ml

*Fig. A8.1* Distribution of asbestos dust exposure levels in different manufacturing industries (based on four-hour personal sampling data obtained in the period Nov. 1972–Feb. 1978)

*Table A8.2* World production of asbestos. Annual figures as at August 1978

| | *Tonnes* |
|---|---|
| USSR | 2 650 000 |
| Canada | 1 572 000 |
| Southern Africa | 783 000 |
| Europe | 353 000 |
| China | 250 000 |
| USA | 150 100 |
| South Central America | 130 000 |
| Australia | 80 000 |
| Others | 50 350 |
| Total | 6 018 450 |

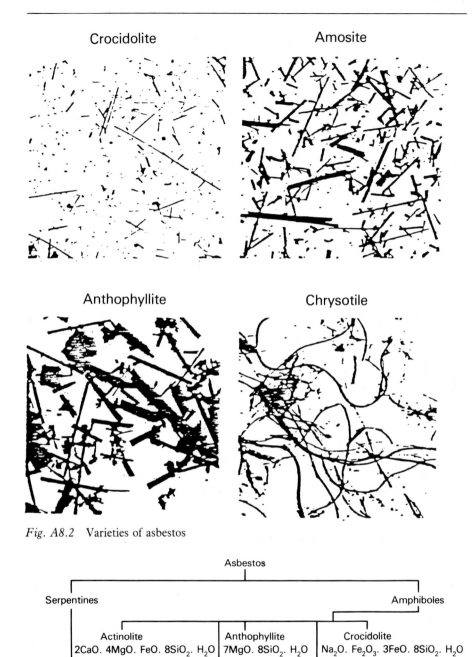

Fig. A8.2   Varieties of asbestos

Fig. A8.3   Varieties of asbestos and their chemical composition

*Table A8.3* Imports of asbestos to the United Kingdom by fibre type. Percentages calculated with 1946 as base

| Year | Serpentines Chrysotile | | Amphiboles Crocidolite | | Amosite | | Anthophyllite | | All | | Total Asbestos | |
|---|---|---|---|---|---|---|---|---|---|---|---|---|
| | Metric tonnes | % | Tonnes | % | Tonnes | % | Tonnes | cent | Tonnes | % | Tonnes | % |
| 1946 | 50 700 | 100 | 1000 | 100 | 2 700 | 100 | — | — | 3 700 | 100 | 54 400 | 100 |
| 1955 | 123 000 | 243 | 6800 | 680 | 12 300 | 456 | — | — | 19 100 | 516 | 142 100 | 261 |
| 1965 | 147 000 | 290 | 3400 | 340 | 22 600 | 837 | 100 | — | 26 100 | 705 | 173 100 | 318 |
| 1975 | 120 000 | 237 | — | — | 19 200 | 711 | 200 | — | 19 400 | 524 | 139 400 | 256 |

*Table A8.4* Production and consumption of crocidolite by product group (Estimated UK consumption by principal product groups)

| Year | World production | UK imports | Textile products | Thermal insulation | Spray | Asbestos cement | Battery cases | Others |
|---|---|---|---|---|---|---|---|---|
| 1910 | 1 341 | 500 | 100 | 400 | — | — | — | — |
| 1920 | 2 801 | 750 | 100 | 650 | — | — | — | — |
| 1930 | 4 972 | 1 000 | 100 | 900 | — | — | — | — |
| 1940 | 8 075 | 2 655 | 127 | 300 | 907 | — | 1 288 | 33 |
| 1950 | 28 805 | 5 267 | 229 | 197 | 1508 | 574 | 2 634 | 125 |
| 1960 | 83 659 | 4 006 | 117 | 64 | 272 | 2 130 | 1 423 | — |
| 1970 | 137 235 | 563 | — | — | — | — | 635 | — |
| 1975 | 164 727 | Nil | — | — | — | — | — | — |

*Table A8.5* Estimated usage for chrysotile asbestos in the United Kingdom from 1880 to 1976 (tonnes)

| | 1880 | 1890 | 1900 | 1910 | 1920 | 1930 | 1940 | 1950 | 1960 | 1970 | 1973 | 1976 |
|---|---|---|---|---|---|---|---|---|---|---|---|---|
| 1. Asbestos cement–building uses | — | — | — | 1 000 | 9 000 | 12 500 | 29 000 | 42 000 | 58 500 | 49 000 | 55 600 | 42 400 |
| 2. Asbestos cement–pressure and other pipes | — | — | — | — | — | 300 | 4 000 | 12 000 | 10 000 | 8 000 | 7 800 | 7 000 |
| 3. Fire-resistant insulation board | — | — | — | — | — | — | — | 500 | 1 000 | 4 000 | 3 000 | 2 700 |
| 4. Other insulation products incl. spray | 10 | 500 | 2 000 | 2 600 | 3 400 | 3 000 | 5 000 | 6 000 | 5 000 | 1 700 | 1 300 | 200 |
| 5. Jointings and packings | 60 | 400 | 1 400 | 2 000 | 3 200 | 3 200 | 6 200 | 6 500 | 7 000 | 9 000 | 11 400 | 10 000 |
| 6. Friction materials | — | — | — | 100 | 1 000 | 1 500 | 3 000 | 6 000 | 10 000 | 17 000 | 18 500 | 15 600 |
| 7. Textile products not in (5) and (6) | 10 | 100 | 600 | 1 000 | 1 500 | 2 000 | 4 000 | 6 000 | 7 000 | 7 300 | 6 000 | 6 300 |
| 8. Floor tiles and flooring | — | — | — | 50 | 300 | 400 | 1 000 | 5 500 | 12 500 | 19 000 | 16 200 | 15 800 |
| 9. Moulded plastics and battery boxes | — | — | — | — | — | — | 300 | 2 000 | 2 000 | 3 000 | 2 200 | 800 |
| 10. Fillers and cements (felts, millboard, paper, underseals, etc.) | reinforced — | — | — | 50 | 1 600 | 2 100 | 9 500 | 16 500 | 18 000 | 21 000 | 25 300 | 28 400 |
| Total | 80 | 1 000 | 4 000 | 6 800 | 20 000 | 25 000 | 62 000 | 103 000 | 131 000 | 139 000 | 148 000 | 129 200 |
| Approx. chrysotile tonnage imported | 80 | 1 000 | 4 600 | 6 800 | 25 000 | 22 000 | 88 000 | 111 000 | 142 000 | 132 500 | 171 000 | 130 000 |

*Table A8.6*  Breakdown of usage of asbestos fibres in the United Kingdom in 1976

| Usage | Chrysotile | | Amosite | | Anthophyllite | | Total | |
|---|---|---|---|---|---|---|---|---|
| | *Tonnes* | *Per cent* | *Tonnes* | *Per cent* | *Tonnes* | *Per cent* | *Tonnes* | *Per cent* |
| Asbestos cement for building | 42 400 | 32.8 | 500 | 3.6 | — | — | 42 900 | 30.0 |
| Asbestos cement for pipes | 7 000 | 5.4 | 1 100 | 7.9 | — | — | 8 100 | 5.7 |
| Fire resistant boards | 2 700 | 2.1 | 11 800 | 84.3 | — | — | 14 500 | 10.1 |
| Other insulation products | 200 | 0.1 | 200 | 1.4 | — | — | 400 | 0.3 |
| Jointings and packings | 10 000 | 7.8 | — | — | — | — | 10 000 | 6.9 |
| Friction materials | 15 600 | 12.1 | — | — | 50 | 50 | 15 650 | 10.9 |
| Other textile products | 6 300 | 4.9 | — | — | — | — | 6 300 | 4.4 |
| Floor tiles | 15 800 | 12.2 | — | — | — | — | 15 800 | 11.0 |
| Plastics and battery boxes | 800 | 0.6 | 400 | 2.8 | — | — | 1 200 | 0.8 |
| Fillers and reinforcements★ | 28 400 | 22.0 | — | — | 50 | 50 | 28 450 | 19.9 |
| Totals | 129 200 | 100.0 | 14 000 | 100.0 | 100 | 100.0 | 143.300 | 100.0 |

★ Including felts, millboards, paper, filter pads for beverages, underseals, mastics, adhesives, coatings, etc.

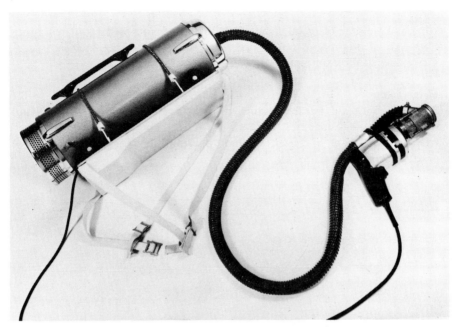

*Fig. A8.4* Portable dust-extraction unit attached to a power drill (an example of one of the many safety precautions used when working with asbestos)

Acetylene[1] (CH–CH)

TLV: None quoted.

**First-aid measures:**
1. Remove the patient to fresh air.
2. Keep a clear airway.
3. Artificial respiration and the administration of oxygen may be called for.
4. Evacuate to medical care.

*General data*
Grade II Chemical
Pure acetylene is a colourless, odourless gas but commercial grades have a gar-lic-like odour due to such impurities as phosphine, hydrogen sulphide and ammonia.

*Uses*
It is mainly used in blow torches for the cutting and welding of metal.

*Hazards*
Acetylene is a non-toxic gas but is an asphyxiant, i.e. it will not support life. Its main hazard lies in its highly explosive characteristics.

319

*Precautions*

Cutting and welding of metal should only take place in a well ventilated atmosphere. Special precautions need to be taken in tanks or other enclosed spaces to guard against the explosion hazard.

*Acute poisoning*

Acetylene is non-toxic, but heavy concentrations have anaesthetic properties and may render a patient unconscious. If the gas is in a very impure state the symptoms of phosphine or hydrogen sulphide poisoning may also be present (see appropriate Hazard Data Sheets).

*Chronic poisoning*

Is unknown.

*Factories Act References and Regulations*

Section (4); s. (30); s. (63).

Ammonia[1] ($NH_3$)

TLV 50 p.p.m., 35 mg/m$^3$

**First-aid measures:**

1. Remove from further exposure into fresh air.
2. Drenching of contaminated skin and irrigation of eyes with water and removal of contaminated clothing.
3. Immediate medical attention.

*General data*

Grade II Chemical

A colourless gas or aqueous solution with a highly irritant odour. The gas possesses a significant fire and explosion risk.

*Uses*

(a) Ammonia is produced as a by-product in the distillation of coal, i.e. in coke ovens. It is removed from the crude gas by distillation in the by-product plant and reacts with sulphuric acid in the 'salt route' to form ammonium sulphate.

(b) Ammonia is used to provide reducing atmospheres in certain furnaces to prevent scale forming on the surfaces of the hot metal, e.g. in Strand Annealing. It is delivered by tanker in either the anhydrous gaseous form or as a concentrated aqueous solution. After pumping into storage tanks it is dissociated catalytically using steam under pressure in the 'Cracking Plant' and the nitrogen and hydrogen so formed feed the furnace.

(c) In acid recovery section of Pickling Plant.

*Hazards*
The main hazard is accidental exposure to sudden high concentrations as a result of valve failure, leakage, etc. Fire and explosion hazards are also significant. The problem on coke ovens is relatively minor.

*Acute poisoning*
Ammonia is a caustic alkali and can affect man by:
1. Inhalation – causing chemical burns of the upper respiratory tract. The symptoms, therefore, are severe burning pain in the throat, etc. difficulty in breathing, and a cough with copious watery sputum.
2. Contact – involving skin or eyes, etc. This causes immediate burning pain in the affected areas with redness and swelling of eyes and mucous membranes and, to a lesser extent the skin.

Acetic acid[1] ($CH_3COOH$)
*Synonyms*: vinegar; ethanoic acid
TLV: 10 p.p.m., 25 mg/m

**First-aid measures**:
1. Remove from atmosphere.
2. Artificial respiration and oxygen therapy may be needed.
3. Remove contaminated clothing.
4. Wash skin and eye splashes copiously with water.
5. Induce vomiting if swallowed.
6. Seek immediate medical aid.

*General data*
Grade II Chemical
It is a colourless liquid with a pungent odour. It is closely allied to acetic anhydride $(CH_3CO)_3O$ which has a sharper odour and is more corrosive.

*Uses*
It is used in the food and canning industry as a preserving agent and in the dyeing and pharmaceutical industries.
 It is also used in the production of plastics, resins, and other chemicals such as organic acetates.

*Hazards*
The principal hazard is irritation of skin, eyes and respiratory tract.
Where the acid is concentrated (glacial acetic acid) skin burns can be deep and take a long time to heal.

*Precautions*

1. Enclosure of process where possible.

2. Good natural ventilation.
3. Provision of protective clothing for protection of eyes and skin.
4. Facilities for washing eyes and skin with water.
5. Storage of acetic acid away from heat in glass or stainless steel containers.
6. Training operatives in handling techniques.

*Acute poisoning*

1. Severe skin burns with concentrated (glacial) acetic acid.
2. Irritation of respiratory tract with cough.
3. Irritation of eyes.
4. If swallowed – pain, vomiting, diarrhoea and shock.

*Chronic poisoning*
1. Swelling of eyelids.
2. Thickening and cracking of skin particularly on palms of hands.
3. Chronic catarrh.

*Factories Act references and regulations*
Section (4); s. (30)); s. (58); s. (63).


Butane[1] ($C_4H_{10}$)
TLV: None quoted.

**First-aid measures:**

1. Remove to fresh air.
2. Artificial respiration and oxygen if called for.
3. Evacuate to medical care.

*General data*
Grade II Chemical
It is an odourless, colourless gas which is heavier than air, and is flammable.

In its natural state (North Sea Gas) it is mixed with methane, ethane and propane.

*Uses*
As a fuel in both industry and the home. In the latter case a 'stink' gas has to be added to aid detection. In industry it is stored in cylinders under high pressure and used for cutting and welding torches. It is also used as refrigerant.

*Hazards*
There is a high fire and explosion risk. The toxic hazard is minimal but the gas is an asphyxiant and will not support life. It has mild anaesthetic effects insufficient to cause unconsciousness. If the liquid is splashed on the skin it causes

local freezing.

*Precautions*
Cylinders of gas should be stored away from heat. If used in enclosed spaces there must be adequate ventilation.
A Code of Practice is needed for welding and cutting operations.

*Acute poisoning*
Mild symptoms of asphyxia – rarely unconsciousness. Local freezing if splashed on the skin.
Mild irritation of nose and throat.

*Chronic poisoning*
Systemic effects are unknown. Continued skin exposure to liquid splashes will cause drying and cracking of skin.

*Factories Act references and regulations.*
Section (4); s. (30); s. (63).

Carbon dioxide[1] ($CO_2$)
TLV 5000 p.p.m., 9000 mg/m$^3$

**First-aid measures:**

1. Remove the patient to fresh air.
2. Give oxygen or artificial respiration if breathing has ceased.
3. Obtain immediate medical help.
4. Skin burns. Apply a first aid dressing and seek medical attention.

*General data*
Grade II Chemical
Carbon dioxide is a colourless, odourless, inert gas at normal temperatures. It is a white snow-like solid when compressed and cooled.
The gas is non-toxic but will not support life. It is heavier than air. About 300 p.p.m. are found in normal air and over 50 000 p.p.m. in the lungs. Increased concentrations of carbon dioxide in the blood cause the breathing rate to increase. Carbon dioxide is evolved in enclosed spaces and tanks where organic matter is decomposing.

*Uses*

1. Gas shielded welding.
2. Shell moulding in foundries.
3. As a refrigeration medium (dry ice).
4. Fire extinguishers.

5. For purging pipelines, vats, silos, tanks, etc. prior to welding or cutting operations to void explosive gases.
6. As a laboratory agent.
7. As tiger tops for ingot moulds.

*Hazards*
Carbon dioxide is an asphyxiant gas, i.e. it does not support life. Effects attributed to the presence of carbon dioxide are usually due to oxygen deficiency. Contact with carbon dioxide snow (dry ice) causes skin burns.

*Precautions*

1. Proper handling and storage techniques for $CO_2$ cylinders.
2. Approved methods of testing and entering enclosed spaces, tanks, etc. where $CO_2$ may have collected.
   (See D.E.P. Technical Data Note No. 18)
3. Protective clothing for those handling $CO_2$ snow (dry ice).

*Acute poisoning*

1. Respiratory distress – gasping for breath.
2. Loss of consciousness followed by death.
3. Burns of skin where exposed to $CO_2$ snow. The part becomes cold, white and anaesthetic.

*Chronic poisoning*
It is unknown in ordinary industrial practice.

Carbon Monoxide[1] (CO)
TLV: 50 p.p.m., immediately hazardous to life 3500 p.p.m.

**First-aid measures:**

1. Remove to fresh air (rescuers required to wear breathing apparatus).
2. Artificial respiration (mouth to mouth method) and oxygen. Cardiac massage if the heart is not beating.
3. Obtain medical assistance.
4. The patient should be made to rest.

The Medical Officer or Nurse will advise on further treatment.

*General data*
Carbon monoxide is a colourless, odourless gas which is highly poisonous. It is found in many gases used or produced in the Steel Industry in the following concentrations:

| | |
|---|---|
| Blast furnace gas | 22–30% |
| Coke oven gas | 6% |
| Producer gas | 29% |
| Town gas up to | 15% |
| B.O.S. gases leaving the vessel up to | 70% |
| Cupola stock gas (iron foundry) | 13–20% |
| Petrol engine exhaust gas: | |
|     cruising | 1% |
|     idling | 7% |
| Diesel engine exhaust gas: | |
|     cruising | 0.2% |
|     idling | 4% |

Natural gas, propane and butane contain no carbon monoxide if burned in free air. If burned in restricted air with a cooler flame, carbon monoxide is produced and may reach dangerous concentrations.

*Hazards*

When inhaled carbon monoxide is absorbed by the blood and combines with haemoglobin in the red cells. The effective quantity of haemoglobin available for carrying oxygen is reduced, leading to oxygen starvation of the tissues – particularly the brain cells.

*Precautions*

(a) All employees exposed to carbon monoxide must be warned of its toxic effects, instructed in safe working methods, the use of breathing apparatus, rescue techniques and first aid (artificial respiration).

(b) When work is to be carried out in potentially dangerous areas, it should be in accord with a code of safe working practice. When possible a 'Permit to Work' system should be adopted. This applies particularly when entering enclosed spaces, i.e. vats, gas mains, etc.

(c) Trained rescue men must be available on each shift.

(d) Facilities for treatment of carbon monoxide poisoning must be available at all times.

(e) Breathing apparatus of the self-contained or compressed airline variety must be provided and properly maintained. Men required to use the apparatus must be instructed and have regular practice in its use.

(f) Apparatus for the detection of carbon monoxide in the atmosphere must be provided. (Consult Medical Department and Industrial Hygiene Laboratory.)

Detector tubes are suitable for single spot tests.

Where the hazard is severe and regular (i.e. blast furnace areas) continuous sampling instruments should be used.

(g) The products of combustion including exhaust gases from petrol engines should be vented to the outside atmosphere.

*Acute poisoning*
The effects of inhaling carbon monoxide depend on the following factors:–

(a) The concentration of carbon monoxide.
(b) The duration of inhalation.
(c) The personal susceptibility of the individual.
(d) The degree of exertion. Heavy work increases the hazard.
Concentrations up to 100 p.p.m. may be inhaled for indefinite periods without producing obvious symptoms. However, concentrations of between 50 and 100 p.p.m. can depress mental performance. When 100 p.p.m. is exceeded symptoms can range from frontal headache, nausea, fatigue and dizziness to unconsciousness and death depending on the factors listed above.

*Chronic poisoning*
There are no known accumulative effects of carbon monoxide, i.e. it is completely excreted after each acute episode.

*Factories Act references and regulations*
Section (30); s. (63).
BM Factory Inspectorate Booklet No. 29, *Carbon Monoxide Poisoning – Causes and Prevention*.
BS 4276: 1968, *The Selection, Use and Maintenance of Respiratory Protective Equipment*.

Carbon tetrachloride[1] ($CCl_4$)
*Synonym*: tetrachloromethane
TLV (skin): 10 p.p.m., 65 mg/m$^3$

**First-aid measures:**

1. Remove to fresh air.
2. Artificial respiration with oxygen if required.
3. Remove contaminated clothing.
4. Wash the skin thoroughly with water.
5. Summon medical aid.

*General data*
Grade II Chemical
It is a heavy, colourless, non-inflammable liquid with a chloroform-like odour and a burning taste. It is decomposed by heat into phosgene ($COCl_3$), i.e. by fires or smoking.

*Uses*
1. A dry cleaning agent.

2. Fat, oil and grease solvent.
3. Paint remover.
4. Fumigant.
5. As a refrigerant and in the manufacture of Freon (another refrigerant), and DDT.
6. In fire extinguishers (see precautions below).
7. In laboratories.

*Hazards*
1. It is a narcotic causing drowsiness and unconsciousness.
2. It is a potent liver and kidney poison, especially in long-term exposure. Alcoholism causes increased susceptibility.
3. When used in fire extinguishers it may be converted into phosgene (q.v.).
4. It is absorbed by inhalation, by mouth and through intact skin.

*Precautions*

1. Substitute trichloroethane $C_3H_3Cl_3$ or perchloroethylene $C_2Cl_4$ where suitable i.e. for degreasing and dry cleaning.
2. On the rare occasions where it is used, enclosure or properly designed exhaust ventilation is necessary.
3. In confined spaces, exhaust ventilation and fresh air respirators should be used.
4. Smoking should be forbidden near tanks containing carbon tetrachloride.
5. Fire extinguishers containing carbon tetrachloride should be replaced by modern ones containing less hazardous substances, e.g. powder type or bromochloromethane (see appropriate Hazard Data Sheet).
6. Clear labelling of containers e.g. carbon tetrachloride BEWARE-POISON

*Acute poisoning*
Acute poisoning may result from inhalation or by drinking the liquid.

Signs and symptoms

1. Drowsiness and dizziness leading to unconsciousness and delirium. In some cases death may be very rapid.
2. In milder cases the symptoms resemble 'gastric flu' with nausea, colic and vomiting.
3. There may be a delay in onset of symptoms up to 8 days, even in severe cases.

*Chronic poisoning*

1. Drowsiness and increasing inertia.
2. Nausea, vomiting and diarrhoea.
3. Jaundice.

4. Passing of scant quantities of urine which may be blood stained.
5. Swelling of ankles.

The presence of any of these symptoms after exposure calls for immediate medical investigation.

*Factories Act references and regulations*
Section (4); s. (30); s. (63).

Unconsciousness is notifiable to the Chief Inspector of Factories under the heading of gassing.

Toxic Jaundice is also a notifiable industrial disease.


Caustic soda[1] (NaOH)
*Synonym*: sodium hydroxide
TLV: $2 \text{ mg/m}^3$

**First-aid measures**

1. Remove from exposure.
2. Remove all contaminated clothing.
3. Deluge the exposed skin and eyes with water, followed by buffered phosphate solution.
4. If swallowed give copious draughts of water to drink.
5. Refer for medical attention immediately.

*General data*
Grade II Chemical
It is a white deliquescent solid which dissolves readily in water. It is strongly alkaline.

*Uses*

1. As a general reagent in laboratories.
2. For water treatment.
3. Degreasing agent. Many proprietary degreasers are strongly alkaline due to caustic soda.
4. In the processing of by-products from coke ovens.
5. Molten caustic soda for descaling stainless steel.

*Hazards*
Caustic soda is corrosive to all body tissues in all concentrations. The degree of burning is proportional to the concentration and the length of exposure, varying from dermatitis in low concentrations to deep and serious burns with the solid material.

*Precautions*

1. Proper handling techniques must be instituted wherever men are exposed, including unloading bulk supplies from vehicles. These consist of impervious protective clothing including gloves and wellingtons and eye protection.

   Arrangements must be made for skin drenching and eye washing at all handling stations.
2. Fume cupboards with air extraction.

*Acute poisoning*
Is normally confined to tissues which have been directly exposed to splashes.
   It is possible for solutions of caustic soda to be swallowed in error when it acts as a corrosive poison.
   Inhalation of fume and dust may cause irritation of the nose and lungs.

*Chronic poisoning*
Exposure to weak solutions of caustic soda over a long period may lead to dermatitis.

*Factories Act references and regulations*
Section (4); s. (55).

Isocyanates ($C_6H_3CH_3$ $(NCO)_2$)

TLV: 0.02 p.p.m., 0 14 mg/m$^3$

**First-aid measures:**

1. Lung irritation calls for removal from the area and seeking of medical advice.
2. Skin contact – wash thoroughly with soap and water.
3. Eye contact – wash with water and refer for medical care.

*General data*
Grade II Chemical
There are two main groups of compounds:

1. Tolylene diisocyanate (TDI) of high volatility.
2. Diisocyanate diphenylmethane (MDI) of low volatility.

The isocyanate group is chemically highly reactive and will combine with many organic compounds. When combined with a resin it forms a high molecular weight polymer of the polyurethane type.

*Uses*

1. As a bond in moulding sand in foundries.
2. Incorporated in paints and varnishes.
3. Polyurethane foams are used in thermal insulation in the lower temperature ranges, electric wire insulation and as acoustic cladding.

*Hazards*

1. Organic isocyanates require careful handling because of their chemical reactivity. Although oral toxicity is low they are irritant when inhaled.
2. From paints containing isocyanates (polyurethane paint) especially if used in confined spaces or for marking hot material.
3. In the casting bay of foundries where isocyanates have been used to bond moulding sand.

*Precautions*

1. Bulk quantities should only be handled under good ventilation conditions.
2. Protective clothing including gloves and goggles should be provided.

*Acute poisoning*
By inhalation – isocyanates both irritate and sensitize the respiratory tract. The attacks may occur at work or in bed at night.

Symptoms

1. Cough and tightness of chest.
2. Breathlessness.
3. Fever and sweating.

*Chronic poisoning*
Once sensitization to isocyanates has occurred exposure to small quantities can precipitate an acute attack of breathlessness and lung irritation.

*Factories Act references and regulations*
Section (4); s. (30); s. (63).

Lead[1] (Pb) and its compounds
TLV: Metallic lead 0.2 mg/m$^3$, tetraethyl lead 0.075 mg/m$^3$

**First-aid measures:**
Nil

*General data*
Grade II Material
Lead is a dense silvery metal. It is used as a teaming addition in the steel industry to make a free cutting steel. Also to be found in Babbitt's metal used to line rolling-mill bearings.

Scrap burning may produce lead poisoning because of red lead paint on girders, ship plates, railway coaches, etc.

Molten lead baths are used in wire drawing and in tempering mild steel strapping.

Lead melts at 327°C, fumes at 350 °C and boils at 1620 °C.

Tetraethyl lead is an anti-knock compound added to petrol. Inhalation of petrol or exhaust fumes in an enclosed space is dangerous from both carbon monoxide (see Hazard Data Sheet) and the lead content.

*Hazards*
Lead poisoning is usually caused by inhalation of minute particles of lead fumes and dust which are absorbed by the bloodstream from the lungs, and finally deposited in the bone marrow. Lead is only slowly released from bone and thus has an accumulative effect causing chronic poisoning.

Lead can be swallowed in food contaminated by dirty hands but this hazard is only mildly toxic compared with inhalation.

*Precautions*

1.  Substitution is highly desirable but has not so far been found possible from a metallurgical viewpoint.
2.  Siting of plant to avoid contamination of other parts of the factory.
3.  Good ventilation and efficient extraction plant are essential.
4.  The wearing of approved and well-fitting respirators may be necessary if the above precautions are not wholly successful. (Not well tolerated.)

    NB – Cloth and gauze pads over nose and mouth induce a false sense of security and are useless.

5.  Protective overalls which can be discarded at meal times and on going home may be helpful.
6.  Provision of washing facilities including hot water, soap and towels. Hands need to be washed before eating or smoking.
7.  No food to be consumed in the neighbourhood of any of these lead processes.

8. Wetting of dust before sweeping up.
9. Periodic air sampling. Consult Medical Department and industrial Hygiene Laboratory. Maintain workroom atmospheric pollution below 0.2 mg/m$^3$

*Acute poisoning*
Low risk – unknown in the steel industry.

*Chronic poisoning*
High risk in scrap burning, deseaming of billets and ingots and patenting of wire and strip.

The main effects are found in the digestive system (colic, constipation) the blood (anaemia) and the nervous system (weakness of wrist and ankles), headaches and pains in the joints.

Periodic medical examinations should be undertaken. Consult Medical Department.

*Factories Act references and regulations*
None of the specific lead regulations apply to the steel industry since none of the scheduled processes are conducted within the industry.
Section (1); s. (58); s. (63); s. (64); s. (82).
See D.E.P. Technical Data Note No 16.

Paraffin[1] and its derivatives CH$_3$(CH$_2$) × CH$_3$

TLV: None quoted

**First-aid measures:**

1. As for non-corrosive poisons – make the patient vomit.
2. Remove to hospital, preserving a specimen of the vomit.

*General data*
Grade II Chemical
Paraffin and its derivatives come from the distillation and fractionation of petroleum.

*Uses*
Paraffin oil or kerosene is used as a lamp oil and as fuel in jet engines. It is a solvent of grease and dirt. The higher paraffins include liquid paraffin (medicinal) soft paraffin – petroleum jelly (dressings for burns), and paraffin waxes.

Within the British Steel Corporation (BSC) it is most likely to be met with as a solvent for greases and oil in engineering workshops and garages.

*Hazards*
It is a defatting agent of skin leading to dry cracking and dermatitis.

It might be drunk in error.

*Precautions*

1. It should always be kept in a well-labelled container.
2. Plastic clothing and gloves should be used where it is to be handled regularly.
3. It should never be used to remove grease and dirt from skin.

*Acute poisoning*
Almost unknown and always accidental.

*Chronic poisoning*
The only aspect to be met with in BSC is a dry cracking skin leading to dermatitis.

*Factories Act references and regulations*
Section (58).

## Accidents to children on construction sites.[2]

These Guidance Notes replace the series of Technical Data Notes (TDN) produced by HM Factory Inspectorate and the CEMA's Notes of Guidance produced by the Employment Medical Advisory Service.

The Notes are published under five subject headings: Medical; Environmental; Chemical Safety; Plant and Machinery and General.

Existing TDN and CEMA's Notes of Guidance will be progressively brought into new groupings.

### Introduction

A survey in the Factory Inspectorate in 1976 produced accounts of 28 fatal accidents to children on construction sites in an 18-month period. 22 boys and 6 girls, including eight five-year-olds or younger, were killed. The largest single cause, 15 deaths, was falling into holes and being drowned or trapped by falling earth; five accidents involved vehicles and seven were caused by materials on sites falling over on to children. From these known cases an average figure of twenty child deaths a year on construction sites can be estimated. This is similar to the number killed on farms and railways and also to the number of adults killed in some high risk areas of construction work.

### Practical precautions

The practical precautions which an occupier should take are listed below. They were drawn up keeping two things in mind; firstly, that no legislation can prevent all accidents to children and secondly, that the younger the child the greater the degree of protection owed to him.

*Exclusion of children and site perimeter fencing*
The first line of defence is to take all reasonably practicable steps to prevent children entering construction sites either on foot or as passengers in vehicles.

At all construction sites where it is reasonably practicable a fence should be erected enclosing all the construction operations. The fence should not be capable of being easily climbed. To this end it should be either close boarded or provided with mesh not exceeding 30 mm. Support posts should be firmly anchored.

Access openings should be gated and kept locked at all times when the site is unoccupied and a reasonable degree of surveillance of the gates should be exercised when they are open. The fencing should be properly maintained and materials should not be placed or stacked in the vicinity of the fence in such a way as to provide easily climbed access over the fence. Suitable warning notices should be fixed to the fencing. This standard is no more than is already adopted by many firms for security reasons and where it is fully implemented it is not proposed that any of the further precautions listed below should normally be invoked.

*Precautions where site perimeter fencing is not possible*
At some construction sites it may not be reasonably practicable to erect a perimeter fence. Each case should be judged on its merits, but obvious examples are very long excavations on motorway sites and a new housing estate which is partly occupied. In such cases the following precautions should be taken:

*Guarding of edges of excavations etc*
All excavations, holes or openings exceeding 2 m in depth and those exceeding 1 m in depth where water is likely to collect should be filled or securely covered immediately work in them is ended. Where they are left open and unattended their edges should be fenced at every accessible part by a barrier of chestnut paling or similar type to a height of 1 m from the ground.

*Vehicles and plant*
All vehicles and plant with moving parts should be effectively immobilized when left unattended.

*Stacking of materials*
All materials which would be liable to cause injury if they fell should be stacked or stored in such a way to prevent their easy displacement. Temporary but secure and stable racking should be used when appropriate.

*Electricity and other energy sources*
Electrical supplies to all equipment which is not required to be energized when

334

the site is unoccupied should be locked off, or switched off at isolators in a locked building or enclosure, at the end of work for the day. Supplies to equipment which is kept energized, e.g. floodlights, pumps, etc. should be installed in such a way that access cannot be gained to live conductors except by the use of special tools. Gas supplies should be similarly isolated or protected and cylinders of compressed gases of any kind should be placed in locked enclosures unless they are of such a size, so located or secured that they cannot be easily moved or their valves opened without the use of special tools. Special tools for electrical or gas supplies should be kept under lock and key when the site is unattended.

*Other hazardous materials*
Any chemical or other material which could be harmful to children should be kept in a locked enclosure when the site is unoccupied.

*Access to elevated areas*
All ladders giving access to elevated areas should, when the site is unoccupied, have the first run removed and placed under lock and key. All loose ladders on the site should be similarly chained or enclosed and locked.

Statutory requirements

Section 3 of the Health and Safety at Work Act 1974 requires every employer or self-employed person to conduct his undertaking, so far as is reasonably practicable, in such a way that other persons, including the public, are not exposed to risks to their health and safety.

Bibliography

A discussion of duties owed to trespassers is contained in the Law Commission 'Report on Liability for Damage or Injury to Trespassers and Related Questions of Occupiers' Liability for Damage or Injury to Trespassers and Related Questions of Occupiers' Liability', Cmnd 6428, HMSO.

Further information

This Guidance Note is produced by HM Factory Inspectorate. Further advice on this and other publications produced by the Executive is obtainable from any Area Office of the Health and Safety Executive or from HMSO bookshops.

Current legal and administrative controls for the general public

| Relevant legislation, etc. | General remarks | Summary of the relevant provisions |
| --- | --- | --- |
| Public Health Act 1936 and 1961 | Statutory nuisance provisions of Act may apply | 1 Local Authorities (LAs) responsible for the control of asbestos emissions.<br>2 Use of asbestos in the construction of buildings is covered by the Building Regs 1976 made under the Public Health Acts. These Regs apply in whole of England and Wales except inner London where the London Building (Constructional) Bye Laws apply. Similar Regs apply in Scotland and Northern Ireland. |
| Public Health (Scotland) Act 1897 | S.16 (General nuisances) | LAs have a responsibility for (1) any accumulation or deposit of mineral refuse which is noxious, or injurious, or dangerous to health; (2) any work, etc. injurious to the health of the neighbourhood or so conducted as to be injurious or dangerous to health; (3) LAs have a duty to inspect their area from time to time to identify nuisances. |
| Clean Air Acts 1956 and 1968 | Emissions of dust from furnaces covered | Any asbestos in dust from a furnace can be subject to some element of dust control. |
| Control of Pollution Act 1974 | Act provides framework for a systematic and co-ordinated approach to waste collection and disposal | 1 LAs have powers to require information from any works about emissions to air at intervals of 3 months or more.<br>2 A waste disposal site licensing regime now operates. |
| Merchant Shipping (Dangerous Goods) Rules 1965 | The carriage of dangerous goods and substances as cargo on UK registered ships is regulated and controlled under these rules | Specific advice on carriage and packing of individual substances is given in the International Maritime Dangerous Goods Code. |

| | |
|---|---|
| Merchant Shipping Act 1970 | Powers are available under s.19 to make regulations to secure safe working conditions and practices | 1 The Dept. of Trade's recommendation made in the *Code of Safe Working Practices for the Safety of Merchant Seamen.*<br>2 The Department of Trade have issued Merchant Shipping Notices on asbestos. |
| Deposit of Poisonous Waste Act 1972 | | 1 Disposers of most types of asbestos waste should notify the responsible authority.<br>2 It is an offence to deposit poisonous noxious or polluting waste on land in such a way that it is liable to give rise to an environmental hazard. |
| Rivers Prevention of Pollution Acts 1951 and 1961 | There is a similar Act in Scotland | Any discharge of liquid effluent to controlled waters from asbestos works requires the consent of the relevant Water Authority in England or Wales or River Purification Board in Scotland. |
| Consumer Safety Act 1978 | | There is no legislation dealing specifically with the use of asbestos in consumer products but there is power to introduce such legislation in the Act. |
| Food Drugs Act 1955 England and Wales | | There are similar Acts in Scotland and Northern Ireland; while there are no specific statutory limits laid down in UK for the levels of asbestos in food, this Act will apply to any question of contamination. |
| Water Act 1973 | | Water Authorities supply water and LAs should see the water is wholesome. |
| Health and Safety at Work etc. Act 1974 | | S.3 obliges employers and self-employed persons to conduct their undertakings in such a way as to ensure, so far as is reasonably practicable, that persons not in their employment who may be affected thereby are not thereby exposed to risks to their safety. |

---

*First-aid training*[3] *(Factories Act 1961)*

After the 30 June 1967, for the purpose of Regulations 5 and 9, a person trained in first-aid treatment must either:

(a)  be a Registered or Enrolled Nurse within the meaning of the Nurses Acts 1957 and 1961 or the Nurses (Scotland) Acts 1951 and 1961; or

(b)  be the holder of a certificate in first aid issued within the immediately preceding period of three years by, or is otherwise recognized as being qualified in first aid treatment by, a training organization.

In these Regulations, the expression 'certificate in first aid' does not include any certificate in first aid of a kind which is issued to persons under the age of fifteen years, whether or not any such kind of certificate is also issued to persons aged fifteen years or over.

For the purpose of Regulation 7, the expression 'training organization' means the St John Ambulance Association of the Order of St John, the St Andrew's Ambulance Association, the British Red Cross Society, or any other body or society approved for the purposes of these Regulations.

The expression 'approved' means approved for the time being by certificate of the Chief Inspector.

The following particulars must be recorded in respect of any person who is required to be a person trained in first aid treatment to the standard required by Regulation 7, namely:

(a)  his name;

(b)  the nature and date of his qualifications;

(c)  the date on which evidence of his qualifications was inspected by the person undertaking the operations or works to which these Regulations apply.

The record required by Regulation 7 (4) must be securely fixed inside the first aid box and must be open to inspection by any Inspector of Factories. Extracts from or copies of such record must be sent to the Inspector as he may require for the execution of his duties under the Factories Act 1961.

*Ambulances (Factories Act 1961)*

Where a contractor employs more than 25 persons on a site, he must:

(a)  within 24 hours of employing more than 25 persons notify in writing the local health authority in whose area the site is situated of:
The location and address of the site and the nature of the operations or works and the probable date of the completion;

(b)  provide and maintain a sufficient number of suitable stretchers;

(c)  appoint a responsible person or persons who must always be available during working hours to summon an ambulance if needed and the contractor must ensure that legible copies of a notice indicating such persons and containing instructions on the making of emergency telephone or radio calls are affixed in one or more prominent positions on the site.

In these Regulations, the expression 'local health authority' means in the case of sites situated outside Greater London, a local health authority for the purposes of the National Health Service Act 1946, and any joint board performing the function of a local health authority under that Act to make provision for an ambulance service and, in the case of sites situated in Greater London, the Greater London Council.

Where telephonic or radio communication with an ambulance station as required by Regulation (8.1) cannot be easily provided, a motor vehicle constructed or adapted so as to be able to carry a stretcher must be provided at or near the site. A card showing the address of the nearest hospital must be provided and kept in a prominent position in the vehicle.

### First-aid rooms *(Factories Act 1961)*

Every contractor who employs more than 40 persons on a site where more than 250 persons are employed, must provide and maintain in good order a properly constructed and suitable first-aid room. A first-aid room must:

(a)  be at or near the site and conveniently accessible;
(b)  have smooth interior surfaces;
(c)  be used only for the purposes of treatment and rest; and
(d)  be in the charge of a person trained in first-aid treatment to the standard required by Regulation 7, who must always be readily available during working hours.

A first-aid room must be equipped with at least:

(a)  a sink having smooth impervious internal surfaces with hot and cold water always available;
(b)  a table with a smooth impervious top;
(c)  means of sterilizing instruments;
(d)  a supply of suitable dressings, bandages and splints;
(e)  a couch;
(f)  suitable and sufficient stretchers including a sling stretcher;
(g)  sufficient blankets and hot water bottles; and
(h)  a foot bath or basin and bowl suitable for use as a foot bath. [9.2]

### Office staffs

In calculating the number of persons employed for the purposes of the Regulations 5 to 9, any persons working in an office erected at the site and in connection with the operations or works must be included on the following basis:

(a)  for every 3 such office workers 1 person shall be included;
(b)  for any fraction of a unit of 3 persons, where the fraction consists of 2 persons, 1 person shall be included, and where it consists of 1 person that person shall be left out of account [10.1 and 10.2]

In relation to persons to whom this Regulation applies, the references in Regulation 4 to a contractor shall be construed as including references to the employer of such persons.

### Shelters and accommodation (*Factories Act 1961*)

Subject to the provisions of Regulation 11(2), there must be provided at or in the immediate vicinity of every site for the use of the persons employed thereon, and conveniently accessible to them:
Adequate and suitable accommodation, which must be kept in a clean and orderly condition and which must not be used for the deposit or storage of materials or plant:

(a)  for taking shelter and for depositing clothing not worn during working hours, which accommodation must contain:
Where more than 5 persons are employed, adequate and suitable means of warming the persons and drying wet clothing, or
Where 5 persons or less are employed, reasonably practicable arrangements for warming the persons and drying wet clothing
(b)  for the deposit of protective clothing and which must have facilities for drying such clothing if it has become wet.
(c)  housing sufficient tables and seats for taking meals, with facilities for boiling water and, where a contractor employs more than 10 persons on the site and heated food is not available, facilities for heating food.

And, subject to the provisions of Regulation 11(2), there must be provided at or in the immediate vicinity of every site for the use of the persons employed thereon, and conveniently accessible to them, an adequate supply of wholesome drinking water clearly marked 'Drinking Water'      [11(1) and 11(4)]
Every contractor must provide facilities for washing, and:

(a)  where at least 1 man is employed for more than 4 consecutive hours they must be adequate and suitable.
(b)  where more than 20 persons are employed or there are reasonable grounds for believing that the works will not be completed within 6 weeks, they must include:
• Adequate troughs, basins or buckets in each case having a smooth impervious internal surface;
• Adequate and suitable means of cleaning and drying;

- A sufficient supply of hot and cold or warm water.
(c)  where more than 100 persons are employed and there are reasonable grounds for believing that the works will not be completed within 12 months, they must include:
  - Four washbasins for the 100 persons, and 1 for every unit of 35 persons thereafter or fraction of such unit;
  - adequate and suitable means of cleaning and drying;
  - a sufficient supply of hot and cold or warm water. [12(1), 12(2) and 12(3)]

### Sanitary conveniences

Every contractor must provide where sufficient urinal accommodation is also provided, at least 1 suitable sanitary convenience for every 25 persons in his employment on the site up to the first 100, and 1 for every 35 persons thereafter.
[13(1) and 13(2)]

In calculating the numbers under paragraph 372, fractions of the units 25 or 35 shall be reckoned as 25 or 35 as the case may be.        [13(3)]

Every sanitary convenience must:

(a)  be sufficiently ventilated;
(b)  not communicate directly with the workroom or messroom;
(c)  except in the case of urinal, be under cover and so partitioned off as to secure privacy;
(d)  except in the case of a urinal, have a proper door and fastening;
(e)  in the case of urinals, be so placed or screened as not to be visible from any other place;
(f)  be conveniently accessible;
(g)  be maintained and kept clean; and
(h)  have effective lighting provided.        [14(1), 14(2), 14(3) and 14(4)]

Where both men and women are or are intended to be employed on a site, the sanitary convenience must afford proper separate accommodation for persons of each sex.        (14(4)

### Inspections and tests [4]

The Factories Act 1961 requires that the following inspections and tests must be carried out in building operations and works of engineering construction.

Working places

| Description | Reg. | Frequency |
|---|---|---|
| Inspection of excavations: (shaft, earthworks, tunnel). | G.P. 9(1) | At least once every day while persons employed. |
| Inspection of tunnel faces, working ends of trenches more than 2 m deep, or bases/crowns of shafts. | G.P. 9(1) | At the commencement of every shift. |
| Thorough examination of those parts of excavations, etc. likely to have been affected by the use of explosives; or near to substantially damaged supports or unexpected falls of material. | G.P. 9(2) (a), (b) | Before any persons are employed in such parts. |
| Thorough examination of all parts of excavations, shafts, tunnels, etc. | G.P. 9(2) (a) | Within the seven days immediately preceding any person employed therein. |
| Inspection of materials used for timbering or the support of excavations. | G.P. 10(1) | On each occasion before they are taken into use. |
| Inspection of materials used for making or fixing cofferdams or caissons. | G.P. 17(2) | On each occasion before the materials are taken into use for the purpose. |
| Inspection of cofferdams and caissons. | G.P. 18(1) | At least once on the same or the preceding day, before persons employed. |
| Thorough examination of cofferdams and caissons. | G.P. 18(1) (a), (b), (c) | Before any person is employed therein; since the use of explosives likely to have affected the strength or stability; or following any substantial damage; or in any case within the immediately preceding seven days. |
| Tests of working places or approaches where the atmosphere might be poisonous or asphyxiating. | G.P. 21(2) | Before any persons are employed therein. |
| Inspection of a scaffold erected by another employer. | W.P. 23 | Before use. |

## Lifting operations

| Description | Reg. | Frequency |
| --- | --- | --- |
| Inspection of lifting appliances and all their parts, as far as their construction permits. | L.O. 10(1) (c) | At least once every week. (The driver can carry out this inspection if he is competent for the purpose.) |
| Examination of anchorages or ballasting of cranes. | L.O. 19(3) | On each occasion before the crane is erected. |
| Test of the anchorages or ballasting arrangements of cranes. | L.O. 19(4) | Before crane taken into use; after each erection of crane; whenever arrangements changed. |
| Examination of crane anchorage or ballasting arrangements. | L.O. 19(7) | After exposure of the crane to weather conditions likely to have affected stability. |
| Tests and thorough examinations of cranes, crabs or winches, except hoists. | L.O. 20(1), (2) | Within the previous four years of being taken into use, and since undergoing any substantial alteration or repair likely to affect its strength or stability. |
| Tests and thorough examinations of pulley blocks, gin wheels or shear legs (except hoists) used for raising or lowering one tonne or more. | L.O. 28(1), (2) | Before initial use and after undergoing any substantial alterations or repairs. |
| Thorough examination of all lifting appliances except hoists. | L.O. 28(3) | Within the fourteen months previous to being taken into use; and since undergoing any substantial alterations or repair. |
| Tests and automatic safe load indicators on jib cranes. | L.O. 30(1) | After erection or installation, but before being taken into use. |
| Inspection of automatic safe load indicators on jib cranes. | L.O. 30(1) | Intervals of not more than one week when crane in use. |
| Tests of mobile crane automatic safe load indicators. | L.O. 30(2) | Before the crane is taken into use; after the SLI has been dismantled; also after it has had anything done to it which may have affected its proper operation. |
| Inspection of mobile crane automatic safe load indicators. | L.O. 30(2) | At intervals of one week or less when the crane is in use. |

Lifting gear and hoists

| Description | Reg. | Frequency |
|---|---|---|
| Test and examination of chains, ropes and lifting gear. | L.O. 34(1) (b) | Before being used in raising or lowering or as a means of suspension. |
| Test and thorough examination of chains, rings, links, hooks, plate clamps, shackles, swivels or eye bolts. | L.O. 35 | Before being used; and also after any repairing, lengthening or altering. |
| Thorough examination of ropes, chains or lifting gear in general use. | L.O. 40 | At least once within the previous six months when used for raising or lowering, or for suspension. |
| Thorough examination of ropes, chains or lifting gear not in general use. | L.O. 40 | When necessary. |
| Tests and thorough examinations of hoists manufactured or substantially altered/repaired after the 1 March 1962. | L.O. 46(1) (a) | After such manufacture, alteration or repair, but before any use. |
| Tests and thorough examinations of hoists used for carrying persons. | L.O. 46(1) (b) | Before use; since last erected, or since height of cage travel increased. (Whichever was the latest.) |
| Thorough examination of all hoists. | L.O. 46(1) (c) | During the six months before the hoist was taken into use. |
| Inspection of all material for any scaffold. | W.P. 8 | On each occasion before being taken into use. |
| Inspection of any scaffold, including boatswain's chair, cage, skip, or similar plant or equipment. | W.P. 22(1) | During the previous seven days, and since exposure to weather conditions likely to have affected its strength or stability. |

*Note*: Chains and slings made from 13 mm (½ inch) bar or smaller must, when in use, be annealed or subjected to some appropriate form of heat treatment every six months. For all other chains and lifting gear the period is fourteen months. Chains and lifting gear, not in regular use, or used only on hand-operated lifting gear, need be annealed or subjected to heat treatment only as necessary. (Lifting Operations Regulation 41.)

# Decommissioning nuclear reactors[1]

Decommissioning requires that nuclear facilities permanently withdrawn from operational service be put into a safe condition to protect man and the environment, the ideal ultimate objective being complete removal and disposal. The UKAEA in conjunction with other organizations has for the past five years been examining the development issues and practical aspects of dealing with nuclear facilities no longer required in the UK. The objective is to include all types of nuclear installations but attention has been directed initially to nuclear power stations. Close liaison has been maintained with the Generating Boards.

At the present time world experience of decommissioning nuclear reactors is comparatively limited. A number of early, low power, units have been closed down and taken to various stages of decommissioning. The largest reactor to be completely dismantled to date was the Elk River Boiling Water Reactor (22.5 MWe) in the USA. There is, however, a wealth of practical experience of working under active conditions during plant maintenance, modification and adaptation which is directly relevant to the type of work involved in decommissioning.

International liaison is maintained through a technical committee of the International Atomic Energy Agency, which has concluded that there are no unsurmountable technical problems to decommissioning. Within the European Community a Commission proposal for a collaborative R & D programme on topics specific to decommissioning is currently under consideration.

Within the UK the UKAEA reactors in support of the power development programme together with the currently operating 26 Magnox reactors in 11 stations totalling some 5 GW will probably be retired by the end of the century. The timing of withdrawal from service will be dictated by development programme requirements in the case of UKAEA reactors and by economic and technical considerations in the case of commercial reactors. Decommissioning aspects were not a primary concern in the design of these facilities, but future designs will take this factor into account to reduce, where practical, the complexity of decommissioning problems.

The UKAEA selected the Windscale Advanced Gas Cooled Reactor (WAGR) as the initial reactor for decommissioning studies and a similar study is being undertaken by the CEGB of a typical steel pressure vessel Magnox station.

## Decommissioning options

Three generally accepted stages of decommissioning have been identified from national and international studies. For the current classes of UK reactors these have been interpreted as:

*Stage 1* Shut down, remove fuel, remove coolant and make safe. Maintain under surveillance.

*Stage 2* Reduce installation to the minimum practical size without penetrating into those parts which have high levels of induced radioactivity. Ensure the integrity of the reactor primary containment and biological shield to prevent personnel and environmental hazard. Maintain under surveillance.

*Stage 3* Complete removal of the reactor and all other plant and waste off-site followed by the return of the site for redevelopment or general use by the public. No further requirement for surveillance.

These stages, each of which establishes a safe condition, define the status of the reactor in terms of its physical state and required degree of surveillance. Accepting that complete removal of the facility is the ideal ultimate objective two main options are open: to proceed to Stage 1 or 2 and to delay Stage 3 operations to allow radioactive decay which will ease dismantling, or to proceed continuously from reactor closure to Stage 3. The decision as to which option to adopt will be influenced *inter alia* by the dose commitment to persons during dismantling operations, the economic attraction of reusing all or part of an existing site, and environmental considerations.

## Radioactive inventory

Decommissioning of a nuclear power station compared with conventional types of industrial installations is unique, due to problems associated with radioactivity. It should, however, be recognized that radioactivity is limited to specific areas and that a large proportion of a nuclear power station has no associated activity and can be decommissioned and disposed of using conventional methods.

To identify the development issues and practical aspects of decommissioning requires among other data, a knowledge of the total radioactive inventory and its decay together with its distribution within the system. The radioactive inventory includes:

(i) neutron-induced activity in the fixed structure of the plant.

(ii) neutron-induced activity of removable components remaining in the reactor after defuelling, e.g. control rods.

(iii) contamination around the primary cooling circuit arising from activated corrosion products or burst fuel.

(iv) contaminated/activated operational waste arising during the life of the reactor and stored in designated facilities.

Estimates for (i) and (ii) can be made by calculation but the accuracy which can be achieved is dependent upon the assumed chemical composition, in particular the abundance of trace elements which become radioactive, of the construction materials. For UK reactors currently being studied these are essentially mild steel, stainless steel, concrete and graphite. The composition of the last is well defined due to the 'nuclear' specification required for its use and analytical control. The specifications for WAGR steels were nominal and the decision was taken to extend them, after consultation with UKAEA metallurgists, to include reasonable quantities of inevitable trace elements. The abundance of trace elements in concrete is controlled principally by the aggregate which in turn is dictated by the geographical source. The concrete composition adopted is based on a nominal specification modified by measurements carried out on samples from the WAGR biological shield.

The calculation of the inventory for WAGR was based on a mean flux in the moderator of $5.7 \times 10^{13}$ n/cm$^2$/sec at a nuclear load factor of 0.7 for a period of 15 years. Although a calculated inventory is considered adequate as a basis for technical judgements it should be validated and corrected if necessary by physical measurements of samples wherever possible from within the reactor. Item (iii) is dependent upon the operational history of the reactor and can only be estimated on the basis of sampling. Item (iv) should be identified from records. In the case of WAGR, operational waste is disposed of as it arises to general facilities on the Windscale site.

## WAGR activation and contamination

Figure A9.1 is a diagram of WAGR indicating the main features of the reactor and its ancillary plant. The major neutron-induced activity occurs in the steel pressure vessel and the steel structure within it, which have collectively a mass of approximately 600 tonnes of mild steel and 40 tonnes of stainless steel. Also within the pressure vessel is some 300 tonnes of graphite forming the core moderator and reflectors, together with the neutron shield situated above the latter. The degree of activation varies within the pressure vessel due to neutron attenuation by internal components. The induced activity is concentrated in the steelwork, which incorporates the bulk of the stainless steel, in the immediate proximity of the core. The significance of the stainless steel is that it has a higher proportion of cobalt and nickel than mild steel and the overall inventory is influenced by the radioactive isotopes of these two elements. The neutron-induced activity and its decay with time, of the pressure vessel and its internal structure, is shown in Fig. A9.2. The initial decay over the first 40–50 years is dominated by Fe-55 (half life 2.6 years) and Co-60 (half life 5.27 years) which are then superseded by Ni-63 (half life 92 years) as the principal isotope. The exponential decay of the system over this second phase therefore is much reduced. The radio nuclides resulting from neutron irradiation are exclusively βγ and no α active nuclides are produced. From Fig. A9.2 it can be seen that the β decay

347

*Fig. A9.1*   The advanced gas-cooled reactor at Windscale

follows the total curie decay but the $\gamma$ activity stabilizes at a virtually constant value after about 100 years.

The degree of activation of the main concrete biological shield and its mild steel reinforcement which surrounds and supports the pressure vessel on internal corbels will vary with location. The maximum depth of activation of the concrete measured from the internal face is approximately 1 metre. The mass of the biological shield is approximately 4000 tonnes of concrete containing some 200 tonnes of mild steel reinforcement. It is calculated that after seven years' decay following shutdown the active portion will consist of around 750 tonnes of concrete and 90 tonnes of the inner reinforcing steel.

The four heat exchangers, each 20 metres high by 7.3 metres diameter and weighing 150 tonnes, are external to the main reactor biological shield. They are not exposed to direct neutron irradiation but are, however, contaminated internally with Co-60, Cs-137 and Cs-134. The degree and distribution of this contamination is monitored on a routine basis.

## Decommissioning practice

The prelude to any decommissioning of nuclear reactors is the removal of the fuel and its contained fission products. This significantly reduces the radioactive

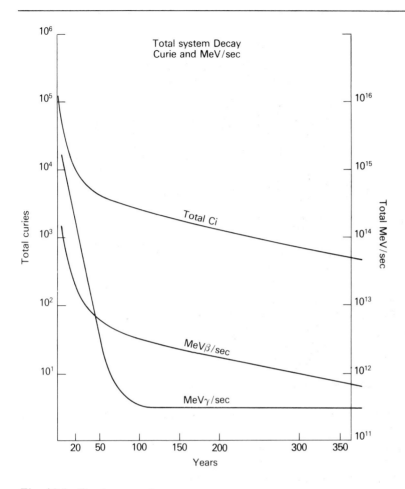

*Fig. A9.2* Total system decay

content of the system leaving the bulk of the residual activity as neutron-induced and therefore in a safer form within the central region of the reactor protected by the massive concrete biological shield structure.

*Stage 1* Decommissioning to this stage consists essentially in sealing the pressure vessel with plugs in the fuel element channels after fuel removal, and securing the integrity of ancillary circuits. This in effect renders the reactor safe and substantially intact on a 'care and maintenance' basis, backed by the appropriate degree of monitoring. This stage is the most economic to achieve but will attract high maintenance costs particularly if this stage is of long duration.

*Stage 2* The decommissioning of WAGR to this stage would include the removal of all plant external to the reactor proper, together with the reactor containment building and all plant and equipment within it, outside the reactor biological shield but including the heat exchangers. The residual structure, which is the reactor biological shield containing active components of the reactor within the sealed pressure vessel, would be a 15 metre diameter by 15 metre high right cylinder. This would occupy about one-fiftieth of the present WAGR site area and would also reduce the visual impact by a factor of six based upon the presented vertical area compared with the 41 metre diameter containment building which currently dominates the WAGR complex.

The most economic Stage 2 situation would be to leave the plant with both the pressure vessel and the interspace between the latter and the biological shield filled with air. No external ancillary operating plant would be required except for monitoring purposes. The following aspects relating to a long-term Stage 2 condition have been considered:

(i) *Temperature* The residual heating in the system associated with activity after two years' shutdown is less than 1 kW. Assuming no forced cooling of the graphite and applying a simplified model based on pessimistic assumptions it was calculated that the graphite temperature would not exceed 40 °C. This temperature is well below the minimum graphite operating temperature (230 °C) and hence there is no possibility of spontaneous energy release from the graphite, or of its combustion. Graphite temperature monitoring would be maintained as a safety measure.

(ii) *Structural integrity* This is basically dependent upon the corrosion of steel. Since the site is coastal a pessimistic corrosion rate of 0.075 mm per year on each exposed surface (i.e. 0.15 mm total thickness) was assumed. Ignoring corrosion retardant factors such as temperature due to residual activity, major component failure periods have been estimated. It is concluded that the integrity of the reactor pressure vessel and its supports would be satisfactory for at least 100 years.

The sealing of penetrations through the biological shield resulting, for example, from cutting through gas ducts to release the heat exchangers, is essential. The top of the biological shield would be capped with concrete with an access provided to enter the reactor top void space for inspection.

The biological shield is a large reinforced concrete structure and judging from available experience of this material no significant problems of deterioration should arise for at least 50 years if it were left exposed to weather. This period could be substantially extended by the construction of a relatively lightweight structure around and braced to the biological shield to afford protection.

(iii) *Radiological Aspects* No radiation hazard should exist at the external face of the biological shield after fuel removal and all penetrations have been sealed and checked.

Throughout the Stage 2 condition, corrosion, both within the pressure vessel and external to it, could produce loose particulate activity. This would be entirely contained within the sealed biological shield the penetration of which by particulates to create an environmental hazard is discounted. The possibility of radiolytic chemical reactions within the pressure vessel between the air constituents and materials of construction, such as graphite, cannot be discounted

(a)

(b)

*Fig. A9.3*  Aerial views of a part of the Windscale site showing the advanced gas-cooled reactor in the left foreground: (a) as it is today; (b) as it might appear at a late stage in the decommissioning of the reactor. Conceptually, the whole area now occupied by the reactor might eventually be returned to 'green field' condition

absolutely. They are unlikely to occur to any significant degree since the radiation fields are relatively low; the reactor vessel and the interspace between the pressure vessel and its biological shield would, however, be equipped with sampling points for routine atmosphere monitoring.

The barrier to any contamination reaching the surrounding ground water is the steel diaphragm floor beneath the reactor, which would require to be made weather-tight at ground level with provision made for access, maintenance, and monitoring.

Access to within the biological shield of the reactor under Stage 2 conditions would only be available through facilities engineered to permit monitoring or inspection. These entrances would be secured and only used by authorised persons. A boundary fence would be erected around the structure.

The engineering requirements to establish Stage 2 have been examined and no major problems have been identified except for the dismantling of the contaminated heat exchangers. These will require to be handled under special shielding and contamination control conditions.

The establishment of a Stage 2 situation will attract a higher initial cost than for Stage 1 but to offset this the long-term cost of maintenance and surveillance will be considerably reduced.

*Stage 3* The two factors which dominate the technical approach to Stage 3 decommissioning are the radiological hazards which will require to be countered during dismantling operations, and the availability of suitable disposal facilities for the dismantled components. During the period between reactor closure and dismantling of active components radioactive decay will occur and so reduce the radiological problems.

A feasibility study has been carried out of the Stage 3 decommissioning of WAGR as a continuing process from reactor closure. The study took account of engineering requirements, radiological aspects and waste management and concluded that on technical grounds such an operation could be undertaken safely and efficiently. The study proposed that a demolition plan should be prepared on the basis of engineering logic. The plan should then be examined against the known or assessed magnitude of radiation/contamination problems which will arise at the various demolition stages; and that consideration then be given to their solution by methods – such as remote handling, shielded working or controlled access – which do not entail modification to the engineering logic. Only if at particular stages such methods prove impracticable will there be a departure from the strict engineering logic and the overall plan amended accordingly.

In broad outline the plan proposes the initial removal of inactive components, other than those associated with services which must be retained to a later date. With the same qualification, the active components external to the pressure circuit would then be removed, followed by removal of the internal structure within the pressure vessel, and of the pressure vessel. The concrete biological shield would be demolished in a manner which would segregate the active and inactive sections. The final operations would be to dismantle the steel reactor containment building, clear the site and back fill the reactor foundations.

A team is now developing a detailed decommissioning plan on the basis of the feasibility study, which includes conceptual engineering studies for remote handling equipment and the modification of existing facilities for dismantling and waste management. It is relevant to comment that demolition will not need research into any new technology; but existing techniques will require development to adapt them to meet special dismantling problems.

It is important to appreciate that the engineering logic differs between leaving decommissioning at Stage 1 or 2 for an unspecified period, and continuing to Stage 3, particularly in the retention and adaptation of existing plant facilities. Hence if the policy relating to the fate of the reactor can be declared well in advance of retirement it should be possible to select the optimum plan for decommissioning. The cost of direct Stage 3 decommissioning must exceed those of Stages 1 and 2 but no continuing costs are involved.

## Decommissioning wastes and disposal

Effort will be applied during decommissioning to salvage the maximum quantities of materials suitable for recycling or reuse from all areas of the site. Such materials will be subject to rigorous monitoring before release. There will however be large quantities of materials which due to their radioactive content cannot be released and will require controlled disposal. The routes currently available are disposal to land and to sea, but at this juncture no firm statement can be made of overall UK policy. This topic is under consideration in the current review of the Government White Paper *Control of Radioactive Wastes* (Cmnd 884) – which is an advisory document and forms the basis of UK practices. The recommendations of the review cannot be anticipated but work has been carried out to assess the practical application of the options.

## Costs and timescales

The removal of fuel from a reactor, which is the initial operation leading to a defined decommissioning stage, will in the case of WAGR extend over a period of about three years. The time required beyond this period to complete Stages 1 and 2 will be of the order of a further one and three years respectively, and in the case of continuing progression to Stage 3 from reactor closure the corresponding extension is about five years. Indicative costs, excluding the cost of defuelling (which is an operational charge) and with no allowance made for the value of recovered plant and scrap, have been assessed. For Stages 2 and 3 these costs represent less than 10 per cent and 15 per cent respectively of the current replacement cost for WAGR at around £70 m.

353

## Conclusion

This article has concentrated on WAGR, which differs in design and size to commercial stations. Although the detail and scale of operations will differ, the general principles which have been discussed are applicable.

Decommissioning has not been a primary consideration in the past, but more attention is now being given to both the design and specification of materials of reactors to ease the problems of dismantling, and also to power station layouts to optimize land re-utilisation.

From the studies summarized in this article and those carried out in other nations there are no technical reasons to suggest that nuclear power stations withdrawn from service cannot be rendered safe and ultimately removed.

# References

## Chapter 1

1. NFDC, Brochures, (1972 to 1981) *History and Services*.
2. *NFDC Archive material*.
3. *NFDC Regional Structure Map*.
4. Companies Act 1929 (4), Limited by Guarantee 26.2.46.
5. JAC, Committee structure, Report, *Health and Safety in Construction*.
6. BS, 94:1971, *Committee Structure*.
7. Ministry of Defence, 1968, 'Blue book', *Military Aid to Civil Community*.
8. NFDC, Form of Contract (revised 1974)
9. DICB, *Working Rule Agreement* (1980 edn)
10. DOE/PSA, *General Conditions of Contract for Demolition* (Extract, p. 4, sec. 16. Fair Wages, etc.)
11. Labour only Sub-contractors, 'Lump labour in perspective', *Contract Journal*, 25.7.74, pp. 20–3.
12. House of Commons, *Treasury Report*, by J. Gilbert, April 1974.13.
13. The Phelps–Brown Report, HMSO 1968; University of Manchester Science and Technology Report, *Building Industry Wages Structure*, 1973; Price Commission, *Construction Panel Board*, HMSO, 1974; Misslebrook Report 1974, *Contract Journal*, 13.6.74; Command Paper 5034, July 1972, paras 145 and 147; Pay and Conditions (other than civil engineering and building), *Construction Report No. 93*, Nov. 1968; Command Paper 3838, para. 31, p. 10; House of Commons (Hansard extract) 18.5.73, col. 1900/1932.
14. Ministerial Circular, 75/75 DOE, 136/75 Welsh Office.
15. Finance Circular, 46/75 Scottish Office.
16. PSA Policy Committee, B and CE sub-committee, Contract Circular BSEC (75), 28 Appendix 2, 9.10.75.
17. DDIR, Records and Reports, 1975 to 1980, Applications and annual returns.
18. Restrictive Trade Practices Act 1956–1968, as amended.
19. Institute of Demolition Engineers, Explanatory leaflet.

## Chapter 2

1. Author's own experience while in control of local authority contracts along with ver-

bal reports from other authorities.
2. Builders price books, Hutchinson's and Spon's – limited guidance.
3. Statutory Regulations: Health and Safety at Work etc. Act 1974; Factories Act 1961, s. (127 (7)); Public Health Act 1961, s. 29; London Building Act (Amended) Act 1939; Building (Scotland) Act 1959, s. (6 (1) & 6 (2))
4. NFDC – Form of Contract.
5. NFDC – Specification.
6. GLC – Procedure and Standard Specification.
7. BS, CP94:1971, s. 1 to 3, pp. 6–22.
8. DDIR, Report and records of inspection 1975 to 1980.

## Chapter 3

1. BS, CP94:1971, *Formation and Structure*.
2. Ministerial Circular 109/72, Secretary of State for the environment to Local Authorities on Code of Practice, November 1972.
3. BS, CP94:1971, (Author's interpretation), s. 1 to 5.
4. HMSO, *Report on Control of Demolition*, by G. Dobry, 1974.

## Chapter 4

1. BS, CP94:1971, s. 4, pp. 24–8.
2. DOE, Research 1972, updated by CITB statistics 1979.
3. 'Demolition of pre-stressed structures', by D. A. Andrews, *Construction News*, 1970, pp. 26–7.
4. EEC Report, *Research into Reuse of Concrete*, No. V.S.18, 1.2.1977.
5. DDIR, Records and inspection reports.
6. HMSO, *Safety in Construction* – Demolition, No. 6E, 1973.
7. JLC Report, *The Demolition of Pre-stressed Concrete Structures*, 1975, pp. 3–32.
8. HMSO, *Repairs of Drums and Small Tanks – Explosion and Fire Risk*, No. 32, 1970 (revised 1975).
9. 'Crocidolite and the construction industry', published in *Protection* June 1974, vol. 11 (6) p. 5.
10. NJA Committee on Health and Safety in *Chemical Industry Training Manual*, March 1977, interpretation and extracts.
11. HMSO, Guidance Notes, *Lead*, 1973 (revised 1976).
12. DOE, TDA Note 47, pp. 1–10.
13. HMSO, *Dust explosions in Factories* No. 22, 1970 (revised 1976).
14. Asbestos Research Council, Pamphlets and data sheets.
15. HMSO, Asbestos Regulations 1969.
16. HMSO, *Health Precautions in Industry – Asbestos* No. 44, 1976.
17. HMSO Health and Safety Executive Report, *Asbestos*, 1979, vols 1 and 2.
18. 'United Kingdom Atomic Energy Authority', by W. H. Lunning, reprint from *Atom*, No. 265, Nov. 1978.

## Chapter 5

1. CITB, *Complex Scaffold* (training manual), 1975.
2. Longman Technical Services, Construction and Civil Engineering, *Construction Technology*, by R. Chudley, vol. 2, part 3, pp. 16–25.

## Chapter 6

1. HASAWA 1974, *T & GWU Safety Handbook*, 1978 pp. 5–24, 83, 84, 92–96, 101–103.
2. Factories Act 1961 plus amendments.
3. Public Health Act 1961 s. 29, plus HMSO -SI No. 421, 1960 and SI No. 1530, 1968.
4. Safety, Health and Welfare Regulations, SI No. 1145, 1948 (revoked).
5. HASAWA 1974, *A Simple Interpretation for the Construction Industry*, by Douglas Short (1978 edn).
6. HMSO, JAC Report, *Safety in Demolition Work*, May 1979.
7. NFDC, Accident Reports, 1969–1975.
8. HMSO, Social Security Act 1975, Accident Book.
9. HMSO, – Factories Act 1961, General Register.
10. HMSO, SI No. 804–1980, *The Notification of Accidents and Dangerous Occurrences Regulations 1980*.
11. HMSO, SI No. 1580, *Construction (General Provisions) Regulations 1961*.
12. HMSO, – SI No. 1933–1971, *The Employers Liability (Compulsory Insurance) Exemption Regulations 1971*.
13. HMSO, – SI No. 1117–1971, *The Employers Liability (Compulsory Insurance) General Regulations 1971*.
14. Accident Reports, DDIR records 1975 to 1980.
15. NJAC on Health and Safety in Chemical Industry, Tables.
16. Health and Safety Executive, Report 1974.
17. Health and Safety Executive, Accident Reports 1974/5.
18. HMSO, Protection of Eyes Regulations 1974.

## Chapter 7

1. CITB Publication, *About the Construction Industry Training Board*, pp. 1–11.
2. HASAWA 1974, s. 2(2) (c).
3. CITB, Press release 30.11.78. Demolition Training Group.
4. Demolition, 'Art and science', by R. G. Price, *Civil Engineering*, vol. 67, No. 789, April 1972, pp. 384–5.
5. HMSO, Command Paper 5034, Robens Report, July 1972.

## Chapter 8

1. DDIR, Records of Inspection 1975–1980.

2. Demolition, 'Art and science', by R. G. Price, *Civil Engineering*, vol. 67, No. 789, April 1972, p. 384.
3. HASAWA 1974, s. (2(2) (c) ).

## Chapter 9

1. DDIR, Records of Inspection 1975–1980.
2. DDIR, Annual Subscription Returns 1975–1980.
3. Prices and Incomes Board, Report No. 93, *Pay and Conditions in the Construction Industry* (excluding building and civil engineering), 1968.

## Chapter 10

1. 'Future problems in demolition', by E. A. Akan, *Civil Engineering*, vol. 67, No. 789, April 1972, pp. 377–81.

## Appendix 8

1. CITB, *Demolition Training*, 1978.
2. HMSO, Guidance Note G.S.7, June 1977.
3. NJAC, *Health & Safety in Chemical Industry*.
4. CITB, *Demolition Training*, 1978.

## Appendix 9

1. 'Decommissioning nuclear reactors', by W. H. Luning, *Atom*, No. 265, Nov. 1978.

## Bibliography

*Research and Location of Information*, by R. I. Almond, 1973 (revised 1974, 1977 and 1980).

# Bibliography I

## Breaking

Silencing concrete breakers, *Architect and Building News* **232**, 27 Sept. 1967: 545

Demolition problems, (Allen, A. L. W.), *Building* **226** (6833), 24 May 1974: 91

Demolition of large reinforced concrete building, (Noble, P.), *Concrete* **5**(9), Sept. 1971: 295–6

Britain's oldest concrete cooling towers: demolition technique features record times, *Concrete* **6**(5), May 1972: 28–9

Demolition air hammers ride crawler drill carriages, *Construction Methods and Equipment* **47**(2), Feb. 1965: 162–4, 166

Air hammer works high to bring concrete wall low, *Construction Methods and Equipment* **49**(5), May 1967: 70–2

Changes in technology, *Construction Plant and Equipment* **2**(3), Nov. 1973: 43

Rocking the foundations, *Construction Plant and Equipment* **1**(10), June 1973: 48–9

No drama at the gasworks, (Patey, D. R.), *Contract Journal* **250**(4867), 14 Dec. 1972: 32–3

Research gives lie to popular belief: silenced breakers not inefficient, *Contract Journal* **217**, 29 June 1967: 1007–8

Concrete breakers must be quieter, *Engineering* **203**, 30 June 1967: 1050

'Copter wields a headache ball: demolished masonry walls of 20-storey steel frame grain bin, *Engineering News-Record* **169**, 27 Sept. 1962: 19

Hydraulic guillotine beheads concrete piles, *Engineering News-Record* **172**, 21 May 1964: 92–3

Excavators shatter cost factors with impactor, *Excavating Contractor* **62**(11), Nov. 1968: 22–3

The durability of prestressed concrete with reference to a structure under demolition, (Andrews, D. A.), Federation Internationale de la Precontrainte, 6th International Congress, Prague, 6–13 June 1970

Rock breaker scores on demolition work, *New Civil Engineer* (27), 8 Feb. 1973: 40

Tough high-up demolition job, *Roads and Streets* **111**, June 1968: 54

## Concrete

Demolition methods for reinforced concrete (O'Neill, D. B.), Advances in Concrete: a symposium, Birmingham, 28–29 Sept. 1971: Concrete Society

Decoupage et demolition du beton, (Cormon, M.), *Batir* (153), 1966: 20–7

Demolishing concrete – today and tomorrow, *Concrete* **6**(12), Dec. 1972: 41

Demolition – post-tensioning still the bogeyman, *Concrete* **7**(2), Feb. 1973: 42

Demolishing prestressing, *Concrete* **8**(6), June 1974: 62–3

Cutting and demolishing concrete structures, *Concrete and Constructional Engineering* **58**(1), Jan. 1963: 49–51

Explosive answers to concrete demolition posers, *Contract Journal* **249**(4860) 26 Oct. 1972 32–3

Everlasting eyesores: pulling buildings down, (Moynahan, B.), *Journal American Concrete Institute* **70**(2), Feb. 1973: N8;N9

Demolition of concrete houses, (Fjosne, A), *Nordisk Betong* (5), 1973: 10–14

The demolition industry's approach to the demolition of modern structures (Griffiths, P. A.), *Structural Engineer* **52**(6) June 1974: A5–A9

## Concrete: breaking

Silencing concrete breakers, *Architect and Building News* **232**, 27 Sept. 1967: 545

Demolition problems, (Allen, A. L. W.), *Building* **226**(6833), 24 May 1974: 91

Demolition of a large reinforced concrete building (Noble, P.), *Concrete* **5**(9), Sept. 1971: 295–6

Britain's oldest concrete cooling towers: demolition technique features record times, *Concrete* **6**(5), May 1972: 28–9

Demolition air hammers ride crawler drill carriages, *Construction Methods and Equipment* **47**(2), Feb. 1965: 162–4, 166

Air hammer works high to bring concrete wall low, *Construction Methods and Equipment* **49**(5), May 1967: 70–2

Changes in technology, *Construction Plant and Equipment* **2**(3), Nov. 1973: 42

Research gives lie to popular belief: silenced breakers not inefficient, *Concrete Journal* **217**, 29 June 1967: 1007–8

No drama at the gasworks (Patey, D. R.), *Contract Journal* **250**(4867) 14 Dec. 1972: 32–3

Concrete breakers must be quieter, *Engineering* **203**, 30 June 1967: 1050

Hydraulic guillotine beheads concrete piles, *Engineering News-Record* **172**, 21 May 1964, 92–3

Excavators shatter cost factors with impactor, *Excavating Contractor* **62**(11), Nov. 1968: 22–3

The durability of prestressed concrete with reference to a structure under demolition, (Andrews, D. A.), 6th International Congress of the Federation Internationale de la Precontrainte, Prague, 6–13 June 1970

Rock breaker scores on demolition work, *New Civil Engineer* (27), 8 Feb. 1973: 40

Tough high-up demolition job, *Roads and Streets* **111**, June 1968: 54

## Concrete: cutting (abrasive)

A plant for cutting reinforced concrete (in Russian), (Cherkashin, Y. A.), *Beton I*

*Zhelezobeton* (1), 1973: 40–1

Diamonds help in bridge modernisation, *Better Roads* **38**(9), Sept. 1968: 26–8

The use of a diamond drill for drilling through reinforced concrete, (Sinclair, S), *Civil Engineering and Public Work Review* **49**(581), Nov. 1954: 1192

Using a diamond drill in drilling through reinforced concrete, (Sinclair, S.), *Civil Engineering and Public Works Review* **54**(640), Nov. 1959: 1301–2

Using the diamond drill for drilling through reinforced concrete, (Sinclair, S.), *Civil Engineering and Public Works Review* **58**(678), Jan. 1963: 67–71 and 58 (679), Feb. 1963: 227–9

Drilling and cutting concrete and other hand materials, (Boyes, R. G. H.), *Contract Journal* **239**(4769), 28 Jan. 1971: 335–7 and 239 (4770), 4 Feb. 1971: 469, 472

Portable concrete sawing machine, *Engineer* **219**, 19 Mar. 1965: 517

New York drillers take care of their diamond bits, *Industrial Diamond Review* **29**, July 1969: 290–3

Sweden's civil engineers turn to diamond, (Minten, F.), *Industrial Diamond Review*, **29**, Sept. 1969: 367–9

The use of diamond blades in the concrete industries, *Modern Concrete* **34**(5), Sept. 1970: 65–6

Plant engineers jack up floor, cut basement door through concrete girder, (Girard, G. W.), *Plant Engineering* **15**, Mar. 1961: 133–4

Concrete sawing trims time on repairs, *Engineering* **18**, Aug. 1964: 135

## Concrete: cutting (electro)

Electron beam cutting of rocks and concrete, (Schumacher, B. W.), *Electron and Ion Beam Science and Technology*, proceedings of the 3rd International Conference, Boston, 5–8 May 1968, 447–8

Thermo-electric method of cutting concrete, (Pavlov, B. A.), *Mekhanizatsiya Stroitelstva* **22**(10), 1965: 8–9

## Concrete: cutting (thermal)

Removing concrete – cutting by laser, (Scott, B. F. and Jones, J. W.), *Advances in Concrete*, a symposium, Birmingham, 28–29 Sept. 1971: Concrete Society

Cutting and drilling holes in concrete by means of a flame thrower, (Bachus, E.), *Bauingenieur* **37**(2), 1962: 47–9

Drilling and cutting concrete by oxygen, (Nielsen, K. E. C.), *Beton-Teknik* **23**(2) 1957: 56–62.

Thermic boring – a method for the boring and severing of concrete, (Casey, E. T.), *Civil Engineering and Public Works Review* **58**(679), Feb. 1963: 217–9

Thermic lancing, (Kaybore Thermic Lancing Co. Ltd.), *Civil Engineering and Public Works Review* **67** (789), Apr. 1972: 389, 391

Clearing old concrete off the site, *Engineering* **185**, 7 Feb. 1958: 191

Thermic lance removes shipping hazard, *Engineering* **204**, 27 Oct. 1967: 668

Burning concrete, *Engineering News-Record* **158**(10), 1957: 74

Thermic lance boring, (Dinsdale, R.), *Heating and Ventilating Engineer* **43**, Nov. 1969: 228–9

Concrete demolition by powder lancing, *Illustrated Carpenter and Builder* **148**(4281), 18 Sept. 1959: 3006

Thermic boring of concrete and reinforced concrete, *Indian Concrete Journal* **40**(12), Dec. 1966: 499–500, 511

Thermic boring gives silent demolition, *Muck Shifter* **25**, Aug. 1967: 28–9

Cutting concrete by flame jet, (Brichkin, A. V.), *Promyshlennoe Stroitel'stvo* **42**(2), 1965: 29–30

Powder lancing cuts cost of difficult concrete demolition job, *Roads and Streets* **101**, Apr. 1958: 158

Powder-lance cuts thick concrete with saving, *Roads and Streets* **104**, Mar. 1961: 117

Thermic drilling of concrete and stone, (Lebrun, M.), *Structural Engineer* **25**(2), Feb. 1947: 57–76 and 25 (10), Oct. 1947: 443–51

Use of oxygen thermal cutting for demolishing, (Gabriel, D.), *Travaux* (456), 1973: 25–6

Powder-lancing cuts 18-inch concrete doorways, *Welding Engineer*, **46**, Feb. 1961: 45

Powder lancing clears way for new radiation lab., *Welding Journal*, **37**. Mar. 1958. 237–8

## Concrete: cutting (water-jet)

Jet Cutting Technology, (British Hydromechanics Research Association), proceedings of the 1st International Symposium, Warwick, 5–7 Apr. 1972, 37 papers

## Concrete: explosives

Demolition by dynamite, *Architectural Forum* **108**, Apr. 1958: 136–7

Demolition of reinforced concrete by explosives, (Batifoulier, R.), *Batir* (158) 1967: 38–44

Bridge demolition at Oroville Dam, *Civil Engineering* (U.S.) **36**(4), Apr. 1966: 32–3

Blasting mass-concrete at Grand Coulee Dam, (Granger, J. R.), *Civil Engineering* (U.S.) **41**, Aug. 1971: 28–31

Well-placed dynamite neatly drops three buildings, *Construction Methods and Equipment* **41**(2), Feb. 1959: 98, 104–5, 108–9

'Air-gap' blasting method demolishes concrete walls, *Construction Methods and Equipment* **46**(9), Sept. 1964: 100–2

Explosives placed without drilling break up piers, *Construction Methods and Equipment* **50**(1), Jan. 1968: 77

Massively reinforced warehouse brought down in 7 seconds, (Gomolak, L.), *Construction Methods and Equipment* **50**(12), Dec. 1968: 64–7

Blasting act is dynamite, *Construction Methods and Equipment* **51**(5), May 1969: 123

Shaped explosives cut reinforced piles quickly and efficiently, (Smith, L.), *Construction Methods and Equipment* **53**, Mar. 1971: 61–3

51. 8M cooling tower blown up, *Contract Journal* **230**, 28 Aug. 1969: 925

Demolition by controlled blasting, *Engineer* **204**(5306), 4 Oct. 1957: 489

Push steelwork as demolition ends, (Turney, H.), *Engineering and Contract Record* **72**(5), May 1959: 87–9

D.H.O. demolition test removes old overpass, *Engineering and Contract Record* **77**(2), Feb. 1964: 53

A look at how to blast concrete, *Engineering News-Record* **159**(19), 7 Nov. 1957: 104–5

Going, going, going, gone: demolition of Washington D.C.'s terminal refrigeration warehouse, *Engineering News-Record* **164**(16), 21 Apr. 1960: 28–9

Dynamite solves tough salvage problem, (Hallstead, W. F.), *Explosives Engineer* **37**(3), May–June 1959: 88–90

Controlled blasting solves difficult problem, (Hallstead, W. F.), *Explosives Engineer* **38**(4), July–Aug. 1960: 120–2

Controlled blasting demolishes stubborn buildings, (Hallstead, W. F.), *Explosives Engineer* **38**(6), Nov.–Dec. 1960: 181–3

Removing old concrete? Try air-gap explosive demolition, (Teller, A. E.), *Plant Engineering* **21**, Nov. 1967: 120–1

Six-second blast topples stack in carefully measured fall: preshooting did the trick, *Power* **113**(9), Sept. 1969: 67

Turbine foundations removal fast and safe way, (Conway, W. C.), *Power Engineering* **65**, June 1961: 60–1

Breaking concrete foundations by blasting, (Aleksandrov, V. E.), *Promyshlennoe Stroitel'stvo* **44**(7), 1967: 19–22

Dynamite did it where drop ball was out of bounds, (Hallstead, W. F.), *Roads and Streets* **102**(6), June 1959: 69–71

Precision blasts make short work of old piers, *Roads and Streets* **111**(6), June 1968: 59, 102

Outstanding technical achievement at Kariba, (Mather, D. D. N.), *South African Mining and Engineering Journal* **68**(3363), 26 July 1957: 1451, 1453, 1455

## Concrete: Microwaves

Removing concrete – cutting by microwaves, (Smith, J. L.), *Advances in Concrete* a symposium, Birmingham, 28–29 Sept. 1971: Concrete Society

Demolition by radar waves, *Concrete Construction* **10**(2), Feb. 1965: 40

Microwaves break up rock and concrete, *New Scientist* **14**(289), 31 May 1962: 443–4

## Concrete: plant

The Nibbler, *Construction Plant and Equipment* **2**(9), May 1974: 67

## Concrete: splitting

New concrete demolition technique, *Concrete Construction* **15**(8), Aug. 1970: 284

## Cutting (*abrasive*)

Diamonds help in bridge modernization, *Better Roads* **38**(9), Sept. 1968: 26–8
The use of a diamond drill for drilling through reinforced concrete, (Sinclair, S.), *Civil Engineering and Public Works Review* **49**(581), Nov. 1954: 1192
Using a diamond drill in drilling through reinforced concrete, (Sinclair, S.), *Civil Engineering and Public Works Review* **54**(640), Nov. 1959: 1301–2
Using the diamond drill for drilling through reinforced concrete, (Sinclair, S.),*Civil Engineering and Public Works Review* **58**(678), Jan. 1963: 67–71 and **58**(679), Feb. 1963: 227–9
Drilling and cutting concrete and other hard materials, (Boyes, R. G. H.), *Contract Journal* **239**(4769), 28 Jan. 1971: 335–7, and **239**(4770), 4 Feb. 1971: 469, 472
Portable concrete sawing machine, *Engineer* **219**, 19 Mar. 1965: 517
Chain becomes a saw to demolish wreck, *Engineering News-Record* **176**, 14 Apr. 1966: 39, 41
New York drillers to take care of their diamond bits, *Industrial Diamond Review* **29**, July 1969: 290–3
Sweden's civil engineers turn to diamonds, (Minten, F.), *Industrial Diamond Review* **29**, Sept. 1969: 367–9
The use of diamond blades in the concrete industries, *Modern Concrete* **34**(5), Sept. 1970: 65–6
Plant engineers jack up floor, cut basement door through concrete girder, (Girard, G. W.), *Plant Engineering* **15**, Mar. 1961: 133–4
Concrete sawing trims time on repairs, *Plant Engineering* **18**, Aug. 1964: 135

## Cutting (*electro*)

Electron beam cutting of rocks and concrete, (Schumacher, B. W.), *Electron and Ion Beam Science and Technology*, proceedings of the 3rd International Conference, Boston, 5–8 May, 1968, 447–68
Thermo-electric method of cutting concrete, (Pavlov, B. W.), *Mekhanizatsiya Stroitelstva*, **22**(10), 1965: 8–9

## Cutting (*thermal*)

Removing concrete: cutting by laser, (Scott, B. F. and Jones, J. W.), *Advances in Concrete*, a symposium, Birmingham, 28–29 Sept. 1971: Concrete Society
Cutting and drilling holes in concrete by means of a flame thrower, (Bachus, E.), *Bauingenieur*, **37**(2), 1962: 47–9
Drilling and cutting concrete by oxygen, (Nielsen, K. E. C.), *Beton-Teknik* **23**(2), 1957: 56–62
Thermic boring – a method for the boring and severing of concrete, (Casey, E. T.), *Civil Engineering and Public Works Review* **58**(679), Feb. 1963: 217–19
Thermic lancing, (Kaybore Thermic Lancing Co. Ltd.), *Civil Engineering and Public Works Review* **67**(789), Apr. 1972: 389, 391
Clearing old concrete off the site, *Engineering* **185**, 7 Feb. 1958: 191

Thermic lance removes shipping hazard, *Engineering* **204**, 27 Oct. 1967: 668

Burning concrete, *Engineering News-Record* **158**(10), 1957: 74

Thermic lance boring, (Dinsdale, R.), *Heating and Ventilating Engineer* **43**, Nov. 1969: 228–9

Concrete demolition by powder lancing, *Illustrated Carpenter and Builder* **148**(4281), 18 Sept. 1959: 3006

Thermic boring of concrete and reinforced concrete, *Indian Concrete Journal* **40**(12), Dec. 1966: 499–500, 511

Thermic boring gives silent demolition, *Muck Shifter* **25**, Aug. 1967: 28–9

New power tool cuts all materials using oxygen and metallic powder, (Burch, R. L.), *Power Engineering* **63**, Sept. 1959: 74–5

Cutting concrete by flame jet, (Brichkin, A. V.), *Promyshlennoe Stroitel'stvo* **52**(2), 1965: 29–30

The jet-piercing process: the application of high-temperature flames to the penetration of rocks, (Just, G. D.), *Quarry Managers' Journal* **47**(6), 1963: 219–26

Powder lancing cuts cost of difficult concrete demolition job, *Roads and Streets* **101**, Apr. 1958: 158

Powder-lance cuts thick concrete with saving, *Roads and Streets* **104**. Mar. 1961: 117

Thermic drilling of concrete and stone, (Lebrun, M.), *Structural Engineer* **25** (2), Feb. 1947: 57–76 and 25(10), Oct. 1947: 443–51

Powder-lancing cuts 18-inch concrete doorways, *Welding Engineer* **46**, Feb. 1961: 45

Powder lancing clears way for new radiation lab. *Welding Journal* **37**, March 1958: 237–8

Dual-flow plasma torch, (Browning, J. A.), *Welding Journal* **43**, Apr. 1964: 275–9

## Cutting (*water jet*)

Jet Cutting Technology, (British Hydromechanics Research Association), proceedings of the 1st International Symposium, Warwick, 5–7 Apr. 1972, 37 papers

## Dismantling

Bridge dismantled without falsework, *Civil Engineering* (U.S.A.) **30**, Aug. 1960: 48–9

Lift-bridge replaced under traffic, (Collard, A. A.), *Civil Engineering* (U.S.A.) **31**, May 1961: 36–9

Tearing down to build up, (Moxley, R. L.), *Compressed Air Magazine* **68**, Aug. 1963: 6–13

Leaving behind a steel skeleton: stripping the facade from Times Tower Building in New York City, (Moxley, R. L.), *Compressed Air Magazine* **69**, Apr. 1964: 4–10

Toppling a Texas tower, *Compressed Air Magazine* **69**, Oct. 1964: 4–7

Demolition – new job for tower cranes, *Construction Methods and Equipment* **42**(4), Apr. 1960: 240–5

Down comes London Bridge, *Contract Journal* **224**, 15 Aug. 1968: 745

Demolition of Cannon Street Station roof, (Holt, H. P.), *Engineer* **207**(5376), 6 Feb. 1959: 208–11

Push steelwork as demolition ends, (Turney, H.) *Engineering and Contract Record* **72**(5),

May 1959: 87–9

Seven Bridge, Sharpness; disaster and demolition, (Barnwell, F. R. L.), *Journal of the Permanent Way Institution* **87**(2), Oct. 1969: 104–8

London Bridge: demolition and construction, 1967–1973, (Mead, P. F.), *Proceedings of the Institution of Civil Engineers* **54**, Feb. 1973: 47–69

Bridge demolition project reverses construction process, *Public Works* **101**, Aug. 1970: 92

New bridge piers built as old ones come out, *Roads and Streets* **111**, July 1968: 58–60

## Explosives

Demolition by dynamite, *Architectural Forum* **108**, Apr. 1958: 136–7

Demolition of reinforced concrete by explosives, (Batifoulier, R.), *Batir* (158), 1967: 38–44

Controlled blasting – constructive destruction, (Darpress (Industrial) Ltd.), *Building Technology and Management* **8**, Feb. 1970: 18–19

Controlled vibration in blasting at close quarters: modernisation of power plant of New York City transit system, (Samuel, R.), *Civil Engineering* (U.S.A.), **28**, Jan. 1958: 35–7

Bridge demolition at Oroville Dam, *Civil Engineering* (U.S.A.) **36**, Apr. 1966: 32–3

Blasting mass-concrete at Grand Coulee Dam, (Granger, J. R.), *Civil Engineering* (U.S.A.) **41**, Aug. 1971: 28–31

An ancient form of energy adapted to modern practice, (Swinnerton, H. A.), *Civil Engineering and Public Works Review* **67**(789), Apr. 1972: 387–9

Demolitions, metal and pile cutting (Westwater, R. and Morris, G.), in Comrie, J (ed), *Civil Engineering Reference Book*, 2nd edn, Butterworths, 1961, 4 vols, Vol. 2, pp. 519–22

Well-placed dynamite neatly drops three buildings, *Construction Methods and Equipment* **41**(2), Feb. 1959: 98, 104, 105, 108, 109

'Air-gap' blasting method demolishes concrete walls, *Construction Methods and Equipment* **46**(9), Sept. 1964: 100–2

Explosives placed without drilling break up piers, *Construction Methods and Equipment* **50**, Jan. 1968: 77

Massively reinforced warehouse brought down in 7 seconds, (Gomolak, L.), *Construction Methods and Equipment* **50**, Dec. 1968: 64–7

Blasting act is dynamite, *Construction Methods and Equipment* **51**, May 1969: 123

24 hour job: blast main span and clear channel, *Construction Methods and Equipment* **51**, Sept. 1969: 119

Shaped explosives cut reinforced concrete piles quickly and efficiently, (Smith, L.), *Construction Methods and Equipment* **53**, Mar. 1971: 61–3

51.8M cooling tower blown up, *Contract Journal* **230**, 28 Aug. 1969: 925

Demolition by controlled blasting, *Engineer* **204**(5306), 4 Oct. 1957: 489

Experimental studies of effects of blasting on structures, (Edwards, A. T. and Northwood, T. D.), *Engineer* **210**(5462), 30 Sept. 1960: 539–46

Push steelwork as demolition ends, (Turney, H.), *Engineering and Contract Record* **72**(5), May 1959: 87–9

D.H.O. demolition test removes old overpass, *Engineering and Contract Record* **77**(2),

Feb. 1964: 53

A look at how to blast concrete, *Engineering News-Record* **159**(19), 7 Nov. 1957: 104–5

Pittsburgh building razed in ten seconds, *Engineering News-Record* **161**(2), 10 July 1958: 29

Going, going, going, gone: demolition of Washington D.C.'s terminal refrigeration warehouse, *Engineering News-Record* **164**(16), 21 Apr. 1960: 28–9

Dynamite fells Texas tower No. 2, *Engineering News-Record* **171**(4), 3 Oct. 1963: 21

Explosives cut cost of razing smokestacks, (O'Neill, J. J.), *Explosives Engineer* **35**(2), Mar.–Apr. 1957: 48–51

Dynamite solves tough salvage problem, (Hallstead, W. F.), *Explosives Engineer* **37**(3), May–June 1959: 88–90

Controlled blasting solves difficult problem, (Hallstead, W. F.), *Explosives Engineer* **38**(4), July–Aug. 1960: 120–2

Controlled blasting demolishes stubborn buildings, (Hallstead, W. F.), *Explosives Engineer* **38**(6), Nov.–Dec. 1960: 181–3

Experiments in plate cutting by shaped high explosive charge, (Zaid, A. I. O. et al), *Journal of Mechnical Engineering Science* **13**(1), Feb. 1971: 13–25

Breakage of scrap moulds using explosives, (John, I. H.), *Journal of the Iron and Steel Institute* **209**, Feb. 1971: 96–9

Can't pull it down? – blow it up!, *Muck Shifter* **23**, Oct. 1965: 28–30

Three fast demolition techniques, *Muck Shifter* **25**, Aug. 1967: 26–7

Background to blasting for civil engineers, (Stenhouse, D.), *Muck Shifter* **25**, Nov. 1967: 35

(1) Blow them up to knock them down. (2) Engineering with explosives charges. (3) Blasting on a beach to improve its facilities, (Leach, G.), *Municipal Journal* **72**(3705) (3706) (3707), 21 Feb. 1964: 569–73; 27 Feb. 1964: 646–7; 6 Mar. 1964: 743–4

Further studies of blasting near buildings, (Northwood, T. D. et al), *Ontario Hydro-Research Quarterly* **15**(1), 1963: 1–10

Controlled applications of explosives in demolitions, (Swinnerton, H. A.), *Permanent Way Institution Journal* **83**(3), 1965: 154;5

Removing old concrete? Try air-gap explosive demolition, (Teller, A. E.), *Plant Engineering* **21** Nov. 1967: 120–1

Thar she goes! dynamiting obsolete stacks is quick, safe and economical, (Hallstead, W. F.), *Power* **104**, Jan. 1960: 176–7

Six-second blast topples stack in carefully measured fall: pre-shooting did the trick, *Power* **113**, Sept. 1969: 67

Turbine foundation removal fast and safe way, (Conway, W. C.), *Power Engineering* **65**, June 1961: 60–1

The use of explosives for demolitions, (Brook, D. H. and Westwater, R.), *Proceedings of the Institution of Civil Engineers* **4**, Division 3(3), 1955: 862–86, 887–99

Operation David: the demolition of a Goliath crane, (Lumbard, D. and Styles, D. G.), *Proceedings of the Institution of Civil Engineers* **35**, Oct. 1966: 293;312

Breaking concrete foundations by blasting, (Aleksandrov, V. E.), *Promyshlennoe Stroitel'stvo* **44**(7), 1967: 19–22

Dynamite + imagination and experience = economy, (Hallstead, W. F.), *Public Works* **90**, July 1959: 129–31

Contractor produces movie on demolition, (Hallstead, W. F.), *Public Works* **91**, Apr. 1960: 209

Obsolete bridge is 'cut down' with explosives, *Railway Track and Structures* **64**(4), Apr. 1968: 25–7

Dynamiting did it where drop ball was out of bounds, (Hallstead, W. F.), *Roads and Streets* **102**(6), June 1959, 69–71

Careful blasting removes old lift bridge, *Roads and Streets* **103**, Sept. 1960: 130–1, 133

Shaped blasting charges speed demolition job at refinery in Wood River, *Roads and Streets* **105**, Mar. 1962: 100

Precision blasts make short work of old piers, *Roads and Streets* **111**, June 1968: 59, 102

Bridge demolished safely with explosive cord, *Roads and Streets* **113**, Aug. 1970: 67

Shaped explosives charges demolish bridges with economy and safety, *Roads and Streets* **114**, Sept. 1971: 78–81

New twist on explosives; improve safety with them, *Roads and Streets* **116**, May 1973: 138–9

Precision blasting safely chops big smokestack down, *Roads and Street* **116**, Dec. 1973: 64

Outstanding technical achievement at Kariba, (Mather, D.), *South African Mining and Engineering Journal* **68**(3363), 26 July 1957: 1451, 1453, 1455

Controlled explosives . . . their uses as a 'fine art', (Swinnerton, W. G.), *Structural Engineer* **52**(6), June 1974: A17–A19

Shaped charges 'deep six' a bridge, *Western Construction* **45**(6), June 1970: 88, 90, 106

## Management, education and research

*A Bibliography on Demolition Structures* (Tibbetts, D. C.), *Canada National* Research Council, Division of Building Research, 1953

Lipsett Brothers: biggest wreckers in the building world, *Architectural Forum* **120**, Jan. 1964: 76–7

Demolition contracting: form of direct contract, *Building* **200**(6147), 10 Mar. 1961: 469

Loose fit versus demolition, *Building* **255**(6797), 7 Sept. 1973: 98

What goes up must come down, (Barfield, J.), *Building* **226**, (6828), 19 Apr. 1974: 81–2

Business techniques and plant demolition, (Breiner, M. B.), *Chemical Engineering Progress* **68**, Mar. 1972: 78–9

Demolition: erecting a framework: results for a BRS survey, (Akam, E. A.), *Civil Engineering and Public Works Review* **67**(789), Apr. 1972: 377–81

Demolition: the art and the science, (Price, R. G.), *Civil Engineering and Public Works Review* **67**(789), Apr. 1972: 383–5

Site clearance, in Seeley, I. *Civil Engineering Quantities*, S.I. edn, Macmillan, 1971, pp. 96–104

*Civil Service Examination Passbook: Senior Demolition Inspector*, (Rudman, J.), National Learning Corp. (U.S.A.)

*Civil Service Examination Passbook: Supervisory Demolition Inspector*, (Rudman, J.), National Learning Corp. (U.S.A.)

Demolition, (Higgins, L. R.), *Construction Methods and Equipment* **55**(1), Jan. 1973: 58–65

Demolition contractors launch apprenticeship scheme, (Allison, S. B. et al.), *Contract Journal* **184**(4291), 21 Sept. 1961: 1439

Demolition builds big business, *Contract Journal* **247**(4837), 18 May 1972: 302, 303, 308

Demolition firms in pay break-away move, *Contract Journal* **250**(4862), 9 Nov. 1972: 35

Demolition, (Patey, D. R.), *Contract Journal* **253**(4888), 1973: 35–55

*Demolitions*, (War Office), H.M.S.O., 1958 (Royal Engineers, Supplementary pocket-book, No. 4)

Wrecking – its just building in reverse, *Engineering News-Record* **152**(21), 27 May 1954: 42–4, 46–7

World's fair postlude: the demolition crews take over, *Engineering News-Record* **175**(17), 21 Oct. 1965: 18–19

Fair demolition to yield test data, *Engineering News-Record* **175**(26), 23 Dec. 1965: 17

Severn Bridge, Sharpness: disaster and demolition, (Barnwell, F. R. L.), *Journal of the Permanent Way Institution* **87**(2), Oct. 1969: 104–8

Legal aspects of demolition, (Powell-Smith, V.), *Local Government Chronicle* (5583), 22 Mar. 1974: 264–7

Man behind the mattock, *Muck Shifter*, **23**, Oct. 1965: 31–3

Guard profits with insurance, (Lever, H.), *Muck Shifter* **25**, Aug. 1967: 30–1

Demolition/general conditions of contract where demolition is to be let as a separate contract, *Specification*, Architectural Press

Present and future trends in the demolition industry, (Griffiths, P. A.), *Structural Engineer* **51**(6), June 1973: A9–A19

## Masonry: breaking

'Copter wields a headache ball: demolished masonry walls of 20-storey steel framed grain bin, *Engineering News-Records* **169**, 27 Sept. 1962: 19

## Masonry: explosives

Explosive cut cost of razing smokestacks, (O'Neill, J. J.), *Explosive Engineer* **35**(2), Mar.–Apr. 1957: 48–51

Thar she goes! dynamiting obsolete stacks is quick, safe and economical, (Halstead, W. F.), *Power* **104**, Jan. 1960: 176–7

## Metals: cutting (abrasive)

Chain becomes a saw to demolish wreck, *Engineering News-Record* **176**, 14 Apr. 1966: 39, 41

## Metals: cutting (thermal)

Changes in technology, *Construction Plant and Equipment* **2**(3), Nov. 1973: 43

Dual-flow plasma torch, (Browning, J. A.), *Welding Journal* **43**(4), Apr. 1964: 275–9

## Metals: dismantling

Bridge dismantled without falsework, *Civil Engineering* (U.S.A.) **30**(8), Aug. 1960: 48–9

Lift-bridge replaced under traffic, (Collard, A. A.), *Civil Engineering* (U.S.A.) **31**(5), May 1961: 36–9

Tearing down to build up, (Moxley, R. L.), *Compressed Air Magazine* **68**, Aug. 1963: 6–13

Toppling a Texas tower, *Compressed Air Magazine* **69**, Oct. 1964: 4–7

Demolition of Cannon Street Station roof, (Holt, H. P.), *Engineer* **207**(5376), 6 Feb. 1959: 208–11

Push steelwork as demolition ends, (Turney, H.), *Engineering and Contract Record* **72**(5), 1959: 87–9

Severn Bridge, Sharpness, disaster and demolition, (Barnwell, F. R. L.), *Journal of the Permanent Way Institution* **87**(2), Oct. 1969: 104–8

Bridge demolition project reverses construction process, *Public Works* **101**, Aug. 1970: 92

New bridge piers built as old ones come out, *Roads and Streets* **111**, July 1968: 58–60

## Metals: explosives

24 hour job: blast main span and clear channel, *Construction Methods and Equipment* **51**, Sept. 1969: 119

Shaped explosives cut reinforced piles quickly and efficiently, (Smith, L.), *Construction Methods and Equipment* **53**, Mar. 1971: 61–3

Dynamite fells Texas tower No. 2, *Engineering News-Record* **171**, 3 Oct. 1963: 21

Dynamite solves tough salvage problem, (Hallstead, W. F.), *Explosives Engineer* **37**(3), May–June 1959: 88–90

Experiments in plate cutting by shaped high explosive charges, (Zaid, A. I. O. et al.), *Journal of Mechanical Engineering Science* **13**(1), Feb. 1971: 13–25

Breakage of scrap moulds using explosives, (John, I. H.), *Journal of the Iron and Steel Institute* **209**, Feb. 1971: 96–9

Operation David: the demolition of a Goliath crane, (Lumbard, D. and Styles, S. G.), *Proceedings of the Institution of Civil Engineers* **35**, Oct. 1966: 293–312

Obsolete bridge is 'cut' down with explosives, *Railway Track and Structures* **64**(4), Apr. 1968: 25–27

Careful blasting removes old lift bridge, *Roads and Streets* **103**, Sept. 1960: 130, 131, 133, 130, 131, 133

Shaped blasting charges speed demolition job at refinery in Wood River, *Roads and Streets* **105**, Mar. 1962: 100

Bridge demolished safely with explosive cord, *Roads and Streets* **113**, Aug. 1970: 67

Shaped explosives charges demolish bridges with economy and safety, *Roads and Streets* **114**, Sept. 1971: 78–81

Shaped charges 'deep six' a bridge, *Western Construction* **45**(6), June 1970: 88, 90, 106

## Microwaves

Removing concrete – cutting by microwaves, (Smith, J. L.), *Advances in Concrete*, proceedings of a symposium, Birmingham, 28–29 Sept. 1971: Concrete Society.

Demolition by radar waves, *Concrete Construction* **10**(2), Feb. 1965: 40

Microwaves break up rock and concrete, *New Scientist* **14**(289), 31 May 1962: 443–4

## Plant

Hobgoblin: demolition breaker uses hydraulic impulse method, rubs at lower noise level, *Compressed Air Magazine* **73**, Dec. 1968: 18

Demolition – new job for tower cranes, *Construction Methods and Equipment* **42**(4), Apr. 1960: 204–5

Demolition air hammers ride crawler drill carriages, *Construction Methods and Equipment* **47**(2), Feb. 1965: 162–4, 166

The Nibbler, *Construction Plant and Equipment* **2**(9), May 1974: 67

Portable concrete sawing machine, *Engineer* **219**, 19 Mar. 1965: 517

Wrecking crane for arctic conditions, *Engineering* **190**(4934), 11 Nov. 1960: 665

Here are two ways to knock down old buildings, *Engineering News-Record* **162**, 19 Mar. 1959: 46–7

'Copter wields a headache ball: demolished masonry walls of 20-storey steel framed grain bin, *Engineering News-Record* **169**, 27 Sept. 1962: 19

Tall scaffold makes tower demolition safe: wreckers hammer down walls of New York's famed Times Tower, *Engineering News-Record* **172**: 30 Apr. 1964: 24–5

Hydraulic guillotine beheads concrete piles, *Engineering News-Record* **172**, 21 May 1964: 92–3

Chain becomes saw to demolish wreck, *Engineering News-Record* **176**: 14 Apr. 1966: 39, 41

Stinger brings down walls fast, *Engineering News-Record* **177**, 24 Nov. 1966: 40

Excavators shatter cost factors with impactor, *Excavating Contractor* **62**(11), Nov. 1968: 22–3

Claw multi-purpose demolition tool, *Excavating Contractor* **63**(4), Apr. 1969: 42–4

Versatile air power speeds work on site, *Muck Shifter* **24**, Aug. 1967: 34–5

Use of modern machinery in construction industry, (Wright, D. F.), *Municipal Engineering* **147**, 5 June 1970: 1203–5

Rock breaker scores on demolition work, *New Civil Engineer* (27), 8 Feb. 1973: 40

Landfill compactor-loader aids urban renewal demolition, *Public Works* **101**, Dec. 1970: 88

Tractor-shovels do whirlwind right-of-way demolition, *Roads and Streets* **106**, Mar. 1963: 40–1, 100

Wheeled tractors handle massive demolition job, *Roads and Streets* **116**, June 1973: 138–9

Big equipment speeds small job, *Roads and Streets* **116**, Dec. 1973: 26–9

Old bridge deck removed fast with tailored equipment, *Roads and Streets* **116**, Dec. 1973: 58–60

Steel scaffolds demolish accidents in demolition work, *Safety Maintenance* **115**, Mar. 1958: 21

## Safety and regulations

Silencing concrete breakers, *Architect and Building News* **232**, 27 Sept. 1967: 545

The right to demolish: control under local authorities, (Jolley, K. T.) *Builder* **201**, (6179), 20 Oct. 1961: 743

President attacks demolition pirates, *Construction Plant and Equipment* **1**(9), May 1973: 4

*Construction Regulations Handbook*, 8th edn. (Royal Society for the Prevention of Accidents), Rospa, 1970

*Construction Safety*, (National Federation of Building Trades Employers, N.F.B.T.E., 1972

'Cheap Jack' demolition hazards – and results, (Goldman, R.), *Contract Journal* **226**, 7 Nov. 1968: 65–6

Council accused of negligence, *Contract Journal* **226**, 28 Nov. 1968: 467, 470

*Demolition*, (British Standards Institution) C.P. 94: 1971

*Demolition and Repair of Storage tanks: Fire Precautions and Fire Fighting*, (Home Office), Technical Bulletin 1972, No. 2, Department of the Environment.

Obsolete nuclear power stations: no major problems in demolition, (Bainbridge, G. R.), *Electrical Review* **179**, 16 Sept. 1966: 421–2

Almost too hot to handle: Mexico City's general hospital, *Engineering News-Record* **163**, 30 July 1959: 43

Excavation, demolition, shoring and under pinning, (British Standards Institution) C.P. 2004: 1972: *Foundations*, pp. 122–8

*Guide to the Construction Regulations, 1961 and 1966*, (Federation of Civil Engineering Contractors and National Federation of Building Trades Employers)

Lead poisoning in demolition work, (McBride, W. W. and Proctor, E. G.), *Industrial Medicine and Surgery* **31**, Jan. 1962: 31–2

Demolition and dangerous structures, (Goldman, R.), *Journal Institution Municipal Engineers* **96**(9), Sept. 1969: 272–3

Control of noise from building and demolition sites: noise rating and statutory limitation of noise from machinery; extension of noise legislation to statutory undertakers, *Journal Institution of Municipal Engineers* **100**(8), Aug. 1973: 212

New safety requirements for demolition operations, *Magazine of Standards* **41**, Apr. 1970: 45–50

Accident problem, (Short, D.), *Muck Shifter* **23**, Oct. 1965: 43–4

Fly by night demolishers cut prices and safety, *Municipal Engineering* **150**(13), 30 Mar. 1973: 684

Structural collapses during erection or demolition, (Short, W. D.), *Proceedings of the Institution of Civil Engineers* **36**, Mar. 1967: 507–22; 38, Dec. 1967: 679–735 and 42, Jan. 1969: 143–52

Public Health Act 1961 9 & 10 Eliz. 1. Ch. 54. H.M.S.O., 1961 (1970 reprint)

New twist on explosive: improve safety with them, *Roads and Streets* **116**, May 1973: 138–9

You can't live there – its radioactive, (Pullin, M. W. and Forrester, P. E.), *Royal Society of Health Journal* **93**(5), Oct. 1973: 271–3

Fire protection during demolition, *Safety Maintenance* **128**, July 1964: 32–4

Erection and demolition of structures, (Brueton, G. R.), *Safety on Construction Sites*, proceedings of a conference, London, 12–13 Mar. 1969, Institution of Civil Engineers, pp. 57–69

*Safety on the Site*, 2nd edn, (Whyte, B. A. C.), United Trade Press, 1970.

Demolition: safety code, (Wells, H. V.), *Structural Engineer* **52**(6), June 1974: A11–A15

*The Safe Cleaning, Repair and Demolition of Large Tanks for Storing Flammable Liquids*,

(Department of Employment), Technical data note No. 18, 1973.


## Salvage

Out of the ashes, *Progressive Architecture* **47**, Feb. 1966: 195–7


## Splitting

New concrete demolition technique, *Concrete Construction* **15**(8), Aug. 1970: 284


## Stone: breaking

Rocking the foundations, *Construction Plant and Equipment* **1**(10), June 1973: 48–9


## Stone: cutting (abrasive)

Drilling and cutting concrete and other hard materials, (Boyes, R. G. H.), *Contract Journal* **239**, 28 Jan. 1971: 355–7 and 239, 4 Feb. 1971: 469, 472


## Stone: cutting (thermal)

The jet-piercing process: the application of high-temperature flames to the penetration of rocks, (Just, G. D.), *Quarry Managers Journal* **47**(6), 1963: 219–6


## Stone: dismantling

Leaving behind a steel skeleton: stripping the facade from Times Tower Building in New York City, (Moxley, R. L.), *Compressed Air Magazine* **69**, Apr. 1964: 4–10
Demolition – new job for tower cranes, *Construction Methods and Equipment* **42**(4), Apr. 1960: 204–5
Down comes London Bridge, *Contract Journal* **224**, 15 Aug. 1968: 745
London Bridge: demolition and construction, 1967–1973, (Mead, P. F.), *Proceedings of the Institution of Civil Engineers* **54**, Feb. 1973: 47–69


## Stone: plant

Tall scaffold makes tower demolition safe: wreckers hammer down walls of New York's famed Times Tower, *Engineering News-Record* **172**, 30 Apr. 1964: 24–5

## Survey of journals

Those journals which have contained the greatest number of articles over the past twenty years, have been selected and are listed below:

|  | No. of references |  |
|---|---|---|
| *Engineering News-Record* | 15 | (American) |
| *Contract Journal* | 11 | (UK) |
| *Roads and Streets* | 11 | (American) |
| *Construction Methods and Equipment* | 10 | (American) |
| *Construction Plant and Equipment* (formerly *Muck Shifter*) | 9 | (UK) |
| *Civil Engineering and Public Works Review* | 8 | (UK) |

Approximately one-third of the items in the bibliography appeared in these six core journals of the demolition industry. However, very important articles can occur in journals not renowned for their coverage of demolition, e.g. Thermic drilling of concrete and stone, by M. Lebrun. *Structural Engineer* **25**(2), Feb. 1947: 57–76 or, The use of explosives for demolitions, by D. H. Brook and R. Westwater, *Proceedings of the Institution of Civil Engineers* **4**, Section 3(3), 1955: 862–86, 887–99. In order to be aware of these papers, it will be necessary to scan special indexing services such as *British Technology Index*, published monthly by the Library Association, or, *Current Information in the Construction Industry*, selected by the library service of the Property Services Agency, which is published twice each month by the Department of the Environment; American publications are covered by *Engineering Index*, a monthly abstracting service, and *Applied Science and Technology Index* which appears eleven times per year. Each of these services is heavily subscribed in this country and it should be possible for everybody to locate a library receiving all of them.

# Bibliography II

The thermic cutting of reinforced and prestressed concrete (in French) (Malier, Y.), *Annales de l'Institut Technique du Batiment et de Travaux Publics* (353), Sept. 1977: 92 −112

Architectural salvage, *Architects Journal* **165**(12), 23 Mar. 1977: 530−3

Shattering of concrete carriageways by means of hydraulic hammer (in German), (Kuhn, H.), *Baumaschine und Bautechnik* **22**(4), Apr. 1975: 107−10

Machine demolition = safe demolition (in German), *Bauwirtschaft* **31**(24), 16 June 1977: 1207−9

Current state of technology of scaling, cutting and demolition concrete structures (in German, (Linder, R.), *Betonwerk und Fertigteil-Technik* **43**(6), June 1977: 313−17

*Blasting Code*, (New Zealand. Department of Labour), D.O.L., 1978, 63 pp.

Demolishing has become a question of know-how and inventiveness, (in Dutch), (Basart, R. C.), *Bouw* **33**(21), 14 Oct. 1978: 45−7

Accounting for demolition, (Fox, G. T. J.), *British Water Supply* Jan. 1974: 10−11

Planned obsolescence and demolition of tall buildings, (Irwin, A. W. and Bain, W. R. L.), *Build International* **7**(6), Nov./Dec. 1974: 549−61

Legal controls on demolition, (Powell-Smith, V.), *Building* **227**(47), 22 Nov. 1974: 103−4

The master blasters, *Building* (25), 18 June 1976: 72−3

Harder they fall, *Building* **232**(121), 25 Mar. 1977: 52−3

Minefields for demolishers, *Building* **236**(4), 26 Jan. 1979: 40−1

Sweeping away the new slums, (Rimmer, G.), *Building* **237**(3), 27 July 1979: 24−7

Downtown demolition U.S.A., (Dober, R. P.), *Building* **239**(28), 11 July 1980: 31−3

Demolition of high rise flats by controlled explosives, (Kriebel, T. S.), *Building Technology and Management* **18**(4), Apr. 1980: 3−6

Demolition: ends and means, (O'Brien, J.), *Chartered Surveyor* **109**(9), Apr. 1977: 293−5

Falling flat on its base, *Civil Engineering*, June 1975: 13

Cutting concrete down to size, (Mussanif, A. A. B.), *Civil Engineering*, June 1975: 37, 39

Down the chimney: part 2, *Civil Engineering*, Sept. 1975: 13

Demolition today, (Griffiths, P. A.), *Civil Engineering*, Sept. 1975: 63

Building up trouble in store, (Lance, A. G.), *Civil Engineering*, Sept. 1975: 67

Demolition methods and equipment, (Musannif, A. A. B.), *Civil Engineering*, Sept. 1975: 69

Helicopter erected tower crane demolishes buildings, (Schrader, C. R.), *Civil Engineering* (A.S.C.E.) **45**, May 1975: 60–2

*Code of Practice for Noise Control on Construction and Demolition Sites*, (British Standard Institution), B.S. 5228: 1975, 35 pp

*Code of Practice for the Safe Use of Explosives in the Construction Industry*, (British Standards Institution), B.S. 5607: 1978, 26 pp

Chopping down a smokestack, *Compressed Air Magazine* **79**, Feb. 1974: 6–9

Demolition of post-tensioned concrete, (Lindsell, P.), *Concrete* **9**(1), Jan. 1975: 22–5

Perspective of a demolition contractor, (Hope-Smith, J. F.), *Concrete* **9**, Dec. 1975: 14–16

At one fell stroke, (Barfoot, R. J.), *Concrete* **10**(9), Sept. 1976: 14–15

What goes up, (Turley, R.), *Concrete* **11**(4), Apr. 1977: 14–16

Techniques of concrete demolition, (Hartland, R. A.), *Concrete* **13**(3), Mar. 1979: 19–23

. . . and then they were gone, *Concrete* **13**(11), Nov. 1979: 25

Fall of a tower, (Cupial, J.), *Concrete* **13**(9), Sept. 1979: 27–41

Demolition: a pattern for registration, (Powell-Smith, V.), *Contract Journal* **274**(5072), 18 Nov. 1976: 52–3

Brains and brawn beat Post Office poser. (Demolition of Wimpole St. Sorting Office, London), (Heywood, P.), *Contract Journal* **287**(5187), 1 Feb. 1979: 29

Released tension spells danger (dangers in demolishing post-tensioned structures), (Heywood, P.), *Contract Journal* **287**(5187), 1 Feb. 1979: 31

Climber collars cooling tower cut down, (Heywood, P.), *Contract Journal* **290**, 23 Aug. 1979: 25–27

Raze or repairs? (Heayes, N.) *Contract Journal* **293**, 24 Jan. 1980: 17–19

*Noise control on construction and demolition sites*, (Gregory, R. E.), Construction (D.O.E.) Mar. 1978: 2–5

Bridge erection method is reversed for dismantling, (Bloomberg, R.) *Construction Methods and Equipment*, July 1974: 68

Long-reaching adjustable hydraulic breaker machines demolish concrete structures, *Construction Methods and Equipment* July 1974: 69

Underwater construction: removing obstacles underwater, *Construction Methods and Equipment* **57**, July 1975: 60–1

Demolition: some problem areas, (Griffiths, P. A.), Letter to *Construction News* (5395), 13 Feb. 1975: 9

The explosive art in Britain and in Austria, *Construction News* (5446), 12 Feb. 1976: 2

Dam being demolished while Wales dries up, (Winney, M.), *Construction News* (5475), 2 Sept. 1976: 14–15

ICOS wall blasted on a tight London site, (Barstow, G.) *Construction News* (5510), 12 May 1977: 26–7

Explosion reduces 26-storey building to rubble, *Construction News* (5533), 20 Oct. 1977: 1–2

Demolition man's hazard: but no labels yet on stressed structures, (Winney, M.), *Construction News* (5597), 1 Feb. 1979: 20

P.S.C. demolition – 'no problem', (Harris, A. J.), *Construction Magazine*, Jan. 1975: 5

Safe, systematic demolition, (Jolley, D.), *Construction Plant and Equipment* **4**(6), Feb. 1976: 47

Demolition of cooling towers, *Construction Plant and Equipment* **4**(6) Feb. 1976: 58

Brute force without ignorance, *Consulting Engineer* **39**(2), Feb. 1975: 39–41

Destruction for progress, (Phillips, P.), *Consulting Engineer* **39**(2), Feb. 1975: 41–3

The gentle gelly merchant, *Consulting Engineer* **39**(9), Sept. 1975: 61

The engineer's role, (Lindsey, D. A.), *Consulting Engineer* **41**(11), Nov. 1977: 26–7

New Malden house, *Consulting Engineer* **41**(11), Nov. 1977: 29

*Demolition*, (Browne, M. A.), Institute of Building, 1979, 48 pp

*Demolition and Construction Noise*, (Building Research Establishment), B.R.E., 1975, 4pp. (Digest 184)

*Demolition and Dismantling Industry Register* 1979, D.D.I.R., 1979, 34 pp

*Demolition guide for building and engineering work under the Construction Act 1959*, (New Zealand, Department of Labour), D.O.L., 1974. 22 pp. (Safety in construction, No. 23)

*Demolition Waste*, (Environmental Resources Ltd.), Construction Press, 1980

*Development of Predictive Criteria for Demolition and Construction Solid Waste Management*, (Chatterjee, S.), Chatterjee & Associates 1976, 1577 Beaver Ridge Drive, Kettering, Ohio 45429

*Demolition and construction noise*, D O E Construction, March 1976: 26–7

*Drilling and Sawing Concrete with Diamond Tools*, (De Beers Industrial Diamond Division), De Beers, 1974, 12 pp, (Diamond information, L.34)

Pioneer A.E.C. reactor dismantled safely, *Electrical World* **181**, 1 May 1974: 41–2

Preserving historic facade takes tricky underpinning, *Engineering News-Record* **197**(16), 14 Oct. 1976: 27–8

Blast drops bridge weight costs, *Engineering News-Record* **198**, 13 Jan. 1977: 11

Blasting scheme saves $6 million, *Engineering News-Record* **198**, 3 March 1977: 11

*Explosives in Demolition*, (Nobel's Explosive Co. Ltd.), I.C.I. 1975, 8 pp.

*Demolition*, Financial Times, 29 May 1975: 2 pp.

Implications of recent changes in legislation for the operations of the gas industry, (Swindells, E.), *Gas Engineering Management* **17**, Mar. 1977: 67–80

Noise and the environment, *Gas Engineering Management* **19**, Mar. 1979: 109–10

Shrinking giant (North Thames Gas – Kensal Green Works), *Gas World* **181**, Dec. 1976: 671–2

Demolition training, (Whaley, P.), *Industrial and Commercial Training* **11**(2), Feb. 1979: 75–7

Concrete building that defies wreckers, *Journal of the American Concrete Institute* **70**, Dec. 1973: N19

The process of demolition using a carbon gas discharge, (Cormon, P.), *Le Batiment Batir* (12), Dec. 1978: 42–3

Demolition et destructions des betons, (Venuat, M.), *Le Moniteur* (26), 28 June 1975: 85;90

*List of Authorised Explosives*, (Health and Safety Executive), HMSO, 1978, 29 pp

Demolition processes in reinforced concrete. (in French), (Cubard, J. C.), *Materiaux et Constructions* **10**(57), May–June 1977: 127–39

The Nibbler: a new concept in concrete breaking, (Musannif, A. A. B.), *Municipal Engineering* **151**(46), 15 Nov. 1974: 2231–4

Industry must face up to demolition risks, (Lucas, S.), *New Civil Engineer* (345), 24 May 1979: 30, 31, 33

Wariness is just good sense, (Holmes, E. W.), letter in *New Civil Engineer* (397), 12 June 1980: 51

Wariness is just 'British ignorance' (Carr, H.), letter in *New Civil Engineer*, (401) 10 July

1980: 37

The dangers of unbonded tendons, (Harris, Sir A.), letter in *New Civil Engineer*, (403), 24 July 1980: 36

Demolishing tendons safely, (Smith, M.) letter in *New Civil Engineer* (405), 7 Aug. 1980: 31

Noise control (B.S. 5228 Code of Practice), *Occupational Safety and Health* 5, July 1975: 18

How to manage a plant demolition project and dispose of surplus equipment, (Law, D. G.), *Plant Engineering* 29, 3 Apr. 1975: 61–3

Economic feasibility of concrete recycling, (Frondistou-Yannas, S. and Itoh, T.), *Proceedings of the American Society of Civil Engineers* 103(ST4), Apr. 1977: 885–99

Safer destruction? *Protection* 15(8), Aug. 1978: 25;6

*Protection of the Environment During Demolition Activities*, (United States Army. Waterways Experiment Station), (Report No. AD–772 920/HX)

*Quieter Demolition Techniques*, (Musannif, A. A. B.), B.R.E., 1975, 7 pp. (Current paper 66/75)

The resource potential of demolition debris in the United States, (Wilson, D. G.), *Resource Recovery and Conservation* 1(2), 129–40

Gutted building stabilized by guy wire/load cell system for razing, *Roads and Streets* 117, Oct. 1974: 102

Un-construction takes skills, planning and machine performance, *Roads and Streets* 118, Aug. 1975: 100–1

Controlled explosives, (Hutchinson, R.), *Structural Engineer* 54, Aug. 1976: A7–A8

Industry comes of age, (Ogden, V.), *Structural Engineer* 54, Aug. 1976: A9–A10

*Safety in Demolition work: Report of the Sub-committee of the Joint Advisory Committee on Safety and Health in the Construction Industry*, (Health and Safety Executive), HMSO 1979, 24 pp

Implications of new laws on building noise control, *Surveyor* 146, 10 Oct. 1975: 29

*The Demolition of Pre-stressed Concrete Structures: A Report by the Joint Liaison Committee of the N.F.D.C.* (National Federation of Demolition Contractors), N.F.D.C., 1975, 22 pp.

Demolishing Itaipu's Arch Cofferdams, (Monteiro, R. and Peyfuss, K. F.), *Water Power and Dam Construction* 31(11), Nov. 1979: 91–4

# Index

379